Children, Adolescents and Death

The topic of death and related issues (such as grief) often begins with questions. When the questions come from, or are about, children or adolescents, they bring an additional component . . . the fear some adults have of giving a "wrong" answer. In this context a wrong answer is one that can cause more harm than good for the child or adolescent who asked the question. This book provides information that can be used to address death-related questions from children and adolescents. It also looks at questions from caring adults about the way children or adolescents view death and the grief that follows a death or any major loss.

Children, Adolescents and Death covers topics that start with early studies of childhood grief and progress to expression of grief in cyberspace. There is no one answer to most of the questions in this book. There are contributors from a number of continents, countries, cultures and academic disciplines, each of whom brings a unique view of the issues they discuss. There are presentations of practical interventions that others may copy, upon which they can build. There are a number of chapters that look at death education in both family and school settings. This work contains ideas and techniques that can be of value to parents, educators, counselors, therapists, spiritual advisors, caring adults and, of course, will be of the most benefit to those who ask the most questions . . . the children and adolescents themselves.

Robert G. Stevenson is a senior professor in the graduate counseling program of Mercy College in New York. He has published over 60 journal articles and book chapters and edited/authored several books. His most recent is *Final Acts: End of Life, Hospice and Palliative Care* (Baywood, 2013). He holds a BA (Holy Cross), MA (Montclair State University), and MAT and EdD (Fairleigh Dickinson University). He developed the first independent course on death education at the high school level and taught it for 25 years. He is a member of the International Work Group on Death, Dying and Bereavement and the Association for Death Education and Counseling. He received the 2013 Robert Fulton Founder's Award from the Center for Death Education and Bioethics. He co-founded a community grief support center, the Jamie Schuman Center, in Hillsdale, NJ. He worked as a counselor in Paterson, NJ for five years with parolees reentering society from state prisons and adolescents in recovery. He received the Defense of Freedom Medal from NY State for his work in the NY Guard after 9/11.

Gerry R. Cox is professor emeritus of sociology/archaeology at the University of Wisconsin–La Crosse. He served as the Director of the Center for Death Education & Bioethics. He has over one hundred publications including twenty-five books. He has served as editor of *Illness, Crisis & Loss* and for *The Midwest Sociologist*. He is a member of the International Work Group on Dying, Death, and Bereavement, the Midwest Sociological Society, the American Sociological Association, the International Sociological Association, Phi Kappa Phi, and Great Plains Sociological Society, and the Association of Death Education and Counseling. He served on the board of Directors of the National Prison Hospice Association.

Praise for *Children, Adolescents and Death*

"In this brilliantly researched book, the greatest experts have shared their skillfully blended tools into a volume of readable, compelling, and penetrating insights. What a magnificent contribution for all who are concerned with the grief experiences of children and youth!"

—Rabbi Earl A. Grollman, DHL, DD, Author, *Talking about Death: A Dialogue between Parent and Child*

"When the student is ready, the teacher will appear. We're all too ready, hungry for this book of readily accessible resources and action plans to help support children and ourselves in this current net-age fraught with disasters, man-made and natural."

—Sandra Bertman, PhD, FT, Author, *Facing Death: Images, Insights & Interventions; Grief and the Healing Arts: Creativity as Therapy*

"This book provides a comprehensive look at the issues faced by bereaved children and adolescents. It presents, in detail, what we know about grieving children, as well as specific ways to facilitate their mourning process. There is something here for everyone—bereaved parents, school personnel, mental health workers, and all who are faced with the normative but often challenging behavior of grieving kids. Readers can select from a potpourri of topics that pertain to their current questions and interests."

—J. William Worden, PhD, ABPP, Co-Director, Harvard Child Bereavement Study, Author, *Children & Grief: When a Parent Dies*

Children, Adolescents and Death
Questions and Answers

Edited by Robert G. Stevenson
and Gerry R. Cox

NEW YORK AND LONDON

First published 2017
by Routledge
711 Third Avenue, New York, NY 10017

and by Routledge
2 Park Square, Milton Park, Abingdon, Oxon, OX14 4RN

Routledge is an imprint of the Taylor & Francis Group, an informa business

© 2017 Taylor & Francis

The right of Robert G. Stevenson and Gerry R. Cox to be identified as the authors of the editorial material, and of the authors for their individual chapters, has been asserted in accordance with sections 77 and 78 of the Copyright, Designs and Patents Act 1988.

All rights reserved. No part of this book may be reprinted or reproduced or utilized in any form or by any electronic, mechanical, or other means, now known or hereafter invented, including photocopying and recording, or in any information storage or retrieval system, without permission in writing from the publishers.

Trademark notice: Product or corporate names may be trademarks or registered trademarks, and are used only for identification and explanation without intent to infringe.

Library of Congress Cataloging-in-Publication Data
A catalog record for this book has been requested

ISBN: 978-0-89503-922-4 (hbk)
ISBN: 978-0-89503-923-1 (pbk)
ISBN: 978-1-315-26623-7 (ebk)

Typeset in Times New Roman
by Apex CoVantage, LLC

Contents

Foreword vii
   Charles A. Corr

SECTION 1
Knowledge of Death 1

CHAPTER 1
**Children and Death: What Do They Know and When Do
They Learn It?** 3
   Robert Stevenson

CHAPTER 2
**Death Version 2016: How Children and Adolescents are Learning
and Grieving in Cyberspace** 25
   Illene Noppe Cupit and Olyvia Kuchta

CHAPTER 3
The Disenfranchised Grief of Children and Adolescents 37
   Kenneth J. Doka

CHAPTER 4
**Trauma and Grief in Early Life: A Model for Supporting Children,
Adolescents, and Their Families** 45
   Dianne McKissock

CHAPTER 5
Family Therapy and Traumatic Losses 69
   Stephanie Rabenstein and Darcy Harris

SECTION 2
Coping with Death at Home and at School 89

CHAPTER 6
Children and Death: Coping through Humor, Art, and Music 91
   Gerry Cox

CHAPTER 7
"Oh, Those Poor Children!": Borrowing Historical and Biographical Loss Narratives of Grieving Children 107
Harold Ivan Smith

CHAPTER 8
Child Development: An Existential Journey 121
Neil Thompson

CHAPTER 9
Children, Adolescents, and Catastrophic Loss: The Role of Spiritual Care. 133
Peter Ford

CHAPTER 10
Helping Bereaved Children in the Schools. 153
Linda Goldman

CHAPTER 11
A School Counselor's Role in Bereavement Counseling. 173
Arthur McCann

SECTION 3
Death and the Family 187

CHAPTER 12
Seasons of Love: Measuring a Child's Life After Suicide 189
Janet S. McCord and Rebecca S. Morse

CHAPTER 13
Dealing with Loss and Grief of Minority Children in an Urban Setting . . . 203
Fernando Cabrera and Robert Stevenson

CHAPTER 14
When a Grandparent Dies 219
Richard Gilbert

CHAPTER 15
Difficult Conversations: Children, Adolescents, and Death 235
Carolyn Cullen

CHAPTER 16
The Presence of Absence: The Struggle for Meaning in the Death of a Child 247
Robert A. Neimeyer and Wendy G. Lichtenthal

Appendix: Questions and Answers 263
Contributors 267
Index 275

Foreword

Charles A. Corr

Sometimes it seems that we can never learn enough about children and adolescents' encounters with death, loss, grief, and mourning. Why is that? I think there are several reasons, most of which have to do with failings on the part of the adults who interact with children and adolescents. Here are five such reasons for us to ponder.

First, some adults appear to hold the view that children really do not have encounters with death and loss early in their lives. This view is naïve and unrealistic. Loss is experienced by an infant as early as when a nipple is withdrawn during breastfeeding or when adults turn away from a child to attend to other things and the child begins to cry. Later in life, a pet might die or a favorite stuffed toy might go missing. (In my experience during a lengthy career in teaching university courses on death, dying, and bereavement, many college students have shown a clear ability to offer vivid descriptions of their earliest childhood experiences with death and loss, as well as about the adults who were or were not helpful in such situations.) At any time in a child's life, a parent or grandparent might die, not to mention a friend or teacher. (Our children found the death of the janitor at their school to be particularly significant, because they knew him as the person who helped them enter and leave school when the sidewalks were icy and he replaced the light bulbs in a darkened and somewhat scary room.) In our society, television and other media provide a daily diet of graphic (and often highly unrealistic) portraits of violence, war, and death. And even young children can often show adults how they are connected to events around the globe through myriad electronic devices that are capable of linking them to tragedy and sadness at the touch of a button. Any youngster who can form an attachment (and that is everyone) can experience loss when or if that attachment is severed. Any adult who believes children live in a world that is untouched by loss and death is imagining a fantasy land unlike the real world of everyday life.

Second, despite all that we have learned, there still seem to be adults who believe that, even if events involving death and loss actually do occur, children (and perhaps early adolescents) are too innocent to have any real awareness of such events in their lives. If children don't know about such events or are thought to be unable to understand them, these adults seem to think there is no need to talk with or educate such supposedly innocent youngsters about loss and sadness. The problems with this mistaken adult view are twofold: (a) If we do not discuss such events with young children, when will be the appropriate time to do so? When will there ever be a magical moment when children will morph from complete ignorance to at least some questions that betray a real need to know? (b) We always need to be wary of interpretations of childhood that excuse adults from having to engage with children on important matters of life and death because such interpretations are typically self-serving in the ways they leave adults off the hook from having to help real children in difficult situations.

Third, another reason why we as adults need to learn more about children and their encounters with death and loss is because whatever the limits there may be in children's understandings of such events, children are almost always aware of the emotional currents that surround them. Even if a child doesn't fully understand what is happening (and who of us ever does completely understand death-related events?), he or she is likely to have a partial, often distorted, grasp of such events and, more importantly, is likely to be sensitive to the emotional cues that adults deliberately or unwittingly give out in such circumstances. When adults are upset, crying, and making efforts to hide things from children, the children often sense that something bad is happening. Indeed, what is happening must be a really bad thing if it cannot be shared. And in the egocentric world of childhood, perhaps the bad thing is the result of something the child did? In short, a child's fears about the unknown can often be more difficult to cope with than what is actually happening. So, by failing to permit a child to be part of the events that are occurring in a family or in a community (in an appropriate way, of course), adults may isolate the child in a frightening world of self-doubt and scary speculation.

Fourth, one of the key responsibilities in development and maturation throughout the life span is to come to know one's own strengths and limitations and to learn how to cope with the events of life. If we raise young children in a greenhouse environment in which nothing difficult or challenging ever happens, how can we expect them to develop effective coping skills that will serve them throughout their later childhood and the remainder of their lives? There is a legitimate place for protecting children from actual harm, but misguided protectionism reveals obvious dangers. Children who are prevented from appropriate involvement in events associated with loss will be stunted in their emotional or psychological growth and will not have any practice in coping in the future with the unexpected challenges that will inevitably confront them. In addition, they will likely come to believe that they have no one to help them in meeting such challenges and no trust that there are adults to whom they can turn for assistance. It is far better from an early age to help children gradually develop effective coping skills in ways that suit their developmental capacities, their needs, their personalities, and the actual worlds in which they live.

FOREWORD

Fifth, adults need to continue this supportive work for their children throughout childhood and into adolescence and young adulthood. Adults may not realize that it is we who locate youngsters in our families, our schools, and our communities. As our youngsters continue to develop and gradually become more and more their own persons, our level of influence over them typically lessens and alters. The media, their peers, their life experiences, and the world around them all become increasingly more influential. That does not mean, however, that there is no further need to teach and support our offspring and members of younger generations. We can continue to provide a constructive presence in their lives, whether as parents or grandparents, teachers and school administrators, adults who work in such professions as law enforcement and the media, or those who establish social policy in our communities. To make these constructive contributions to children and other young people, we always need to learn more about helping them understand and cope better with death, loss, grief, and mourning.

In this volume, the editors have brought together a collection of chapters by knowledgeable contributors that can assist adults, whether they are parents, community members, or professionals who work with children, to guide and support youngsters in the ways that are needed in the 21st century. The need is great because the issues are not just about death, dying, or bereavement; they are about life and living, about how the young people we help today (or do not help) will live out their lives. What we as adults need to do is to sensitize ourselves to the different ways individual children experience and express their reactions to death and loss, and to help such children lead more effective and more fulfilling lives. The chapters in this book can assist a variety of adults—especially parents, school personnel, and healthcare providers—to engage in that work in more useful ways in a variety of situations. We need not think of the contents of this book as dark and scary—helping children to achieve their full potential in the face of significant challenges is a rich and rewarding work.

SECTION 1

Knowledge of Death

This section contains chapters that can help to answer the following questions:
- What do children know about death and grief?
- When and how do they learn this?
- What are things children "need" to know about death and grief?
- What impact can this information have on the lives of children?
- When are children "capable" of experiencing grief?
- In what ways do the expression of grief by children and by adolescents differ from that of adults?
- What are the latest findings about children and teens and their computer activities that relate to grief and loss?
- To what extent do children and adolescents use social media and computer-related communications and activity to communicate about and to learn about death?
- What are the least understood aspects of childhood grief and trauma?
- What do grieving and traumatized children need?
- What are the key aspects of the "Infinity Model" of bereavement counseling?
- How is the grief of children and adolescents different after a death caused by traumatic means?
- What specific things can help facilitate a child's expression of grief?

CHAPTER 1
Children and Death: What Do They Know and When Do They Learn It?

Robert Stevenson

The title of this book refers to the fact that the topic of "children and death" has long produced more questions than answers. What do children know? When and how do they learn it? What particular things do children "need" to know? What is the impact of such knowledge on the lives of children? These questions have now been openly discussed and, at times, heatedly debated for decades. These discussions/debates started primarily in the United States, Canada, and Europe, but increasingly the points they raised are being examined in countries and cultures throughout the world. This chapter will focus on early studies as a starting point. The bulk of my experience comes from working with children in the United States and Canada, and with the staff of Merimna, an agency that works with bereaved children and their families in Greece. However, to see this as a topic that impacts only children in North America and Europe is a mistake. That is why I will refer to studies from around the world. Perhaps the best source for such information is the 5-volume series from Baywood entitled *Death and Bereavement Around the World*. This series is cited throughout the chapter.

Adults like to see childhood as an idyllic time, filled with joy and innocence. While this mental image may be well intentioned, the reality of life for most children is quite different. Life brings changes to every child and many of these changes involve loss. The most profound loss a child must face is the death of someone they love. Because some adults try to maintain an image of innocence and joy, they want to believe that children do not need any special knowledge about death and grief. This is especially true in the United States and Canada. However, such a belief can leave children isolated and forced to cope on their own when a death occurs.

THE FIRST QUESTION

Why? The first question children most frequently ask has been and continue to ask is, "Why?" When it follows a death it is most poignant. Why did he/she die? Why do things like this happen? When adults attempt to answer these questions, other questions arise—more "whys." If the questions are asked in a school, a new question arises. Why tell children about this before they need to know it? All of these questions are legitimate and reflect concern on the part students, educators, and parents. They are important to the young person asking the question. They deserve honest answers.

In 1972 I developed the first high school course on death and grief in the United States. I then taught the course for 25 years until I retired from secondary school teaching. Our knowledge about children and death has come a long way in the decades since the start of that course. We certainly know more now than we did in the early 1970s. Research has been more widespread and more countries are actively involved in providing answers. However, there are still disagreements, and despite the efforts of international associations, not every country is at the same point in understanding the needs of, and developing a response to, the needs of children.

WHAT DO CHILDREN KNOW AND WHEN DO THEY KNOW IT?

The earliest answers to these questions come from England (Sylvia Anthony) and Hungary (Maria Nagy). Sylvia Anthony's seminal work, described in two books—*The Child's Discovery of Death* (1940) and *The Discovery of Death in Childhood and After* (1972)—found that before age 2 a child does not understand the meaning of death. Anthony (1940, 1972) stated that after age 2, children think often of death. She identified a "magical" component in much of this thought. Anthony believed that much of a child's thought about death was connected to aggressive impulses. This and "magical" thinking created a situation in which the child believed his or her thoughts to be a factor that could actually "cause" death. This led some to experience feelings of guilt for having had thoughts of death. The result was that children tried to avoid thinking of death, but found it was something that could not be avoided. When children asked questions about death and saw anxiety in adults, or found them reluctant to answer their questions, this also fed feelings of personal blame and guilt. Worse, it also caused some children to avoid asking their questions about death, especially at home.

Maria Nagy identified three stages in the child's understanding of death. Her work, conducted through the 1940s in Hungary, was brought to a wide audience by Herman Feifel's work *The Meaning of Death* (1959). Nagy said that an infant has no concept of anything beyond itself, certainly not mortality. If the child experienced anything when a death occurred, it was a feeling that something the child wanted or needed was "absent." This feeling does not really constitute a conscious "understanding" of death.

By age 3, the child understands that there is a thing called death. This is the first stage in a child's "understanding" of death. Children have seen death. For most, it is a pet or animal, but for others, the sight of death means dead people. These are children who have seen people torn apart by cruelty and war or delivered by death from the suffering of disease. These children have seen death, but from about 3 to 5 or 6 the child believes that death is a type of separation. Death can be seen as "diminished life" from which one can return. It is "reversible."

In the second stage, from 6 or 7 to about 10 years of age, the child makes the abstract idea of death into a concrete person, place, or thing. Children may see death as a "deathman" figure in black or as a cemetery, a weapon (such as a gun or knife) or most commonly a dark place. It is a big part of the reason for the fear of the dark that so many children experience.

The child reaches the third stage by about age 10. The child takes on an "adult" understanding of death. Death is seen as final, inevitable, and will one day be personal. This adult understanding means that death is

- Universal: All things that live will one day die, even the child himself/herself.
- Irreversible: People who die can no longer return.
- Nonfunctioning: The body no longer functions at any level. Death is not a form of diminished life. There is no life left.

For over 70 years, the work of Nagy has held up well. Her work was with children in an Eastern Europe that was torn by war. Direct exposure to death in a wartime environment may accelerate the process and dispute the approximate time frames given by Nagy, but most still develop from ignorance about death to knowledge of death through a similar developmental process. There is a belief that these three points are necessary for a child to reach an "adult" understanding of death. More recently than Nagy, Stephen Gullo also described the three parts of an adult understanding of death as knowing that death is "final, personal and irreversible" (Gullo & Plimpton, 1985). Age ranges, rather than stages, now describe how children understand and cope with death. However, it is important to remember that an individual child's concept of death is a function of that child's developmental level more than a function of the child's chronological age.

With a basic understanding of the way children come to find a meaning for death, there are questions that logically follow. What experiences do children typically have with death? What questions do children ask about death? How can their questions best be answered? Who is best to answer these questions? Should they be answered by parents, by guardians, by educators (including spiritual advisors), or by all of these people working together?

THE CHILD'S EXPERIENCE OF DEATH

Edna St. Vincent Millay, in her well-known poem, described childhood as "The Kingdom Where Nobody Dies" (1997). However, the actual experience of children shows that it is not the case. They see death in the body of a dead pet or in that of a wild animal. They see a passing funeral procession. They learn of death through their stories and games. They see death whenever they watch television. And for many children, they see human death firsthand. The children of Northern

Ireland, Bosnia, Israel, Palestine, Rwanda, Afghanistan, and Iraq know of death because many have see it so often. So too have children in the wake of a tornado, hurricane, flood, or other natural or man-made disaster. However, there are different ways in which adults respond to this reality and there are differences for children as well.

In the United States, through the second half of the 20th century, there were attempts to shield children from the knowledge of death. This paralleled the separation of old age, dying, death, and funeral rituals from the home. The rise of the nuclear family limited the child's contact with older adults. The rise of the funeral service profession and separate funeral "parlors" sought to take death and mourning out of the American home. It then became possible to exclude children from the rituals that accompanied a death. One study found that children ages 8–12 thought about death and, at the same time, were afraid to talk about it (Zweig, 1983). This was said to be a result of the mystery that adults imposed on death.

During the last quarter of the 20th century, as children returned to greater participation in funerals and the rituals that follow a death, they became more willing to ask their questions and to discuss their thoughts and fears about death. Zweig noted cultural differences among American children. African American children were more likely than Caucasian children of the same age to think of death as "transitory" and to see death as a person, or "deathman." Caucasian children did "personify" death, but were more likely to see it connected to a place or thing. (Stevenson, 1984). African American children were also more likely to attribute the cause of death to some form of aggression. Studies by Sigel (1970), and Carter (1971) also found this association of death and aggression by African American children. The automatic connection of death and aggression appears to diminish as children enter their teens.

One of the greatest differences among cultures involves funeral rituals. In the United States there is disagreement as to whether or not children should be allowed to attend funerals. European American families at first had children present but established a pattern that eventually isolated children from wakes, funerals, and if possible, from grief in any form.

Jewish traditions have been modified and now combine traditional observances with new findings about childhood grief. Ronald Trojcak states that

> Although children who have not reached the age of mitzvot—twelve for girls and thirteen for boys—are not obligated by any of the mourning rules, the tendency in most instances of a child suffering a loss of a parent or sibling is to involve her to the extent possible in the rites. Although it used to be common practice to shelter children from death and cemeteries, mental health professionals now consider it far better for a child to attend the funeral, watch the burial, rend her garment, sit shivah, and even recite kaddish for her parent or sibling. Children, too, need opportunities to express their love and grief openly, and Jewish mourning rites offer that to them. (2002)

Native American traditions differ in their practice regarding their children and their involvement with, or isolation from, rituals connected to dying and death. Among the Apache, the fear of death was communicated to children at an early age. Traditional Apache practice did not allow children to be around the dying or even view the dead and prevented children from associating with other children who were grieving. Children would seldom be around a dying person or at a funeral, since the Apache generally feel that children are to be protected from the ravages of illness and death (Cox, 2002). Unlike the Apache, the Lakota want the children to be present. However, death by suicide is viewed differently. In such cases, the death is not to be discussed near children and they are excluded from any rituals. Native American culture places much value on children. Prayers and rituals were performed to give health and life to children (Cox, 2002). Throughout the 20th century, African American children have been likely to attend wakes (the traditional watch over a dead body) and funerals (Zweig, 1983). The ability of children to play a role in funerals and grief rituals exists in many cultures. In the Hindu tradition of India, children are permitted to attend funerals. They are not shielded from witnessing death or even attending a cremation.

In Greece, there is an even split about whether children should have contact with dying people. According to tradition, parents are supposed to protect and shield their children from death. Young children are not allowed to attend the funeral or visit the gravesite during the memorial services. The children are perceived as vulnerable and are thought to be unable to deal with the grief and loss directly. Greek parents are not to show their grief openly when their children are present, regardless of the age of the child. Clearly, this is changing. Today more Greeks believe that children should take part in funerals, and most would allow children an active role in mourning (Papadatou & Iossifides, 2002).

In Eastern Europe, Polish children were allowed by more than half of the parents to observe a dead body. About half (45%) believe that children should not know much about death and should avoid contact with dying people, and almost the same number of people think they should be allowed to do so. More than 90% believe that children should take part in funerals (Rogiewicz & Ratajska, 2002). In Russia, the problem of children and death, whether the death of a child or a death in the family, is also not openly handled. Typically, adults in these cases tend to shield children from the death experience, so losses, even of close relatives, are concealed from children. Russian researchers found that children become aware of death and its inevitability even if they have never witnessed dying. However, because it is not discussed, children end up trying to cope with their fear of death alone (Artemieva, 2002).

In Japan and Korea, it is expected that people will, whenever possible, die at home. Of necessity, children will be present and have some part in rituals. It is believed that, "if a person does not attend, it is considered a very shameful act and in fact, a great sin. Moreover, dying away from home should be avoided as the soul of deceased cannot be comfortable" (Kubotera, 2002).

The differences regarding children attending funeral rituals can become emotional. However, it may not be as important an issue as some have believed, since it is less a factor in the child's view of death than the ability of the child to discuss death openly.

THE ROLE OF PARENTS

In most cases, children will feel more comfortable learning about death and discussing questions with their parents who, after all, should know their own children better than most so-called experts. This is an area in which parents/guardians, educators, and spiritual advisors should cooperate to reinforce each other as all parties try to help the children involved. This is not an "either/or" situation. Many children need care in all areas of their lives when trying to cope with a major loss, such as with the death of a loved one. It is always appropriate for a parent or guardian to pass on personal and family traditions of faith and to tell children what he/she believes about an afterlife. This is true in virtually all cultures.

In North America, such lessons cannot be taught in a public school setting without the risk of violating the personal beliefs of many families. Students can speak of their beliefs, but that is not the same as a presentation by a caring adult who can answer the "Why?" that often follows such explanations. In the United States, even the media cooperate with denial about major issues for children. An example of this can be seen in the way the Children's Television Workshop deals with issues related to children and HIV in two countries, South Africa and the United States.

In South Africa, there was a new character introduced on *Sesame Street*. Her name is Kami (which means "acceptance" in Tswana). Kami is a character with HIV and the show sometimes deals with her status. When Kami appeared, several Senators actually warned Public Broadcasting stations not to have such a character on any shows broadcast in the United States (POZ, 2002). In the United States, it seems denial can be institutionalized and maintained by force when threatened. If educational institutions have their content censored (even indirectly), it becomes even more important that parents have current, accurate information to share with their children, even when there are others who see the topic as controversial.

Parents ask what they should say when children ask challenging questions. Typically, a child asks two questions about death: Why do people die? Will you (the parent) die? A third, often unspoken, question is, If you die, what will happen to me?

Why Do People Die?

When my own son asked me this many years ago, I was hard-pressed at that time to know exactly what to say to one so young. I gave a response I had first heard suggested at a conference at Columbia-Presbyterian Medical Center in New York. I answered, "People die because they are so hurt or so sick or so old that their bodies just won't work any more. Sometimes they can be helped by doctors or by nurses or by their family. But sometimes things are just so bad that they can't live any more, and then they die." This answer works well in most cultures because it deals with the physical reality of death. It allows a parent to add whatever cultural or religious beliefs they believe appropriate to the answer. A Christian might say that death exists because it is "the wages of sin," as it says in the Bible. However, in cultures that believe human beings are perfectible after several lifetimes that answer would not be helpful.

Will You Die?

Many children ask this question of a parent or guardian. When they do, they are also asking (even if they do not say it at the time), "If you do die, what will happen to me?" My own son asked a variation of this. When I told him about why people die, he looked at me for a long time and asked, "Are you old?" He had decided that I didn't look sick or hurt so he narrowed his concern to age. When I explained that I was older than him and older than my students, but I was younger than his grandparents, I went on to say a bit more. I told him that his mother and I would do all we could to stay with him and care for him for as long as we could, but that if anything ever did happen to us, his aunt and uncle would be there to care for him and love him. He seemed comfortable with that answer and, many years later, said that he still remembered that day, had understood the answer at that time, and never really felt it was necessary to bring it up again. However, he also said that he knew that, if he needed to, he could have asked the question again at any time. There are two points here that can be helpful for parents. First, answer a child's question in the best way you can, using what you know. And second, be honest in your explanation, even if it means saying, "I don't know" at times.

Parents ask, "How should I tell my child about a death?" and "How do children try to cope with feelings about death?" The answer to the first question is simple—tell the truth. Tell them what happened and do it in an honest, direct manner. One group of teens, when they were asked this question, offered several suggestions. They said such information should be kept simple. The meaning of words should be clear. Platitudes should be avoided. The adult should be sure that the child understands the meaning of what has just been said. Misunderstanding can lead to hurtful fears and mistaken beliefs. Parents should allow their children to ask any questions the children have and should try to answer them as honestly as they can.

Finding an answer to the second question is a bit more complicated. While a person may demonstrate different coping styles in different situations, it is theorized that each person has a primary coping style to which he/she will turn in times of extreme stress. When working with children in New York City, Steven Gullo identified six basic coping styles: accepting, defying, facilitating, submitting, altruistic, and optimistic. These are developed in childhood and carried through life. Each coping style has both positive and negative aspects.

Acceptor

The acceptor is like a living version of the serenity prayer. That prayer asks for "serenity to accept what cannot be changed, the courage to change what can be changed, and the wisdom to know the difference." Each person has only a limited amount of energy. These children want to know where they can direct their energy to best deal with the problems they face. They may ask seemingly endless streams of questions about their situations. The questions can become tiring or annoying, but if parents refuse to answer them or dismiss them, these children can withdraw and reject any further support or even communication.

Defier

Defiers are *angry*, and this anger produces energy. They see death as terribly unfair. The fact of death as an end to life makes them angry. Defiers typically take the energy produced by this anger and use it to work toward positive goals. A defier can accomplish many things, but with so much anger, there is always a chance that the energy-producing emotions can boil over and lash out in a destructive outburst. The growing number of violent outbursts by young people have been linked by some to this style of coping.

Facilitator

Facilitators have such a strong need to feel in control that they may, consciously or unconsciously, bring about the very result they most fear. The result is often not one they want, but they will accept (or even produce) it to believe it happened because they were in control. When it comes to death, facilitators may engage in risk-taking behaviors, even life-threatening behaviors, to have the resulting feeling of control when (and if) they survive.

Altruist

Altruistic individuals sacrifice personal issues to work for the greater good. It is the condition of the group (class, team, family, church, community, etc.) that matters, and they will not allow personal needs to interfere with helping that group. For children, the group most commonly becomes family or school.

Optimist

These children believe that they can achieve any goal they set for themselves. They can often achieve more than others think possible. However, if they do not reach the goals they have set, the resulting disappointment can be devastating.

Submitter

Submitters believe that they are helpless. It is "others" who control the events in their lives. They may have been "taught" by events or by abuse that they are in fact helpless. However, the issue here is often guilt. If they are helpless, they need not feel responsible for some past event (or even for the feelings that came after that event). They escape the emotional "down" of guilt, but it is at the cost of never experiencing the "high" of joy or happiness.

Strong feelings by themselves may create a need "cope." This can cause a person to draw on one or more of the coping styles discussed above, often one of the first the individual developed at a young age. After a death, there are many losses experienced by young people. The attempt to find a place for these events, to integrate these losses into the personality is a purpose of the grief process. The emotions most often present in grief are helplessness, hopelessness, loneliness, guilt, anger, and fear.

- Helplessness: The feeling that there is nothing that the child can do to overcome or avoid the unpleasant feelings.
- Hopelessness: The belief that things are bad and these unpleasant feelings may never diminish or go away.
- Loneliness: The feeling of absence of a loved one or the experience of a loss that others seem unable to recognize.
- Guilt: Comes from the "I should or should not have . . ." reactions that a child experiences after a death. The child is troubled by kind acts that were left undone or by unkind acts for which the child has not been forgiven and for which he/she believes that no forgiveness is now possible, either from the deceased or from him/herself.
- Anger: Comes from the belief that the situation is "unfair" or that it is the result of the actions or plans of a third party who has not been held accountable. In the United States, the terrorist attacks of September 11, 2001, created this type of anger in children. Children, along with their parents, teachers, and counselors, gave examples of anger. Their anger was directed at the perpetrators of the attacks, at their countries, at their religion and culture, and even at their own government for "allowing" such events to occur. This anger was blamed for a rise in reported episodes of violence in New Jersey schools after September 11. However, anger can also be seen as a "surface" emotion that can conceal a deeper and stronger feeling, namely, the feeling of fear. It has long been seen in coping with the problems of alcoholism and drug abuse that there can be tremendous anger in that population. Fear is often the underlying cause of this anger.
- Fear: This fear may be fear of a loss of control, fear of losing love, or a fear of losing respect. The fear of losing control may prompt the belief that the child is losing control of the present and also losing the ability to make decisions that influence his/her future. The fear of losing love may cause a feeling that the individual is losing connection to others—losing the ability to love and be loved. The fear of losing respect can cause anger over a loss of self-respect or from the belief the child has lost respect from others. When these fears are present for children and teens, many find that they cannot sleep, become short tempered (often with those closest to them), have periods of extreme sadness, become apathetic, and in some cases, experience somatic complaints. While most children do not experience these problems after a death, many do. In addition, some teens will seek to self-medicate with alcohol or drugs. Others withdraw into an apathetic stupor, seeming to lose interest in all but assigned tasks and sometimes even in those. In those who seek or are referred for help, fear is often identified as a major concern.

The *fear of a loss of control* is not as great a problem for young children as it is for teens. Adolescents are trying to establish themselves as independent adults, and this fear comes from an unwillingness to return to the dependence of childhood. The *fear of losing love* hits home most strongly with young people who have suddenly lost a loved one. They were also aware that a death could occur at any time with no warning and strike another loved one. More of their family or friends could die. Finally, after a death, some children worry that they might not be up to the challenges they face now and in the future. They experience *a fear of losing respect*—self-respect, and the respect of others if they are not able to carry on.

One intervention that has been successful in helping children to face these fears has been the belief that, "In every fear lies the opportunity for courage." Parents and teachers can remind the child that if there were no fear, no one would ever have a chance to be "brave." The child who feels fear now has the opportunity to be brave by showing courage.

Following a death, emotions may be strong enough in themselves to warrant concern. The same emotions are also present in individuals who may be at risk of suicide. Only the emotion of *worthlessness* is needed to create the possibility of suicide. Worthlessness, along with the feelings of "normal" grief, can create a situation from which the individual sees no escape and one in which they feel only pain.

Clearly, it is important to help children understand death and grief. The topic may make some uncomfortable, but avoiding the topic can cause far worse consequences. Worse still can be the stories that some parents offer to their children. Statements that a loved one "went to sleep" or "is on a trip" may confuse and anger the child and can complicate the grieving process.

The decision of what to say about a death and when to say it is one that is best made by a parent. However, if parents avoid facing this issue, children may call upon others for answers to their questions. This is not limited to the United States. In Poland, one study shows that in situations in which children were included in the bereavement process, many parents tried to be sensitive, patient, understanding, and caring. They talked to the children and made efforts to prepare them for the death and to prepare them for the rituals that would follow the death. They tried to explain the nature of death and, if they were believers, passed on their faith in an afterlife. However, there were also parents who tried to limit the grief of children. These parents tried to organize activities diverting the child's attention from the illness, avoided the subject, or concealed the fact of the death by taking the child away from the home. These parents hid their emotions from their children and exhibited ineffective ways of behaving such as

- Concealing death: Avoiding conversations, lack of interest, or respect for children's experiences and showing impatience. In China, there is a hesitancy to speak of death in the presence of children and there are still families that tell children their deceased father has gone to work in some far place to spare them the news of death (Martinson, 2002).
- Frightening with death: Threatening children with ghosts, dead people, and passing on the knowledge about death in a harsh manner (Rogiewicz, 2002).

Myra Lipman of the New York Parents League has stated that "schools cannot assume the entire responsibility for a child's death education nor can they ignore the matter entirely. There should be effective home-school communication so that parents know what information is being presented to their children" (Stevenson & Stevenson, 1996). Starting in the early 1970s, death education courses came into existence across the country. They were found to make the school a focal point for helping concerned parents with specific needs to contact appropriate support groups in their community.

THE ROLE OF SCHOOLS

A school is seen as a place that provides answers to the questions of students. When educators tackle the questions related to death, it can be seen as an extension of the school's normal function. Further, the school is a place of learning, and "learning" to grieve effectively, even once, can give a student a vital life skill. The topic of children and death is one that became a focal point of my career as an educator and counselor. Since the first time I stood in front of a group of students, I have sought to provide them with information and skills that would be useful to them as they tried to answer the questions of their own lives. My own preparation was as a history/social studies teacher. As with many educators and parents, as I first began to explore the topic of children and death, I had no idea where this journey would lead.

"Perspectives on Death" was a course title first used by Berg and Daugherty in 1972. Their groundbreaking teaching module was 30 sessions in length. The 30 sessions were to be taught in a course such as health or "life science" and included ten guest speakers, two field trips, and three test days. This left only 15 sessions of classroom instruction. The course that I helped to develop included a field trip and testing, but the curriculum offered over 40 days of classroom instruction. Then, at the request of the students themselves, the death education course was expanded to a semester (18 weeks), with over 80 days of classroom time.

The title of the course shows a concern that seems to be common in the United States. The word "death," although not a problem for students or parents, bothered some board members. Thus, the course title, "Perspectives on Death," became "Contemporary Issues of Life and Death." In the school's written curriculum statement, this became, simply, "Contemporary Issues" and the administration and board of education pretended it was simply a "current affairs" course. For over 25 years this elective course was filled to capacity. These adolescents had questions about dying, death, and grief and found some answers in the death education course.

The school is a natural support system in every culture. The members of a school community typically spend many hours there each week. Depending on the country, the time can vary from 35 hours to 70 hours or more spread over five to seven days. Schools maintain contact with members of this "community" at other times as well. Students and teachers work together, play together, and share the knowledge they gain about life. With such close proximity it is easy to come to know others very well, their strength and weakness, success and failure, happiness and sorrow. Students may say they are there because it is required, that they have no choice. However, this does not explain the many hours spent there with classmates and teachers outside of the regular class hours. It cannot explain why students in some schools who have lost a loved one want to return to the school to be here with their friends and teachers. They return there because they see the school as a place where they will receive support in dealing with important issues in their lives.

Dying, death, and grief are life events that many young people face on a regular basis. Perhaps they always have faced these issues and we have only recently become aware of their effect on children. Some children deal with loss on a daily basis. In the United States, it is widely held that as many as one child in every class will have a parent die by age 18. One in every 900 teens dies each year from accident, suicide, homicide, or illness. Some children experience the death of a teacher, while others must learn to cope with sibling death (stillbirth, miscarriage), family change (separation/divorce/remarriage), life-threatening illness (self or family member), serious physical injury, violence, the fear of violence, and the loss of "security" (Stevenson, 2009).

Children may also undergo emotional numbing, guilt, anger, difficulty concentrating, and fear of the future. Emotional numbing can vary from a brief period of shock to a reaction in which children believe, in effect, that if feelings hurt like this, they will withdraw into themselves and refuse to feel anything at all. Guilt and anger can be seen as two sides of the same coin. These two feelings are often linked in grieving people and may result in apathy (a withdrawing from life) or in acting out. This acting out from guilt and/or anger may be directed at others through verbal or even physical attacks. It can also be directed back at the student him/herself in a pattern of "accidents" or as punishment-seeking behavior.

Grieving students may work on assignments at home or in school in the same way as they previously did but the results may be far less satisfying. Their minds are, to put it simply, "on other things." Their loss is paramount and academic work takes a backseat to it. Or academic work may be dismissed entirely because it has become meaningless in the face of death. The grieving students simply cannot concentrate.

The future is unknown and children may fear they will be unable to cope with additional losses that could arise in this unknown future. Examples of this fear may be seen in children who resist any further changes in their lives or their environment. However, the future requires every person to be able to make decisions. No decision can be better than the information upon which it is based. If we want children to be able to make effective decisions for their own lives, we need to include information about loss and grief in their knowledge base.

The label "death education" has been applied to a wide range of student experiences. It does not simply refer to any course in which the word "death" is mentioned or discussed. An English class that was reading Shakespeare's *Hamlet* or *Romeo and Juliet* may not be dealing with this in a context of death education. Death education is defined as a *formal curriculum that deals with dying, death, grief, and loss and their impact on the individual, the community, and on humankind*. After decades of death education courses in schools, it has become clear that educators and students can benefit from having the study of death and loss in the curriculum.

A curriculum is a "statement of priorities." The curricula in our schools reflect what we hold most important. In many countries, the classes, units, and curricula that deal with loss and grief have come to be known as death education. This title may be a bit too narrow to properly describe what these curricula have become. In death education courses, students learn to deal with loss of all types. However, death education is used so widely that it may be better to understand its full meaning than to change it to "loss education," even though that is what it has now become. Clearly, parents are the first and in most cases best teachers of their children. However, it can be stated with certainty that a single death of a student, teacher, parent, sibling, or community member can affect the function of a school. The other losses that accompany a death will certainly affect the function of any school in which they occur. The impact of a death and grief in a school may

- impair the academic performance of students,
- shorten the attention span of students,
- cause "problem" behavior. Such behavior may include attention-seeking (or punishment-seeking) behavior, acting out, apathy (withdrawal from life), behavior that copies an absent loved one, a drop in grades, and/or poor health (with frequent absence or visits to the school nurse or to a doctor).

These student reactions are further complicated when their expression is delayed. In children and adolescents it is not unusual in some cases for such a delay to last as long as 5 years. It then may be quite difficult to understand the change in a child's behavior, especially when a teacher does not know of the effects caused by the death so many years ago. Furthermore, one affected child can produce a disruptive pattern that can impact on an entire class, and one such class can have an impact on an entire school. For these reasons, the topic of death was given a place in many school curricula.

When dealing with grief, school children may react in any of a variety of ways. Grief, although a healing process, does produce anxiety in the grieving individual and may impact friends and classmates as well. The effects of anxiety on schoolwork have been shown by a number of researchers, including Gaudry and Spielberger (1971). Students experience a shorter attention span and difficulty in concentrating that may be accompanied by a drop in grades. In varying degrees, many of these students perceive themselves to be "helpless" in coping with crises. They may show signs of depression, increased episodes of daydreaming, or they may withdraw from socialization with peers. These children and adolescents also report somatic complaints more often than their peers. All of these possible disruptions in the learning process and classroom routine make a teacher's role more difficult. Ignoring these very real difficulties being encountered by students will only magnify their effect. Although many of the tasks connected to coping with grief take place following a death, the time to prepare to carry out these tasks is before the death occurs. Clearly, there is a role for schools and teachers to play in helping children learn about death.

Death education developed more quickly in the United States, but other countries were not far behind. In Canada, it was Sandra Elder who helped found school support groups in a number of secondary schools and who expressed the need for death education when she said,

Grief is a human process to be experienced. It is *not* an illness to be treated. It is important to learn to grieve, as it is to learn arithmetic, language or science. Children witness and feel changes in their lives, often without the skills to express their fears and pain. Grief is a life skill to be learned and lived. (Elder, 1994)

In Greece, Danai Papadatou and her staff at Merimna provide support for grieving children and families. As part of their work, they are working with teachers and counselors from throughout Greece to help them to understand the ways children understand death and cope with grief. Their work is important enough that Merimna was the recipient of a grant from the European Union to train educators and counselors in specific ways to assist the children in their care.

In England, the BBC aired a program in 1988 and in Canada and Australia in 1989 called *The Facts of Death*. It examined death education in the United States, but was not aired in the United States until 1993–1995 and then was limited to public broadcasting stations. The program, produced by David Willcock, inspired a number of parents and educators to contact the educators shown in the broadcast and the people at the BBC. They stated that they did not have such programs in their country and they expressed an interest in starting such courses in English schools. Willcock stated that he had been a skeptic, but that he emerged from his project with a belief that there was a place in secondary schools for death education. He cautioned that such courses should be led by the needs of students and not shaped by the voices of critics or the whims of individual educators (Willcock, 1988). His one concern was that the topic not become a formal part of the education curriculum for very young children. He felt, and many educators would agree, that at a young age, it is not the children but their teachers who need to be taught about grief and shown how it can be acknowledged and grieving children helped in schools.

In Belgium, the Life and Death at School (LeDoS) Project takes just the type of position that Willcock proposed. This project was established to help teachers be better able to help their students. It was found that teachers could not avoid encounters with loss. Unfortunately, for many of those teachers, the fear of talking about death was immense and often it prevented them from helping their students. The Life and Death at School Program helps and stimulates teachers to be sensitive to feelings of loss among the children. They are invited to dwell upon their own experiences of loss to better understand mourning tasks and processes. The program uses a scenario with six possible storylines for working with bereavement in the event of a death in a child's family (Somers, 2002).

GUIDELINES FOR SCHOOL SUPPORT

The following responses have been used in schools in Europe, Canada, and the United States. They have been shown to be a helpful guide to those who seek to create a supportive atmosphere for a school community dealing with issues of death or of grieving students. These are not things to do just after a death. If implemented in advance, their presence helps the school community to fulfill its role as a support system for each of its members. It is important to remember that these guidelines were developed in working with students in America and Europe. However, parents and educators in Asia, Africa, and South America have found them to be a helpful starting point in developing guidelines of their own. What is important is that concerned adults start now to establish guidelines that can be implemented now to prepare for the time when they will be needed.

Know What Support Already Exists

In many areas there are now organizations with programs that provide assistance for just this type of situation. The Association for Death Education and Counseling (ADEC), based in the United States, is an international organization that has provided help in creating an atmosphere of support in schools following a loss. ADEC is an important resource for educators. The Rainbows program, founded by Suzy Yehl Marta, is used in homes and schools across the United States and Canada to join family and educators in support of the young people both seek to support. In Athens, Greece, Merimna has begun to train educators from throughout Greece so that these men and women can be a source to support to their colleagues, their students, and their communities. In Canada, John Morgan established the King's College Center for Education About Death and Bereavement in London, Ontario. The Center sponsored annual conferences on aspects of loss and grief until 2002. With John Morgan's retirement, the organization of the annual conference was taken over by Robert Bendiksen and Gerry Cox of the University of Wisconsin-LaCrosse and the conference location shifted in 2003. In British Columbia, the late Sandra Elder helped found Living Thru Loss, an organization that helps run support groups for bereaved students in schools. Concerned adults should learn about such programs, where they are, and how they can be contacted should the need arise.

Have Procedures in Place to Inform Students
When a Loss Occurs

In the United States, this was thought to be so important that the National Association of Secondary School Principals published a protocol for informing the school community of a death (Stevenson & Powers, 1987). The news will be painful no matter what is done, however, prior planning for such an event can help keep that pain to a minimum by avoiding mistakes, usually well-intentioned, that could make the reaction worse. This is important for children of all ages.

Find a Place in the Curriculum for Issues
Connected to Loss

Death education occurs regularly for students. They see it in their lives and those of their friends. What is needed is not such informal "education" but information delivered in a systematic, measurable way. As was said earlier, a curriculum is a statement of priorities. Find ways to include necessary information about loss, grief, and coping in the formal curriculum.

Every culture has stories about death and dying. Many are told regularly, even to very young children. In Judeo-Christian tradition, death was created as a punishment for human disobedience. In Indonesian tradition, God offered man immortality, but the gift was rejected because man did not hear the offer. In Melanesian mythology, death came to the world because the gods decided that old people, with their wrinkled skin, were too ugly to live. In Sumer, death was the "freezer" of all human affection, turning love to hate for the living in the hearts of ghosts (Jobes, 1962). Telling stories to "explain" death is an old tradition. Fortunately, today there are many stories that deal with death and the emotions that accompany it. They relate to all types of death and are aimed at a variety of developmental stages and cultural backgrounds.

Provide Positive Role Models

Parents, teachers, and other concerned adults model ways to deal with loss and sadness. They can show children that grief hurts, tears are "normal," and that emotions need not be "avoided," and this modeling can be seen as effective teaching.

Avoid Silence

Social critic Phyllis Schlafly has been quoted as saying, "Anything they [teachers] do is apt to be far worse than doing nothing at all" (Bordewich, 1988). It has been found that silence can magnify the feelings of helplessness, hopelessness, and loneliness, which are part of all grief reactions and can add feelings of worthlessness. In this way, "silence" may actually strengthen all four of the emotions present in many suicide attempts (Stevenson, 1987, 2002).

Be Aware of the Importance of Nonverbal Communication

All of us must be aware of the many ways in which we communicate. Our attempts to speak with children can be influenced by location (where we speak), time (when we speak) and space (distance between us as we speak). We should be aware of all of the factors that have an impact on our communications with children. Location should be one in which children feel most comfortable or least threatened. In school, this is typically the child's classroom, not an auditorium, cafeteria, or assembly hall. The best time to speak about a death is as soon as the entire staff has been informed and knows what to tell students about what has happened. It is not good to postpone such communication, but it can also be a mistake to speak out too quickly and spread misunderstanding or rumor. Body language varies widely from one culture to another. Any guidelines must take this into account. For example, adults in the United States expect children to maintain eye contact with them. Typically, a teacher will interpret averting the eyes as a sign of disinterest or even disrespect. However, when speaking with adults, Japanese students avert their eyes as a sign of respect. This is but one example of the need for a multicultural approach to effective communication.

Create Rituals to Acknowledge the Reality of Changes

Rituals or memorials need not be traditional or formal, but it is important to show students that a change such as a death in the school community does not simply happen without other changes taking place as well. By taking time to mark that change with some ritual, some rite of passage, we confirm that this change has happened and that the child's reactions to that change are justified. If we try to "deny" that a change has taken place, we should not be surprised when children adopt coping mechanisms that attempt to do the same and continue that "denial."

When rituals take place following a death, parents should be kept informed of all that takes place so that they remain the primary support for their children. Classroom rituals have involved lighting candles, drawing pictures, sharing memories, or in the case of a student death, creating a memory book as a gift for the parents and family. Other rituals may involve donation of books or other equipment to the school in the name of the deceased (with an accompanying ceremony), a gift to charity in the name of the deceased, or in many countries that do not have the prohibition against religion in schools that exists in U.S. public schools, a religious ceremony.

Give Abstract Concepts Some "Concrete" Form

Often some small item can provide comfort and courage to grieving students. A cross or other religious symbol, a polished stone, a doll or some other object can be an amulet (warding off evil) or a talisman (helping the possessor to accomplish some difficult task). A plastic "lens" can be used to explain to students how an event can be a lens that changes the way the world looks to them. Using a lens (which can multiply and rearrange the image in front of them) is a concrete way to explain what happens when we grieve or when we suffer from a loss or other sudden change in our lives. The power in an object or a ritual comes not from the thing itself but from the caring person who introduces it and from the way in which it is used. If nothing else, it serves as a reminder to the students that there are still people who care about them and are still there to help them if they are needed.

Promote Helping Others as a Way to Overcome Negative Feelings

One class of students raised money with candy sales in school. The money was regularly sent to local charities in the name of deceased loved ones. A notification was then sent to survivors that a gift had been made in their loved one's name. This ritual had benefits at many levels and continued at the students' request for several years. It was important enough to the students that they continued it even after their teacher's retirement.

Other students wrote, and had published, a series of articles for other young people on topics such as children attending funerals, teachers helping grieving students, and the grief that follows a death from AIDS. They learned they did not need to listen only to "others." Their opinions had enough value that they, themselves, could *be* "others" when they helped their peers.

Offer Support for All Ages

The students in my death education class published several articles discussing what schools could do for students from a student perspective. We regularly received calls from parents who wanted help for bereaved children and wanted to ask these students (high school juniors and seniors) to suggest or to evaluate a response. It is clear that schools do not have all the answers to any problem, but they do have information that many parents find useful. When the school can act as a clearinghouse for such information, there is no need to reinvent the wheel.

Provide Security and Structure

With one part of life "out of control" because of a loss, children and adolescents need to be able to feel that they still have some control in other areas of life. It is not unusual for students to attend class immediately after a loss and to try to go through the day in as "normal" a manner as possible. This gives them a feeling of "control" over this part of life. However, to force children to behave in a routine manner after a death or other major loss when they do not wish to do so removes the very feelings of control we are trying to reinforce. School policies must acknowledge that an "individual" person is always more important than a "general" policy and each student must be aware that this is true.

Plan to Cover a Full Range of Possible Responses

Planning should be directed not only at schoolwide response after a death or other loss but at things a teacher may do with an individual student. Teachers should know that an individual child might have an increased need for attention. If asked questions by students, teachers should be honest and avoid platitudes, avoid speaking of blame for the death, listen (and not feel the need to try to solve all of the grieving student's problems or to make everything "all right"). Help students to understand grief and to set priorities.

Help Each Child at His/Her Own Developmental Level

There are materials available to help students understand and cope with loss. Books about losses, such as death and divorce, exist in abundance. They are geared to many ages, developmental levels, and even to specific cultural/ethnic groups. A book that is very good for a middle school student or class may miss the mark entirely if read to second graders. Teachers and parents should know *in advance* what is contained in any story they share with a child. There are death/loss curricula for high schools, middle schools, and elementary schools. These are not automatically interchangeable. Material aimed at younger students can be used with older students, but the reverse is not equally true. A classic book that pointed out the developmental differences in student grief and highlighted possible ways of dealing with grief in ways appropriate to the level of the student is *Discussing Death: A Guide to Death Education* by Gretchen Mills (1975). It does not provide a curriculum but offers instead the information that can be the basis for creating classes to aid grieving students.

Help Children and Adolescents to Externalize Thoughts/Feelings

Provide ways for students to "get out" the thoughts and feelings they may otherwise keep bottled inside. Drawing pictures, writing, reading stories related to loss or grief (called "bibliotherapy"—book therapy—by some), or storytelling can all be helpful techniques in giving grieving students an opportunity for needed catharsis—an emotional cleaning out. One exercise my students found most helpful was the burning of "secrets." Each student was given a paper. They were asked to write on that paper something they wished to "leave in the past." Or they could write down (externalize) some secret that felt they could not share with anyone else. Each student was asked to write "something," no matter what, so that those with items to get rid of would not feel singled out. They could write something important to them or just write that they had nothing to say.

The papers were then crumpled into balls and placed in a small can (with holes punched at the bottom). They were taken outside and then burned as a way of getting rid of any bad feelings connected with the thought the student had written down. The first time I tried it I was not sure precisely how the students might react. They insisted on watching until they were sure that there was nothing left but ashes. From that day on, every class asked when they too could have that special class. It seems that more students than we realize have painful thoughts and feelings they are looking for a way to "release." (Note: This exercise has been used with children ages 8 and older. With young children, it is important to take all necessary time to include a warning about safety. Explain that they should only do this with adults to help.)

Remember That the Impact of a Loss on Students May Affect Others as Well as the Children

As time passes, most members of the school community will grieve, recover, and move on from a loss and its aftermath. It may seem that, since the death of a student has a clear impact on that child's teacher, to stress this point is only to belabor the obvious. However, teachers in the roles of caregiver and educator may have difficulty taking time to tend to their own needs. When a child dies, teachers often spend long hours helping children and parents and in seeking training to be more effective in that role. Such a death also places an emotional strain on teachers as well as on students and parents. It is important that schools acknowledge this situation and that they take time to acknowledge the change that has occurred for staff as well as for students.

Assume a Partnership Role

The partnership of parents and teachers and other members of the community at-large is vital in assuring a caring atmosphere for students in which learning can flourish. In addition, every teacher and school should have another "partner" when called on to assist students following a death. Each school should develop a partner school that can be called upon for help when a death or other loss affects a school community. Typically such a partnership involves joint staff development so that the educators in both schools get to know each other before some crisis occurs. They then can work out ways in which the school coping with the aftermath of a death can draw on needed support from the partner school. Teachers too may at times need a partner. A teacher coping with personal losses may not be able to give full attention to the needs of grieving students and may require the assistance of a colleague at such a time. Partners can also discuss and evaluate attempted interventions and constantly improve their ability to assist students. There is not just one way to assist students—no one way to best deal with questions about a death or with the grief that follows.

FINAL THOUGHTS

Children who have experienced bereavement have special needs. A well-known psychologist once said of her own grief, that "knowing why you hurt doesn't make it hurt less." It should be added, however, that such knowledge could keep you from hurting more than you have to. If this is true for adults, it is even more so for bereaved children who have lost someone precious to them. To keep the hurt from being worse than it has to be, parents, family members, and educators have found it helpful to create procedures to employ when the need arises. In this way, plans are formed when the pressures of time and emotional distress are at a minimum. School policies, staff training programs, and even appropriate readings for use by (or with) students can be put in place in advance of need. This is not "therapy." These steps may have a therapeutic effect on some students, but actual therapy is work best left to healthcare professionals. In teaching these children about death and grief, about the feelings they will encounter, we accomplish something else. When we teach students about loss and grief we do not cure emotional illness. What these lessons can "cure" is ignorance—the ignorance of children, the ignorance of adults. These lessons might well lessen the pain such ignorance may cause.

REFERENCES

Anthony, S. (1940). *The child's discovery of death*. London, UK: Paul, Trench, Trubner.
Anthony, S. (1972). *The discovery of death in childhood and after*. New York, NY: Basic Books.
Artemieva, T. V. (2002). The problem of death and a system of "death education" in Russia. In J. Morgan & P. Laungani (Eds.), *Death and bereavement around the world: Volume 1: Religious traditions*. Amityville, NY: Baywood.
Behrens, R. et al. (1967). *A descriptive study of elementary school children who have suffered a major loss*. Master's thesis, Simmons College of Social Work.
Berg, D. & Daugherty, G. (1972). *Perspectives on death*. Baltimore: Waverly Press.
Bordewich, F. M. (1988, February). Mortal fears: Courses in "death education" get mixed reviews. *Atlantic Monthly, 261,* 30–34.
Carter, W. B. (1971, Winter). Suicide, death and ghetto life. *Life Threatening Behavior, 1*(4), 264–271.

Cox, G. R. (2002). North American native care of the dying and the grieving. In J. Morgan & P. Laungani (Eds.), *Death and bereavement around the world: Volume 1: Religious traditions.* Amityville, NY: Baywood.

Elder, S. (1994). Support groups in the schools. In R. Stevenson (Ed.), What will we do? Preparing a school community to cope with crises. Amityville, NY: Baywood/

Feifel, H. (Ed.). (1959). *The meaning of death.* New York, NY: McGraw-Hill.

Gaudry, E., & Spielberger, C. (1971). *Anxiety and educational achievement.* Sydney, Australia: Wiley.

Gullo, S. V., & Plimpton, E. H. (1985). On understanding and coping with death during childhood. In S. V. Gullo, R. R. Patterson, J. E. Schowalter, M. Tallmer, A. H. Kutscher, & P. Buschmans (Eds.), *Death and children: A guide for educators, parents and caregivers.* Dobbs Ferry, NY: Tappan Press.

Jobes, G. (1962). *Dictionary of mythology, folklore and symbols.* New York, NY: Scarecrow Press.

Kubotera, T. (2002). Japanese religion from folklore perspectives: Critical comment on Kunio Yanagida's ideas of the spirit of the dead. In J. Morgan & P. Laungani (Eds.), *Death and bereavement around the world: Volume 4: Asia and Australasia.* Amityville, NY: Baywood.

Laungani, P. (2002). Hindu spirituality in life, death, and bereavement. In J. Morgan & P. Laungani (Eds.), *Death and bereavement around the world: Volume 1: Religious traditions.* Amityville, NY: Baywood.

Martinson, I. (2002). Dying, death and grief: Glimpses in Hong Kong and Taiwan. In J. Morgan, & P. Laungani (Eds.), *Death and bereavement around the world: Volume 4: Australia and Australasia.* Amityville, NY: Baywood.

Mills, G. (1975). *Discussing death: A Guide to Death Education.* Carlsbad, CA: ETC Publishing.

Morgan, J., & Laungani, P. (Eds.). (2002a). *Death and bereavement around the world: Volume 1: Religious traditions.* Amityville, NY: Baywood.

Nagy, M. (1959). The child's view of death. In H. Feifel (Ed.), *The meaning of death.* New York, NY: McGraw-Hill.

Papadatou, D., & Iossifides, A. M. (2002). Dying and death in the Greek culture. In J. Morgan & P. Laungani (Eds.), *Death and bereavement around the world: Volume 1: Religious traditions.* Amityville, NY: Baywood.

POZ. (2002, November). Takin' it to the street: We're all over AIDS. *POZ.*

Rogiewicz, M. & Ratajska, A. (2012). Dying, Death, Funeral, and Grief in Poland. In *Death and bereavement around the world: Europe (Death, Value and Meaning.* Amityville, NY: Baywood

Sigel, R. S. (1970). An exploration into some aspects of political socialization: School children's reactions to the death of a president. In R. S. Sigel. (Ed.), *Learning about politics: A reader in political socialization.* New York, NY: Random House.

Somers, P. (2002). Living and dying is an art, even in Belgium. In J. Morgan & P. Laungani (Eds.), *Death and bereavement around the world: Volume 3: Europe.* Amityville, NY: Baywood.

Stevenson, R. G. (1984). *Curing death ignorance: A death education course for secondary schools.* Unpublished doctoral dissertation.

Stevenson, R. G. (1987). The fear of death in childhood. In J. E. Schowalter, P. Buschman, & P. R. Patterson (Eds.), *Children and death: Perspectives from birth through adolescence.* New York, NY: Praeger.

Stevenson, R. G. (2002). *What will we do? Preparing a school community to cope with crises* (2nd ed.). Amityville, NY: Baywood.

Stevenson, R. G. (2009). Children and death around the world. In J. Morgan & P. Laungani (Eds.), *Death and bereavement around the world, Volume 5: Reflective essays*. Amityville, NY: Baywood.

Stevenson, R. G., & Powers, H. L. (1987, May). How to handle death in the school. *Education Digest*.

Stevenson, R. G., & Stevenson, E. P. (Ed.). (1996). *Teaching students about death: A comprehensive resource for educators and parents*. Philadelphia, PA: Charles Press.

St. Vincent Millay, E. (1997). The kingdom where nobody dies. In *Collected poems*. Cutchogue, NY: Buccaneer Books.

Trojcak, R. (2002). The Jewish Foundation to the Christian belief in resurrection. In J. Morgan & P. Laungani (Eds.), *Death and bereavement around the world: Volume 1: Religious traditions*. Amityville, NY: Baywood.

Willcock, D. writer/producer (1988). *Everyman Series: The Facts of Death*. London, England: British Broadcasting Corporation.

Zweig, A. R. (1983). Children's attitudes toward death. In J. Schowalter, P. R. Patterson, M. Tallmer, A. H. Kutscher, S. V. Gullo, & D. Peretz (Eds.), *The child and death*. New York, NY: Columbia University Press.

CHAPTER 2
Death Version 2016: How Children and Adolescents are Learning and Grieving in Cyberspace

Illene Noppe Cupit and Olyvia Kuchta

Isn't it ironic that in such a death-phobic society as the United States death is an omniscient presence on the Internet? Death lurks on all of our electronic devices, from cell phones to tablets. Typing in the keywords "Death and Dying" in the Google search bar will yield about 177,000,000 results in approximately 0.20 seconds. The sites run the gamut from casket building to computerized games featuring death. In addition there are virtual cemeteries, memorial websites, online support groups, information about death (from both questionable and reputable sources), YouTube videos featuring cross-cultural practices as well as actual assisted suicides, and numerous reports of mortality statistics. Even comics featuring death and dying are found on the Internet: referring to the cyberworld we now inhabit, the "Grim Reaper" reports that going online to find his victims has replaced his house calls.

Perhaps more influential than the compendium above are the use of social media sites, which, broadly defined, are websites or computer-based applications that support social interaction through posts, the sharing of information, user-generated commentary, and visual data such as photos and videos (Marwick & Ellison, 2012). There has been such an upsurge of such sites that it is difficult to keep track of who is using which site and for what purpose. Perhaps the most reputable source for such data is the Pew Research Center, which in May 2013 published its most recent national survey of technology use among 12–17-year-olds and their parents (Madden et al., 2013). Some of the key findings of this report are as follows:

- 78% of teens now have their own cell phones and almost half (47%) of them have smart phones, or phones with Internet connections.
- 23% of teens now own a tablet computer.
- 95% of teens use the Internet.
- 8 in 10 adolescents who are online use social media.

- 93% of teens either own a computer or have home access to a computer. Sharing a home computer with other family members is fairly common, as 71% claimed that they do so.

There are several sites that are popular among older children and adolescents, including Facebook and Twitter. The Pew report (Madden et al., 2013) found that most teens favor Facebook, with 94% of the teens who use social media maintaining a Facebook profile and 81% claiming that Facebook is the social media site that is most often used. In addition, Twitter use is growing—fully 26% also have a Twitter account, with smaller numbers attracted to Tumblr and Instagram. Findings in the Pew Report, as well as other reports claim that adolescents are migrating to social networking sites other than Facebook and Twitter, including Instagram and Snapchat, perhaps in response to the "takeover" of the more "traditional sites" by their parents and other adults. Finally, the popularity of social media sites has led to the development of new sites (e.g., ScuttlePad) explicitly pitched to children younger than 13 years old, the age requirement for membership in Facebook. Thus, expectations of social media literacy and usage are extended downward to young children.

As new social media opportunities emerge and as teens move from one computerized venue to the next, it may become increasingly more difficult for adults to supervise and monitor their Internet activity. The prevalence and salience of such Internet activity is a dominant force in the intellectual, social, and emotional development for older children and adolescents. Cyberspace occupies all dimensions of the ecological life space of children and adolescents, affecting their most intimate interactions as well as providing a cultural context for their development. As Sofka (2014) notes, youth's involvement with technological communication defines their generation (i.e., they are considered "digital natives," whereas older generations are "digital immigrants"). More importantly, social interactions and identity exploration frequently occur in a virtual universe, so the social and psychological consequences of the use of such devices must be considered in the study of child and adolescent development.

NARRATIVE PSYCHOLOGY, MEANING-MAKING, TEENS, AND TECHNOLOGY

Although modern technology via mobile devices lures all age groups, the appeal to adolescents and emerging (young) adults is obvious. We refer to young adults as "emerging adults" to represent an age group (approximately 18 to 24 years) bordered by adolescence on one side and adulthood on the other (Arnett, 2004). What is it about texting, using social networking sites, "googling" (a noun, a verb, and a framework for the universe) everything under the sun that makes this so appealing to this cohort? Narrative psychology and the theory of reconstruction of the self through storytelling provide a useful organizing framework. According to this theoretical perspective, individuals find coherence in their experiences through the use of narrative, which enables them to find a sense of order, meaning, and coherence to their understanding of their selves in a temporal sequence of past, present, and future (Crossley, 2000). It is a phenomenological, reconstructive perspective that examines the structure of a narrative, with its beginning, middle sections (involving plot twists and resolutions), and anticipated endings. Through this self-narrative, individuals gain a sense of identity and an understanding of who they are in their place and time (Crossley, 2000). These self-narratives are continually being revised as a result of social interactions and the flow of life, but it is during periods of developmental transition (e.g., adolescence and young adulthood) when such narratives especially need reconstruction. A death, particularly when it is traumatic, typically demands active processing of one's self-narrative and reconstruction of the autobiography (Neimeyer, 2011). It is the means by which the adolescent tries to comprehend who he or she is now without the parent, friend, or sibling. This occurs at all age levels, but perhaps this process is where new technologies lure the adolescent and emerging adult. We contend that it is through writing and communicating about the events, about oneself and others via the various Internet-based modalities, that narratives reflect continual processing and reprocessing in a social context (Crossley, 2000).

The Internet also serves as a treasure-trove of information and misinformation about death (Cupit, Sofka, & Gilbert, 2012). For example, Seligson (2014) describes a popular Youtube channel, "Ask a Mortician," established in 2011, which allows for videos to be posted discussing questions from anything ranging from "How do you become a mortician?" to "Can you bake cremated remains into a chocolate cake?" It is inevitable, therefore, that the Internet may be the resource for children, adolescents, and emerging adults to learn and communicate about one or more of the multiple facets of death and dying. In particular, identity reconstruction, mean-making about death, and connection seeking is the draw for such cohorts, and the Internet facilities these processes in many ways. This is because many features of social networking sites and other Internet-based sources form an easy synthesis with the normative developmental advancements of this portion of the life span. And it is the integration of Internet use and the specific features of adolescence that help to inform how older children, adolescents, and emerging adults turn to the computerized world via social media sites, chat groups, blogs, search engines, and other computer-mediated communications to create a new developmental picture of their encounters with death and dying.

THE DEVELOPMENTAL TASKS OF ADOLESCENCE AND THE INTERNET

According to Blos (1979), adolescence is best understood as sequential phases (early, middle, late), each associated with core tasks. In our contemporary adaptation of this perspective, which includes adolescents' involvement with technology, early adolescence (approximately ages 10–14) heralds the chief developmental task of emotional separation from one's parents, as is evidenced by the primacy of peers as a source of emotional support and identity development. For many young teens, texting, social media sites, and venues of expression such as blogs are a desirable way to connect with friends and distance themselves from their elders. Adolescents may be horrified by the thought that their relatives wish to "friend" them, and they devise strategies to avoid their watchful eyes. Of course, this also means that in case of their experiencing death or a life-threatening illness that such distancing may render them isolated from adult help. Social media, in this case, can be an attractive lure to receive such social support, especially because it is removed from the embarrassment of unpredictable face-to-face interactions. It provides the young adolescent with an opportunity to work on the narrative with his or her "friends" rather than with adults. As the narrative gets co-constructed with one's peers, so does the adolescent receive affirmation (or sadly, disconfirmation), which helps to sort out the identity concerns in relation to death.

In a second phase (middle and late adolescence—approximately 15–18 years), the adolescent moves toward gaining a sense of independence, competence in making decisions and setting goals, and developing a sense of self in terms of a more realistic identity and set of values. Many years ago, sociologists posited that the self develops out of social interaction. According to Mead (1934), the self emerged from imagining ourselves how others perceive us—" the looking glass self." Later, David Elkind (1967) proposed that adolescents, in the throes of egocentrism, carried about an "imaginary audience," observing and perhaps judging all that they did, said, and wore. Has the mirror and that judgmental Greek chorus migrated to Facebook, Snapchat, and Twitter? Is that why adolescents (and increasing numbers of children) feel compelled to record and photograph everything? Do such accounts affirm that an event happened and offer the opportunity for feedback? Thus, while still communicating via social media, the Internet becomes a way to receive feedback about oneself, and a "place" where teens increasingly turn for information and resources in the decision-making process. They also receive and send posts and links that provide information of interest to themselves and to their peers. Adolescents use social media sites for their identity explorations in a variety of ways. The death of a loved one is a defining event for most people; for the adolescent, that death may become who they are, particularly when they are in the acute phases of their grief or working through a life-threatening illness. Mentally processing identity issues may thus take place online, as the adolescent writes of death and dying and what it personally means for him or her. Posting pictures, articles, videos, and blogs provides a means of self-expression and storytelling. The story gets told and retold so that a communal sequence of events, sense of meaning about what had happened, and the place of one's own thoughts and emotions and evolving sense of self in this context emerges. An evolving self in the context of death and loss emerges out of this process. As Kasket (2012) notes, social media sites such as Facebook allow us to co-construct our identities as well as our sense of existence.

The final phase is posited as a newer "stage" of development, stemming from contemporary economic and social forces. Blos (1979) referred to "late adolescence," but current economic and social factors have led Arnett (2004) to propose a newer stage, termed "emerging adulthood." Spanning roughly ages 18–24, it is a period characterized by instability, transience, and intense self-focus in preparation for the more adult responsibilities of love and work that follow. Emerging adults are fully expected to be technologically proficient and connected, and are expected to know how to access and use social networking sites appropriately. Thus, adolescent/ emerging adult "cyberculture" is cohort defining and affords a location for social interaction, a private space to develop independence, a means for self-expression and exploration, and a community, which may be especially important when teens and emerging adults feel disenfranchised or marginalized (Sofka, 2009). Emerging adults may find that the Internet provides a "participatory culture," whose open membership encourages the sharing and exchanging of information (Jenkins, Purushtoma, Weigel, Clinton, & Robison, 2009; Sofka, 2009).

Of course, neatly dividing adolescent development into these three phases is an oversimplification. Developmental issues, as well as how they interact with encounters with death, reach peaks and valleys over all of these years. In addition, cutting across these dimensions in terms of how they interact with technology is the immediacy of the process, particularly rewarding to the adolescent whose time perspective and sense of immediate gratification do not necessarily match the adult world's relationship with time. It is within this milieu that children's adolescent and emerging adult use of the Internet for their encounters with death and dying can now be understood.

ADOLESCENCE DEVELOPMENT, DEATH, AND TECHNOLOGY

During the adolescent years, conceptions of death undergo a significant evolution to a closer approximation of a "mature" understanding (Noppe & Noppe, 1991). Such understanding operates in conjunction with intense emotional responses that many adolescents experience with regard to death. Adolescent cognitive and affective development come into play in conjunction with increased experiences of loss and death. Although popular culture portrays these years as the zenith of vitality, possibility, and limitless opportunity laden with fun, the truth is that many adolescents are deeply aware of their nondeath losses. They lose, for example, their belief that they can grow up to be anything that they want to be, their trust in the adults around them, and a simpler worldview, which includes death only coming to the aged (Noppe & Noppe, 1991). They are concerned about the continuity of life on the planet and become aware of a personal legacy that they hope to someday leave. Such ruminations play an important role in understanding their life span and the life spans of others, wherein death becomes the end marker in a more realistic way. Is it possible that some of the risk-taking behavior, devil-may-care attitudes of this age period, and fascination with death themes in popular music (Plopper & Ness, 1993) and fiction (e.g., the Harry Potter series, the *Twilight* series, and the zombie population explosion in videos) partially reflect both embracing and a thumbing of the nose at the Grim Reaper?

Many of these changes, sadly, also are a result of increased encounters with death. Some of these are normative as grandparents and other elders in the teens' lives die.

But the increase in peer death due to violent, sudden, and tragic means cannot be denied. For example, whereas in the general U.S. population the leading cause of death is cardiovascular disease, for adolescents (aged 15–24 years) it is death due to unintentional injuries (e.g., car accidents, firearm accidents), homicide, and suicide (CDC, 2014). Human-induced deaths also are the leading causes of adolescent death throughout the world (Balk, 2014; Cupit & Meyer, 2014).

The moral here is that although adolescents look like adults in terms of their mature understandings of what death means, their own personal experiences (which at times may be traumatic), their sense of vulnerability and invulnerability, and their need to carve personal identities apart from conventional thinking and their behavior (including using technology and social media in this context) makes them look different in terms of their approach to death (Corr & Corr, 2013).

For example, a recent article in the *New York Times* (Seligson, 2014) addresses how young adults are redefining mourning via the Internet. Profiling young adults grieving over the death of parents and friends, the article zeroes in on many positives of social media as it offers a place of support for those grieving through innovative means. These means can get as creative as receiving a mix tape for submitting an online essay about an experience of loss. The founder of "Lisa Frank Mixtape," Zoe Feldman, has found this system to be incredibly helpful for people experiencing grief. Positively reinforcing the bereaved for sharing their grief experiences helps them to realize that there are rewards for sharing their narratives as they themselves receive benefits from the narratives of others. "One person wrote and said it's like being part of a weird, sad tribe" (Seligson, 2014, para. 11). But tribes have rituals, social norms, and their stories, and they impart a sense of identity and belonging to which many adolescents and emerging adults gravitate.

ADOLESCENT COPING WITH GRIEF, DYING, AND LOSS: TRAVERSING FACEBOOK, TWITTER, AND OTHER THANATECHNOLOGICAL REALMS

The most popular form of computer-mediated communications among adolescents and emerging adults are social networking sites, which largely are public websites that allow users to share communications and view the communications of others with whom they are connected in some fashion (Marwick & Ellison, 2012). The power of such social networking sites is that the content is persistent (does not disappear from cyberspace), easily replicable, is of a large scale in terms of the possible numbers of individuals who can view the material, and is characterized by "context collapse," in other words, different groups of people (e.g., social class, ethnic backgrounds, age groups, degree of "real-life" interaction, educational, and professional levels) all are lumped together into a few groups such as "contacts" or "friends" (Marwick & Ellison, 2012). Within this wide dispersal of interpersonal communications, we find that adolescents, who tend to be very private about intense emotion-laden experiences, seem to have no qualms about airing their feelings in such a public venue (Walrave, Vanwesenbeeck, & Heirman, 2012).

Such public airing of one's thoughts and feelings about the death of close friends, celebrities, and even individuals unknown to the writer on social networking sites (DeGroot, 2014) seems to be fairly common for today's adolescents. Mourning on these sites is therefore a public affair, uncontrolled in terms of who may receive access and comment, and co-constructed in the sense that the story about the deceased changes with the writings of various mourners. Across the globe, funeral rituals and practices evolved to allow such mourning in public spaces, as it enables the community of mourners to receive a sense of social consolidation (Kastenbaum, 1977). Adolescents, who may shun public funeral ceremonies (and view them with disdain), nonetheless engage in public mourning rituals via the Internet wherein perhaps they gain their own cohort-driven sense of social consolidation. But postings are not subject to the nuances, social cognitions, and modifications of communications that are typical of face-to-face interactions (Marwick & Ellison, 2012) and are not easily restricted to certain viewers.

FACEBOOK

Users of Facebook establish a home page that usually has pictures, profiles of oneself, ways to contact others ("friends"), and a "wall" where the user can self-post and see the postings of others. When someone dies, and if Facebook is notified, that account, and wall become "memorialized," meaning that it can no longer be changed or accessed by anyone other than the current list of friends. These friends, however, are able to view and post on the wall and communicate with others via their postings. Thus, the memorial Facebook evolves as the story of the deceased continues to be modified and changed, and the mourners gain a sense of community via the timeline and a continued relationship with the deceased (Kasket, 2012). Such postings offer a treasure-trove of data as to how contemporary adolescents mourn and seek social support via their technology. For example, Kasket (2012) analyzed the content of the Facebook postings of adolescents who died in car accidents and also interviewed three individuals with regard to their experiences with these posthumous writings. One of the themes that emerged from such analysis was the expression of the belief that the deceased was receiving the Facebook message: "I know u can read this, it just sux that u can't talk back . . . thanks for letting me talk to u again" (Kasket, 2012, p. 65).

Another important theme that emerged from Kasket's (2012) analysis was that Facebook was used to maintain the relationship with the deceased (Klass [2006] referred to this as "continuing bonds"): "A piece of who he was is still going to live on, his heartbeat will always be with his family . . . but for the rest of us, as a friend, or the people who sat next to him in class, it's a way for them to remember him too . . . to feel connected ('Ruby')" (Kasket, 2012, p. 66).

Such communications also suggested that the mourners received solace by being a member of an Internet community, particularly by reading the posts of others. So Clare says, "I shared comforting quotes and lyrics that I found. Anything that helped me, I put up there in hopes that it would help someone else" (Kasket, 2012, p. 66).

Similar themes of adolescents' messages on a social networking site were also found by Williams and Merten (2009), who examined comments and blogs of teenagers to 20 profiles of now-deceased teenagers. The researchers found that over the course of a year, the number of comments decreased, with these comments becoming less emotionally intense with time. Most importantly, Williams and Merten found that such comments were directed toward the deceased and not other users on the site. The authors also observed that images, poems, statements of coping, and humor peaked and valleyed during landmark days (i.e., holidays, birthdays, and major life events). The content of the comments ranged from declarations of love and missing the deceased, events in honor of the deceased, and comments of coping strategies. What was especially noteworthy about the findings of Williams and Merten was the active emotional and mental processing and self-reflections that were imbued in these messages. Adolescents reminisced, described the trajectory of their grief, discussed current situations, and waxed philosophical about theology, life, and death. In other words, they created and reworked their narratives over time.

The replicable, large-scale, persistent, and context-collapsible nature of social networking sites also means that Facebook memorial pages may be available to those who have no "real" connection to the deceased and yet feel some sort of bond in a remote and virtual manner, people who DeGroot (2014, p. 78) calls "emotional rubberneckers." These observers became active posters as well, either noting their remote relationship with the deceased or connecting with the death in some personal way (DeGroot, 2014). Thus, emotional rubbernecking provides an outlet for nonbereft adolescents to learn about the affective and tangible consequences of death, relate these to their own personal experiences as they construct their own values with regard to death, and work on their own sense of identity construction as they self-disclose on the memorial walls. As in the case of the "actual mourners," the private becomes public in a voyeuristic way. Looking across the results of these studies, it is evident that adolescents are actively constructing narratives of the death—their relationships with their deceased friends that are attempts to form a cohesive story during a period of life characterized by transition and self-exploration. This is "meaning-making" at its best, in a virtual universe (Cupit et al., 2012).

Along with Facebook, there are other emerging online venues where adolescents manifest their grief. Many adolescents are switching from Facebook to new versions of social media that their parents have not yet embraced. A recent study done by researchers at GlobalWebIndex found that daily Facebook use for adolescents has declined (Peterson, 2013). This research has shown that while Facebook still remains popular, other media sites such as Twitter, Snapchat, Vine, and Tumblr are increasing in popularity.

TWITTER

Many adolescents are using Twitter in combination with a multitude of other forms of social media. The challenge of reducing the story to a few lines may inhibit and oversimplify the complexity of grief as well as one's self-narrative. Conversely, there are positives with using Twitter because it is so instantaneous, forward, and does not demand much cognitive and affective energy. The status updates, or "tweets," can be used as a form of reassurance for adolescents who may be looking for a sanctioned way to grieve in comparison with their peers—a form of minimalist meaning-making. The continuous tweets can maintain a conversation about a person who is deceased as a form of remembrance. Such shared memories and comments may be a way of promoting and maintaining the legacy of the deceased (Sanderson & Cheong, 2010).

OTHER THANATECHNOLOGICAL VENUES

During World War II, servicemen would note their presence on the many fronts of the war by drawing a cartoonish character with the expression, "Kilroy was here," as seen in Figure 2.1 (Brown, 2001).

Stories need audiences and making a permanent notation helps to acknowledge one's selfhood, particularly under duress and under times of identity transition. It should not be surprising, therefore, that taking a "selfie," or a photo of oneself using a mobile device, has increased in popularity. The Pew Center for Internet Research reports that 91% of teens have posted a selfie (Madden et al., 2013). Should this also include taking a selfie at a funeral? The practice has become an area of contention because it becomes one of intent in which the reason behind the selfie is questioned.

Figure 2.1. Kilroy was here.

Whereas adolescents may engage in this practice as an affirmation of their presence at a funeral, their elders view this as disrespectful behavior. Some argue that the intention of taking a selfie at a funeral is as a token of love or remembrance. Selfies, as a pictorial narrative, can also be a way to tell one's online community that an important person in one's life is now deceased. Especially for adolescents, who are highly connected to online communities, selfies become a way to share a connection with others, receive feedback, and reformulate identity through meaning construction. Because adolescents are searching for reassurance as they strengthen their identity, a selfie can be valuable when an adolescent is vulnerable, such as when at a funeral (Gibbs, Meese, Arnold, Nanson, & Carter, 2015). Adolescents may use the selfie to illustrate the narrative and connect with other people about this significant event happening in their lives. Although others may view such behavior as offensive, adolescents may even point to President Barack Obama, who was seen taking a selfie with two other world leaders at the funeral of South Africa's Nelson Mandela in 2013.

Additionally, another popular social media website is YouTube, a website to where users can post and watch videos. Recent research complied by Pew Research Center found that 24% of adolescents post videos of themselves (Madden et al., 2013). The prevalence of adolescent use of YouTube is important when it comes to the expression of grief responses. Because contemporary social media has evolved to be more than just a source of information, postings on YouTube may be particularly important in facilitating emotional expressions (Lee, 2011). YouTube is shown to offer a way for the emotional needs of a bereaved user to be met (Lee, 2011). According to Lee's (2011) analysis using media systems dependency theory, bereaved adolescents depend on this online environment to help them to cope with their loss.

CONCLUSIONS: EMBRACING SELF-NARRATIVE VIA TECHNOLOGY

In this chapter, we have argued that there are many ways in which adolescents and emerging adults (digital natives) who are seeking information about death and/or coping with loss and grief are using contemporary technology. Of course, it is important to acknowledge that not all of the information is accurate or helpful—some is quite sensationalistic, and some may be harmful to a vulnerable young person. Caring adults need to help adolescents and those on the cusp of adulthood to recognize misinformed and dangerous online sources and to help them learn what is safe and not safe to post on various sites. Educators and parents also must be aware that the age of use of social networking sites is moving downward (Madden et al., 2013) and that younger adolescents also tend to have fewer privacy concerns (Walrave et al., 2012).

Yet embedded within adolescents and emerging adults' extensive use of technology is the need for self-exploration, identity development, self- and peer-reflection, and social connection. They are using their stories, via the many different forms of communication on their mobile devices, to make sense and coherence out of emotionally disruptive events at a time when they are working hard to find their place in their own life span. It is important, therefore, for individuals who are involved with these cohorts, such as educators, parents, and clinicians, to be aware of the significant role that technology plays in the lives of young people. It is not helpful to shake one's head in dismay at how stuck youth are to their cell phones and tablets, especially at difficult times such as when they are struggling over an encounter with death. Rather, it behooves us to embrace the technology, work at being technologically literate, and encourage adolescents and emerging adults to share what they have written. Sofka (2014, p. 219) says it well:

> Inviting adolescents to share tales of their adventures in the digital world, whether the genre of the tale turns out to be a drama, a comedy, or a horror story, is a useful way to help process these experiences and to alleviate one's own worries or fears about the impact of digital technology on an adolescent's social and emotional well-being.

REFERENCES

Arnett, J. J. (2004). *Emerging adulthood: The winding road from the late teens through the twenties.* New York, NY: Oxford University Press.

Balk, D. (2014). *Dealing with dying, death and grief during adolescence.* New York, NY: Routledge.

Blos, P. (1979). *On adolescence.* New York, NY: Free Press.

Brown, J. E. (2001). Kilroy. *Historical dictionary of the U.S. Army.* Westport, CT: Greenwood. Retrieved from https://books.google.com/books?id=ygqNt3ra-vYC&pg=PA264&dq=kilroy+was+here+1939&hl=en#v=onepage&q=kilroy%20was%20here%201939&f=false

Centers for Disease Control and Prevention (CDC). (2014, February 13). *FastStats: Deaths and mortality.* Retrieved April 16, 2014, from http://www.cdc.gov/nchs/fastats/deaths.htm

Corr, C. A. & Corr, D. M.. (2013). *Death & dying, life & living* (7th ed.) Belmont, CA: Wadsworth.

Crossley, M. L. (2000). Narrative psychology: Trauma and the study of self/identity. *Theory Psychology, 10,* 527–546.

Cupit, I. N., & Meyer, K. J. (2014). Accidents and traumatic loss: The adolescent experience. In K. Doka (Ed.), *Coping with loss in adolescence* (pp. 117–138). Washington, DC: Hospice Foundation of America.

Cupit, I. N, Sofka, C. J., & Gilbert, K. R. (2012). Dying, death, and grief in a technological world: Implications for now and speculations about the future. In C. J. Sofka, I. N. Cupit, & K. R. Gilbert (Eds.), *Dying, death, and grief in an online universe* (pp. 47–60). New York, NY: Springer.

DeGroot, J. M. (2014). "For whom the bell tolls": Emotional rubbernecking in Facebook memorial groups. *Death Studies, 38,* 78–84. doi: 10.1080/07481187.2012.725450

Elkind, D. (1967). Egocentrism in adolescence. *Child Development, 38,* 1025–1034.

Gibbs, M.., Meese, J., Arnold, M., Nansen, B., & carter, M. (2015). #Funeral and Instagram: Death, social media, and platform vernacular. *Communication and Society, 13,* 255–268.

Jenkins, H., Purushotma, R., Weigel, M., Clinton, K., & Robinson, A. J. (2009). Confronting the challenges of participatory culture: Media education for the 21st century [White paper]. *MacArthur Foundation.* Retrieved May 21, 2008, from https://mitpress.mit.edu/sites/default/files/titles/free_download/9780262513623_Confronting_the_Challenges.pdf

Kasket, E. (2012). Continuing bonds in the age of social networking. *Bereavement Care, 31*(2), 62–69. doi: 10.1080/02682621.2012.710493

Kastenbaum, R. J. (1977). *Death, society, & human experience, Part 4*. New York, NY: Mosby.

Klass, D. (2006). Continuing conversations about continuing bonds. *Death Studies, 30*(9), 843–858.

Lee, C. S. (2011). Exploring emotional expressions on YouTube through the lens of media system dependency theory. *New Media Society, 14*, 457–475. doi: 10.1177/1461444811419829

Madden, M., Lenhart, A., Cortesi, S., Gasser, U., Duggan, M., Smith, A., & Beaton, M. (2013, May 21). Teens, social media, and privacy. *Pew Research Center*. Retrieved April 15, 2014, from http://www.pewinternet.org/2013/05/21/teens-social-media-and-privacy/

Marwick, A., & Ellison, N. (2012). "There isn't wifi in heaven!" Negotiating visibility on Facebook memorial pages. *Journal of Broadcasting & Electronic Media, 56*(3), 378–400. doi: 10.1080/08838151.2012.705197

Mead, G. H. (1934). *Mind, self & society*. Chicago, IL: University of Chicago Press.

Neimeyer, R. A. (2011). Reconstructing meaning in bereavement. In M. Watson & D. Kissane (Eds.), *Handbook of psychotherapy in cancer care* (pp. 247–258). Hoboken, NJ: Blackwell.

Noppe, L. D., & Noppe, I. C. (1991). Dialectical themes in adolescent conceptions of death. *Journal of Adolescent Research, 6*, 28–42.

Peterson, B. (2013, November 12). Where are the Facebook teens going? *globalwebindex*. Retrieved April 2, 2014, from http://blog.globalwebindex.net/facebook-teens

Plopper, B. L., & Ness, M. (1993). Death as portrayed to adolescents through Top 40 rock and roll music. *Adolescence, 28*(112), 793–807.

Sanderson, J., & Cheong, P. H. (2010). Tweeting prayers and communicating grief over Michael Jackson online. *Bulletin of Science, Technology & Society, 30*, 328–340.

Seligson, H. (2014, March 21). An online generation redefines mourning. *The New York Times*. Retrieved April 18, 2014, from http://www.nytimes.com/2014/03/23/fashion/an-online-generation-redefines-mourning.html?_r=0

Sofka, C. J. (2009). Adolescents, technology, and the Internet: Coping with death in the virtual world. In D. E. Balk & C. A. Corr (Eds.), *Adolescent encounters with death, bereavement, and coping* (pp. 155–170). New York, NY: Springer.

Sofka, C. (2014). Adolescent use of technology and social media. In K. J. Doka & A. S. Tucci (Eds.), *Helping adolescents cope with loss*. Chicago, IL: Quality Books.

Walrave, M., Vanwesenbeeck, I., & Heirman, W. (2012). Connecting and protecting? Comparing predictors of self-disclosure and privacy settings use between adolescents and adults. *Cyberpsychology: Journal of Psychosocial Research on Cyberspace, 6*(1), article 3. doi: 10.5817/CP2012-1-3

Williams, A. L., & Merten, M. J. (2009). Adolescents' online social networking following the death of a peer. *Journal of Adolescent Research, 24*, 67–90. doi: 10.1177/0743558408328440

CHAPTER 3

The Disenfranchised Grief of Children and Adolescents*

Kenneth J. Doka

INTRODUCTION

One of the perennial debates in psychology is the question of when children are capable of grief. According to some, particularly those who take a psychoanalytic approach, true mourning does not occur until a child has fully developed an identity in adolescence. Others hold that children are capable of grief once they achieve object consistency, around the age of 3. I have always liked Worden's (2009) comment—that *all* children are capable of grief but that they express their grief in different ways than adults.

Worden's position affirms two major points. First, it reminds us that from the earliest ages children form attachments and can experience significant loss when these attachments are severed. Second, it also recognizes that children are still developing—cognitively, emotionally, spiritually, behaviorally—hence, they are likely to express their grief differently at different stages of their development.

But even if we understand and recognize that children do grieve, we do not always acknowledge all their losses. Like adults, sometimes children's grief is disenfranchised; although they grieve, others around them do not acknowledge their right to mourn.

This chapter explores the disenfranchised grief of children. Beginning with a brief overview of the concept of disenfranchised grief, I then consider the types of losses that children may experience that might be disenfranchised. Finally, I offer suggestions for helping children cope with disenfranchised grief.

DISENFRANCHISED GRIEF

In every society there are norms or rules that regulate behavior. From the time we are born, we are constantly taught these rules—how and what to eat, ways to dress, how to behave toward other people.

---

*This chapter draws from previous material published by the author (see Doka, 1995).

But we learn other sets of rules as well—"feeling" rules, which govern the ways we are expected to feel (see Hochschild, 1979). We make reference to these rules all the time. "I have every right to feel angry." "I know I shouldn't feel guilty." In each of these situations, feeling rules are evoked that affirm or contrast our own feelings with some accepted norm.

In fact, we can broaden the concept of feeling rules to a more general sense of internal rules. For just as there are norms that govern external behaviors, there are norms that focus on internal states. These go beyond feeling rules to norms that govern how we are expected not only to feel but to think and to believe.

Some of these internal rules define who, what, when, and how someone is supposed to grieve. In most Western societies, these norms define *grief* narrowly. We have a right to grieve when family members die; in many businesses, workers are accorded time off when members of the immediate family die.

Yet our attachments extend beyond the family. But when we grieve the loss of those loved ones, our grief is likely to be disenfranchised; it is not openly acknowledged, socially supported or sanctioned, or publicly shared. Sometimes one may disenfranchise oneself out of shame or guilt. For example, a man involved in an extramarital affair may never be able to acknowledge the relationship or his grief over the loss should his lover die. Even if he did, others may not acknowledge his right to grieve.

In earlier books on disenfranchised grief (Doka, 1989, 2002), I described four different contexts of disenfranchised grief. The first context includes unrecognized relationships. In many relationships outside kin, the closeness of the attachment is often not appreciated. The loss of a friend or a lover, for example, may be devastating, yet at best the friend may be expected to support family members. Death can even engender grief when it ends relationships that existed in the past (e.g., that with an ex-spouse) or never involved actual interactions (that with a celebrity).

A second context of disenfranchised grief involves losses that are not recognized as significant. Abortion, perinatal loss, the loss of a pet, all can be grieved. Many nondeath-related losses such as incarceration, divorce, adoption, or placement in foster care may cause grief reactions that are unrecognized by others.

In the third context, grievers are not recognized as being capable of feeling grief. The grief of the very young, the very old, or the mentally or developmentally impaired is often unacknowledged. Fourth, certain types of deaths can be so shameful that even grievers with a socially legitimate right to grieve may be reluctant to acknowledge their loss. Examples of disenfranchising deaths include suicide, alcohol- or drug-related deaths, or victim-precipitated homicide. Given the stigma attached to the disease, many grievers may feel that they cannot publicly acknowledge the loss of someone who died of AIDS, depriving themselves of the opportunity to mourn or seek support.

A fourth context describes grievers who do not grieve in socially expected ways. For example, this can include individuals who are perceived as either too stoical or emotional in their expression of grief.

Whatever the context, each of these losses shares one similar characteristic. In each there is a sense that those experiencing the loss have no right to grieve. Their grief is disenfranchised.

THE DISENFRANCHISED GRIEF OF CHILDREN

Like adults, children, too, can be disenfranchised grievers, often for the very same reasons. Like the rest of us, children have a circle of people with whom they are exceedingly close. Friends are an extremely important part of their social world. Writing in his novella "The Body" (which later became the basis for the 1986 movie *Stand by Me*), Stephen King (1982) reflects that we never have friendships as strong as those in childhood. Perhaps it is because adults simply do not have the time for friendships that children do. Children and adolescents can literally spend scores of hours each week developing, maintaining, and nurturing their friendship ties.

Given the extensive investment children place in friendships, the death of a friend can be devastating. Not only is it a frightening reminder of vulnerability and mortality, it is also the loss of a key relationship, a part of the child's identity. Children will grieve these losses intensely. But the adults around them may not recognize the great significance of the loss. In one case, for example, Joey's parents were deeply troubled by the fact their 9-year-old son seemed to accept the loss of his grandmother so well but was devastated when his friend Todd drowned on vacation. They failed to recognize that, while his grandmother played only a small part in his life, Todd was one of Joey's most significant ties. From daily rides to school to weekend sleepovers to after-school sports, Joey and Todd were inseparable. Teachers, coaches, neighbors, and supportive adults may also be part of the child's world, and children may grieve their deaths deeply as well.

Relationships with noncustodial parents are also likely to be more significant than others recognize. I investigated the reactions of children to the deaths of their noncustodial parents, particularly parents who had had minimal connection to the child (Doka, 1986). Many of these children did feel grief, not only for the death of their natural parent, but also for the ties that never had an opportunity to develop. Mark is a good example of this. Mark was not yet born when his parents divorced. His father never saw him or even acknowledged him as his son. When his father died 10 years later, Mark's mother could not understand her son's grief. Mark grieved the relationship that never was and now never would be. With his father's death, Mark's fantasy of an eventual reconciliation died as well.

Even negative attachments can be grieved, when the relationship is a strong one. Louie was an aggressive, sometimes bullying sixth grader. When he died in a car accident, his teacher was surprised that one of the children most affected was Keith, a child Louie often tormented. Keith felt very guilty about the death since he often had publicly wished Louie would die or disappear. Even when the death was announced to the class, one classmate turned to Keith and loudly whispered, "I'll bet you're glad." While the attachment between the two boys was negative, it was still an attachment.

Children are attached not only to their own intimate network but to the wider world as well. Often they are caught up, as some adults are, in the lives of celebrities: witness, for example, some of the adolescent and preadolescent magazines and posters that decorate children's bedrooms. The deaths or illnesses of rock stars, presidents, or other heroes may cause a deep sense of grief. Many adolescent youths, for example, grieved with Magic Johnson when he announced he was infected with HIV.

A second type of disenfranchised grief is that of unrecognized loss. For example, a common unrecognized loss in adolescence may be that of abortion. Not everyone who has an abortion experiences a grief reaction, but some do. Those who are likely to do so include those who are having an abortion for the first time, those who are ambivalent about the choice or were pressured by others to select abortion, or those who viewed the pregnancy as a solution to another problem. Adolescent girls are very likely to possess some or all of these factors that place them at risk. And sometimes it is not just the adolescent girl but the boy as well who feels a sense of loss.

One of the most common, most significant, and often unrecognized losses in adolescence is the loss of a romantic relationship—breakups of boyfriends and girlfriends. In his surveys of college freshmen, Louis LaGrand (1986) found that this was the loss cited as most significant by the largest number of respondents. Many adults, however, were unresponsive to the feelings of grief that such breakups generated.

Losses do not always have to be that of humans. From films such as *Lassie* and *National Velvet* to *Free Willy* we have celebrated the bond that children can have with animals. The loss of a pet causes a grief that parents and adults may not always appreciate. The ways that adults respond to what may be the child's first significant loss may teach children patterns that they may seek to use in subsequent deaths. For example, denying the child's grief and seeking to obtain a quick replacement may unwittingly teach the child that grief should be suppressed and that, when one faces a loss, one should seek immediate replacement. It is better to allow the child to mourn the loss and later, when he or she is ready, seek another pet. The child should be reminded that this pet, even if the same species and breed, is different than the pet that died, reinforcing the idea that each individual, and each loss, is unique.

There may be other losses, too, that children experience and grieve in childhood. The loss of childhood innocence or idealism may itself be grieved. Zupanick (1994), for example, suggested that children who grow up in dysfunctional families may grieve the loss of perceived normalcy.

As children grow older, they may grieve the loss of opportunity. Tom, for example, grieved deeply when he was cut from his high school varsity team. To Tom, that loss meant that he was not likely to fulfill his dream of a professional sports career.

Children experience many losses that are not due to death but are losses nonetheless. Parents, relatives, or friends divorce; friends move. People they care about may change, sometimes in the course of development, sometimes because of other factors such as drug or alcohol abuse or incarceration. Even graduations can be ambivalent experiences encompassing both pride and loss. Children and adolescents may also be placed in or removed from foster care. Foster children, foster families, and foster siblings and natural families and siblings may all be touched by loss. In all these cases, these losses may remain unrecognized by others, the child's or adolescent's grief disenfranchised.

Divorce can represent a major loss for many children. It is often complicated by the fact that children may have many ambivalent feelings about the divorce, for example, regretting the separation but being happy that any open conflict has ended. Children, too, have to mourn the loss of the one parent while simultaneously building a new relationship with that parent. They may be struggling with other feelings such as guilt and anger. And they may be struggling alone, disenfranchised by others, themselves mourning. Children can even delay their own grief, feeling that they need to support others.

Another significant yet unacknowledged loss can result from the incarceration of a parent. Joy (2014) notes that the losses the children experienced were extensive. Not only did they lose a relationship with a parent but secondary losses as well. For example, the incarceration of a parent might involve a significant loss of family income.

Because of their ages, even children or adolescents grieving the loss of family members can be unrecognized grievers. This is particularly likely to happen to very young children. People often assume that preschool children cannot understand death and must be protected from it. When a death occurs, these children may not have an opportunity to participate in rituals, nor may their capacity to grieve even be acknowledged by others.

Developmentally or mentally impaired adolescents or children may have similar experiences. When her mother died, Jenny's family did not even notify the group home where the 19-year-old resided. They reasoned that, since she was mentally handicapped, she would not understand what had occurred and would burden them during a difficult time. Similarly, John's parents tried to shield John, a hospitalized 14-year-old schizophrenic, from his brother's death.

We also may disenfranchise young children or developmentally or mentally impaired adolescents since they express grief differently than expected. Crenshaw (1991) speaks of the "short sadness span" of children, the fact they often find it intolerable to hold uncomfortably strong emotions for long periods. Their grief then may by expressed in short intensive outburst followed by periods during which they seem unaffected by loss. But while young children or developmentally or mentally impaired youths may grieve differently, they still grieve.

Finally, there are disenfranchising deaths. Children are not immune to shame, and certain types of deaths carry a stigma that children may hesitate to bear. Paul, an upper-class 13-year-old, and Maria, and impoverished 15-year-old, have each lost a brother to AIDS, and both are too ashamed even to acknowledge the loss to others. Their grief is similar to Jessica's, whose sister committed suicide, and to Ty's, whose father died while committing a robbery. Joy (2014) describes the grief of children whose fathers were executed. As Joy notes, few of the children wished to openly address the arrest, trial, or subsequent execution. In each case, the shame of the death has impaired the individual's ability to grieve. In each case, the grievers disenfranchised themselves. Unwilling to share their losses with peers or supportive adults, they grieve alone.

One can be disenfranchised in more than one way at once. For example, 19-year-old Jerome was doubly disenfranchised. He could not share the fact that his mother's foster children are HIV infected. He realized that disclosure not only violated the foster agency rules but would also create problems for him and his family in the neighborhood. When his young foster brother was removed and hospitalized, later to die, he did not feel free to share his grief over the loss of his first "kid brother," whom he loved deeply. But even if he had, others might not recognize the loss of a foster brother as significant.

These examples are not meant to be exhaustive. Readers will recognize other significant losses that may be disenfranchised. Children may experience grief in a wide variety of situations and contexts that may be unrecognized by others.

HELPING CHILDREN COPE WITH DISENFRANCHISED GRIEF

Children can be assisted in dealing with disenfranchised grief in the same way that they can be helped in dealing with their loss. By respectfully listening to the child, allowing the child to share his or her grief, adults not only provide genuine support but teach effective coping.

Adults may have to validate children's grief and to help them recognize and interpret their sense of loss. This means acknowledging the loss and stressing that the child's grief is a normal reaction to the loss experienced.

Children, too, need an opportunity to participate in grieving. Rituals set aside to commemorate a loss can be a powerful way to give feelings focus and recognize grief. Children should not then be immediately excluded from funeral or other memorial rituals; rather they should be offered choices on whether and how to participate. In order to make meaningful choices, children will need information about what to expect in the rituals as well as possible options. It is also essential that adults are there to support the adults and manage the child at the ritual. If parents are intimately involved in the ritual or actively grieving, that may mean assigning the task to someone who has the time, relationship, and ability to focus on the child.

As other chapters will emphasize, varied expressive activities, therapeutic ritual, and grief groups often are very useful in offering children and adolescents grief support. These interventive strategies can be particularly valuable when grief is disenfranchised.

It takes courage to grieve. For the child, it takes courage to recognize and cope with uncomfortable feelings. For the adult, it takes courage to trust the child to do so. Yet there is little alternative. Children, as well as adults, form all sorts of attachments that are severed in all kinds of ways. When these attachments are broken, there is grief. The challenge for adults is to recognize the full scope of children's attachments and grief and to honor their grief as best they can.

REFERENCES

Crenshaw, D. (1991). *Bereavement: Counseling the grieving through the lifecycle.* New York, NY: Continuum.

Doka, K. J. (1986). Loss upon loss: Death after divorce. *Death Studies, 10,* 441–449.

Doka, K. J. (1989). *Disenfranchised grief: Recognizing hidden sorrow.* Lexington, MA: Lexington Press.

Doka, K. J. (1995). Friends, teachers, and movie stars: The disenfranchised grief of children. In E. Grollman (Ed.), *Bereaved children and teens: A support guide for parents and professionals* (pp. 37–45). Boston, MA: Beacon Press.

Doka, K. J. (2002). *Disenfranchised grief: New directions, challenges and strategies for practice.* Champaign, IL: Research Press.

Hochschild, A. R. (1979, November). Emotion work, feeling rules and social support. *American Journal of Sociology, 85,* 551–573.

Joy, S. (2014). *Grief, loss, and treatment for death row families: Forgotten no more.* Lanham, MD: Rowman & Littlefield.

King, S. (1982). The body. In *Different seasons.* New York, NY: Viking Press.

LaGrand, L. (1986). *Coping with separation and loss as a young adult.* Springfield, IL: Thomas.

Worden, J. W. (2009). *Grief counseling and grief therapy: A handbook of the mental health practitioner* (4th ed.). New York, NY: Springer.

Zupanick, C. (1994). Adult children of dysfunctional families: Treatment from a disenfranchised grief perspective. *Death Studies, 18,* 183–195.

CHAPTER 4
Trauma and Grief in Early Life: A Model for Supporting Children, Adolescents, and Their Families

Dianne McKissock

BACKGROUND

The practice model described in this chapter was developed at the National Centre for Childhood Grief in Sydney, Australia, which is known publicly as *A Friend's Place* so that children won't feel stigmatized when asked where they are going. Co-founded as a charitable service by my husband, Mal, and me 21 years ago, it was financially supported solely from our teaching fees for the first 15 years. Children between the ages of 3 and 18 years are seen free of charge. The Bereavement C.A.R.E. Centre, our adult service, shares the same building and was similarly founded and funded 36 years ago, but is now our private practice. Children initially received counseling from the Bereavement C.A.R.E. Centre but it became clear that in order to raise community awareness of the needs of bereaved children and to act as their advocates, we could be more effective in the context of a specialist service. Initially staffed solely by volunteers, the service now pays sessional fees to professional counselors who are helped by trained support workers. Staff currently consists of an office manager, a coordinator of counseling services, 5 specialist children's bereavement counselors, 4 adult's counselors who see parents and other caregivers, and 10 support workers. All those involved work part time.

INTRODUCTION[1]

Trauma and grief are part of early life experience for many of our community's children, adolescents, and their families. Sudden or expected death; chronic illness; separation and divorce; loss of home, country, or financial security; domestic

---

[1] The words "child" and "children" will be used in speaking about both children and adolescents. No matter what our age, we are all somebody's child.

violence; child abuse; natural disasters; and media images all too frequently scar the ideal, innocent landscape of childhood.

The outcome is not all doom and gloom. There are abundant success stories in the arts, politics, business, science, and community service, of traumatized or grieving children who go on to become successful, fulfilled adults. Availability of safe places and people, compassionate care, and constructive survival strategies have the ability to help children and adolescents learn to live with grief and develop valuable life skills. While the focus of this chapter is on grief from death-related loss, the clinical principles involved and the model described can be adapted and applied to loss and trauma from any cause.

Aim

This material was written as a guide for caring professionals and volunteers involved in the care of children, who want to develop the best possible ways of minimizing long-term harm from traumatic life events.

Target Group

Information included here may have particular relevance for those involved in hospital- or community-based palliative care who hope to develop bereavement support services for the children and siblings of their patients. It is also hoped that psychologists, social workers, pastoral care workers, school counselors, and teachers will be able to apply whatever aspects of the described practice model are appropriate in their own situation. Ethical principles included provide guidelines for determining suitable referral sources for individual children.

The Model

The theoretical aspect of the model that underpins this chapter—Chaos Theory—is derived from physics. Chaos Theory aptly describes the out-of-control, "all over the map" experience of most bereaved people and the conscious and unconscious endeavors of the individual or family system to restore balance, to re-create the old and familiar order. Of course, this is not possible. The role of skilled and compassionate others is to "hold" or support the person or destabilized system until a new order is established. For those interested, a detailed description of Chaos Theory as it applies to bereavement can be found in other publications by the author (McKissock, 2004; McKissock & McKissock, 1998, 2003).

The following images illustrate the natural, narrative order in which uncomplicated clients share their experiences, hopes, and fears, and rehearse for their changed future. Once the client's unique rhythm of contact with, and need for distraction from pain is revealed, the counselor facilitates the process by asking sensitive and creative questions that stimulate a kind of tai chi movement from the "event" to memories of the past. These memories can bring the deceased or former self to "life," and time in the "future loop" allows expression of fears, hopes, and rehearsal,

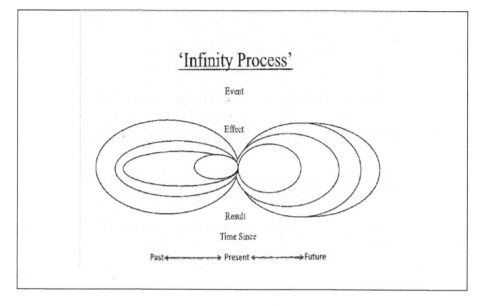

Figure 4.1. Infinity model.

ensuring that the client gradually develops "them centered" strategies for managing grief and facing their changed future.[2]

The broadly systemic, clinical practice aspect of the model, called the Infinity Model (illustrated above) has that title because grief is infinite, dynamic, nonlinear, and the process is descriptive, not prescriptive. It shares some features of the Dual Process Model developed by Stroebe and Schut (1995, 1999). Aspects of the present, past, and future are consistently and creatively woven and rewoven through storytelling and other empowering strategies to rebuild the web of broken dreams, helping young people to live with, and in, a world that for them has been changed forever. Movement from the pain of the present to memories of the past and rehearsal for the future serves a double purpose—temporary relief from intensity and reduced fears of "getting stuck." Key aspects of the model involve the belief that grief makes children, adolescents, and adults into an exaggerated version of their nonbereaved selves, that emotional and at times functional regression are core, universal aspects of grief, and that passionate sadness is a more accurate description of most grief responses than the frequently used inappropriate label of "depression."

Positive reframing when appropriate is used to enhance young people's understanding of events and of their own responses. Children are taught how to recognize and label their own emotional reactions to events, to sensory stimuli, and to the

---

[2] The narrative process with young children is not smooth and usually involves small story "grabs" over numerous sessions, eventually gathered together by the counselor into the familiar infinity "shape."

words of others. They learn how to "pass" when asked voyeuristic questions, how to eventually take control of their story instead of feeling controlled by it, and how to distract when "enough is enough." Each child, each family's natural rhythm of contact with, and distraction from pain is identified and respected. Painful events are not avoided, nor are they forced into focus. Whatever naturally surfaces as foreground is dealt with in whatever way seems right for this child—this family. Finally, the power of retrieved, positive memories is consistently highlighted as an important tool to sustain connection with the person who has died.

FAMILIAR OR "NORMAL" GRIEF REACTIONS IN CHILDREN AND YOUNG PEOPLE

Put simply, children's grief responses at different developmental "stages" might be summarized as

- Ages 2–4: Death is experienced as abandonment. The child believes death is reversible—regressed behavior is intended to elicit care.
- Ages 4–7: Death is often personified (e.g., the Grim Reaper). Some children still think death is reversible. They may feel responsible for the death—magical thinking.
- Ages 7–11: Death may be seen as punishment for bad behavior, bad thoughts. Children in this age group have a reasonable understanding of the permanence of death. They have the ability to mourn more openly. They may ask a lot of questions, regress, or act out.
- Age 11–18: There is a more adult approach with traditional mourning. May experience anger or what can appear to be depression. Regressive behavior and biological changes may stimulate rebellion and acting out. They may find it easier to talk to someone outside the family.

These responses are generally well known in theory, going back to Maria Nagy in the 1940s (as described in Stevenson's earlier chapter), but are less understood and accommodated in practice. Many grieving children claim to feel misunderstood by adults and by their peers. They tend to be referred for help, often reluctantly, when their behavior causes concern at home or at school. Parents may be surprised and anxious when their child doesn't appear to be grieving; doesn't cry; is irritable, rebellious, or withdrawn; or sometimes if they appear to be getting on with life "as if" the painful event had not occurred. Conversely, parents may also worry if the child is regressed and clingy, cries a lot, or shows changes in their eating or sleeping patterns.

Teachers and school counselors might encourage parents to seek counseling for their child as a result of inattention in the classroom (daydreaming), crying over seemingly trivial occurrences, or aggressive behavior toward another child. These may be good reasons for making a referral for a grief "check up," or continuing support, but are all normal responses.

NORMAL, BUT LESS UNDERSTOOD, GRIEF RESPONSES OF CHILDREN

I will begin with regression because it has already been mentioned here.

Regression

Regression refers to a belief developed through many decades of observation and thousands of hours of clinical experience at our Centre, that grieving and traumatized people, no matter what their age, can regress emotionally and functionally. When asked, most bereaved people describe their internal age as anywhere from 8 to 15, while others who may have been abused, neglected, abandoned, traumatized, or experienced loss at an earlier age, describe feeling pretty much the age they were when the event occurred. Initially, the feeling and behavior appears to be persistent, ebbing and flowing sometimes many times during any given day, week, month, eventually moving to intermittent as grief becomes more familiar (McKissock, 1998, 2009). Regression can be reexperienced whenever grief becomes foregrounded. Older children and adults, even some young children, find the concept understandable, accurate, and normalizing, and when asked, "How old do you feel inside right now?" are usually able to readily identify an age.

This core concept is not judgmental or patronizing. In fact, it facilitates compassion, explains behavior, and identifies appropriate counselor strategies. As with anyone who is or feels young and vulnerable, the counselor may initially do some things "for" the client, moving to do things "with," still later simply retaining "fingertip support."

Passionate Sadness vs. Depression

Passionate sadness may be a more accurate term to describe grief reactions after the death of someone with whom the bereaved has shared a relationship with a high degree of centrality. Grief and depression may share many of the same observable and felt features—sleeplessness, restlessness or lethargy, crying, sighing, feeling hopeless, unable to find meaning in life, being self-focused, changed eating patterns, a range of physical symptoms such as nausea, aches and pains, breathlessness—but they are not the same. The old adage "What looks like a duck and walks like a duck is not necessarily a duck" applies here. It is almost impossible to differentiate between sadness and depression in the first 6 months after a painful and/or traumatic event. Later, it can be easier for a skilled clinician to do so. Adults are often inappropriately diagnosed and medicated for experiencing or demonstrating normal responses. When this occurs in the case of young children and adolescents, it can border on abuse. The possible long-term consequences can, and should, generate concern. There is no literature currently available that supports the use of chemicals in "treating" bereaved children.

Fight, Flight, Freeze Responses

In crisis situations, the nature of the crisis, biology, personality, and family modeling influence the way we all respond, as does the availability of competent help and the behavior of those around us. Initially, body chemistry primes us for fight or flight, or overloads our circuits so that we feel "rooted to the spot," unable to do anything. Later, versions of these responses will be experienced and acted out in a learned rhythm that may seem unfamiliar and frightening because of its intensity. Regression, as previously mentioned, exaggerates previous ways of being and doing, and makes us feel vulnerable. We may feel at the mercy of our reactions instead of feeling in control.

A calm, compassionate, and skilled bereavement counselor can explain and normalize reactions. The bereaved or traumatized child or young person can gradually be helped to regain a sense of control over what is controllable, while learning to live with the truth that no matter what we do or believe, some things in life are outside our control.

Loss of Self-Esteem

Current literature tends to identify loss of self-esteem as an indicator of complicated grief, or grief with pathological undertones. Personal experience over 35 years suggests that it is a rare person, no matter what age, who does not experience a loss of self-esteem, especially in the first months to years after a significant bereavement or trauma. Loss of self-esteem is a normal grief reaction and much of this response can be attributed to regression—a feeling of "not fitting our skin." From our regressed "self," we are vulnerable to the kind of internal dialogue that says "I should have been able to . . ." or "I shouldn't have done, said or thought. . . ." All these are versions of "It's my fault" or "I should be able to do or be, better." We have observed that this kind of guilt-laden dialogue at times, though not always, can be related to age and gender. Some children and adults blame themselves for the illness, death, or traumatic event, while others attribute blame to other people, "things" or circumstances. Perhaps anger allows some to feel more in control and able to act, to do or say something when everything in their world feels out of control. The sad part of this kind of response is that it does not elicit the type of caring as does a reaction of sorrow or guilt. Sadness and guilt tend to give helpers a role that can appease some of their feelings of helplessness.

Whether initial reactions are anger, sadness, guilt, or fear, children, young people, and their families gradually regain self-esteem as they survive the "firsts" of everything—the first seasonal changes, birthdays, anniversaries, and significant events. They gradually rebuild a history of solving problems and develop more understanding about their changed "self" and the changed world they now live in. Self-esteem returns as they tentatively take some pride in their achievements.

Heightened arousal can be anticipated and is considered normal with the first impact of bereavement or trauma, and in the days and weeks following the event. What is less understood, and therefore more vulnerable to "diagnosis," is the duration of this reaction. Children, young people, and adults gradually gain understanding of their reactions, regain some sense of control, and learn ways of distracting themselves, managing the discomfort of heightened arousal. Everything can be going along just fine when some simple thing that was not anticipated can tip the scales. More understandable perhaps, media images, reminders of a death or traumatic event, and sensory stimuli all have the power to restimulate fight, flight, or freeze responses. It is as if an on/off switch remains hypersensitive for a very long time, perhaps for years, or in some cases, forever.

Tendency to Catastrophize

When something awful occurs in the life of a child or young person, they lose many things, including innocence. Past security may have come from believing that life was predictable, that someone (initially parents) was in control. That belief can be shattered when grief or trauma becomes part of their lives. Initially, any stimulus that carries reminders of the "event," of their loss, has the power to raise anxiety that something awful is about to happen—again. Everything may appear worse than it is, bigger, more threatening. All of that is understandable from a regressed perspective. While the tendency to catastrophize gradually reduces in intensity in a supportive environment, the bereaved and/or traumatized child may retain a lifetime vulnerability to responding in this way when sick, tired, or stressed.

TENDENCY TO HYPOCHONDRIASIS OR SOMATIZATION OF GRIEF

Our experience with children coming to *A Friend's Place* has been that those whose parents die suddenly, particularly from undiagnosed illnesses such as brain tumor, heart disease, embolisms, ruptured aorta, and the like are particularly vulnerable to somatizing grief. The child's trust in others' ability to notice and correctly interpret signs and symptoms is severely challenged, leaving them with the belief that if they aren't hypervigilant, the same fate might befall them. Every ache and pain, every swelling, every tremor can seem like a warning of something sinister taking place. This tendency can also occur when a sibling dies in similar circumstances or a parent dies from an illness with particularly distressing, observable symptoms like MND, MS, and other neurological diseases.

Parents who may feel understandably concerned often tire of providing reassurance that the child only has a cold, a bruise, or a headache that can be explained. Such parents are encouraged to listen with compassion, provide information and reassurance, a medical checkup if concern continues, then a distraction with an enjoyable activity. We suggest that when the child is old enough to understand, parents explain what is happening, what they are doing and why, so that children's self-awareness is sufficiently increased to enable them to become active participants in their own care. We at *A Friends Place* believe that the child is most empowered when they understand the reasons why they are vulnerable to worrying about their health, know that this may always be so, particularly when they are overtired or stressed, but that they can learn to manage their anxiety. Recognizing and expressing what is happening, differentiating between what needs further attention and what doesn't, and learning to distract with pleasant activities is a good life skill to develop, irrespective of trauma and grief.

WHO MAY NEED SUPPORT?

Bereavement support services should be available to all grieving children, young people, and their families, and not restricted to those deemed to be "at risk." It appears fashionable at the moment, possibly from the perspective of economic rationalism, to attempt to develop screening procedures that identify those most in need of follow-up after significant loss. There are a number of fundamental concerns about this method of determining service provision. The first concerns the possibility of questionnaire insensitivity; second, the potential lack of clinical experience and interpretive skill of those administering the questionnaires; third, the possibility of stigmatizing those deemed to be at risk; and finally, depriving grieving children, young people, and families who are deemed to be "coping," of support that may have immeasurable preventive health value.

From a systemic perspective, it is important to question an implied "illness" focus when grief is a natural and healthy response to a painful event. In ordinary, nonbereaved families, children often complain that it is the problem children who gain a disproportionate share of parental attention. Might this not also be true if bereavement support services focus attention only on those considered to be at risk—the so-called problem people? Bereaved children and families whose outward behavior might indicate the ability to cope, might well be left with the question "What do we have to do to get the attention we also need? How bad do we have to feel?"

Service providers often fear the cost of making support services available to *all* grieving and/or traumatized children. Their concern is understandable, particularly when there are so many other worthy demands on health services. The suffering of grieving children is often unseen or misunderstood and can easily be diminished if comparisons are made with children who have severe behavioral or psychiatric problems, or obvious physical disabilities.

Assumptions may be wrongly made that the family will take care of its grieving children—difficult to do when adults are grieving the same loss, feel empty and powerless, and perhaps have little understanding of childhood grief. Not all children and their families want or need bereavement support services, particularly in the long term. What they do want and need is an informed and compassionate social environment, the right to choose or not choose to access counseling and support services, the right to feel considered and cared for, and not discriminated against just because they appear to be coping. Many children who come to *A Friend's Place* only need one 2-hour session with a skilled bereavement counselor. At the end of this assessment and therapeutic session, the child or adolescent, as well as their parent or guardian, may feel sufficiently reassured to "go it alone." They will leave feeling understood and supported, their reactions and experiences "normalized" by a knowledgeable and compassionate other. Questions will have been encouraged and answered, their own personal coping style validated, or perhaps some new or healthier strategies suggested for managing their grief. It is enough for many young people and their families just to *know* there is help available if needed—at the end of a phone, on a safe website, or via email. In our experience, it is very rare indeed for grieving families to overuse available care.

WHEN SHOULD SUPPORT SERVICES BE PROVIDED?

Many caring people and services are unsure about the best time to offer counseling or other support. Initially, most people need TLC and practical help from relatives and friends when they are feeling regressed and vulnerable. Outside support usually requires the capacity to get oneself from A to B, to sit still, to think relatively clearly, and to absorb information. Based on support experiences at *A Friend's Place*, we believe that somewhere between 4 and 8 weeks after the event is the optimum time to begin, but it is important to accommodate individual differences. Around the 4–8 week mark, body chemistry seems to change, numbness wears off, family and friends return to their usual responsibilities, and everything seems to be getting worse. Fearful of overburdening others and perhaps losing existing support, grieving people may begin to keep feelings, thoughts and needs "under wraps," or turn to outside sources for help. This is usually a good time for support services to make contact, or for friends and relatives to give information about available resources. However, for some, the event may have been so traumatic, or their internal and/or external resources so fragile, that help is needed much earlier. Sometimes, just being given an appointment, even with a waiting period, can "hold" those who find themselves in emotional territory that is frightening and unfamiliar.

Children tell us that support in a school setting usually lasts around 4 weeks, at which time their peers tend to get fed up with the amount of attention the grieving child receives, feel uncomfortable about making comments or asking questions, lose interest, or believe the child or teen is now "over it." Sometimes help isn't sought or needed until much later—perhaps months, or even years. The effect of a new developmental stage, a significant life event, news items, or some unanticipated sensory stimulation may bring the event or grief back into sharp focus, almost as if it is happening all over again. This can be confusing and concerning for the child or teen and for their families or teachers. Occasionally, a young person may not feel on safe enough ground to be receptive to outside help until they have regained some feeling of control over their lives. For some, increased language and conceptual skills make it possible for them to use help offered without feeling dumb or stupid.

At *A Friend's Place*, we have a different "when" for individual and group counseling or support. All children, teens, and their families first receive individual counseling. It is important for the counselor to know and understand the client, the event, their history, and resources, in order to determine the best way of helping "this client"—"this family." We do not include children in support groups until they are emotionally ready to cope with competing for attention, and are believed to be "group children." Traumatized children and teens are often "reluctant grievers" and may have great difficulty telling their story. Others have difficulty stopping the flow of words. For these reasons, and many others, it is probably best that these children be seen individually for an extended period before being considered for inclusion in a support group.

HOW LONG SHOULD SUPPORT BE PROVIDED?

Support needs to be available for as long as necessary, that is, until the child or adolescent demonstrates their ability to build life around pain, to be "in life." The end of an individual or group counseling experience should ideally include an "open door." Many children and families need booster sessions from time to time, as life events and developmental changes return grief into foreground or change its nature. Support that is withdrawn too soon has the potential to undo all the positives that have already been achieved. Fears about creating dependency are rarely justified. If clear boundaries are set and maintained from the beginning of the therapeutic relationship, children and their families eventually take pride in "finding their own feet" in a very changed world. They often gain strength just from knowing that "fingertip support" is genuine and available if they temporarily lose confidence.

We are aware that many services operate differently. For example, those providing group support only may have closed groups and a structured program consisting of perhaps 6–8 sessions, with the potential for a follow-up session sometime later. These programs can certainly be helpful, as are most opportunities to tell important stories and express feelings in a safe setting. It is often believed that open-ended services such as those at *A Friend's Place* are costly and impractical, depriving more needy people in the community of available help. This is not our experience. The use of skilled volunteers and a variety of low-key supportive strategies such as books, pamphlets, email, websites, phone calls, and such often allow grieving families to feel supported just by knowing they can access help whenever needed. In more than 20 years of providing a specialist service for children, and more than three decades for grieving adults, we have rarely experienced anyone overusing or abusing the service.

WHERE SHOULD SUPPORT BE PROVIDED?

The answer is, in a safe place. Ideally, counseling and support services should be provided in an environment that makes the client feel protected and the counselor empowered. When families are experiencing emotional chaos, it is important for those helping them to control what is controllable. The environment may initially be one of the only controllable aspects. Many people are employed to provide outreach services and in that capacity are expected to do home visits. If that is the case, it is important to be clear and realistic about aims and time frame, to pay particular attention to the issue of boundaries, and as much as is possible, define a therapeutic space where interruptions can be controlled or minimized (McKissock, 2004). The same applies to visiting children in a hospital setting where privacy may be difficult.

In most instances, formal counseling and group work for all ages is more easily controlled for safety, privacy, and freedom from interruption in the counselor's familiar territory. This may be in private counseling rooms, a suitable building in the grounds of a hospital, a community health center, a church or community hall, a tent in the desert if necessary, or in a school setting. When asked to provide crisis services (e.g., after sudden deaths like suicide or accidents) in unfamiliar venues such as schools or other community settings, there are important questions to ask before agreeing. These include (a) Is my/our physical presence the best way to meet the need? (b) Is this the best setting to provide compassionate care? (c) Is it the right time? (d) Are we the best people to respond, or would others be preferable in this case? (e) What are the possible legal ramifications of involvement? and (f) the all-important Could this service be provided in 100 similar settings? (See Important Principles of Clinical Practice for further details.)

It is important for each service provider to formulate a clear policy around this and other support issues so that rational answers to requests are possible even when emotions are affected by dramatic or unusual circumstances. We are often asked to provide "in-house" counseling in schools or workplaces after sudden, dramatic deaths or traumatic events, and our response is usually to encourage familiar people to provide opportunities for debriefing, with our support "from the sidelines." We attend to the needs of the caller, rehearse next steps in the process, and offer to be on standby for phone contact if needed. Our physical presence is rarely needed once calm is restored, information provided, and the caller is assured of the availability of external resources when appropriate.

WHO DOES, COULD, OR SHOULD PROVIDE SUPPORT SERVICES?

These points may be determined by (a) the belief system of those in policy-making or management roles, (b) provider knowledge and skills, (c) geography, and (d) available resources.

Based on the above, we are likely to find bereavement counselors, or group leaders, who are salaried psychologists, social workers, medicos, nurses, teachers, and pastoral care workers. The salaried team may be extended with the addition of skilled professionals who offer their services as volunteers, and kind and caring souls who have undergone training and supervision to ensure they are competent support workers. The use of skilled volunteers is an invaluable way of extending the support team and of addressing some of the cost fears discussed earlier. The motivation of some folk who feel "called" to provide their services for bereaved and traumatized children might be dubious, and highlights the need for a sound selection and training process.

Loving parents have a need and a right to ensure that their children and adolescents receive care from safe, competent, compassionate, and well-trained professionals and volunteers. It is important that everyone involved in the care of vulnerable children and young people should have first undergone a background check through the appropriate channels nationwide to ensure that no one has a criminal record. Parents, and at times referring professionals, find it helpful if service providers have photos as well as professional and relevant personal details of all counselors and other support staff available on their website. This enables parents to do some checking up before committing their child or themselves, and to get a feel for the kind of people who create the character of the service.

The following list of desirable counselor qualities is presented as a guide for those selecting service providers, for those referring children and their families, and for parents who want to find the best care available for their child. Counselors should

- Have relevant professional qualifications plus a working knowledge of grief, loss, and trauma, and the needs of bereaved children and young people;
- Believe children are lovable and vulnerable, despite behavior that suggests otherwise.
- Believe life is worthwhile;
- Believe painful events can be survived and integrated in our lives if we help each other;
- Have a good sense of humor;
- Be able and willing to enter a child's world;
- Recognize their own strengths, weaknesses, and prejudices;
- Have fulfilling personal relationships;
- Know what books to read and where to find needed information;
- Believe in the value of effective, supportive clinical supervision.

A more detailed list of desirable qualities can be found in McKissock (2004, pp. 10–11).

IMPORTANT PRINCIPLES OF CLINICAL PRACTICE

Clinical supervision refers to a supportive process that gives the counselor or group leader what they give the child, including safety, compassionate understanding, truthful information, acknowledgment of strengths, creative management strategies, encouragement, and confidentiality. As with the children in our care, the only time supervision confidentiality should be broken is when safety issues are involved—the safety of the counselor or group leader, or the safety of children in their care. Confidentiality should be discussed openly at the beginning of the supervisory relationship and be part of the written or tacit contract.

Boundaries refer to the ethical requirement of all counselors to include a clear sense of personal space and respectful behavior so that children and their families can safely entrust themselves to the counselor's care, knowing that their vulnerability will not be exploited. While the counselor provides an important function of companionship and may develop an intimate relationship with the child, young person, and their family, they are not "friends." All counselor behavior should demonstrate an awareness of this line of demarcation (McKissock, 2004; McKissock & McKissock, 1999).

The "Rule of 100" is a useful "test" counselors can apply when they are moved by a particular child, story, or event to go beyond the call of duty. It may involve something as simple as offering someone a lift to the train station, taking a child shopping or to a sporting event, or responding to a call for help from a teacher after a student has died in dramatic circumstances. The first example involves legal and insurance complications as well as the capacity to change the dynamic of the counselor/client relationship; the second has the power to change not only the counselor/client dynamic, but the dynamic of the whole system—sibling rivalry comes to mind; and the third example involves an examination of how best to use scarce resources to help not only this teacher, this school, these students, but teachers, schools, and students in a much wider area.

Could we offer a lift to 100 clients? Could we take 100 children to an event? Could we respond to the needs of 100 teachers in crisis? 100 schools? 100 students? Could any of us deal with 100 phone calls interrupting our sleep? If the answer is no to 100, then other solutions need to be found. We may on the other hand answer yes to the question as it applies to grieving or traumatized students, if the students are older, for example, middle school to senior high school students. They may be able to gather in an auditorium, with their teachers and school counselors, so that important information can be given, questions asked, responses normalized, and management strategies explained. The situation would be quite different with very young children and might best be dealt with by providing the service for parents and teachers who could then do the same—with support—for children in their care.

Cultural and religious sensitivity means being open and able to learning from each child, each family, cultural and religious expectations and norms, how their culture or religion supports, impacts on, or is affected by their grief. It does not mean taking a course or reading tomes about particular cultures or religions so that one can appear knowledgeable. Further information about all of these principles can be found in McKissock and McKissock (1999, 2003) and McKissock (2004).

A STRATEGY OUTLINE FOR SUPPORTING BEREAVED/TRAUMATIZED CHILDREN AND/OR ADOLESCENTS

Therapeutic strategies may include individual counseling, group support, therapeutic rituals, a website, email facilities, a chat room, text messages, brochures and booklets, a library, special events, question and answer sessions, telephone or text contact, advocacy in legal or education systems, and information sessions for teachers and the medical profession. Caregivers such as parents, grandparents, school counselors, psychologists, social workers, general counselors, doctors, nurses, and lawyers often value access to phone or email support and consultation.

Networking and information exchange with similar services in other states or countries can prove invaluable for counselors, children, adolescents, and their families, decreasing feelings of loneliness or of feeling "different." Public seminars, speaking at conferences, speaking to the media after specific events, and writing articles for publication in magazines and local newspapers can all be broadly effective ways of raising community awareness of the needs of grieving children.

WHAT GRIEVING/TRAUMATIZED CHILDREN AND ADOLESCENTS NEED

Bereaved and traumatized children and adolescents need and have the right

- To be safe—emotionally, physically, and spiritually—to be treated with sensitivity, understanding, and respect
- To ask questions, no matter how confronting for adults;
- To be given truthful information and answers to their questions in age-appropriate language;
- To be included, to be encouraged, supported, and involved in delivery of diagnosis and prognosis, in providing care for a dying relative, in decision making about funerals, rituals, and memorialization;
- To have familiar routines maintained to create a sense of security and control over what remains controllable;
- To choose when they will tell their story and to whom they tell it;
- To express feelings in a way that is safe for them while respecting others' rights;
- To be connected to others who share and understand their experience;
- To remember loved ones who have died and to sustain their connection with them;
- To feel valued, despite family trauma and grief;
- To hope that life will be fulfilling, despite the pain and loneliness of grief;
- That adults will model effective ways of living with painful experiences;
- To have opportunities for enjoyment without being judged as unfeeling;
- To sustain hope—to have things to look forward to.

THE FRIEND'S PLACE MODEL OF SERVICE DELIVERY

Support services for grieving or traumatized children and young people might occur as a combination of the approaches or strategies already described, or as a single aspect, depending on perceived need and available resources. Any service could be described as appropriate if it addresses the needs of its target group. It is ideal if it does so effectively.

In Australia, a model for such service delivery is the children's bereavement service known as *A Friend's Place*, described in this chapter. It is also known as the National Centre for Childhood Grief (the NCCG). It offers services similar to those available through the Dougy Center in America, Merimna in Greece, Winston's Wish in the UK, and the Jessie & Thomas Tam Centre in Hong Kong. All of these facilities share a similar philosophical perspective. Differences in each service reflect appropriate adaptations to local characteristics and to the availability of financial and practical resources.

A Friend's Place grew out of the Bereavement C.A.R.E. Centre in Sydney and became a specialist charitable service for children in January of 1994. Support offered is as close to the ideal as possible in the circumstances. That is, the service is not government funded and is currently dependent on some team members being prepared to provide their skills free of charge, while those with more specialized skills are paid sessional fees. All counselors have appropriate professional qualifications and extensive professional and life experience.

Whom Does the NCCG See?

Clients include bereaved or dying children between the ages of 3 and 18 years and their families, and children and young people whose parent, sibling, or other close relative has a terminal illness.

Is There a Cost Involved?

Some donations are received and appreciated. After an initial assessment session for parents or guardians, all children and young people are seen free of charge until the age of 18.

How Does a Child, Adolescent, or Family Access The Service?

Families can find simple information on a website, or information may be passed on to the grieving family by the school, general practitioner, friend, or relative. Potential clients don't need a referral, but parents or guardians need to make personal contact with the Centre. An answering machine is sometimes used and counselors return calls ASAP. Contact can also be made via fax or email.

Parents or guardians (of children under 16) are seen before appointments are made with a child or young person. This assessment and support session is usually conducted on a fee-for-service basis by consulting professionals. Fees are reduced for those with financial difficulties and no child is denied access to this specialist service on financial grounds. Sessions are usually of 2 hours in duration. An appointment is made with the child as soon as possible after their parent or guardian has been seen and these sessions are also approximately 2 hours. Decisions about how best to help this child, this family, are made after both sessions have taken place.

ASSESSMENT—WHAT IS RIGHT FOR EACH CHILD, ADOLESCENT, OR FAMILY?

Not all children, young people, or families need, or will benefit from, professional help, especially in the form of formal counseling groups. What they need is awareness that help is available and accessible in whatever form best suits their needs. The first line of assessment is to determine if this family might receive the greatest benefit from being given written information or advice and support via telephone or email. Many parents just want to let us know what they have done so far and ask for reassurance that they are on the right path, or perhaps they need advice about how to deal with specific behavior. Others ask for or agree to have a session for themselves so that they can engage with the Centre and are able to receive from their counselor what they may then give to the child or children in their care. In some instances, reinforcing and supporting the parental role is all that is required, particularly when children are very young.

Whatever form family help may take after the initial assessment (phone or face to face), parents or guardians of children and young people under the age of 15–16, as already mentioned, are always seen first for a 2-hour assessment session so that the child's grief can be understood and supported in a relationship context. It is imperative that we understand the parent or guardian's grief, ensure that they are receiving appropriate support for their own needs, and engage with them to develop a trusting relationship so that the environment supports whatever the child gains from counseling. In that way, the child experiences teamwork as an important statement of their role in the family and of their social value. The nature and quality of parental/guardian care the child receives after bereavement or traumatic experience is one of the greatest determinants of long-term outcome (Silverman & Worden, 1993). For this and many other reasons, it would be remiss of any bereavement support service to omit parents or guardians from the assessment process, inclusion in the "helping team," or from receiving ongoing support for their own needs. First sessions with a parent/guardian and later the child may indicate that individual counseling is the best way of addressing identified needs, at least for the time being.

INDIVIDUAL COUNSELING

Children and young people seen individually at the Centre usually begin with sessions every three to four weeks, with family email and phone support available between sessions as required. The space between sessions is gradually increased, always with the possibility of change if the space seems too long or short. If children are traumatized, sessions may be more frequent to begin with until trust is securely established and the child or young person feels more secure, then spaces gradually increased. When trauma is involved, it is important not to retraumatize by pressuring children to tell distressing details of their story. However, they are assured that there is nothing their counselor is unwilling to hear or understand. Emphasis is usually on sensory soothing and helping children and young people learn strategies for managing anything that is intrusively affecting their ability to be fully engaged in life.

Bereavement counseling is not like psychotherapy wherein regular counseling may be required in order to uncover what has been long hidden. In bereavement or trauma, the event is new, the purpose of counseling is to help clients live with what has occurred, not to create change, although change may occur as a by-product. We believe that enough life needs to happen between sessions to help the child/young person and their family develop a history that demonstrates their ability to survive, knowing that a helping hand is available to grab hold of should they fear stumbling. Life happening, along with skilled counseling, minimizes the likelihood that they or the counselor will feel as if they are going over the same spot in the same story.

Each session ends with some fun, physical activity, and, with younger children in particular, may include the parent or guardian. Their inclusion symbolizes teamwork, demonstrates that it is possible to be sad or anxious and still have fun, and facilitates reentry into everyday life after being in the rarified atmosphere of the counseling venue. The counseling relationship does not have a finite ending, usually tapering off over time, always with the knowledge that "booster" sessions can be arranged as needed if, as already explained, grief is brought back into focus by life events or developmental milestones.

SUPPORT GROUPS

Roughly 50% of children being seen at the Centre at any given time are assessed, or self- assess, as group children. The others are seen individually. Some children may be seen on an individual basis initially, later participating in a group. Groups are not for everyone, nor is everyone right for support groups. (Full assessment guidelines are provided in McKissock, 2004, pp. 43–57.) In an assessment session, usually lasting around 2 hours, the counselor wants to learn important things about the following before including children/young people in a support group:

- The child's current story
- Relationship ability
- Level of impulse control
- Frustration tolerance
- Emotional capacity
- Social skills
- Medical history
- Loss history

If the child assessed is able to understand and keep rules around respect, can tolerate some frustration, is not overly shy, can form a trusting relationship with their counselor, appears to be socially and verbally competent for their age, does not have uncontrolled ADHD, does not have any serious behavior or health problems, then a support group might be an appropriate way of providing care. As bereaved children who are regressed and vulnerable generally don't accommodate strangeness or difference easily, we choose to see children with obvious difficulties on a one-to-one basis. Groups are labor intensive, not a cheap way of providing care for the maximum number of people. Our groups of young children consist of 10 participants and four to five leaders, while groups for teens (14 years plus) may be facilitated by two or more competent leaders.

Bereavement support groups can be open ended or closed (with a set program for a time-limited period), or a combination. Groups at *A Friend's Place* are a combination. They are closed in the sense that participants are expected to make a commitment for at least a full school term, but open because the program is ongoing and new participants can join as soon as there is a vacancy. Groups are held fortnightly, with an optional, concurrent group for parents or guardians. Children usually remain in their group until they feel ready, or their behavior suggests they are ready, to graduate. The shortest stay to date has been one school term, the longest 5 years. Graduation ceremonies, meaningful "rites of passage" adapted from those used at the Dougy Center in Portland, Oregon, acknowledge the graduate's courage and ability to live with grief and are poignant for all involved. Descriptions of these ceremonies can be found in McKissock (2004), along with outlines of the structure and sample session content.

The structure of sessions remains constant to create security, the content changing according to group needs. Participants are included in groups experiencing similar losses (e.g., death of a parent or death of a sibling), even though the manner of death may be different. Children experiencing grief from separation and divorce are not combined with those experiencing death-related loss. The Centre operates on the principle that homogenous groups tend to work much better than those that are heterogeneous. It has been found that competition—the "my loss is worse than yours" version—can be minimized. Children bereaved by homicide are kept separate and usually have one or two full-day sessions per year, in addition to individual counseling. The separation from children bereaved in other ways is because we have found that homicide, particularly when the murderer has not been jailed, or involving one parent killing the other, raises the anxiety level of other children.

Groups for adolescents have predominantly been held as a full-day session during school holidays. This seems to work best for young people who have heavy commitments to school work, sports, and social activities. We recognize that the need to remain part of their existing group, to feel "normal" despite their experiences of loss or trauma, is an important part of their survival. However, some of our overseas colleagues have a different experience and provide weekly or fortnightly groups for adolescents, often closed, for a set period of time. These seem to work best when the counselors/services have a close relationship with local schools and conduct groups in a school setting or a setting close to the school.

WHAT HAPPENS IN INDIVIDUAL OR GROUP COUNSELING SESSIONS?

Each session begins with a focus on "engagement" or reengagement. Children and young people are encouraged to share current interests and events in their lives—a version of show and tell. This provides an opportunity to demonstrate *for* themselves and *to* others more of the whole person they really are and their increasing ability to live with grief. They do not want to be defined simplistically and inaccurately as "that bereaved or traumatized child."

Every session involves sharing some aspect of their story. Storytelling will be facilitated in whatever way seems right for this child on this occasion. For very young children, storytelling about a painful event or feeling is likely to be in short "grabs"—a sentence or two, sometimes only a few words, occasionally just in body language or the nature of play. Inclusion of play, fun, and physical activity is determined by the age of the child, their mood or needs on the day, the weather, and the ability of the counselor to creatively respond to overt and covert signals, and/or intuitively anticipate what might be helpful.

The Centre has a large, private garden that can be used in fine weather, allowing children to let off steam, to breathe again after courageously focusing on painful aspects of their lives. Use of this outside area provides opportunities for parents to be included in the ending of individual sessions whenever appropriate, enabling us to reinforce the teamwork aspect of bereavement care and facilitating the child's reconnection with their everyday world. (The garden is also frequently used for physical activities at appropriate points in group sessions, but parents are rarely included.) With the child or young person's agreement, and approval of the content, a summary of the session is given to parents or guardians either verbally in the child's presence, or later in an email, particularly if the child is very young. In this way, the importance of teamwork is emphasized without compromising the child's need for confidentiality.

ADOLESCENT SERVICE

Most adolescent clients over the age of 14 who are seen at *A Friend's Place* choose individual counseling. These sessions are supplemented by an opportunity to participate in an all-day group session during school holidays. The focus of these days might be simple information sharing plus a barbecue and chat, or be more specific like a day for "Motherless Daughters," "Fatherless Sons," and so on. Teens are also able to receive email counseling and support or have text-message contact with their counselor and, with parental agreement, will soon be able to connect with other bereaved teens via the chat room we are developing. Until 5 years ago, financial constraints and other scarce resources prevented holding residential weekends such as those found to be very successful in similar services in other countries. In recent years however, we have introduced separate weekend residential adventure programs for girls and boys and hope that at some point family weekends might be a possibility.

OTHER SERVICES PROVIDED BY
A FRIEND'S PLACE

Special days and events supplement the Centre's ongoing program. Sometimes the nature of these days is dictated by identification of a special need, others because they have proved beneficial in the past. On these occasions, clients being seen individually have an opportunity to participate in a group. They can do so, sometimes without having to tell their story, or much of their story, allowing them to feel connected to others who have similar life experiences, minus the threat of being the center of attention. Examples are

- Art therapy: Opportunities for children to experience the pleasure of creating lasting and very personal memorials under the guidance of someone experienced.
- Drama: Under the guidance of experienced drama therapists and in the presence of their familiar counselors, children get to act in a play about death, dying, and bereavement in a real theater. They are encouraged to improvise, to say whatever is in their thoughts and hearts, and they do so in a most inspiring and moving way, to an audience of parents and guardians. Even very shy children can benefit from projecting thoughts and feelings onto a role that allows them some feeling of protection from personal exposure.
- Family picnic: One example being an adventure experience put on by a local four-wheel-drive club. Children, young people, their families, Centre counselors, and special members of the local community get to share a simple, life-focused experience that tends to be an individual experience in a group setting.
- M.U.M.S. (Men Under More Stress): A special day for widowed dads responsible for raising young children. We invite a sensitive, experienced home economist to teach the dads about household budgets, preparing simple nutritious meals and packed school lunches, shopping, and so on. Part of the day is focused on group discussion with a nurse or medico about female issues, such as explaining menstruation to their daughters, talking about sexuality, hormones, and so on, as well as dealing with simple health issues.
- Motherless daughters: A day to share experiences of growing up without a biological parent of the same sex—"secret women's business"—to learn about and experiment with skin care and makeup, fashion, to talk about boys, music, sex—whatever girls wish they could share with their mothers.
- "Remembering Hearts": An annual ceremony open to the general public wherein loved people who have died are memorialized and honored. Messages written on dissolving hearts are floated in Sydney Harbor and other venues while families picnic, enjoy entertainment, and experience the feeling of connection to others who have had similar experiences of grief.
- End of year party: A celebration of life, of survival. A time to honor the people who died, the courage of those who are grieving, and a time to celebrate whatever rituals are relevant to participants, in the presence of others who understand the bittersweet feeling stimulated by those occasions.

As mentioned, there has been no financial support or human resources to allow offering residential weekends to families attending the Centre, although they could be of great value. This idea has been placed in the "desirable but not essential" category.

Seminars and Conferences

When possible, the NCCG provides speakers for conferences and public seminars. These are typically organized by others and there are occasional small seminars held at the Centre. As the Centre is not government funded, and most staff work on a voluntary or minimally paid basis, fees are charged for public presentations. Center seminars are held for a number of reasons, which include

- To help those on a periodic and unpredictable waiting list for appointments. These free seminars enable counselors to "hold clients," and to help them as they wait by providing information, answering questions, suggesting strategies for managing distress, and demonstrating the fact that counselors are sensitive to the effect that waiting may have on a newly bereaved person. It is rare for anyone to have to wait longer than 3–4 weeks, and most people are seen within a fortnight from first contact.
- To raise awareness in the local community. Medicos and staff from local hospitals and health centers may be invited to visit the Centre to familiarize themselves with counselors and facilities, and to ask questions that might help their patient care and referral processes.
- Response to requests from specific community groups, including self-help groups.
- Educational sessions on current or newsworthy aspects of grief.

To assist with costs, a small fee ($20–$50, depending on the length of the seminar and the nature of refreshments) is charged for each participant at all Centre seminars other than those for clients on the waiting list. Clients attend free of charge.

External Supervision

The Centre directors currently provide clinical supervision for professionals from other organizations or private practice whose work involves working with bereaved or dying clients. Supervisees include psychologists, social workers, medicos, school counselors, nurses, chaplains, school counselors, and teachers. Fees apply for these supervision services.

Clinical Consultations and Debriefing

Professionals are able to have free, brief clinical consultations and postsession debriefing via phone or email. Fees apply when consultations are face to face.

Audio-Visual Resources

A Friend's Place has produced a number of books, tapes and pamphlets that can be ordered online, and in future aims to develop a resource library and reading room for community use. Requests for reading lists suitable for children of specific ages or grieving from very specific losses are usually directed to Compassion Books in the United States.

TRAINING FOR PROFESSIONALS AND VOLUNTEERS

Training has been provided by the Bereavement C.A.R.E. Centre. Beginning in 2015, *A Friend's Place* will provide in-house training for volunteers and external training on request. Available courses include

- Core course (3 days): Fundamentals of loss, grief, and an introduction to bereavement counseling; the foundation for all other courses.
- Adults and Grief (3 days): Counseling grieving adults; the environment in which children grieve; introduction to specialist clinical supervision.
- Working with Bereaved Children (6 days): Involves a condensed core course, along with fundamentals of childhood loss and grief; individual and group interventions; and observation of Centre groups.
- Bereavement Support Workers Course (6 months): This involves completion of the 6-day course mentioned above, followed by a 6-month (two school terms) commitment to assisting trained leaders in a Centre bereavement support group. It does not involve working with individual children. Clinical supervision and progress reports are provided free, and at the successful completion of these terms, the graduate is given a Certificate of Competence as a support worker. Academic qualifications are desirable but not essential for this course, which is the foundation for extended and more intensive training.
- Applied Studies in Death, Dying & Bereavement (12–18 months): Apprenticeship Training—Trainees are selected from interested graduates from the Support Workers Course who have the necessary academic qualifications, have demonstrated desirable attributes in working with children, and have been experienced as creative and cooperative team members. This course involves completion of four written assignments, required reading, monthly clinical supervision, and weekly/fortnightly participation in support groups. Trainees sit in with trained counselors in family and individual sessions and gradually develop a caseload of individual clients. Graduation occurs when the trainee is considered competent in individual and group work, and in their knowledge base about loss, grief, and trauma.
- Postgraduate Diploma in Bereavement Counseling—Children (2–3 years): Apprenticeship Training—This course is only suitable for academically qualified professionals wishing to specialize in bereavement counseling. Applications are accepted from graduates of the above course who have demonstrated advanced knowledge and skills, and have the necessary personal qualities to act as children's advocates in educational and legal settings, and to act creatively in all required leadership roles. The course involves up to eight written assignments, active participation in all support groups, carrying an individual caseload, monthly clinical supervision, gaining administrative

experience, and sitting in with the Centre Directors in a variety of settings from clinical to educational. Graduation occurs when the trainee has demonstrated (via a DVD) the level of competence deemed necessary for a specialist bereavement counselor.

Plans for future training courses include further short courses for community volunteers to be conducted over three weekends. This would enable more warm-hearted and competent people currently unable to take leave from the paid workforce to equip themselves to join the Centre's support team.

CONCLUSION

Working with bereaved children and their families is a rewarding experience, which has the potential to stimulate the full range of human emotions. Sometimes challenging, often sad, but balanced by moments of joy and fun, we have found that counselors who have fulfilling relationships in their private lives and opportunities to refill their own "emotional tanks" tend to survive longest in this important area of community service. Like the families they serve, they also have needs and rights. These are summarized in a kind of "Bill of Rights," which counselors are encouraged to use as a checklist for giving feedback to their clinical supervisors or employers from time to time. As a Bill of Rights for those who support bereaved and traumatized children and their families, the following are a good starting point:

- Appropriate training
- A safe and attractive environment in which to provide care—an environment that is ecologically and therapeutically sound
- Supportive clinical supervision—supervision that provides the caregiver the same support that the caregiver is expected to give to those in their care
- Acknowledgment for providing a valuable community service, often at some personal cost.
- Opportunities to have fun, be lighthearted—to maintain balance and sustain hope.

REFERENCES

McKissock, D., & McKissock, M. (1998, 2003). Bereavement counselling: Guidelines for practitioners. *Bereavement C.A.R.E. Centre*. Retrieved from www.bereavementcare.com.au

McKissock, D. (2004). Kids grief: A handbook for group leaders. *The National Centre for Childhood Grief, Australia*. Retrieved from www.childhoodgrief.org.au

Silverman, P. R., & Worden, J. W. (1993). Children's reactions to the death of a parent. In M. S.Strobe, W. Strobe, & R. O. Hasson (Eds.), *Handbook of bereavement: Theory, research and intervention* (pp. 300–316. New York, NY: Cambridge University Press.

Stroebe, M. S., & Schut, H. (1999). The dual process model of coping with bereavement: Rationale and description. *Death Studies, 23,* 197–224.

Helpful Books for Clients

McKissock, M., & McKissock, D. (1988-2012). *Coping with grief Australia.* New York, NY: HarperCollins.

McKissock, D. (1998 & 2009). *The grief of our children.* ABC Books & The Bereavement C.A.R.E. Centre, Sydney, Australia. Retrieved from www.childhoodgrief.org.au

McKissock, D. (2012). The magic of memories [CD], Book of 16 stories, Illustrated Bed Time Story. *The National Centre for Childhood Grief, Australia.* Retrieved from www.childhoodgrief.org.au

Schuurman, D. (2003). *Never the same.* New York, NY: St. Martin's Press.

CHAPTER 5
Family Therapy and Traumatic Losses

Stephanie Rabenstein and Darcy Harris

The recent confluence of the trauma and grief literature is refining our understanding of what can happen with death and loss occurs by traumatic means. Most of the emphasis of research and scholarly writing continues to focus on the process of individuals after exposure to a traumatic event or death. In this chapter, we wish to further the dialogue regarding grief and trauma by expanding the way that trauma is defined and widening the scope from the more mainstream orientation of the individual perspective to the shared experience of the family system. We will begin by exploring the defining features of traumatic losses and briefly discuss three types of complicated grief in families; traumatic grief, prolonged grief, and posthumous disillusionment. We will review the literature that has been written on the topic of traumatic loss within the family context, and describe some of the therapeutic considerations for working with families where traumatic losses of various types have occurred.

TRAUMATIC LOSS

Serge[1] (age 12), his sister Alana (age 10), and youngest brother Miles (age 6) were referred to a child and adolescent mental healthcare outpatient program by the victim services branch of the local police department. According to the headlines four weeks ago, while his family thought he was in a nearby city driving the cab he owned, Dave (the children's father) stormed the home of a local family and stabbed a woman and one of her two children. Dave was killed in a subsequent armed stand-off with police. Nadia, Dave's wife, and the children's mother was tearful throughout the session. She learned about her husband's death when police came to her door insisting that she accompany them to the police station where she was questioned "like a criminal" by detectives for several hours. Alana sat close to her mother, holding on to her mother's arm, dry-eyed and gazing off into a distant corner of the room while Serge and Miles

---

[1] In the case studies presented in this chapter, scenarios and names have been changed and adjusted to protect the identities, confidentiality, and privacy of clients.

played quietly in the sand tray. When asked about how the children were doing, Nadia reported that Serge often sat for hours in his father's cab which was parked in the family's driveway. Alana was "doing well" and with the support of a family friend, was to begin music lessons. Miles was doing "okay too," although all three children slept with their mother nightly. Nadia explained angrily that the police "were lying" about the events surrounding Dave's death. They told her that it seemed Dave was having an extramarital affair with the woman he supposedly killed. Nadia denied that Dave was unfaithful. She described him as an attentive husband and loving father. She suspected that the police killed the woman and her child accidentally during the exchange of gunfire and were blaming Dave. Furthermore, the family bank accounts were frozen during the ongoing police investigation, leaving the family without income and dependent on friends for food and money to pay the bills. When I (S.R.) asked Serge and Alana to tell me a little bit about their father, both began to weep. Miles stormed over from the sand tray, stuck his face in mine and shouted, "Shut up! You are hurting my family! Stop talking! Shut up!"

What is Traumatic Loss?

A common definition of a traumatic event is one that occurs outside of the range of most people's normal life experiences or expectations (Walsh, 2006). While this description is certainly helpful, we believe that whether an experience is traumatic or not is centered upon the perceptions and interpretations made by those who experience it. A traumatic loss may, in fact, be the violent death of a family member, but it may also be any loss that significantly undermines one's sense of safety or that stretches the boundaries of one's assumptions about how the world should work to the point that there are profound feelings of senselessness, meaninglessness, helplessness, powerlessness, loss of control, and distress (Carlson & Dalenberg, 2000; Janoff-Bulman, 1992; Kauffman, 2002). The key aspect of the trauma centers upon a sense of threat to the individual or to someone who is embedded into the attachment system of that individual, along with an inability to protect and prevent harm from occurring. It is important to note that the threat is not limited to the possible loss of physical existence through death, but it may also include loss of one's sense of psychological and emotional integrity. We are careful in our practices to listen for how our clients describe their experiences, allowing them to tell us not only their stories about what happened, but more importantly, how they perceive and interpret the event(s) that occurred.

While deaths that are untimely, sudden, or violent are cited as the most common source of trauma, other types of experiences may also be considered traumatic losses. Traumatic loss situations may include incidents of physical harm or disability; sudden absence; abduction; relationship dissolution; unemployment; immigration; sexual, emotional, or physical abuse; and/or violence (Walsh, 2007). Neria and Litz write,

> The boundaries between traumatic stress, PTSD, complicated or chronic bereavement as a mental health outcome independent of the nature of the loss, and traumatic bereavement (loss by traumatic means) and traumatic grief (the unique mixture of trauma and loss) have not be examined sufficiently. (2003, p. 74)

It is also important to define and differentiate some of these key concepts that we have found helpful in our clinical work. These terms include traumatic loss, traumatic grief, prolonged grief, and posthumous disillusionment.

- *Traumatic loss* is any loss experience that involves a shattering of one's core assumptions about how the world should work, how people should act, and/or about a person's view of himself/herself (Janoff-Bulman, 1992; Kauffman, 2002). Common examples of traumatic losses may include violent deaths, untimely deaths, sudden deaths, events where there has been prolonged suffering (especially when attempts to try to alleviate suffering are ineffective), losses that are ambiguous or stigmatized, multiple loss events, and losses that "trigger" past traumatic events (Walsh, 2007; Webb, 2004).

  Traumatic losses may or may not involve the death of another individual. Some of our clients who experience non-death-related traumatic losses will sometimes describe feeling that what died was something that was "inside" them rather than a person (Harris, 2010). These losses may be symbolic in nature or experiences that result in a loss of safety and security, anxiety about the future, and inability to trust others or one's self (Webb, 2004). The degree of traumatic overlay is related to the depth in which one's assumptive world is challenged or rendered meaningless. Loss experiences may also encompass more than a single, finite event. The literature on nonfinite loss and chronic sorrow (Boss, Roos, & Harris, 2011; Schultz & Harris, 2011) describes losses that are ongoing in nature and that may not have a foreseeable end. Nonfinite traumatic losses are highlighted by a sense of ongoing uncertainty, vulnerability, and vigilance.

- *Traumatic grief*, a form of complicated grief, refers to a death that occurs within the context of an extreme or horrific event, such as a mass disaster, a violent encounter, extreme events, the presence of bodily mutilation, or some grotesque aspect to the death (Chapple, Swift, & Ziebland, 2011; Nader, 2009–2010). Death that occurs as a result of an incident involving one or more of these factors often leads to traumatic symptomatology in the bereaved survivors. However, whether or not this type of event is actually experienced by an individual or family as a traumatic loss must be ascertained by listening carefully to the perceptions and reactions of the family members and not be solely based upon how the clinician views these same events. The key component of traumatic grief is that the emotional, physiological, and cognitive symptoms of trauma are so overwhelming that they impede the bereaved person's capacity to remember the deceased, which is an essential task of grieving. At its worst, real or imagined images of the violent or accidental death overshadow positive or neutral images and memories. The bereaved family members avoid thinking or talking about their loved one in order to manage the horror that is fused to these memories. This can leave the traumatically bereaved frozen between their trauma and grief; unable to move forward with either.

In the literature on children's responses to traumatic loss, Cohen, Mannarino, and Deblinger (2012) define Childhood Traumatic Grief (CTG) as the death of an important person in a child's life that occurs under circumstances that the child perceives as traumatic. Memories of the deceased person trigger overwhelming trauma responses that in turn make it very difficult if not impossible for the child to grieve. At the far end of the continuum, this disorder has the potential to prompt the onset of depression, substance abuse, suicide attempts, psychiatric hospitalizations, and relationship difficulties if left untreated (AACAP, 2010).

- *Prolonged grief*, another form of complicated grief, occurs after a significant interpersonal loss in which death has occurred but not by violent or accidental means. Prolonged grief is defined by the intensity of the bereaved person's attachment to the family member or friend who has died. It is chronic and unremitting. Its defining feature is separation distress that includes "recurrent pangs of painful emotions, with intense yearning thoughts of the loved one" and disbelief about the death, anger, distressing and intrusive thoughts related to the death and avoidance of people or things associated with the loved one (Zisooki & Shear, 2009, p. 69). Holland and Neimeyer (2011) found differences in how distress is experienced when the events surrounding the loss are traumatic (traumatic distress) versus when the loss itself is the traumatic stimulus (separation distress). However, it is important to note that (a) traumatic distress (trauma as it is experienced by the individual related to the events surrounding the loss whether or not the event was violent or accidental) may coexist with separation distress (trauma due to the loss of a central attachment figure), (b) that both descriptions involve significant distress and may be experienced as a threat to the individuals/family's integrity, and (c) the focus should remain upon how the loss is experienced and interpreted by the individual/family to inform clinicians regarding the best point of intervention with the family. Kissane (2014) and Prigerson et al. (2009) emphasize that *prolonged grief disorder* is a pathological form of chronic grief in which "the bereaved become stuck in their sadness, with narrowing of their life" and are in need of intervention (Kissane, 2014, p. 13). Clinical implications for prolonged grief will be discussed later in this chapter.

- *Posthumous disillusionment*, another type of complicated grief, occurs after the death of a significant other when distressing information about events or behaviors come to light that may change core beliefs and feelings about the person who has died. These revelations consequently may change the perception of the nature of the relationship with the deceased (Nader, 2009–2010; Stalfa, 2010). Stalfa (2010) suggests that the sense of betrayal experienced by the survivors is the key moderating variable. This is a relatively new and unstudied phenomenon and yet one we have found to be valuable in our work with families such as Serge's.

Value of a Family Approach

Naomi and Ray referred their 4-year-old daughter, Jacklynn, for treatment because of her extreme difficulties getting to school, using public washrooms, disrupted sleep, and nightmares. It all started when Jacklynn was home sick for 5 days. When it was time for her to return to school, Jacklynn, threw temper tantrums, cried, and begged her parents to let her stay home. Concerned and puzzled, her parents consoled her, asking why she didn't want to return. With wide-eyed intensity, Jacklynn explained that a substitute teacher got mad when Jacklynn ran to the bathroom without asking permission. The teacher followed her into the bathroom, yelled at her, said she was bad, and slapped her buttocks. This incident occurred weeks prior to Jacklynn's illness. Naomi and Ray reported the information to the school. Child Welfare authorities and the police were notified and an investigation took place. The substitute teacher was placed on leave and took an unexpected trip to visit family on the other side of the country. The school maintained their (fallacious) position that, despite the police investigation, since charges had not been filed, no abuse had taken place. Naomi and Ray sought legal counsel but elected to keep Jacklynn at the school since she would have a new teacher for the following year. In treatment, Jacklynn presented with significant posttraumatic stress symptoms and was diagnosed with posttraumatic stress disorder (PTSD). Treatment consisted of trauma-focused play therapy for Jacklynn and child-management skills to help her parents manage both her developmentally appropriate and trauma-based acting-out behaviors. Posttreatment measures indicated that all of Jacklynn's posttraumatic stress symptoms had remitted and were within normal ranges. Yet, as a year of successful treatment drew to close, Naomi and Ray continued, as they had multiple times before, to bring up the possibility of suing the school even though Jacklynn had a very successful year in first grade. News that the substitute teacher was teaching at another institution in the region reignited all of Naomi and Ray's fears and anxieties for Jacklynn's safety and began to interfere with their home life and jobs. Both were hypervigilant and irritable. Naomi presented to the Emergency Department with chest pains while Ray reported disturbing recurrent nightmares in which he attempted to kill the perpetrating teacher. Jacklynn experienced a mild reluctance to attend school and had trouble falling asleep again. Although the treatment team shared their concern for the safety of other children, they were alarmed by the intensity of Noami and Ray's posttrauma symptoms and met with them alone to discuss this.

Historical Perspectives on Family-Focused Trauma Interventions

A family systems approach to the treatment of trauma first began right after World War II (Hill, 1949) and later with veterans in the United States who were returning from conflict in Vietnam (Walsh, 2007). Numerous models of family therapy have been applied to instances in which there has been a traumatic loss in the family system itself (Coulter, 2011) or when one family member has been exposed to a traumatic event and the "ripples" from the experience of the individual have ramifications for others in the family system (Dinshtein, Dekel, & Polliack, 2011; Ein-Dor, Doron,

Mikulincer, Solomon, & Shaver, 2010; Monson, Taft, & Fredman, 2009). These studies demonstrate that the family system can be profoundly affected by traumatic events that individual members have experienced and that it also can moderate the impact of such events on these same individual members. Of further interest is Cohen et al.'s (2012) trauma-focused cognitive behavioral therapy (TF-CBT) for children, in which parental involvement in their child(ren)'s treatment has been found to alleviate symptoms in both children and parents. These researchers have also emphasized that the relief of parental distress has a mitigating effect on children's responses.

Catherall (2004) and Figley and McCubbin (1993) describe the relational stresses within families that occur after war, catastrophic events, violence, and abuse. Barnes (2005) and Matsakis (2004) specifically described the impact upon the family system when one member was exposed to a traumatic incident and relied upon his/her family members for support afterwards. Briere and Scott (2006) indicate that family members are often the "hidden victims" of trauma because their lack of direct exposure may be seen as protective when, in fact, they may be reliving feelings of overwhelming powerlessness, helplessness, and threat daily as the member who witnessed the events firsthand recounts his/her experience in their presence. The literature on PTSD in families seems to indicate a reciprocal relationship when there has been a traumatic event, identifying that supportive family relationships can mitigate some of the effects of the trauma, but adding that traumatized individual family members can traumatize other members of their family (Carlson & Dalenberg, 2000; Coulter, 2011; Ozer, Best, Lipsey, & Weiss, 2003).

Historical Perspectives on Family-Focused Bereavement Interventions

The field of bereavement has a history of family-based interventions. Psychiatrist David Kissane writes that traumatic and other forms of complicated grief "reverberate among the clan" (Kissane, 2014, p. 6). Religion and culture filtered through the family system influence how a family mourns. Family leaders model when, where, and how members express emotion and provide comfort to each other. The transmission of "either compassionate support or avoidant silence" (Kissane, 2014) can be traced through multiple generations. However, similar to the field of traumatology, interventions focused on the family have often taken a backseat to individually oriented treatments and resulted in missed opportunities to access the family as a resource and support (Kissane, 2014, p. 13).

In their work with the bereaved families of cancer patients, Kissane and his associates have developed and validated a screen that identifies families "at risk" for complicated grief and guides intervention. Lichtenthal and Sweeney (2014) identify several individual and family variables that increase families' risk for complicated grief. These factors include family functioning style, member's attachment styles, levels of social support, individual's tendency to express negative affect and instability (neuroticism) predeath marital dependence, the role of the deceased, the family (spouse or parent), and event characteristics (such as who found or identified the body).

Attachment Relationships as Sources of Support

The attachment system functions to preserve a sense of safety and security in the world. Attachment is usually cultivated in the context of primary familial relationships in infants and young children, is reinforced in close relationships as we mature, and it forms the basis for the development of the schemas and perceptions of the world, others, and the self that tend to remain stable through one's lifetime (Janoff-Bulman, 1992). The family is usually the core of the attachment system that forms the foundation for how individuals navigate change, loss, and transition. Typically, the attachment system exists below the level of conscious awareness, and most individuals aren't aware of its importance until a perceived threat activates attachment behaviors, motivating the individual to seek proximity and contact with primary attachment figures (Webb, 2004). An example of how attachment behaviors are triggered in response to a threat is to ask a group of adults in North America what they did upon learning of the events of September 11, 2001. The vast majority will respond that they contacted a loved one immediately, even though their loved one was not directly involved with the events that were unfolding. The desire to establish connection with attachment figures at this time was an example of the activation of attachment behavior in response to a perceived threat and anxiety about safety.

Walsh (2007) states that the effects of trauma can be moderated by whether or not those who are wounded are able to find comfort, reassurance, and a sense of safety with others. Webb (2004) describes the importance of attachment relationships when there is exposure to a perceived threat, indicating that attachment-related behaviors (i.e., need for contact and proximity with those who are closest to an individual) are often activated in such situations in order to provide a sense of security and stability to the individual. Since the activation of the attachment system is often a response to trauma, focusing therapeutic support on the family system where there are usually several significant attachment figures present is an important point of consideration. However, there may be a paradox in situations of trauma, when the sense of vulnerability that accompanies exposure to a threat heightens proximity-seeking behaviors and a need for closeness with attachment figures, while at the same time, trusting others may also be difficult, especially if the traumatic event was due to an intentional act by another individual (Ein-Dor et al., 2010). It is interesting to note that descriptions of disorganized attachment style, characterized by behaviors that are erratic, avoidant, or inconsistent, have been attributed to the effects of unresolved trauma or losses that have occurred within the family system (Liotti, 2004).

More recent research in bereavement indicates that grief is often best facilitated through finding ways to continue the bond with the deceased individual(s) rather than focusing energy on letting go of lost attachment figures. The Continuing Bond theory of bereavement highlights the need for individuals to find ways to remain connected to deceased loved ones through rituals, memories, stories, actions, and objects (Klass, Nickman, & Silverman, 1996; Stroebe, Schut, & Boerner, 2010). Fostering the continuance of a bond with a deceased family member can draw families together at a time when there has been great pain and confusion.

Family Meaning Making

Walsh (2007) states that families need to be involved in "making meaning of the trauma experience, putting it in perspective, and weaving the experience of loss and recovery into the fabric of individual and collective identity and life passage" (p. 210). Allowing families the opportunity to share in this meaning-making experience together can reinforce the shared family narrative and strengthen the relationships between the members of the family system. According to Nadeau, this process (as cited in Lichtenthal & Sweeney, 2014) can support or protect against the creation of complicated grief in a grieving family. When a family can't find a meaning for the death of a member or creates a negative meaning about this loss, the family's adjustment is at risk and intervention is warranted (Lichtenthal & Sweeney, 2014). However, recent research by Davis, Harasymchuk, and Wohl (2012) suggests that family agreement about a loss may be more important to the family's well-being than the positivity of their story.

Secondary Traumatization

Those closest to the traumatized individual are not immune to hearing the stories, feeling the anxiety, and having their own feelings of helplessness and powerlessness as they attempt to support their loved one who has been affected by a traumatic experience. Indeed, the *Diagnostic and Statistical Manual of Mental Disorders, Fifth Edition* (DSM-5) lists the revised criteria for posttraumatic stress disorder as follows:

> Exposure to actual or threatened a) death, b) serious injury, or c) sexual violation, in one or more of the following ways:
>
> 1. directly experiencing the traumatic event(s)
> 2. witnessing, in person, the traumatic event(s) as they occurred to others
> 3. learning that the traumatic event(s) occurred to a close family member or close friend; cases of actual or threatened death must have been violent or accidental
> 4. experiencing repeated or extreme exposure to aversive details of the traumatic event(s) (e.g., first responders collecting human remains; police officers repeatedly exposed to details of child abuse); this does not apply to exposure through electronic media, television, movies, or pictures, unless this exposure is work-related. (APA, 2013)

These revisions reflect the profound implications for families when a traumatic loss has occurred. Parents of traumatized children can themselves be traumatized by watching their children struggle and by their awareness of their children's exposure other family members, not just parents and children can be at increased risk for PTSD through indirect exposure provides a traumatized family member.

According to Briere and Scott (2006), social support is one of the most important variables that determine the impact of a traumatic event on an individual. And for most individuals, the family is the primary source of that social support. Working with families in this context allows for the opportunity to support the individual family members so that the risk of secondary traumatization is minimized. In therapy, family members are supported in their own reactions to the traumatic experience, given an opportunity to offer support to those in the family who need to talk about traumatic material in a safe place, and provided a means to integrate the experiences of all of the members into the family system.

Individuals do not live in a vacuum. Traumatic loss experiences can combine significant grief responses with intense feelings of anxiety, hypersensitivity, withdrawal, jealousy, verbal abuse, anger, and destructiveness. The person who is traumatized might seem very disconnected from the outer world, not be available to his/her family, and may, at times, be perceived to behave in bizarre ways (e.g., flashbacks or extreme startle responses). If there are accompanying avoidance symptoms associated with the loss, routine daily activities such as visiting with friends or taking part in family or children's functions, can be complicated and difficult (Dekel & Monson, 2010). Emotional numbing can affect attachment to children and intimate partners. Irritability and anger associated with living in a heightened state of physiological arousal can add tension and stress to close relationships. Family members report that they "walk on eggshells" fearful of upsetting their loved one who has experienced the traumatic event. These types of responses are commonly reported by families whose loved one has returned from military service in areas of war or armed conflict (Dekel & Monson, 2010; Ein-Dor et al., 2010; Milliken, Auchterlonie, & Hoge, 2007; Monson et al., 2009).

Inclusion of Children in the Process

A family-based approach is often considered ideal when children are involved in a traumatic loss, but implementation of a family session with children intimidates many family therapists. Children often act out the stresses of the family system as 6-year-old Mia demonstrated. If the child who is reacting to family stress is treated in isolation, little headway can occur with the child's therapy unless the underlying family dynamics are also addressed, as we saw with Jacklynn's parents. Children's reactions can be closely related to those of their parents and other family members, and most children rely upon their parents for a sense of safety and security when there is uncertainty or stress (Webb, 2004). Lund, Zimmerman, and Haddock (2002) state that some of the more common reasons why many family therapists often do not include children in the couples or family therapy are (a) the therapist is uncomfortable handling children in the therapy sessions or had no training in work with children, (b) therapists are concerned about difficulties engaging children who are at differing developmental levels, (c) very few child-oriented therapies have been adapted to a family context, (d) concerns that children should not be exposed to adult issues or that the children may be distracting in the session, and (e) the sparse literature available that would provide examples and descriptions of family therapy with younger children.

As discussed earlier, trauma may have an impact upon attachment and the ability of parents and children to remain connected in a meaningful way. Traumatic losses that affect parents' abilities to provide appropriate care and stability in the home may also impede children's abilities to cope. Reactions to traumatic events may include increased parental conflict, family disorganization, and stress from disparate reactions or dyssynchrony of grieving styles, which may all have a negative impact upon children (Cohen et al., 2012). Although they may not be directly exposed to a traumatic event or experience a loss as traumatic, exposure to a parent who is experiencing difficulties coping due to a traumatic loss increases the risk that these children may also suffer anxiety, depression, social impairments, and secondary traumatization (Bernardon & Pernice-Duca, 2010; Brown, 2005; Pynoos, Steinberg, & Goenjian, 1995). Parents may not be aware of the stress and symptoms of the children if they are engulfed by their own reactions. Systemically oriented interventions that are aimed at stabilizing and reorganizing the family system while supporting the experiences of both the parents and children in a safe environment tend to provide the best outcome for children (Bernardon & Pernice-Duca, 2010; Cohen, Mannarino, & Deblinger, 2006; Pernicano, 2010; Tarrier, Sommefield, & Pilgrim, 1999).

Clinical Considerations

The Intersection of Grief and Trauma

When a loss experience has an overlay of trauma, symptoms of reexperiencing in the form of cognitive, emotional, or physiological flashbacks may be triggered when there is a sense of heightened vulnerability or situations that are permeated with feelings of powerlessness or helplessness. At these times, acute physical signs of arousal, intense anxiety, panic, or anger may incapacitate the individual. On the other side of the spectrum, there may be cognitive and emotional numbing, dissociation and avoidance of people, places, or things that trigger traumatic material. In addition, individuals who struggle with exposure to trauma triggers often report being aroused and hypervigilant, experiencing difficulties with sleep, concentration, exaggerated startle responses to stimuli, and difficulties regulating emotions such as anger and rage (Cohen et al., 2012; Coulter, 2011; Nader, 1997; Pernicano, 2010; Rynearson, 2010; Simpson, 1997). When the trauma is accompanied by a significant loss, the intersection of the grief with the traumatic material presents a unique "dance." While typical bereavement responses overlap with some responses to trauma, grief tends to draw individuals into a need for immersion into the loss, manifest by the commonly described behaviors of searching, yearning, and a desire to reminisce, search for meaning, and share memories (Holland & Neimeyer, 2011; Nader, 1997).

Traditional grief therapy and support, that may involve actively remembering the person, talking about memories, sharing feelings, and going deeply into the grief can cause emotional flooding if a as traumatic overlay is present in as is the case with traumatic grief and prolonged grief. However, the avoidance of stimuli, which is a protective response after a traumatic incident, prevents an individual from integrating the loss through these normal grieving responses. Social withdrawal and avoidance may be protective in situations of exposure to trauma, but these responses may intensify the attachment wound that is left by the loss of a loved one. As exemplified in the case study with Miles, Serge, Alana, and their mother Nadia, attempts to reminisce about happy memories of the loved one may potentially lead to a reexperiencing of the trauma as well (Nader, 1997). It is a catch-22 for many individuals. Therapists who work with families in which there are children who are dealing with traumatic grief must be able to recognize when trauma is present and make sure that the work is going slowly enough, without flooding the child, while still touching upon the grief of the child and the other family members (Cohen et al., 2012; Nader, 2008). This can be a very difficult process and requires a great deal of clinical sensitivity.

In our experience with families like Nadia's, struggling with posthumous disillusionment adds another layer of complication to the traumatic grief. In addition to wading through the overwhelming images fused to their husband/father's death, the family was confronted with the alternative narrative presented by the police that Dave was not who his family thought he was. The possibility that Dave was having an affair and could kill as the police suggested cast doubt on the happy memories Nadia, Serge, Alana, and Mia needed to retrieve in order to grieve his death and their related losses. As often is the case, it is the surviving adults in the family who first grasp the significance of the emerging contradictory information and lash out at the deceased and sometimes therapist in rage and pain. While working with a family who was grieving the suicide death of their father, an 8-year-old said, "I don't think I listened enough to Dad, that's why he died." Based on the preliminary information the family provided, I (S.R.) responded, "I think your dad loved you very much, but the depression made him think it would be better if he died." The child's mother leaned toward me and in a controlled, firm voice said, "His father *did not* love him! I found drugs, alcohol, and receipts for massage parlors in his things. He lied. He *did not* love any of his children! If you continue to tell my son that, we will not come back!" A few years later, the family returned for treatment because the boy, now 14 was anxious and depressed. I reminded the mother of this exchange and she remembered it clearly as well. I explained that we now call their experience posthumous disillusionment. "It's kind of helpful to know it has a name and other people go through that his mother commented ruefully."

It is often proposed that when there is a strong presence of both grief and trauma symptoms, the initial focus of the therapy should be upon managing and finding a way to contain the trauma symptoms and the anxiety that is related to them before more grief-focused interventions are initiated (Nader, 1997; Rynearson & Salloum, 2011). It seems reasonable that establishing a sense of safety in the therapeutic environment through the use of containment strategies and some trauma reprocessing should be the priority before exploring the emotionally laden grief-related material in more depth to prevent further flooding and risk of retraumatizing the client(s) in the sessions.

Establishing Safety Within the Family Context

One of the core issues involved with traumatic loss is the heightened level of vulnerability and need for safety that is felt in relation to the loss that has occurred. The therapeutic setting needs to provide a container in which the family members feel safe with the therapist and each other. Issues of safety are associated not just with the events that have led up to the traumatic loss experience, but also with how the family members process their feelings about the loss themselves and with each other. We think the concept of safety encompasses three broad areas:

1. Physical and environmental safety, which involves protection from external threats or further harm.
2. Safety within the family system, which includes how the family members process what has occurred, how they relate to each other, and adjusting the therapy if the family system is the source of the trauma (such as in situations of abuse or domestic violence). This level of safety also encompasses psychological safety for the individual members within the context of family therapy, such as instances where one member is not able to engage fully in the process due to fear, shame, or concerns about potential negative consequences from other family members by his/her participation in the therapeutic process.
3. Safety related to an individual's intrapsychic threshold of tolerance for the process due to the potential for triggering or flooding secondary exposure to traumatic triggers within the context of the therapy.

In situations in which the response of one family member has the potential to destabilize other family members, the therapeutic environment must provide a container for all of the members. This container provides clear boundaries for the material that is covered in the sessions, as well as ground rules for how the sessions are conducted, mechanisms for disengagement if one or more of the members begins to feel unsafe, and recognition and accommodation for members who are more vulnerable, such as children, individuals with special needs, or family members who may be more prone to reexperiencing the trauma or having traumatic symptomatology reactivated during the therapy. In situations wherein one family member recounts a traumatic event in detail, subjecting the other family members to this traumatic material and thus risking secondary traumatization, the therapy needs to offer a safe alternative environment where the traumatized individual can work through his/her feelings surrounding the event, while offering protection and support to the other family members who may be profoundly affected by hearing this material. Working with a family in this way provides an opportunity to acknowledge and contextualize the change in the equilibrium of the family system, while normalizing all the various responses and diverse ways that the family members may be coping with what has happened.

When discussing issues related to safety, it is important to recognize that children rely upon their parents to protect them, model responses to life events, and to establish appropriate boundaries in their everyday interactions (Webb, 2004). If one or both parents are highly emotionally distraught or distressed, the children involved may not only have to process the fact of the loss in the family, but also the fear that may accompany seeing a parent become emotionally overwhelmed and unable to provide a container for their feelings. Nader (1997) describes difficulties in children's ability to cope with trauma if parents are unavailable or unable to be engaged with children due to their own symptomatology. Cohen et al. (2006) state that when a parent's symptoms impinge on "his/her emotional availability or judgement to the point that the therapist believes it is interfering with adequate parenting practices, the parent needs to be referred for his/her own therapy" (p. 36).

Family Resilience and Reality

In her work with families who have experienced traumatic events, Walsh (2007) states that therapy should focus on "a multisystemic, resilience-oriented approach that recognizes the widespread impact of major trauma, situates the distress in the extreme experience, attends to ripple effects through relational networks, and aims to strengthen family and community resources for optimal recovery" (p. 207). While we recognize the reality that not all families possess such innate resilience, many strengths and coping skills can still be identified even in the most disorganized family systems. The emphasis here is upon an approach that recognizes the positive attributes of the family members, along with their attempts to cope with a very difficult experience, even when the family system appears to be overtly dysfunctional. A family that has experienced a traumatic loss event is not doomed to fall apart as a result of disparate reactions and the effects of exposure to trauma on the relationships between its members. Calhoun and Tedeschi (2006) completed research with individuals who struggled with traumatic experiences. The results of their research demonstrated that many individuals who experience traumatic events and losses later report the development of new strengths, untapped potential, creative expression, and innovative solutions after participants experienced trauma of various types. Most families have a great deal of potential to mediate and transform traumatic experiences in the same way.

Within a discussion of family resilience, it is important to connect the strengths-based perspective of most family-oriented therapies to the issues of safety as delineated in the previous section. The reality is that not all families are primarily resilient, especially when there are safety issues or vulnerabilities that relate directly to the family system itself, as discussed previously. In addition, although there is great potential for growth in adversity, not all individuals and families have the resources or innate strengths that allow for this type of outcome to eventually surface in a predominant way. Therapists need to be able to "hold" these two concepts together: the desire to foster a family's growth and resilience in the face of a traumatic loss, while realistically recognizing that not all families will be able to respond in this way.

Intervention Strategies

Assessment

Assessment is always the basis of strong clinical intervention in family therapy. Family therapists believe that it is valuable and important to work with the family as a whole whenever possible because, as the axiom goes, the whole is greater than the sum of its parts. This is of particular importance when the family is traumatized *and* grieving. The family system needs to construct a coherent narrative about the traumatic loss in which each member's experience becomes part of the shared family narrative, especially if the traumatic loss is the sudden, deeply disturbing death of a member. When terrible events occur, treatment may be provided to individuals separately or in subgroups (i.e., parent alone, child alone, the parent and the child who has been identified as the client without siblings) (Lehmann & Rabenstein, 2002). Seeing the family together for assessment can generate verbal and nonverbal information about whether the whole family system is paralyzed by the traumatic loss, or if some members are actively grieving, while others are frozen by trauma. In posthumous disillusionment, this is usually the point in assessment at which family members disclose or hint at information that challenges their individual and collective core beliefs about the deceased. In these cases, the therapist might state that he/she will be meeting with the adult family members separately to discuss more personal or "grown-up issues." An astute therapist recognizes that a young child who leaves her play to crawl into the lap of her weeping father is as important to understanding the family as her mother's story of how the family's older son died in a hit-and-run accident on his way to school.

A carefully conducted, thorough assessment of the family when traumatic loss or grief is known or suspected is vital for several reasons:

1. When the family includes children, particularly very young children 1 to 6 years of age, the therapist is working with the most vulnerable and sensitive family members. The developing coping strategies of a young child may have been further compromised by the traumatic nature of their loss, especially if the deceased is a parent (NCTSN, 2012).
2. Even if a child has not directly experienced the loss as traumatic, the vulnerability of the child's caregiver who has been traumatized will be distressing to the child. Furthermore, depending on the age of the child, the caregiver who is incapacitated by his/her grief may be inattentive to the emotional and sometimes even the physical needs of the child at critical stages of development (Cohen et al., 2006; Hennighausen & Lyons-Ruth, 2007).
3. The overwhelming nature of trauma, especially if it involves abuse in families, has the potential to isolate members and fragment the family's collective story about the events. This fragmentation can be perpetuated by the legal system that prohibits family members from talking to each other when criminal charges are filed and they are witnesses. Crisis intervention programs in domestic violence programs and adult mental health services often work with adults and children separately. In these instances, the family as a unit may never talk about the event or events leading up to the loss (Lehmann & Rabenstein, 2002).

Family therapy provides a forum for the family members to hear each other's perspective of events and feelings, correct misconceptions, and create a coherent family narrative, allowing the family to move forward through their collective and individual grief.

Configurations of Traumatic Loss in the Family System

The complex interplay of an event, proximity to an event, meanings attributed to events, and the role of attachment relationships in families has led us to develop the following definitions that we have found helpful when initially considering family therapy in the context of traumatic loss (Harris & Rabenstein, 2014). These definitions provide guidance throughout the assessment and treatment process, which will be discussed in greater detail later.

Traumatized Families

These are families whose members have collectively experienced the traumatic loss firsthand. The experience of Nadia's family is an example in which all the family members experienced the traumatic loss directly. Nadia and her children had strong, positive relationships with Dave as husband and father before he died. They did not witness his death directly but were subjected to video clips and photos of the house where the deaths took place. Furthermore, they had to come to terms with the police perspective, painfully at odds with some of their happy memories and core beliefs about Dave. In addition, they were faced with multiple traumatic losses including significant financial hardships and a loss of privacy in the small town where they lived.

Traumatized Children

In families with children who have been traumatized, the caregivers and/or attachment figures may or may not have not directly experienced the loss that their child(ren) has/have experienced, and they may not have experienced their child's trauma first-hand but are secondarily traumatized by the event. Jacklynn was alone when she was assaulted by the teacher. However, her distress had a big impact upon her parents, who felt powerless by their inability to protect and comfort Jacklynn. Their view of the world as a place where they could provide the best for their only child and their belief that they could protect her was shattered. Given her young age, they mourned the loss of a sense of certainty in their parenting. When faced with Jacklynn's developmentally appropriate acting out behaviors, they wonder whether it is "normal" or a result of trauma. Parents like Ray and Naomi do not experience the trauma and traumatic loss in the way that their child does, but are most certainly at risk for secondary traumatization as discussed earlier and described in greater detail by Briere and Scott (2009). We have found that providing information to parents about the DSM-5 diagnostic criteria for PTSD that supports the traumagenic nature of secondary exposures can be validating.

Traumatized Parents

These are families in which a caregiver has experienced a traumatic loss but the children have not. In one case example, a father who was a police officer was first on the scene of a horrific car accident involving several cars. One car burst into flames. Despite his best efforts, he could not get the car door open and witnessed the occupants, a family of four with two adolescents the approximate ages of his own children, burn to death. In the aftermath, his entire family dynamic was affected by his traumatic symptomatology.

Understanding these family configurations allows us to structure the sessions in such a way as to allow all participants to contribute without being overwhelmed.

Perspective of the Clinician

Working with clients who are exposed to traumatic events and losses can take a large toll on therapists placing them at risk for secondary traumatization. (Ben-Porat & Itzhaky, 2009; Figley, 1995; McCann & Pearlman, 1990). Training in therapeutic work typically involves a focus on change as the cornerstone toward the resolution of difficulties. Therapists also have their own assumptions about the world, themselves, and their work, which may entail the desire to help relieve the suffering of others. However, there are problematic situations in which suffering is prolonged, or injustices continue and can't be remedied, and when all good intentions and training seem to be ineffectual. In addition, as described earlier, just as family members may be at risk for vicarious trauma by hearing their loved ones' experience of a traumatic loss, therapists are not immune to hearing these accounts as well. The DSM-5 also recognizes this impact. Criteria A4 states,

> Exposure to actual or threatened death, serious injury or sexual violence in one (or more) of the following ways . . . [including] experiencing repeated or extreme exposure to aversive details of the traumatic event(s) (e.g., first responders collecting human remains, police officers repeatedly exposed to details of child abuse). (APA, 2013, p. 271)

When working with clients who have experienced horrific circumstances, therapists are often confronted with issues of cruelty, abuse, injustice, and violation. It is easy for the therapist to identify with the stance of victimization and powerlessness that clients may feel. Gerhart and McCollum (2007) state that while all good therapists desire to help their clients, they must also understand that there is inevitable suffering in life: "It is tempting for us to subtly join [with clients] in their search for the mythical state of pain-free living and embark on an effort to change what is unchangeable" (p. 215).

These authors suggest that the acceptance of suffering as a normal part of life can be a valuable stance in family therapy. They support the cultivation of mindfulness and compassion-based practices in order to be open to the potential growth that can occur as a result of suffering, while at the same time, encouraging therapists to also take an active role in the attempt to relieve the suffering of their clients. Geller and Greenberg (2002) suggest that one of the most effective interventions with clients is that of "being with" rather than focusing on what therapists might "do to" the clients in their practice. They describe a process whereby clinicians can cultivate their ability to be fully present to clients, completely engaged and attuned to their experiences, while not being singularly focused and attached to a specific outcome:

Therapeutic presence also adds to the relationship conditions a sense of grounding, which includes therapists trusting their own felt and expressed experience. With presence, the therapist is as close as possible to the client's experience while maintaining a sense of self as separate and whole. (p. 84)

Therapists who are accustomed to practicing mindful awareness may be better equipped to be fully present and responsive in the therapeutic situation when traumatic material is being discussed rather than quickly jumping in to intervene and reframe the experience because the empathetic bond has drawn them personally into the overwhelming feelings of the client.

CONCLUSION

There is a plethora of recently published research and material on these topics. Many of these publications provide new insights and intervention strategies for working with individuals and families after traumatic loss. We have attempted to summarize some of these current findings and discussions in this chapter, but it is apparent that this is a rapidly evolving field, and clinicians need to maintain currency and clinical competence by regularly availing themselves of current research, literature, and trends in this area.

Therapists who work with families that have experienced traumatic losses and complicated grief must understand how the individual experience of traumatic loss is embedded within the family system, which is also shaped by the structural and political context of the family. They must also be adept at understanding family dynamics as well as developmental factors unique to children who are involved in the process. In addition, they must be able to recognize traumatic symptomatology and be sensitive to the "dance" that occurs when grief and trauma intersect. Finally, they need to know how to create safety within the therapeutic environment and be well-versed in the literature and recent findings related to both trauma and grief.

REFERENCES

American Academy of Child and Adolescent Psychiatry (AACAP). (2010). Practice parameter for the assessment and treatment of children and adolescents with posttraumatic stress disorder. *Journal of the American Academy of Child and Adolescent Psychiatry, 49*(4), 414–430.

American Psychiatric Association (APA). (2013). *Diagnostic and statistical manual of mental disorders* (5th ed.). Washington, DC: APA.

Barnes, M. F. (2005). When a child is traumatized or physically injured: The secondary trauma of parents. In D. R. Catherall (Ed.), *Specific stressors: Interventions with couples and families* (pp. 73–90). New York, NY: Brunner-Routledge.

Ben-Porat, A., & Itzhaky, H. (2009). Implications of treating family violence for the therapist: Secondary traumatization, vicarious traumatization, and growth. *Journal of Family Violence, 24*, 507–515.

Bernardon, S., & Pernice-Duca, F. (2010). A family systems perspective to recovery from posttraumatic stress in children. *The Family Journal: Counseling and Therapy for Couples and Families, 18*(4), 349–357.

Boss, P., Roos, S., & Harris, D. (2011). Grief in the midst of ambiguity and uncertainty: An exploration of ambiguous loss and chronic sorrow. In R. Neimeyer, D. Harris, H. Winokuer, & G. Thornton (Eds.), *Grief and bereavement in contemporary society: Bridging research and practice* (pp. 163–176). New York, NY: Routledge.

Briere, J., & Scott, C. (2006). *Principles of trauma therapy: A guide to symptoms, evaluation, and treatment.* London, UK: Sage.

Brown, E. J. (2005). Efficacious treatment of stress disorder in children and adolescents. *Pediatric Annals, 34,* 139–146.

Calhoun, L. G., & Tedeschi, R. G. (2006). The foundations of posttraumatic growth: An expanded framework. In L. G. Calhoun & R. G. Tedeschi (Eds.), *Handbook of posttraumatic growth: Research and practice* (pp. 1–23). Mahwah, NJ: Erlbaum.

Carlson, E., & Dalenberg, C. (2000). A conceptual framework for the impact of traumatic experiences. *Trauma, Violence, and Abuse, 1,* 4–28.

Catherall, D. R. (2004). *Handbook of stress, trauma, and the family.* New York, NY: Brunner-Routledge.

Chapple, A., Swift, C., & Ziebland, S. (2011). The role of spirituality and religion for those bereaved due to a traumatic death. *Mortality, 16*(1), 1–19.

Cohen, J. A., Mannarino, A. P., & Deblinger, E. (2006). *Treating trauma and traumatic grief in children and adolescents.* New York, NY: Guilford Press.

Cohen, J. A., Mannarino, A. P., & Deblinger, E. (2012). *Trauma-focused CBT for children and adolescents: Treatment applications.* New York, NY: Guilford Press.

Coulter, S. (2011). Systemic psychotherapy as an intervention for post-traumatic stress responses: An introduction, theoretical rationale and overview of developments in an emerging field of interest. *Journal of Family Therapy.* doi: 10.1111/j.1467-6427.2011.00570.x

Davis, C. G., Harasymchuk, C., & Wohl, M. J. A. (2012). Finding meaning in a traumatic loss: A families approach. *Journal of Traumatic Stress, 25,* 142–149. doi: 10.1002/jts.21675

Dekel, R., & Monson, C. (2010). Military-related post-traumatic stress disorder and family relations: Current knowledge and future directions. *Aggression and Violent Behavior,15,* 303–309.

Dinshtein, Y., Dekel, R., & Polliak, M. (2011). Secondary traumatization among adult children of PTSD veterans: The role of mother-child relationships. *Journal of Family Social Work, 14*(2), 109–124.

Ein-Dor, T., Doron, G., Mikulincer, M., Solomon, Z., & Shaver, P. (2010). Together in pain: Attachment-related dyadic processes and posttraumatic stress disorder. *Journal of Counseling Psychology, 57*(3), 317–327.

Figley, C. R. (1995). Compassion fatigue as a secondary traumatic stress disorder: An overview. In C. R. Figley (Ed.), *Compassion fatigue: Coping with secondary traumatic stress disorder in those who treat the traumatized* (pp. 1–20). New York, NY: Brunner-Mazel.

Figley, C., & McCubbin, H. (1983). *Stress and the family: Coping with catastrophe.* New York, NY: Brunner-Mazel.

Geller, S. M., & Greenberg, L. S. (2002). Therapeutic presence: Therapists' experience of present in the therapeutic encounter. *Person-Centered and Experiential Psychotherapies, 1*(½), 71–86.

Gerhart, D. R., & McCollum, E. E. (2007). Engaging suffering: Towards a mindful re-visioning of family therapy practice. *Journal of Marital and Family Therapy, 33*(2), 214–226.

Harris, D. (2010). Introduction. In D. Harris (Ed.), *Counting our losses: Reflecting on change, loss, and transition in everyday life* (pp. xi–xviii). New York, NY: Springer.

Harris, D., & Rabenstein, S. (2014). Family therapy in the context of traumatic losses. In D. W. Kissane & F. Parnes (Eds.), *Bereavement care for families* (pp. 137–153). New York, NY: Routledge.

Hennighausen, K., & Lyons-Ruth, K. (2007). Disorganization of attachment strategies in infancy and childhood. In R. E. Tremblay, R. G. Barr, & R. Peters (Eds.), *Encyclopedia on early childhood development*. Montreal, Quebec, Canada: Centre of Excellence for Early Childhood Development. Retrieved September 5, 2012, from http://www.child-encyclopedia.com/sites/default/files/textes-experts/en/567/disorganization-of-attachment-strategies-in-infancy-and-childhoo.pdf

Hill, R. (1949). *Families under stress*. New York, NY: Harper.

Holland, J., & Neimeyer, R. (2011). Separation distress and traumatic distress in prolonged grief: The role of cause of death and relationship to the deceased. *Journal of Psychopathology and Behavioral Assessment, 33*, 254–263.

Janoff-Bulman, R. (1992). *Shattered assumptions: Towards a new psychology of trauma*. New York, NY: Free Press.

Kauffman, J. K. (2002). Safety and the assumptive world. In J. Kauffman (Ed.), *Loss of the assumptive world: A theory of traumatic loss* (pp. 205–212). New York, NY: Routledge.

Kissane, D. W. (2014). Family grief. In D. W. Kissane & F. Parnes (Eds.), *In bereavement care for families* (pp. 3–16). New York, NY: Routledge.

Klass, D., Nickman, P. R., & Silverman, S. L. (1996).*Continuing bonds: New understandings of grief*. Washington, DC: Taylor & Francis.

Lehmann, P., & Rabenstein, S. (2002). Children exposed to traumatic violence: The role of impact, assessment, and treatment. In A. R. Roberts (Ed.), *Handbook of domestic violence intervention strategies* (pp. 343–364). New York, NY: Oxford.

Lichtenthal, W. G., Cruess, D. G., & Prigerson, H. G. (2004). A case for establishing complicated grief as a distinct mental disorder in DSM-V. *Clinical Psychology Review, 24*, 637–662.

Lichtenthal, W. G., & Sweeney, C. (2014). Families at risk of complicated bereavement. In D. W. Kissane & F. Parnes (Eds.), *In bereavement care for families* (pp. 149–165). New York, NY: Routledge.

Liotti, G. (2004). Trauma, dissociation, and disorganization: Three strands of a single braid. *Psychotherapy: Theory, Research, Practice, Training, 41*(4), 472–486.

Lund, L. T., Zimmerman, T. S., & Haddock, S. A. (2002). The theory, structure, and techniques for the inclusion of children in family therapy: A literature review. *Journal of Marital and Family Therapy, 28*(4), 445–454.

Matsakis, A. (2004). Trauma and its impact on families. In D. R. Catherall (Ed.), *Handbook of stress, trauma, and the family* (pp. 12–26). New York, NY: Brunner-Routledge.

McCann, L., & Pearlman, L. A. (1990). Vicarious traumatization: A framework for understanding the psychological effects of working with victims. *Journal of Traumatic Stress, 3*, 131–149.

McCollum, D. (2006). Child maltreatment and brain development. *Minnesota Medicine, 89*(3), 48–50.

Milliken, C. S., Auchterlonie, J. L., & Hoge, C. W. (2007). Longitudinal assessment of mental health problems among active and reserve component soldiers returning from the Iraq war. *Journal of the American Medical Association, 298*, 2141–2148.

Monson, C., Taft, C., & Fredman, S. (2009). Military related PTSD and intimate relationships: From description to theory-driven research and intervention development. *Clinical Psychology Review, 29*, 707–714.

Nader, K. D. (1997). Childhood traumatic loss: The intersection of trauma and grief. In C. Figley (Ed.), *Death and trauma: The traumatology of grieving* (pp. 17–41). New York, NY: Brunner-Mazel.

Nader, K. D. (2008). *Understanding and assessing trauma in children and adolescents: Measures, methods, and youth in context*. New York, NY: Routledge.

Nader, K. D. (2009–2010). Types of complicated grief. *International Society for Traumatic Stress Studies.* Retrieved August 21, 2014, from http://www.istss.org

National Child Traumatic Stress Network (NCTSN). (2012). *Understanding child traumatic stress.* Retrieved September 5, 2012, from http://www.nctsn.org/resources/audiences/parents-caregivers/understanding-child-traumatic-stress

Neria, Y., & Litz, B. T. (2003). Bereavement by traumatic means: The complex synergy of trauma and grief. *Journal of Loss and Trauma.* doi: 10.1080/15325020490255322

Ozer, E. J., Best, S. R., Lipsey, T. L., & Weiss, D. S. (2003). Predictors of posttraumatic stress disorder and symptoms in adults: A meta-analysis. *Psychological Bulletin, 129,* 52–73.

Pernicano, P. (2010). *Family-focused trauma interventions.* Plymouth, UK: Aronson.

Prigerson, H. G., Horowitz, M. J., Jacobs, S. C., Parks, C. M., Asian, M., Goodwin, K.,. . . Macieiewski, P. K. (2009). *Prolonged grief disorder: Psychomatic validation criteria proposed for DSM-V and ICD-11*: e1000121.

Pynoos, R. S., Steinberg, A. M., & Goenjian, A. (1996). Traumatic stress in childhood and adolescence: Recent developments and current controversies. In B. A. van der Kolk & A. C. McFarlane (Eds.), *Traumatic stress* (pp. 331–358). New York, NY: Guilford Press.

Rynearson, E. K. (2010). The clergy, the clinician, and the narrative of violent death. *Pastoral Psychology, 59,* 179–189.

Rynearson, E. K., & Salloum, A. (2011). Restorative retelling: Revisiting the narrative of violent death. In R. Neimeyer, D. Harris, H. Winokuer, & G. Thornton (Eds.), *Grief and bereavement in contemporary society: Bridging research and practice* (pp. 177–188). New York, NY: Routledge.

Schultz, C., & Harris, D. (2011). Giving voice to nonfinite loss and grief in bereavement. In R. Neimeyer, D. Harris, H. Winokuer, & G. Thornton (Eds.), *Grief and bereavement in contemporary society: Bridging research and practice* (pp. 235–248). New York, NY: Routledge.

Simpson, M. A. (1997). Traumatic bereavements and death-related PTSD. In C. Figley (Ed.), *Death and trauma: The traumatology of grieving* (pp. 3–16). New York, NY: Brunner-Mazel.

Stalfa, F. J. (2010). "Posthumous disillusionment" as a type of complicated grief. *Journal of Pastoral Care and Counseling, 64,* 1–8.

Stroebe, M., Schut, H., & Boerner, K. (2010). Continuing bonds in adaptation to bereavement: Toward theoretical integration. *Clinical Psychology Review, 30,* 259–268.

Tarrier, N., Sommerfield, C., & Pilgrim, H. (1999). Relatives' expressed emotion and PTSD treatment outcomes. *Psychological Medicine, 29,* 801–811.

Walsh, F. R. (2006). *Strengthening family resilience* (2nd ed.). New York, NY: Guilford Press.

Walsh, F. R. (2007). Traumatic loss and major disasters: Strengthening family and community resilience. *Family Process, 46*(2), 207–227.

Webb, N. B. (2004). The impact of traumatic stress and loss on families. In N. B. Webb (Ed.), *Mass trauma and violence: Helping families and children cope* (pp. 3–22). New York, NY: Guilford Press.

Weisaeth, L., & Eitinger, L. (1993). Posttraumatic stress phenomena: Common themes across wars, disasters, and traumatic events. In J. P. Wilson & B. Raphael (Eds.), *International handbook of traumatic stress syndromes* (pp. 69–77). New York, NY: Plenum Press.

Zisooki, S., & Shear, K. (2009). Grief and bereavement: What psychiatrists need to know. *World Psychiatry, 8*(2), 67–74.

SECTION 2

Coping with Death at Home and at School

This section contains chapters that can help to answer the following questions:
- How do children use humor, art, and music in coping with grief?
- How can specific techniques, such as storytelling, bring a child's culture into the grief process?
- How have some famous historical figures integrated grief experienced as children grievers into their live achievements?
- How might historical grief narratives be used with grieving children and adolescents?
- What light can existentialism cast on child development?
- What are the implications of this for professional practice in working with dying or grieving children?
- What are the spiritual and emotional needs of children who have experienced multiple losses during a disaster?
- What are the reactions of children to catastrophic loss, given their stage of development?
- What is a simple but potentially effective action plan for the emotional and spiritual care of children during a disaster?
- What are common signs of grief in children and adolescents?
- What is a Children's Loss Inventory?
- How do children express their grief in school?
- What role can grief play in bullying and violence?
- What do grieving children need in school?
- What can teachers and school counselors do to help grieving children and adolescents?
- What is the impact of the death of a child on school faculty and staff?
- What is the role of a school "crisis team" when death affects a school community?

CHAPTER 6
Children and Death: Coping through Humor, Art, and Music

Gerry Cox

People die. Children will know that people die. As adults, we know, intellectually, that death is a natural part of life, and yet when we are confronted with death, we cry out loud, "Why?" in response; children react with the same emotions as adults, but they tend to react to their grief in much more dramatic ways. In the world today, the deaths of family and friends are not the only deaths that children must face. Terrorism, mass shootings, school violence, war, suicide, and just watching the news on television may cause children to grieve over deaths of people who the child does not even know. What death means to each of us is different. We are all influenced by our experiences and our stage of development. With children, the stage of development is crucial. A toddler's response is quite different than her school-age sister's, and both are quite different than the adolescent, or than adults who often reach for something to read. So do children. Many wonderful books are available for all ages. For children, having someone reading to them is a special time. It is the one time that the child knows that he or she has your undivided attention. It is a time when you can share on the same level. One of the most common questions is whether or not their grief is normal (Thompson, 2012). Parents know their children better than anyone else. They will, hopefully, be able to tell if their child is reacting normally.

AIDING GRIEVING AND DYING CHILDREN

Like adults, children grieve. Like adults, children may suffer from complicated grief. Individuals suffering from complicated grief typically feel overwhelmed, unable to adapt, engage in behavior that is repetitive, or experience extensive interruptions of the healing process that abnormally lengthens their grieving. For children, complicated grief may be presented by the complete absence of grief reactions. Generally, the absence of grief reactions is associated with the broken heart syndrome and masked grief reactions (Marrone, 1997). Robert Stevenson suggests that adults see childhood as a time of growth and learning that should be filled with love and joy, which leads adults to try to shield children from emotional pain and turmoil (Stevenson, 2002). Unfortunately, protecting children does not prepare them for the pain that is part of everyone's life. Contrary to what some may tell you, your child will experience many of the same thoughts and emotions as you. She or he will be sad, angry, preoccupied, lonely, worry, and cry, and yet she or he will probably not let you see these feelings and emotions. Children have many different reactions to grief. A child's grief reflects her or his current stage of development. Depending upon age, telling the child that we lost the head of our family when grandpa died, may cause the child to think that grandpa lost his head. This child will not want to go to the funeral home to see grandpa. A heart attack, forever, and other concepts may or may not have meaning. I am not sure that they always have meaning to me either. A child who just broke up with her boyfriend may also grieve differently. Everyone's grief reaction is colored by what is important at that time in their life.

Grief comes out in intense but brief episodes. After learning of a loved one's death, the child may cry and then suddenly stop crying and ask to go out to play or to go to a friend's house. This is perfectly normal. Children, like us, dip in and out of grief. They seem to know how much pain that they can tolerate at any given moment. When they reach their limit, they simply shut it off and do something else. We may also do this.

Children may regress after a death. Older children may want to suddenly spend more time at home, teenagers may suddenly start fighting with their siblings, younger children may suddenly start clinging, little children may want you to dress or feed them. We all regress in grief. It may be less noticeable in us than in children. Regressing seems to be a cry for attention. We refocus on ourselves and our needs for a time. It is normal.

Children express their grief in actions rather than words. Grief support programs for children typically offer art projects and games to encourage them to express their feelings. Perhaps we could do that more for adults as well. Grieving children often play dead, get buried, play funeral, or whatever. It is okay. Anger might surface as teasing or simply being unreasonable. Have you ever been that way when you were unhappy? William Worden suggests in his "grief-work hypothesis" that emotional ventilation, including crying, mourning, and anger, needs to be expressed before one can begin to heal from a significant loss (Walter & McCoyd, 2009). Children often postpone their grief, or at least parts of it. William Worden and Phyllis Silverman reported that in their study of 125 children, for many children, grief reactions do not surface until the second year after the death of a parent (Worden, 2009). When a sibling dies, changes were found as late as 5 years after the death. Grief can be scary. It may need to be delayed. How many of us bury ourselves in paperwork and financial activities to avoid grief? Children often avoid reminders of the person who died. So do we. Keeping very busy may allow them to do so. We need to help them face their grief and pain. Children often share different parts of their grief with different people. They may tell a grandpa about their anger or fear and their teacher about their crying alone in their room and so forth. Children regrieve when life changes significantly. When your child goes off to college, she or he may want to go to the cemetery. Some of us feel guilty for living and being happy. Having an older sibling go away to school or whatever may trigger regrieving in younger siblings. It also triggers regrieving in parents. Grief does not end. It remains a part of us. How can we manage? While many strategies exist for aiding those suffering from complicated grief, the use of humor, art, and music may be used to aid children.

USING HUMOR, ART, AND MUSIC WITH DYING AND BEREAVED CHILDREN

Children may not be able to express their understanding of death in words, or communicate their feelings with words. Children often make a conscious effort to keep their feelings and other responses secret in an attempt to protect their parents (Robinson & Mahon, 1997). It is not from lack of knowledge that children are silent. Very young dying children do exhibit certain behaviors, which indicates that a child is aware that he or she is dying and what dying means, and like dying adults, dying children are most fearful of being abandoned or rejected during their dying (Marrone, 1997). Colin Murray Parkes reports that very young children who lose their mother not only suffer from the effects of losing their mother but of being lost oneself in a strange environment left with no comprehension of his or her situation, confused, frightened, and lonely (Parkes & Prigerson, 2010). Children may be more likely to suffer from complicated grief because they are often excluded from the normal family coping rituals. These same children observe, overhear, and see sadness in the adults whom they are looking to for support and care. Children who lack the experience and knowledge of how to cope are often insulated from the very adults who could help them learn to cope. The child is often left to grieve without family support. Loneliness is inversely related to self-esteem (Rokach & Brock, 1998). The family that fails to provide the necessary social support to the grieving child may further complicate the child's grieving by helping to foster loneliness and the resulting loss of self-esteem. Children can mourn successfully if supported. Silverstein and Bengtson (1997) found that kinship attachment is important in crisis. Parents and other adults have their own grief to attend to, but they also need to help support children who are also grieving. Various alternatives exist that can help heal children. Cultural beliefs have staying power. Magic aids the healing process yet it is seemingly unexplainable as a form of social support (Coe, 1997). Parents and other adults need to use strategies with children that will provide social support in a nonthreatening manner. Support strategies that are nonthreatening to children might include the use of humor, art, and music. While not an art form, the Internet and what it offers also appeals to children who are grieving. Not only is music available, but all forms of artistic endeavors can be found.

Youth are very much the "net generation"; that is, "net" as short for Internet. For older children, the Internet offers blogs, support groups, online memorials, online counseling, and sharing with others experiencing the same losses. For those who are struggling to find themselves, the Internet offers a way to approach the arts in many forms by offering insights, support, and encouraging mental action.

Children like to deal in abstractions. They also tend to take things seriously. Children will discuss anything. No subject is too painful or forbidden to them. Children tend to fuse together fantasy and reality. Fantasy never diminishes for children. Fairy tales and children's stories provide a social context that can provide insights that are invaluable for a child (Lau, 1996). Other excellent sources of children's fairy tales and stories would include Bettelheim's *The Uses of Enchantment: The Meaning and Importance of Fairy Tales* (1976) and von Franz's *An Introduction to the Interpretation of Fairy Tales* (1970). Stories and folklore can provide a perspective, knowledge, and relationships (Bauman, 1996). Adults develop memories and learned responsibilities while children develop anxieties that are often peculiar to the young. Children often develop separation anxiety that may arise from basic physical needs such as feeding and protection. Children often have a sense of purpose, but it is often vague and may make them feel dwarfed by it all. Most children seem to keep their distance and fail to come to grips with their fears. Scenes remain ingrained in their memories. Intensity of fear may be opposite of to the amount of danger. In the face of these reactions, children who are grieving often attempt to keep their feelings and other responses secret in order to protect their parents who are also grieving (Robinson & Mahon, 1997). Thomas Moore (1992) indicates that our habit of viewing our bodies as machines keeps us from attending to the beauty, the poetry, and the expressiveness of our bodies. Secrets keep us from laughing. Having no taboo topics allows children to face reality. Children and adults who inhibit or hide emotions do not feel better. Suppression of emotions when facing sadness or other negative emotions does not provide relief from that emotion (Gross & Levenson, 1997). Social support is an independent variable that affects people's physical and mental health (Palfai & Hart, 1997). All children, including females, need that support.

Females are generally more likely to feel loved than males (Meyers, 1997). This may affect their grief. They may feel more responsibility to manage their own grief so as to spare the parent or parents who love them. While we assume females to be more expressive than males and because they are generally more mature, most parents are less concerned with their adjustment to grief. Because they appear to be "handling their grief," females often do not get the assistance that they need. Females may be better at "masking" their grief. They, too, suffer from complicated grief. By age 6, female children are twice as likely to experience anxiety disorders as males (Lewinsohn, Gotlib, Seeley, & Allen, 1998). Perhaps because females are generally more mature and responsible than males as children, we tend to focus upon the grief disorders of males. All children need the help of adults when facing grief. Even comic strips are able to make the point that children should be included and that they grieve. Sarah Brabant (1997–1998), in her study of death and grief in comic strips, suggests that even in comics the "ordinariness" of death affirms the impact of death on survivors, the uniqueness of the grieving process for each person, and the variation in time and intensity of the grief process. All who are grieving need social support. Humor, even gallows humor, can provide a sense of social support. Steve Lipman (1991) wrote *Laughter in Hell: The Use of Humor During the Holocaust*. Elie Weisel also discussed the use of humor during his stay in the concentration camps (personal communication). Humor is a reaction to oppressive conditions (Bauman, 1996). Social support does aid coping behavior.

Social support can be exhibited in many ways. Grieving creates tension for children. Grief makes life seem to be without purpose. Loss or separation is a blow to a child's sense of being and purpose. One's health and well-being can be threatened by crisis and loss. Good health and well-being are the core features of life. Leading a life with a purpose, quality interactions with others, self-regard, and mastery lead to positive human health (Ryff & Singer, 1998). Bereavement itself can have health consequences severe enough to require professional intervention (Schut, Stroebe, van den Bout, & Keijer, 1997). Children who may already have difficulty expressing emotion may have the problem compounded if the person who died was the very person who listened (Schut, Stroebe, van den Bout, & Keijer, 1998). To help a child who has difficulty expressing emotions, adults can use several approaches. What kinds of humor, music, art, or whatever might help them?

ART, MUSIC, AND EXPRESSION OF GRIEF

Seemingly, all children like to draw and to express themselves in pictures. Christine Liddell suggests that children in all parts of the world are taught how to interpret pictures (Liddell, 1997). All children offer pictures to adults to display in the home in a special place such as on the refrigerator or other prominent places. As children develop their oral abilities, they seem to draw fewer and fewer pictures. No matter what the level of oral fluency, pictures are a bridge to expression. For children of all ages, pictures hold a special significance (Liddell, 1997).

Music, like art, is another form of expression that does not require oral fluency. The effects of music are greater than the effects of silence (Wilson & Brown, 1997). Music is a therapeutic tool. A religious attitude can be understood or adopted through music. Music has been used throughout history to promote spiritual development (Lowis & Hughes, 1997). An 11-year-old dying of cancer who was creatively gifted applied his creative skills using music to control his pain and give meaning and understanding to his dying (Marrone, 1997).

Children, like adults, are always learning, growing, and developing. Their knowledge, understanding, and reactions to illness, crisis, and loss are also constantly developing and changing. Natural or expressive therapies such as music, art, play, dance, or drama allow the child to be expressive in a less threatening fashion than talking one on one with an adult (Doka, 1995). Children can be asked to relive and revisit through guided imagery, to examine their memories of the person who died, to test memories with reality, to list anxieties or fears, to face anxieties and fears, to engage in fantasy and imagination exercises that might improve coping skills, or to engage in therapeutic rituals that focus on specific behaviors or activities that develop coping skills. Guided drawings are not intended to stifle creativity but rather are designed to improve the drawing capacity and self-expression (Shatil, 1995). Competition can be a problem depending upon the culture.

In urban U.S. schools, children are rewarded for competitive behavior more than in rural schools (Eisenberg & Mussen, 1989). Not only do children learn different styles of competition, but they also will exhibit different coping skills, artistic interest, and styles of responding. No list or single description of activities will ever suffice. Each caregiver must try to determine what kinds of music, art, humor, or whatever might be useful for this child. Males like to give advice or tell others what they might do, while females like to provide emotional assistance and caregiving services (Goldsmith & Dun, 1997). The male child might be asked to draw a picture to aid another child who is having difficulty managing grief. Since you are an intelligent child, what would you say to another child who is having difficulty with grief? The female child might be asked to indicate what kind of care she would give to another who was suffering. Generally, each child will address his or her own needs in reaching out to others. Those who give support to others benefit themselves from giving that support (Jung, 1997).

As adults, there is a strong temptation for us to interpret all drawings, songs, and emotional statements of children. Certainly some aspects of artistic expression do seem to be universal. Cross-cultural studies do seem to show that fear is often expressed by the color black, envy by red, and anger by both black and red (Hupka, Saleski, Otto, Reidl, & Tarabrina, 1997). Children all over the world draw pictures and attach meaning to their pictures. Pictures are a bridge to literacy. Pictures allow those who do not have the words to be able to express themselves (Liddell, 1997).

For adults, the question is what do these pictures mean? Certainly some expressions can easily be interpreted. Cox, Vanden, Berk, Fundis, & McGinnis, (1995), in a study of the effects of the Gulf War on children, used drawings and writings of grade school children to uncover their deepest fears and beliefs about the war. While the differences increased with age and ability to express verbally, females tended to identify with people and emotions while males displayed more aggression.

Care needs to be taken to not read too much into the drawings of children. It is not wise to create problems if none exist. Jonathan Shatil (1995) suggests that the artwork of children should not be judged or be competitive, and that it must instead be light, playful, and tranquil without comparisons or "should." Many art forms exist for working with children of all ages. For children of all ages, fears get worse if nothing is done or attempts are made to overprotect them (Sarafino, 1986). Drawings and other art forms can be used to aid children.

For an excellent demonstration of using drawings with children see, Nancy Boyd Webb (1993), *Helping Bereaved Children: A Handbook for Practitioners*. Another excellent text would be Linda Goldman (1996), *Breaking the Silence: A Guide to Help Children with Complicated Grief: Suicide, Homicide, AIDS, Violence, and Abuse*. Goldman discusses the use of visualization, photography, artwork, clay, toy figures, punching bags, tape recordings, and storytelling; for younger children, the use of sandbox, dolls, dollhouses, drawing materials, and other play materials; for older children, fantasy, play, and creative activities involving more words are more useful (Dyregrov, 1990). Children may want to play funeral, to act out the ceremony with their peers. Children may want to communicate and share with the deceased, draw a picture, write a story, to leave a special gift in the casket (Worden, 1996). Children may want to make a memorial book, to remember anniversaries, special days, or some other means of expressing their grief and remembrance (Pennells & Smith, 1995). Children need to be encouraged to express their feelings in some form to help manage their grief.

Like art, music is also an excellent form of self-expression. Music affects one's mind and body. Joyful music can elevate one's mood and encourage laughter. Deanna Edwards (1993) indicates that music is not just entertainment, but it is also a powerful therapy and teaching tool. Music is more than just sound. It has atmosphere and to some degree dramatic action. As a painter uses physical paints and the sculptor uses clay, the musician uses his or her voice, singing ability, words, message, attitudes, adaptation, and musical ability to provide a musical message for the listener. The listener brings a capacity for hearing, interpreting, and reliving the musical emotions of the creator. For most music, there is an intimate relationship between music and words. The nature of beauty in music does not need words, but the use of words can be powerful. For music to have a message, it must reach the listener with feeling, impulse, craving, wishing, inspiration, and ideation.

Danai Papadatou and Costas Papadatos (1991) suggest that death-related themes are prominent in adolescent music. Music and the arts are part of the life of people in all cultures. Most tend to appreciate most the music of their youth. Regardless of age, people enjoy music. Music, like other art forms, heals. The particular style of music to be used depends upon you. Your favorite music may not help you manage life events, but it will probably help to enrich your day. Each of us tends to find most satisfying the kind of music that we enjoyed while growing up. The heartbeat of the universe may be expressed with the beat of the music. It can speak to us in ways that can reach our inner existence. It can mirror our own heartbeat.

How many people listen to music while exercising, waiting for an airplane, preparing for an athletic contest, or thousands of other activities? Gymnasts use music to enhance their performance. Mothers use music to soothe crying babies. Funeral liturgies use music to heal the loss of loved ones. It is difficult to find a cultural ritual that does not include music. While most are texting, using mobile devices, computers, and other electronic devices, music is still a major part of all cultures.

Each life must also have hope. Life is full of awe and wonder for children, and hopefully for adults as well, but it is also full of pain and suffering. As adults or parents, we try to protect our children from pain and suffering, but we cannot. From the cutting of the first tooth, to ear aches, to death, life is full of pain and suffering. Hope does not come from sweetness and protecting children from poverty, racism, hate crimes, violence, death, and even the suffering of innocents. Hope comes from seeing the goodness in the hearts of people in spite of the suffering and pain that life offers. To sugarcoat life leads to cynicism and despair rather than hope. How could anyone face mobs while walking in peace marches, Nazi's as Anne Frank, the poor as Mother Teresa, or any other act of courage without hope?

Each of us has shortcomings, failings, and makes mistakes, yet life can still be full of hope, dreams, and fulfillment. Perhaps you can save your soda cans and have your child give the bag of cans to a homeless person. The joy in the face of the homeless person may allow your child to learn about hope. Music is a way to increase optimism and hope even in the face of loss and grief!

What can a song do? Some songs help people forget their troubles. Others help them to better understand their troubles. Songs might even help inspire people to act. Perhaps war songs have inspired people to join the military in time of crisis for their nation. Music leads us to dance, to sing, to move in rhythm, to smile, to talk, to enjoy our lives. Music allows the elderly to bring back the magic of their youth. Workers use music to allow them to forget the harshness of their tasks. Like drink and drugs, music can relieve stress, help people forget, inspire, mourn the loss of love or life, and thousands of other emotions.

THE SOCIOLOGY OF THE ARTS

The Sociology of the Arts is the sociological study of people's appreciation of the aesthetic value of objects, actions, images, and sounds. Life has more to offer than shelter, clothing, and other utilitarian necessities. Color, form, feel, design, taste, touch, emotion, desire, and appeal take human experiences to functional pleasure that stimulates the imagination, feelings, sensory experiences, emotions, creative expressions, and feelings. Humans have a sense of and a desire for the aesthetic. As we age, these feelings can be enhanced with music or other art forms.

The arts are an expression of the attitudes and values of the people toward important aspects of their lives. Since people live and act within social settings based upon social relationships, their arts, photography, architecture, poetry, music, sculpture, painting, weaving, carving, opera, drama, and humor are determined to a large extent by social factors. The dominant social class usually sets the standards for cultural tastes. The dominant class with economic, religious, and political power imposed its tastes upon the rest of society. While opera is generally viewed as a "highbrow" elitist form or art, it is not really class bound due to its mix of the comic and serious (Hutcheon & Hutcheon, 1996). What is art for one social class may not be viewed as art for another social class. Creative tattooing and other bodily arts may be snubbed by most in higher social classes. Many in the lower social classes may be less attracted to feminist or gender arts.

With the development of mass communications, mass media, mass education, and mass production, the quality, attitudes, and values of the artistic creations have dramatically changed. The art of the Greek era, the Roman era, the Gothic, Impressionism, or of ancient China provides knowledge of the intellectual, social, and spiritual climates of those cultures. The explosion of the popular arts in modern society, the buying power of youth around the world, the mass production and distribution of products, and lack of emphasis upon the intellectual in art have changed the world of the arts. What is produced in Kansas can be sold in Somalia or anywhere around the world. The original, the special, the unique artistic creation is still available, but mass/pop art is far more accessible. The birth of pop art coincided with the development of mass advertising and with television moving from a luxury to a necessity. Artist Andy Warhol in the 1960s produced art exhibitions with Campbell's soup labels and Coca-Cola bottles. By the 1970s, fields were plowed, planted, and trimmed to offer art only viewable from the sky. Earth art expanded to include creating art that would never be show in studios or galleries. Graffiti led to murals and artistic creations on buildings, underpasses, and railroad cars. Certainly, people try to decorate their homes, offices, schools, churches, and even stores with art. Art is not simply the nonutilitarian.

Much of art is useful. It is difficult to draw the line between the aesthetic and the utilitarian. If my cereal box is artistic, it may sell better. If my packaging of my product is appealing, it sells. Color television changed packaging for advertising. Technology revolutionized art. Because of the technological explosion, the study of the sociology of the arts faces new challenges, dramatic changes, and is possibly a pivotal era in the study of the arts. The changing nature of the economies of the world has vastly changed architecture. As economies struggle, lack of funds will mean that the spectacular cathedral will no longer be built. Buildings in cities no longer exhibit the art of the past. Architecture is a living art and creative structures are being built, but concern over money has changed what architects can create. Concerns about terrorism, floods, hurricanes, fires, or eventual demolition may have more impact on design than beauty or artistic creations. Sports stadiums or other ventures that can make money are often artistic and extravagant in their construction while government buildings, schools, and libraries must be built by the lowest and often least creative builders. The lasting quality of some of the arts seems to have been lost or at least is eroding. At the same time, cartoons, popular music, salon music, illustrations, caricatures, and the protest music of the 1960s and 1970s were not intended to be lasting. Today, one can buy a Van Gogh, an R. C. Gorman, Picasso, or Monet print at Walmart. Yet an original Van Gogh may sell for over $100 million. Art is more available to all, and yet art is less accessible. Private collectors hoard masterpieces. But music is available everywhere. If you have a voice, you can make music regardless of quality.

Not only are children aided through their grief by expression, children who are free to express their own emotions are more apt than other children to approach and assist others who are in need (Eisenberg & Mussen, 1989). Poetry, reflection, meditation, and creative writing allow children and adults to open their minds and hearts to grieve successfully. Thomas Attig, in a beautifully creative book, *Catching Your Breath in Grief . . . and Grace Will Lead You Home* (2012), offers a marvelous example of philosophical writing about grief that should aid those of all ages who are grieving.

The use of the arts allows children to remove the sense of distance between themselves and others; to find relief for depression; to enhance their self-esteem; to lower anxiety, fear, and other feelings of grief; and to achieve a safe level of acceptance of reality. It is not necessary to flood the child with reality, but it is important to support and encourage a reasonable view of what actually occurred (Hemmings, 1995).

CONCLUSIONS

Children of all ages are capable of grieving and surviving loss. Using humor, music, and art are effective ways to provide social support for children who are experiencing complicated grief. Various techniques ranging from storytelling to humor exist for aiding children who are grieving. Support from adults is required for children to maintain their self-esteem and to manage loss. Children need help to make choices. Children need to say goodbye by writing a letter, making a picture, sending up a balloon with a message to their loved one. Adults need to support their efforts. Expressing emotions aids children who are grieving. The use of the arts, the Internet, and family support will aid grieving children of all ages!

APPENDIX I
25 Things That Can Help Children Who Experience Loss

1. **Sacred place**: Create a sacred place. This can be a memory room or spot in a room or hall. It can be a place to keep items of value to the child and to you in a visible, open place.
2. **Journaling and Storytelling**: Journaling or storytelling is another technique to manage loss. Depending upon their age, try to get the child to write a journal of their journey through grief, or if they are too young to write, have them chronicle through drawings or other art forms. Drawing or writing can be a process of discovery. If you draw or write along with the child for any length of time, you will probably state what is in your heart and your mind. You will unearth much that you may not recognize about your own grief for your losses.
3. **Humor**: Humor is an excellent coping mechanism. Laughter helps us find inner peace. Humorous stories, particularly about us, are perhaps the easiest form of humor to use to aid the grieving or the dying. Humor is not the absence of sadness. Humor allows us to view our situations with a different lens, to not take ourselves and our lives so seriously. Laughter helps us find inner peace. This peace is not found by laughing at other people, but laughing with other people.
4. **Music**: Music, like other art forms, heals. Children love music! It is best to use their favorite music rather than yours. Your favorite music may not help them manage their loss, but it could help you manage yours. Each of us tends to find most satisfying the kind of music that we enjoyed while growing up. The heartbeat of the universe may be expressed with the beat of the music. It can speak to us in ways that can reach our inner existence. It can mirror our own heartbeat.
5. **The Arts**: Art, drama, puppeteering, clay, drawing, painting, and other forms of expression, like journaling, may aid children who are attempting to cope with loss.
6. **Friendship**: Friendship is a powerful form of coping. People may be the best source of help. Friends share their joys and their sorrows. Few of us have lives that we would want to trade with others.

7. **Acceptance**: Acceptance is also a coping tool. We must learn to accept each person as he or she is, trust his or her judgment while recognizing that each person, like us, will make mistakes. When your daughter or son chooses a spouse, do not second guess their choice. It is their choice. If you show acceptance and trust, your relationship will be strong. If you question their choice, you will strain your relationship.
8. **Balance**: Balance may also help. Life is a series of blessings and burdens. One must find balance in one's own life. This can mean that one should find the place in life, the job, or vocation that one is called to serve. If one focuses upon making money, one miss the career that would have offered joy and purpose to one's life. If one suicides because of youthful failures, one may miss the joy and purpose of one's life as a grandparent much later. Of course, teaching children about balance is a lifelong journey!
9. **Love**: Love is another tool to help manage loss. People need each other. We cannot survive without one another. Family, friends, spiritual friends give life meaning and purpose. Knowing that friends and family will be there for you is a valuable lesson for children. Love is freely given in spite of mistakes. None of us is perfect. Children are loved in spite of their errors. Learning our heritage is part of this sharing of love. Stories about the great-grandmother who died when you were an infant may show the love that she felt for you even though you don't remember her. The quilt that she made or some other treasure may be a visible sign of her love.
10. **Harmony and Security**: Harmony and security can create a sense of harmony and security for the person experiencing loss. One needs to be secure in the home, school, work, play, and life.
11. **Facing Reality**: Facing reality as it is can also help us to know what things that they can change, what things that they cannot. To accept what cannot be changed and to have the courage to change what can be changed as described in the Serenity Prayer of St. Francis.
12. **Rituals**: Rituals can allow each person to express their spirituality. Family rituals may become a remembrance of the deceased family members and friends as they are offered on special days during the year. Such rituals may also include simply keeping family treasures because they belonged to deceased love ones. It can be making a basket, weaving a rug, a sand painting, or whatever. Rituals support belief and give purpose to faith.
13. **Play**: For children, play is a major method of coping. For adults, work is a major method of coping. Play is a child's work. Just as our jobs can add meaning and purpose to our lives, so too can a child's play add meaning and purpose to a child's life. Children can experience unrestrained joy in play. Perhaps we still feel that kind of joy in our work. Work and play are both spiritual and a source of spiritual growth. Play differs from sport in that it lacks rules. As adults, we impose rules on children and destroy their ability to play effectively.
14. **Prayer**: Another useful tool is prayer. Life itself can be a prayer. One can pray for the animal or plant that gave its life to feed us, for the opportunity to have a job

to support one's family, for one's family, for the earth that provides all that is needed for life, for the universe, for everything in life. Prayers can be ritualized, can take place in religious settings, be memorized, or simply lived. Prayer may also involve rules, but children need to be able to "play" with their prayers.

15. **Forgiveness**: People can also use forgiveness as a coping tool. Each of us has wronged others and been wronged by others. Our spiritual growth also includes moments of forgiving and being forgiven. Remember when you broke your mother's vase that was a gift to her from her mother? You discovered that she actually cared more for you than the vase. The children must be taught that the pain or suffering that one caused is not necessarily forgotten, but that trust and growing together in spite of the betrayal allows us to go on with our lives. After scolding them for breaking the vase, you can give them a hug. Rivalries between siblings, friends, or others must be acknowledged openly and then trust and forgiveness can follow.

16. **Hope**: Each life must also have hope. Life is full of awe and wonder for the child and hopefully for adults as well, but it is also full of pain and suffering. As adults or parents, we try to protect our children from pain and suffering, but we cannot. From the cutting of the first tooth to earaches to death, life is full of pain and suffering. Hope does not come from sweetness and protecting children from poverty, racism, hate crimes, violence, death, and even the suffering of innocents. Hope comes from seeing the goodness in the hearts of people in spite of the suffering and pain that life offers. To sugarcoat life leads to cynicism and despair rather than hope. How could one face a mob in peace marches, Nazi's as Anne Frank, the poor as Mother Teresa, or any other act of courage without hope? Each of us has shortcomings, failings, and makes mistakes, yet life can still be full of hope, dreams, and fulfillment. Perhaps, you can save your soda cans and have your child give them to a homeless person. The joy in the face of the homeless person may allow your child to learn about hope.

17. **Sharing and Caring**: We all need to be taught sharing and caring. As adults, we can experience joy when we share. So can children. The child who offers you a lick of their sucker or ice cream can feel real joy in watching you oblige their offer. Spirituality needs to include sharing and caring for others rather than the usual "me first" ethic of the U.S. culture.

18. **Listening**: Those experiencing loss need to know that we are actually listening to them. Listening, both verbally and nonverbally, will help others cope. We must actually listen. Put down your paper, turn off the television, and give the child your true attention. True listening shows that you really care. Perhaps you may remember being read stories as a child. It may be the last time that you had the undivided attention of your parents.

19. **Spirituality**: Spirituality itself is a coping tool. I am not sure if we can teach others about spirituality. Children may be the best teachers. It seems that they are better teachers for us. A Hopi child understood the conflict with the Navajo tribe better than most adults. She indicated that the battle was over the land. She

said that the Navajo wanted to cut up the land, to farm it, which in her view of spirituality meant to harm the land. To divide the land was to hurt the land. The land deserved its freedom and chance to live. In her spiritual orientation, she felt that the Hopi must protect the spirit and well-being of the land because the land can feel the difference. A Navajo child indicated that the White people who try to amass property and things have a problem. Their problem is that they have so much that they cannot choose what to love or need and are lost because they have no homeland, just houses and things. Another Navajo child facing the ultimate death of her grandmother saw no reason to pray for her to live. She saw that death is not bad. She saw that her grandmother was suffering in life. She prayed for her grandmother to have a peaceful death rather than to pray that she suffer by living longer. Children are our best teachers!

20. **Encouragement**: Encouragement may also help others to cope. Offer encouragement rather than praising, saying that the person is pretty or whatever. Encourage them by focusing upon the process rather than the outcome. Loss in athletics, school, or whatever is not failure. Failing to try is failure. Rather than allowing the other person to say that he or she cannot do something, encourage them to try. Real courage comes from the scars that come from trying to do the seemingly impossible. Have you ever clapped for a Special Olympics participant that you did not even know? Perhaps tears came to your eyes. Sharing is part of encouragement. As part of my training in an Outward Bound program, my feet were tied together, my hands tied behind my back, and I was tossed into the ocean for an hour. Being somewhat afraid of drowning, I was sure that I could not survive, but I did survive. In the process of training for the event, I received encouragement to try. I was told that I would be rescued if I needed to be. Life is a journey. We must all be encouraged to do the seemingly impossible. The struggle together adds much meaning and purpose to life.

21. **Freedom**: We must also instill in others the desire to have freedom. They must become free to live until they die. As dying people, we are not dead. The dying, too, must live life fully. Each day must be lived fully. In our culture we tend to live for the future. We must live for now rather than for someday that may not even happen.

22. **Dreams**: We all need to be taught to try to live our dreams. We need to be aware of the power of dreams to help give meaning and purpose to life. Each day is a blessing. Each day should be better than yesterday and tomorrow better than today. Children do not have much of a past to live for, but we can foster pessimism, cynicism, and doom in children by living in the past rather than living in the present. We must try to live our dreams and strive to accomplish them. Everyone needs something to look forward to each day to have a reason to get up in the morning. Remember the excitement of your own childhood when an anticipated even kept you from sleeping the night before the event that so excited your sense of life?

23. **Miracles**: We need to be taught the power of miracles. Saints tend to live ordinary lives and do ordinary things extraordinarily well. Instead of looking for great miracles in one's life, look for the little ones that make each day what it is. When you have no money for bills or whatever, a friend pays you what is owed or a painting is sold or whatever. When you are tired and nearly falling asleep while driving something occurs to cause you to awaken fully. The beauty of the face of a homeless woman or the singing voice of a developmentally disabled child. The miracle of birth or even death. The first word that your child speaks, the cry when the light shocks them as they leave the womb. What are your life's miracles? They need not be what is a storyline for books or movies and yet maybe they are. Perhaps the greatest miracle is our life. That every human and animal has something to offer and that every life is precious. Are your children a miracle? Are they not precious and special?
24. **Prayer for the dead**: While not true of all religions, for those who practice the Communion of Saints, the relationship with the dead continues. The living can ask for help from those who have died, just as they would ask for their prayers when they were alive. Not everyone that you love is with you at this moment. You can still love them! Clearly, children can be encouraged to continue to love and to have a relationship with those who have died. Roman Catholics, Native Americans, and many other groups encourage relationships with those who have died.
25. **Memory**: Encourage the child to develop memories to treasure into the future. What they choose to remember may not be the highlights that you might treasure, but you can also make videotapes, pictures, items that can be treasured, and stories for the future to help maintain those memories.

REFERENCES

Attig, T. (2012). *Catching your breath in grief... and grace will lead you home.* Victoria, BC, Canada: Breath of Life.

Bauman, R. (1996). Folklore as transdisciplinary dialogue. *Journal of Folklore Research, 33*(1), 15–20.

Brabant, S. (1997–1998). Death and grief in the family comics. *Omega: Journal of Death and Dying, 36*(1), 33–44.

Carey, T. C., Carey, M. P., & Kelley, M. L. (1997). Differential Emotions theory: Relative contribution of emotion, cognition, and behavior to the prediction of depressive symptomatology in non-referred adolescents. *Journal of Clinical Psychology, 53*(1), 25–34.

Coe, R. M. (1997, March). The magic of science and the science of magic: An essay on the process of healing. *Journal of Health and Social Behavior, 38*, 1–8.

Cox, G. R., Vanden Berk, B. J., Fundis, R. J., & McGinnis, P. J. (1995). American children and Desert Storm: Impressions of the Gulf conflict. In D. W. Adams & E. J. Deveau (Eds.), *Beyond the innocence of childhood: Factors influencing children and adolescents' perceptions and attitudes toward death* (pp. 109–121). Amityville, NY: Baywood.

Doka, K. J. (Ed.). (1995). *Children mourning: Mourning children.* Washington, DC: Hospice Foundation of America.
Dyregrov, A. (1990). *Grief in children: A handbook for adults.* London, UK: Kingsley.
Edwards, D. (1993). Grieving: The pain and the promise. In J. D. Morgan (Ed.), *Personal care in an impersonal world: A multidimensional look at bereavement* (pp. 39–72). Amityville, NY: Baywood.
Eisenberg, N., & Mussen, P. H. (1989). *The roots of prosocial behavior in children.* New York, NY: Cambridge University Press.
Goldman, L. (1996). *Breaking the silence: A guide to help children with complicated grief: Suicide, homicide, AIDS, violence and abuse.* London, UK: Taylor & Francis.
Goldsmith, D. J., & Dun, S. A. (1997). Sex differences and similarities in the communication of social support. *Journal of Social and Personal Relationships, 14*(3), 317–337.
Gross, J. J., & Levenson, R. W. (1997). Hiding feelings: The acute effects of inhibiting negative and positive emotion. *Journal of Abnormal Psychology, 106*(1), 95–103.
Hemmings, P. (1995). Communications with children through play. In S. C. Smith & M. Pennells (Eds.), *Interventions with bereaved children.* London. UK: Kingsley.
Hupka, R. B., Saleski, Z., Otto, J., Reidl, L., & Tarabrina, N. V. (1997, March). The colors of anger, envy, fear, and jealousy: A cross-cultural study. *Journal of Cross-Cultural Psychology, 28*(2), 156–171.
Hutcheon, L., & Hutcheon, M. (1996). *Opera, desire, disease, death.* Lincoln: University of Nebraska.
Jung, J. (1997). Balance and source of social support in relation to well-being. *Journal of General Psychology, 124*(1), 77–90.
Komproe, I. H., Rijken, M., Ros, W. J. G., Winnubst, J. A. M., & Hart, H. (1997). Available support and received support: Different effects under stressful circumstances. *Journal of Social and Personal Relationships, 14*(1), 59–77.
Lau, K. J. (1996, Spring). Social structure, society, and symbolism: Toward a holistic interpretation of fairy tales. *Western Folklore, 55,* 233–244.
Lewinsohn, P. M., Lewinsohn, M., Gotlib, I. H., Seeley, J. R., & Allen, N. B. (1998). Gender differences in anxiety disorders and anxiety symptoms in adolescents. *Journal of Cross-Cultural Psychology Abnormal Psychology, 107*(1), 109–117.
Liddell, C. (1997, May). Every picture tells a story—Or does it? *Young South African Children Interpreting Pictures, 28*(3), 266–283.
Lipman, S. (1991). *Laughter in Hell: The use of humor during the holocaust.* Northvale, NJ: Aronson.
Lowis, M. J., & Hughes, J. A. (1997). Comparison of the effects of sacred and secular music on elderly people. *Journal of Psychology, 131*(1), 45–55.
Marrone, R. (1997). *Death, mourning, and caring.* Pacific Grove, CA: Brooks/Cole.
Meyers, S. A. (1997, April). The language of love: The difference a preposition makes. *Personality and Social Psychology Bulletin, 23*(4), 347–362.
Moore, T. (1992). *Care of the soul: A guide for cultivating depth and sacredness in everyday life.* New York, NY: HarperCollins.
Neale, R. E. (1993). Joking with death. In K. J. Doka & J. D. Morgan (Eds.), *Death and spirituality* (pp. 323–331). Amityville, NY: Baywood.
Palfai, T. P., & Hart, K. E. (1997). Anger coping styles and perceived social support. *The Journal of Social Psychology, 137*(4), 405–411.
Papadatou, D., & Papadatos, C. (1991). *Children and death.* New York, NY: Hemisphere.

Parkes, C. M., & Prigerson, H. G. (2010). *Bereavement: Studies of grief in adult life.* New York, NY: Routledge.

Pennells, M., & Smith, S. C. (1995). *The forgotten mourners: Guidelines for working with bereaved children.* London, UK: Kingsley.

Robinson, L., & Mahon, M. M. (1997). Sibling bereavement: A conceptual analysis. *Death Studies, 21,* 477–499.

Rokach, A., & Brock, H. (1998). Coping with loneliness. *Journal of Psychology, 132*(1), 107–127.

Rohde, P., Seeley, J. R., & Mace, D. E. (1997, Summer). Correlates of suicidal behavior in a juvenile detention population. *Suicide and Life-Threatening Behavior, 27*(2), 164–175.

Ryff, C. D., & Singer, B. (1998). The contours of positive human health. *Psychological Inquiry, 9*(1), 1–28.

Sarafino, E. P. (1986). *The fears of childhood: A guide to recognizing and reducing fearful states in children.* New York City, NY: Human Sciences Press.

Saunders, C. (1995–1996). A response to Logue's "Where Hospice Fails—The limits of palliative care." *Omega: Journal of Death and Dying, 32*(1), 1–5.

Schut, H. A. W., Stroebe, M. S., van den Bout, J., & de Keijser, J. (1997). Intervention for the bereaved: Gender difference in the efficacy of two counselling programmes. *British Journal of Clinical Psychology, 36,* 63–72.

Shatil, J. (1995). *The psychography of the child: Development of the psychograpic capacity from drawings to writing, and the means for improvement.* New York, NY: University Press of America.

Silverstein, M., & Bengstson, V. L. (1997, September). Intergenerational solidarity and the structure of adult child-parent relationships in American families. *American Journal of Sociology, 103*(2), 429–460.

Stevenson, R. G. (2002). *What will we do? Preparing a school community to cope with crises* (2nd ed.). Amityville, NY: Baywood.

Thomas, J. B. (1997). Dumb blondes, Dan Quayle, and Hillary Clinton: Gender, sexuality, and stupidity in jokes. *Journal of American Folklore, 110*(437), 277–313.

Thompson, N. (2012). *Grief and its challenges.* New York, NY: Palgrave.

van Aken, M. A. G., & Asendorpf, J. B. (1997). Support by parents, classmates, friends, and siblings in preadolescence: Covariation and compensation across relationships. *Journal of Social and Personal Relationships, 14*(1), 79–93.

von Franz, M.-L. (1970). *An introduction to the interpretation of fairy tales.* Dallas, TX: Spring.

Walter, C. A., & McCoyd, J. L. M. (2009). *Grief and loss across the lifespan: A biopsychosocial perspective.* New York, NY: Springer.

Webb, N. B. (1993). Traumatic death of friend/peer: Case of Susan, age 9. In N. B. Webb (Ed.), *Helping bereaved children: A handbook for practitioners.* New York, NY: Guilford Press.

Wilson, T. L., & Brown, T. L. (1997). Reexamination of the effect of Mozart's music on spatial-task performance. *The Journal of Psychology, 131*(4), 365–370.

Worden, J. W. (1996). *Children and grief: When a parent dies.* New York, NY: Guilford Press.

Worden, J. W. (2009). *Grief counseling and grief therapy: A handbook for the mental health practitioner.* New York, NY: Springer.

CHAPTER 7

"Oh, Those Poor Children!": Borrowing Historical and Biographical Loss Narratives of Grieving Children

Harold Ivan Smith

> The American public seems to have a never-ending taste for reading about the lives of others.
> —Lois Banner (2009, p. 586)

Tonight, all across the planet, the bedtime routine for millions of children will include "Tell me a story." Children will drift off to sleep with fragments of a story wandering the corridors of their imaginations. Some stories will be about brave children tackling all kinds of problems, including dragons. In some families, a parent or relative will read from a well-worn storybook, perhaps passed down from a previous generation.

Publishers and booksellers particularly support storytelling by offering new books on heroes, sports figures, or adventurers. Browse in Barnes & Noble or surf Amazon.com and you will find biographies and history books designed for different reading comprehension levels of children. As a result of exposure to brief biographies on presidents, adventurers, humanitarians, sports figures, soldiers, inventors, and social activists, a seed is planted: I, too, can be strong, courageous, and/or adventurous. The template for a successful book generally follows a brief mention of difficulties encountered during childhood and a strong focus on the subject's adult achievements. More recently, however, children's authors are including details of losses a particular subject has experienced: death, divorce of parents, or acts of trauma. This reality is demonstrated by Cooper (2003) in *Jack: The Early Years of Jack Kennedy* and Nelson (2013) in *Nelson Mandela*.

Caroline Kennedy, in *Poems to Learn by Heart*, notes her mother's intentional effort to expose her daughter to great poetry. Kennedy reflected, "In the ancient world, before books or printed material, children had to memorize the information they needed for navigating, farming, trading, entertainment, and civil life" (2013, p. 11). Cultures "braved-up" their children with stories—magnificent epic heroic narratives—intended to transmit values and to transform fear into courage and survival. I remember the cadence of Alice Cannon, my 5th-grade teacher, reading after lunch the tales of Paul Bunyan. As fifth graders listened and drifted into naptime, Paul Bunyan became real.

Can clinicians and teachers transmit emotional navigational skills for grieving children through stories? Might stories of individuals who have experienced and survived significant trauma during childhood have value to children today? This chapter will examine that possibility.

Too many would-be consolers rely on a cliché—"Oh, children are so resilient!" Some children are resilient; other children are not resilient!

A TALE OF A CHILD-GRIEVER

1884 A child is born into an affluent dysfunctional family. Her mother, a society belle known for her beauty, verbally abuses her daughter: "You are the ugliest thing God ever created!" Due to the father's marital infidelity and substance abuse, the parents separate before the child is age 7.

1892 The child's mother dies of diphtheria. Custody of the three children is awarded to a stern maternal grandmother whose favorite word is, "No." The father is discouraged from seeing his children.

1893 The girl's oldest brother dies of diphtheria.

1894 The father—to whom the 10-year-old girl is devoted—dies under scandalous conditions. The child later recalled, "I was treated like the daughter of a wicked, ruined man. They got the funeral over as quickly as possible" (Levy, 1999, p. 153). The girl was not allowed to attend any of the rituals.

This girl and her brother live with their maternal grandmother and four emotionally unstable unmarried adult aunts and uncles in a psychological "house of horrors." Her grandmother spends her days in a dark bedroom; meals are eaten in total silence. The two uncles, alcoholics, regularly fire pistols near their niece to see her dance. The little girl has no friends and has little contact with her cousins. The family cannot risk other children witnessing the chaos in the home or being injured by the irresponsible uncles. This girl finds refugee in reading in four languages.

Nothing in this early narrative indicates this girl would become well-known and make significant contributions to humanity. On the darkest days, if you had told this orphan,"There *will* be great opportunities ahead for you," why would she have believed you? The world would never have heard of Eleanor Roosevelt if a remarkable teacher at an English boarding school had not intersected her life.

IDENTIFY PARTICULAR ELEMENTS OF GRIEF EXPERIENCE THAT ARE RESPONSIVE TO BORROWING

Compassionate care for grieving children has relied on theoretical constructs that offer rationale and structure for clinical intervention and care. How might narratives from child-grievers "place a face" on the theories and be translatable into a grieving child's life?

I have proposed (Smith, 2004, 2012) the use of borrowed narratives to identify historical/biographical stories of child-grievers who have faced, survived, and sometimes thrived in circumstances comparable to what some children are experiencing today. My contention is that grieving children need stories for identification, inspiration, and reflection. Paradoxically, the emotional wilderness of one grieving child becomes, through a clinician's awareness and transmission, a potential oasis for another child. Neimeyer (1998) insists, "In the telling of our tales we seek help in finding answers, or at least, permission to share [or frame] the burning questions" (p. 54).

Many children experience an overloaded palette of grief: trauma, death by suicide or murder; death as a consequence of poverty; death as a consequence of parental substance abuse; death due to an accident, illness, or natural disaster. Additionally, children survive nonfinite losses that upend their lives, particularly divorce or abandonment. Some children, unfortunately, juggle multiple losses or serial losses. Some children navigate losses that would be difficult for some clinicians to comprehend.

After Gadla Henry Mphakanyiswa died in 1927, his nine-year-old son's possessions were quickly packed. His mother walked him to the home of a chieftain who, by tribal tradition, would now rear the boy. Consequently, within days that boy lost his father, mother, home, school, and playmates. Everything that provided security to this 9-year-old vanished with his father's death! Fortunately, Nelson Mandela survived his childhood (Smith, 2012).

A Tale of a Wise Teacher

Perhaps you are familiar with the Buddhist proverb, "When the student is ready the teacher will appear." In Eleanor's home in New York, something happened—or almost happened! This 15-year-old adolescent found herself on a ship to England to attend boarding school. Although desperately afraid of water, she welcomed this adventure because it put distance between her and a bizarre family.

Madame Marie Souvestre—elderly, dignified, a brilliant "out-of-the-box" thinker—welcomed the new pupil to Allenswood, which attracted the daughters of Europe's elite families. French was the only language spoken at the school. If a student used more than two words of English in the course of a day, she had to confess that lapse before bedtime. Fortunately this girl spoke flawless French and Madame took notice! Soon the girl sat at the head table every night at dinner. This adolescent, who had spent almost no time around other children, flourished in a safe environment and soon became the school's most popular student.

Eleanor accompanied Madame as a companion on trips across Europe. She taught the adolescent to navigate train schedules, exchange money, and secure lodging. More significantly, Souvestre affirmed this girl's spontaneity and nurtured her confidence.

Instruction was rigorous in Souvestre's classroom. If she judged a student's essay less than first-rate or lacking evidence of original thought, she tore it up before the class. Eleanor learned to write well under this regimen.

If you had whispered to Eleanor during this experience, "You will become a great teacher, write bestselling books, host radio shows, and nurture many orphans," how would Eleanor Roosevelt have responded?

Define Techniques for Borrowing Narratives From Historical Grieving Children

A clinician must have a generous awareness of potential children from whom to borrow. But where does a clinician begin to audition stories?

Biographies

Decades after the death of his father, as a political prisoner in South Africa, the one leisure Nelson Mandela was allowed was reading. A childhood love of books impacted his daily life as a political prisoner. Mandela later observed, "If I had not gone to jail and been able to read and listen to the stories of many people . . . I might not have learned how others handled difficult situations" (Cohen & Battersby, 2009, p. 164). How differently Mandela's life might have turned out had his father lived and had he not been encouraged to read?

Ronald Reagan (1990) identified a pivotal experience in his childhood:

> My mother was gone on one of her sewing jobs, and I expected the house to be empty. As I walked up the stairs, I nearly stumbled over a lump near the front door; it was Jack [his father] lying in the snow, his arms outstretched, flat on his back. I leaned over to see what was wrong and smelled whiskey. He had found his way home from a speakeasy and had just passed out right there. For a moment or two, I looked down at him and thought about continuing on into the house and going to bed, as if he weren't there. But I couldn't do it. When I tried to wake him he just snored—loud enough, I suspected, for the whole neighborhood to hear him. *So I grabbed a piece of his overcoat, pulled it, and dragged him into the house, then put him to bed and never mentioned the incident to my mother* (p. 33, emphasis added).

Responsibility and survivability began early for this boy! If you are aware of what Smith (2012) calls a narrative slice, you could loan it to a child navigating a parent, or parent's, issues with substance abuse. You might share the narrative slice with responsible adults in the child's life.

Memoirs

Abigail Thomas suggests that memoir writing "is a way to figure out who you used to be and how you got to be who you are" (2008, p. 2). That concept is demonstrated in a memoir by Natalie Cole. As the daughter of famed musician Nat King Cole, Natalie, age 16 when he died, was never allowed to grieve. "My mother reminded me of Jackie Kennedy. She was perfectly poised, maintaining great dignity amid this profound sadness. We were requested to act the same" (2010, p. 29). This narrative slice might be valuable to an adolescent who has been told, "Get over it! Move on!" or whose grief has been disenfranchised. Unfortunately, Cole's denial had significant consequences. "Some twenty years later," she disclosed in her memoir, "I was told by a wise counselor that I still hadn't mourned the loss. I'm not sure I ever will. My teenage years will forever be defined by my father's death" (p. 99).

A Griever Named Ken

Ken Burns is an award-winning producer of documentary films. His mother was diagnosed with breast cancer when Burns was 3 years old; eight years later she died. Her illness was the dominant thread in Burns' childhood. His father "closed himself off from Ken and his brother, feeling the grief was his alone and *not* the boys'" (Bush, 2003, p. 150). Burns recalled, "There was never a moment in my childhood when I wasn't aware of her impending death and then, after she passed, that she had died" (Bush, 2003, p. 150).

A year after his mother's death, Mr. Burns took his adolescent son to a movie. At one point in the movie, as father and son shared popcorn, Ken's father began crying:

> He hadn't cried when my mom died the year before, and I had never seen him cry. I instantaneously understood that it was the power of the medium that had given him this permission, and I sort of swore on the spot to myself that I would be a filmmaker. (Bush, 2003, p. 150)

Over time, Burns produced a string of award-winning documentaries such as *The Civil War*, *Baseball*, *JAZZ*, *The War*, and *The Brooklyn Bridge* and established the "gold standard" for making documentaries. Barbara Bush recalled a weekend when Burns was a houseguest. As Mrs. Bush and Mr. Burns "walked Millie and then sat and talked and talked" (Bush, 2003, p. 149), Bush described the impact of his mother's death on his childhood. He disclosed that there had been "no services" for his mother. Cremation was chosen by his father. Very tidy. But not psychologically beneficial to a grieving 11-year-old.

Years later, Burns launched a personal documentary. The Burns brothers, given their extensive contacts, identified the funeral home that had handled the cremation. The brothers learned their mother's cremated remains had never been picked up. At some point, her cremated remains had been buried in "a potter's field." The day came when Ken and his brother stood in that cemetery for indigents. On another day, the brothers returned with a minister and finally "had a service" for their mother. Eventually, the brothers had a headstone erected for her.

I uncovered this narrative slice by reading Barbara Bush's *Reflections* (2003). I am fascinated by an insight phrased by Ken's psychologist father-in-law. He asked Ken, "What do you think you do for a living?" Ken responded that he was a documentary filmmaker.

You," his father-in-law countered, "wake the dead! You made Abraham Lincoln and Jackie Robinson and Louie Armstrong come alive." After a pause, he pushed on: "Who do you think you're really trying to awaken?'"

Burns hesitated. "My mother" (Bush, 2003, pp. 149–150). That conversation profoundly impacted Burns and led him to acknowledge his mother's death as a critical element in his own narrative. Sharing Burns' story or stories of other child-grievers might lead a grieving child or adolescent to recognize the significance of their narratives.

Examine Methods to Find Grief Slices in
Biographical/Historical Narratives

After identifying a historical or biographical narrative slice, the clinician asks, not unlike an archeologist studying a specimen, "What have we here? How might this be shared with and valued by a grieving child?"

While visiting the National Library of Vietnam in Hanoi, I stumbled on a wise piece of advice from Ho Chi Minh: "Look wide and think deep" (Nguyen, 2008, p. 194). That practical guidance will be useful in evaluating grief narratives for potential use.

SEARCH TIPS

1: Do an initial Google search on a person. Remember that Wikipedia is only a starting point for gaining an overview of a griever that interests you.

2: Skim/read essays in biographical reference books. Essays in a biographical dictionary or biographical encyclopedia summarize an individual's life in a few pages. Key episodes in their childhood may be mentioned. Three standard sources I have found valuable are

The Dictionary of American Biography Online
The American National Biography
The Dictionary of Canadian Biography Online

The essay on Abraham Lincoln in *American National Biography* focuses primarily on Lincoln's rise to national prominence and the presidency and includes a brief mention of the death of Lincoln's son, Willie, in 1862. However, in McPherson's (1999) *A.N.B.* essay, I learned that Nancy Hanks Lincoln, Abraham's mother, died in 1818, when he was nine. A decade later, on January 20, 1828, Abraham's only sibling, Sally, died in childbirth. Abraham's grief was heightened, the biographer contends, because Lincoln believed an intoxicated physician had caused her death (Burlingame, 2008; Miller, 2006). How did this 18-year-old express his grief? Abe "sat down on a log and hid his face in his hands while the tears rolled down through his long bony fingers." He repeatedly moaned, 'What have I to live for?'" (Burlingame, 2008, p. 45).

Take note of the identity of the author(s) of a biographical essay. What else has he/she written, in this case, on Lincoln; that is, journal articles, biographies, or multiple-volume biographies on Lincoln that might offer a deeper treatment of

Lincoln's grief during childhood? In your initial reading, pay attention to references cited by authors in the essay.

3: Expand your search. Once you have chosen an individual(s) to research—and have made a preliminary judgment call on the individual's potential value to you—expand the horizons of your project. The distinguished biographer Doris Kearns Goodwin (2005) calls this process, "widening the lens" (p. xxii).

4: Read biographies on your subject. Also, explore your subject in biographies written for children or adolescents. For example, when I read on Eleanor Roosevelt, I read Monica Kulling's *Eleanor Everywhere: The Life of Eleanor Roosevelt* (1999), designed for readers in grades 2–4. When my interest turned to *Condoleezza Rice,* I read Linda Wade's *Condoleezza Rice* (2002) in the Blue Banner Biography series.

5: Examine the index in biographies or histories looking for an entry such as "Lincoln, Abraham, *childhood.*" By reading further, you might discover a subentry, "death of mother, 225–231, 241." Check the index for other family members: "*Lincoln, Thomas*" (Lincoln's father) or *Lincoln, William Wallace* (Lincoln's son who died in the White House in February 1862). Frequently, indexes identify in parenthesis or a dash following the name the relationship to the subject of the biography—father, mother, daughter, uncle, grandfather, or such.

6: Read. Read widely. Read wisely. Gregory DeBourgh (2008) suggests that while skimming a journal article on your subject of interest, glance at the article before and after it. Pay attention to the dates of publication to assess recent publications. Newer biographies, for example, may be based on recent research or interpretation unavailable or ignored by previous writers.

7: Explore specialized biographical resources. Specialized encyclopedias or dictionaries, often available in library reference departments, will prove valuable. For example, when I wanted to know something about George Frideric Handel, who composed *The Messiah* and other classic musical works, I began with Hicks' (2001) essay in *The New Grove Dictionary of Music and Musicians* (Vol. 10, pp. 747–813). Here are highlights of a quick read:

- Son of George Handel, a barber-surgeon, and second wife.
- Boy's interest in music discouraged by father.
- George denied access to musical instruments.
- Father insisted, "You are going to study law."
- Handel secretly practiced the clavichord in the attic.
- At age 9, Duke of Saxe-Weissenfels heard George playing and the Duke "persuaded" Handel's father to support the boy's musical talent.
- Father died on February 14, 1697; George was 12.
- Although the death eliminates the barrier to studying music, George assumes family responsibilities.
- At age 18 leaves Halle.
- Wrote *The Messiah* in 1841 in three weeks.
- "Maintenance and education of exposed and deserted young children," Handel proposed a benefit concert. Moreover, for that occasion, Handel composed,

Blessed Are They That Considereth the Poor, which was sung for the next 10 years at fundraising events for that hospital.

Browse reference sections in local public libraries for such well-acknowledged resources.

Examples:

Commire, A. (Ed.). (1999). *Women in world history*. Detroit, MI: Gale.
Hine, D. C. (Ed.). (1993). *Black women in America: An historical encyclopedia* (2 vols). Brooklyn, NY: Carlson.
Malinowski, S. (Ed.). (1995). *Notable Native Americans*. Detroit, MI: Gale.
Oboler, S., & Gonzalez, D. J. (Eds.). (2005). *The Oxford encyclopedia of Latinos and Latinas in the United States*. New York, NY: Oxford University Press.
Saari, P. (Ed.). (1995). *Prominent women of the 20th century*. Detroit, MI: UXL/Gale.
Smith, J. C. (Ed.). (1992). *Notable Black American women*. Detroit, MI: Gale.
Stein, M. (Ed.). (2004). *Encyclopedia of lesbian, gay, bisexual and transgender history in America*. Detroit, MI: Thompson-Gale.
The A to Z of women in world history. (2002). New York, NY: Facts on File.
The encyclopedia of Asian history. (1989). New York, NY: Scribners.
Telgen, D., & Kamp, J. (Eds.). (1993). *Notable Hispanic American women*. Detroit, MI: Gale.

8: Enlist reference librarians in your search. Some librarians read widely in history or biography and may be able to point you to a solid source for further exploration. Many librarians are skilled in advanced research tracking to locate resources for your project.

9: Explore your subject's contemporaries. While Condoleezza Rice is a widely recognized name, the memoirs of her friend Carolyn Maull McKinstry (2011) offers insight into how school children in Birmingham grieved after the bombing of the Sixteenth Avenue Baptist Church in 1963. The death of those four children shaped both girls' lives.

While reading Christina Haag's (2012) *Come to the Edge: A Love Story*, about her friendship with John F. Kennedy, Jr., I discovered that immediately following the death of John's baby brother Patrick in 1963, a grieving president-father showed up with a puppy named Shannon, thinking the dog would distract the children from their grief. John told Haag that when he was a toddler, at times, his mother did not know whether to scold him or the dog for messes or for sweets which disappeared from the table.

> He laughed when he told the story. But his mood darkened when he told of another Shannon, the one he loved best, the one who was irascible. He had been away for part of the summer, and on his return, he found that his mother had given the dog away. "I didn't even get to say goodbye" he said sadly. (2011, p. xvii)

That story may be meaningful to children/adolescents who have had a pet die or given away.

GUIDANCE FOR PRODUCTIVE EXPLORATION

Tip 1: Pay attention to footnotes, endnotes, or asterisks in the text. If you read only the text in a biography or history you may miss a good recommendation for further reading or details that expand the text. Increasingly, editors try to keep endnotes "lean" (Burlingame, 2008, volume II, p. 839) by moving material into endnotes.

Nigel Hamilton, who has written extensively on methodology in biographical research, urges, "Read carefully the bibliographies, footnotes, and endnotes of existing biographical works on your subject, and make a list of all the names mentioned—especially in the author's acknowledgements" (2008, p. 69).

Tip 2: Use caution with secondary sources. If you rely on secondary sources, you trust the accuracy of an author or authors, their editors, and fact-checkers. You also rely on their interpretation of events. Investing time in thoroughly researching primary sources proves valuable for counseling, writing, and speaking. Given length restrictions for articles or chapters, some anecdotes cannot be used. Keep them handy, however, for speaking or counseling opportunities.

Tip 3: Book yourself on an occasional "wild goose chase." What does science fiction have to do with grieving children? A lot if the author had experienced grief as a child. As I skimmed a Wall Street Journal article on Ray Bradbury, a leading writer in this genre, I learned that Tom Nolan, the reporter, had asked Bradbury, "Where do your stories come from?"

> "All my stories are me," Bradbury answered. He elaborated: "When I was 8 years old, I was at the beach in Waukegan and a little girl was building a sandcastle with me. She went in the water and she never came out. She drowned. It was my first experience with death. It upset me terribly. . . . Years later, I remembered that, and I wrote about it; it was called "The Lake." It was published in *Weird Tales*. And all around the world, people wrote to me about that story; and my career was started. I was 26 years old." (Nolan, 2010)

Curious to know more about Bradbury's grief experiences, I turned to Weller's (2005) *The Bradbury Chronicles*. I discovered that Bradbury's childhood had been shaped not just by the girl's death but by a string of deaths: beloved grandfather, uncle, and baby sister. Had I not read the *Wall Street Journal* that day, I would have missed a story that has been meaningful in my writing.

Tip 4: Deputize friends who read history, biography, and memoirs. Ask friends or colleagues who read memoir/history/biography to note the mention of grief and loss issues and to pass that information to you.

Tip 5: Look for the "good steer." Gregory DeBourgh (2008) appreciates individuals who steer someone to a good resource. You might ask professor(s) for direction
- to be a "sounding board" for your ideas;
- to loan editorial "eyeballs" to review your drafts.

MAXIMIZING BORROWED NARRATIVES

1: Let the story "percolate." The grief landscape offers raw materials to be refined into practical narrative slices that might make a difference with a particular grieving child or adolescent. The story you discover and share with contemporary grievers might be critical in sense-making and future-making.

2: A borrowed narrative is more than a string of interesting or trivial facts. Willyn Webb (1999) advocates using "people potential" in counseling. Given the cultural fascination with heroes, personalities, athletes, and celebrities, narratives from their grief experiences may prove valuable. Condolezza Rice was in elementary school in Birmingham when the Sixteenth Avenue Church was bombed in 1963. Five decades later, she experiences a memory residue:

> Those memories of the Birmingham bombings have flooded back to me since September 11 [2001]. And, as I watched the conviction of the last conspirator in the church bombing last month [May 2002] I realize now that it is an experience that I have overcome but will never forget. (Rice, 2002).

Clinicians and grievers can jointly explore the grief of someone the counselee admires. Ask a griever

"How would [Name] react in your situation?"

"How might [Name] counsel you?"

"What might [Name] say that you would find helpful and hopeful?"

"What would you like to ask [Name] about grief?"

3: Know the details of the story before you use it.

That September 15, 1963, a young girl named Carolyn collected Sunday school offerings at the Sixteenth Avenue Baptist Church in Birmingham. Before turning in the collection to the church treasurer, she stopped by the women's restroom where she found four friends primping in front of the mirror.

"You'd better not be late to church," she teased.

Carolyn climbed half-way up the basement steps when a bomb detonated. One mile from the bomb blast, an 8-year-old attending a Presbyterian Church, asked, "What was *that*?" It was the bombing that would forever define her young life and the lives of hundreds of children in Birmingham.

By nightfall she would know that four girls had been killed in the blast. By nightfall she would know that her best friend, Denise McNair, had been decapitated in the blast. Yet the following morning, Monday, this girl and other children went to school as if nothing had happened. Carolyn recalls,

> Days passed, and then weeks, and we simply walked through our same routines—predictable routines disturbed only briefly that Sunday morning.
>
> No one asked me, "Carolyn, are you okay?" "Carolyn, do you miss your friends?" "Carolyn, are you afraid?" "Carolyn, do you want to talk about what happened at church?" Nothing was said—not at home and not at school. (McKinstry, 2011, p. 90)

Finally, one peer admonished her, "Well, frankly, Carolyn, I think you're making more out of this than you should" (McKinstry, 2011, p. 9). This incident, a dominant thread in McKinstry's memoir, is what Worden (2009) calls "antecedent" loss. In this culture, it is too easy to cliché, "Oh, children are *soooo* resilient." But grief is never "done" or "over" or "finished." Children may move forward, but they do not "move on."

PUTTING FACES ON THEORY'S BONES

Theories of grief are valuable in caring for a grieving child. In my experience, however, theories need "faces on the bones." For example, Worden (2009) identifies four "tasks" of grief:

- To accept the reality of the loss
- To process the pain of grief
- To adjust to a world without the deceased
- To find an enduring connection with the deceased in the midst of embarking on a new life

Can you identify a story of a grieving child that illustrates one of these tasks? Certainly, McKinstry (2011) demonstrates the fourth task. McKinstry has found—and kept—an "enduring connection" with the deceased children of the Birmingham bombing. McKinstry believes that had she not been chosen to collect the offerings she would have been with her friends in the bathroom which was the location of the greatest damage.

Through a clinician's skilled use of borrowed narratives, theory comes to life. Sharing borrowed narratives may lead the griever to explore more on that particular individual. Borrowing narratives can increase your potential to impact a griever's life.

CONCLUSION

Eleanor Roosevelt's childhood was shaped by the death of her mother when Eleanor was 8, the death of a brother when she was 9, and the death of her beloved father when she was 10. These were, I would contend, "grief ambushes," which impacted her emotional development. Eventually, in four autobiographies, Eleanor Roosevelt disclosed details of how grief had shaped her childhood, but also how one caring person made a difference. Mrs. Roosevelt concluded that people "read" biography and memoir because they identify a link. "There is nothing particularly interesting about one's own story unless people can say as they read it, 'Why, this is like what I have been through.'" A good memoir, autobiography, or borrowed narrative may lead the reading griever to conclude, "Perhaps, after all, there is a way to work it out" (1984, p. xix).

Just as children at bedtime ask, "Tell me a story," children may ask for a borrowed narrative valuable in their grief work.

REFERENCES

Banner, L. W. (2009). AHR roundtable: Biography as history. *American Historical Review, 114*(3), 579–586.

Burlingame, M. (2008). *Abraham Lincoln: A life*. Baltimore, MD: Johns Hopkins University Press.

Bush, B. (2003). *Reflections: Life after the White House*. New York, NY: Lisa Drew/Scribner.

Cohen, D. E., & Battersby, J. D. (2009). *Nelson Mandela: A life in photographs*. New York, NY: Sterling.

Cole, N., with Ritz, D. (2010). *Love brought me back: A journey of loss and grace*. New York, NY: Simon & Schuster.

Cooper, I. (2013). *Jack: The early years of John F. Kennedy*. New York, NY: Puffin Books.

DeBourgh, G. A. (2008, January). *Interactive instruction: Tips, tools, and techniques to involve learners and promoter reasoning skills*. San Francisco, CA: Mosby's Faculty Development Institute.

Goodwin, D. K. (2005). *Team of rivals: The political genius of Abraham Lincoln*. New York, NY: Simon & Schuster.

Haag, C. (2012). *Come to the edge: A love story*. New York, NY: Spiegel & Grau.

Hamilton, N. (2008). *How to do biography: A primer*. Cambridge, MA: Harvard University Press.

Hicks, A. (2001). George Frideric Handel. In *The new Grove dictionary of music and musicians, Vol. 10* (pp. 747–813). New York, NY: Grove/Macmillan.

Kennedy, C. (2013). *Poems to learn by heart*. New York, NY: Disney Hyperion.

Kulling, M. (1999). *Eleanor everywhere: The life of Eleanor Roosevelt*. New York, NY: Random House Books for Young Readers.

Levy, W. T., with Russell, C. E. (1999). *The extraordinary Mrs. R: A friend remembers Eleanor Roosevelt*. New York, NY: Wiley.

McKinstry, C. M., with George, D. (2011). *While the world watched: A Birmingham bombing survivor comes of age during the civil rights movement*. Wheaton, IL: Tyndale.

McPherson, J. M. (1999). Lincoln, Abraham. In *American National Biography, Vol. 13* (pp. 662–673). New York, NY: Oxford University Press.

Miller, R. L. (2006). *Lincoln and his world: The early years: Birth to Illinois legislature*. Mechanicsburg, PA: Stackpole Press.

Neimeyer, R. A. (1998). *Lessons of loss: A guide to coping*. New York, NY: McGraw-Hill/Primis Custom.

Nelson, K. (2013). *Nelson Mandela*. New York, NY: Katherine Tegen Books.

Nguyen, D. N. (2008). *Ho Chi Minh thought on diplomacy*. Hanoi, Vietnam: Gioi.

Nolan, T. (2010, March 30). Tales from inner space: A cultural conversation with Ray Bradbury. *The Wall Street Journal*, p. D7.

Reagan, R. (1990). *Ronald Reagan: An American life*. New York, NY: Simon & Schuster.

Rice, C. (2002, June 16). *Acknowledge that you have an obligation to search for the truth*. Address to the Graduating Class of Stanford University.

Roosevelt, E. (1984). *Eleanor Roosevelt, with love: A centenary remembrance*. New York, NY: Lodestar/Dutton.

Smith, H. I. (2004). *When a child you love is grieving* (Rev. ed.). Kansas City, MO: Beacon Hill Press.

Smith, H. I. (2012). *Borrowed narratives: Using historical and biographical narratives with the bereaving*. New York, NY: Routledge.

Thomas, A. (2008). *Thinking about memoir*. New York, NY: AARP/Sterling.
Wade, L. (2002). *Condoleezza Rice*. New York, NY: Mitchell Lane.
Webb, W. (1999). *Solutioning: Solution-focused interventions for counselors*. Philadelphia, PA: Accelerated Development.
Weller, S. (2005). *The Bradbury chronicles*. New York, NY: Morrow.
Worden, J. W. (2009). *Grief counseling and grief therapy: A handbook for the mental health practitioner* (4th ed.). New York, NY: Springer.

CHAPTER 8

Child Development: An Existential Journey

Neil Thompson

INTRODUCTION

This chapter explores the subject of child development from an existentialist point of view. Central to existentialist thought is the critique of "essentialism," the tendency to adopt a view of individuals as relatively fixed entities. Existentialism therefore rejects the idea of child development as the description of a process of maturation that produces a relatively fixed "personality."

Dominant approaches to child development are reviewed and their often essentialist assumptions are highlighted. As a counterbalance, an existentialist account of child development is proposed, one that presents childhood and adolescence as socially constructed stages in a lifelong fluid process of self-creation. Some of the main implications of this for professional practice in working with children and young people are also drawn out.

The point is also made that, in responding to the needs of children and young people who are dying or grieving, it is important to have a sophisticated understanding of child development and not rely on the oversimplifications associated with much of the classic work on this subject.

The Developing "Organism"

The use of the term "organism" in this subtitle is intended to reflect the fact that, while human beings are best understood from a holistic, multidimensional perspective (Thompson, 2012), much of the traditional literature relating to child development focuses primarily if not exclusively on the biological dimension. For example, Moore (2005) states that "the concept of development is rooted in the biology of the individual life cycle" (p. 3). Contrast this with my own view, which can be stated as the concept of development is rooted in multiple complementary and sometimes conflicting spheres of influence, biological, psychological, interpersonal, environmental, cultural, structural, political and spiritual. Focusing narrowly on biological matters produces a distorted and limited picture of human development in general and of child development in particular.

Furthermore, human existence can be characterized, from an existentialist perspective, as a dynamic mixture of human agency (the ability to make choices and decisions and act upon the circumstances we find ourselves in) and constraints on our agency (the wider context on which our agency acts). Focusing on biology places considerable emphasis on the constraints, and little or no emphasis on the role, of agency within those constraints. It can therefore be seen as disempowering. In addition, as we shall explore in more detail below, a biological emphasis distracts attention from the significant role of wider sociological factors (Hunt, 2005).

The Influence of Freud

Many approaches to child development have placed considerable emphasis on psychological factors, albeit not without retaining a strong biological focus. Prominent among these has been the work of Freud. He developed a sophisticated theory of psychosexual development which was initially subject to considerable criticism and even ridicule (because of the iconoclastic notion that there were strong elements of sexuality in the psychological development of children [Jones, 1961]) but later became a highly influential theoretical perspective.

Freud's work can be seen as an interesting mix of biological determinism and a more psychologically based approach, which took account of perception and meaning (an important theme to be discussed below). However, we can detect elements of essentialism in both these features. Freud regarded the stages of development as (biologically) universal and therefore took no account of how there may be differences across cultures or in different social settings. In terms of the role of meaning, he drew on fixed symbolism and therefore failed to appreciate the fluidity of meaning. For example, his discussion of the unconscious assumes that symbols (in dreams, for example) are fixed in their meaning and does not take account of the fact that the same symbol can mean different things to different people in different contexts. In both cases, therefore, there was an undue amount of emphasis on fixity.

In addition, Freud laid considerable stress on what he called the "formative years," which he regarded to be the first five years of life. Developmental opportunities beyond this time were deemed to be fairly limited, and changes in a person's psychological approach to their life and problems were assumed to require extensive long-term psychoanalytical intervention. This is a further example of essentialism, with constraints writ large and relatively little role ascribed to human agency.

Beyond Freud

Erikson's work is one example of an influential school of thought that grew out of Freud's work but which differed from it in significant ways (Erikson, 1977). One such difference was that Erikson rejected the idea of development more or less ending after the formative years. He wrote of the "eight ages of man" (the word "man" is significant), which spoke of development as a lifelong process (in eight stages).

Another significant difference was that Erikson rejected Freud's view that the process of development was universal. He recognized the significance of cultural differences and the impact that these could have on a child's development. However, despite this advance, he did not take this far enough, insofar as he neglected other sociological factors. For example, while it was positive that he took account of cultural variation, it was disappointing that he took no account of the potentially detrimental consequences of racism and the implications of this for development. In addition, his use of the term "eight ages of *man*" reflects the fact that he took little or no account of gender and the highly significant differences in experience that a child's gender can bring about.

Attachment Theory

A further example of traditional theoretical approaches to child development is attachment theory. Based on the influential work of Bowlby (1953, 1969, 1973), this approach emphasizes the significance of early childhood experiences of bonding (or "attachment") with one or more key figures and the impact different patterns of attachment can have on later life and overall development. Bowlby's original conception spoke of attachment to the child's mother (1956), but later works have recognized the patriarchal assumptions that underpinned Bowlby's work (see, for example, Howe, Brandon, Hinings, & Schofield, 1999) and have pointed out that it does not have to be the mother who occupies this role.

In its updated form, it continues to be widely used and offers some helpful insights into children's behavior, emotional responses, and interactions. However, as long ago as 1992, Gambe, Gomes, Kapur, Rangel, and Stubbs pointed out that much of the work on attachment has tended to assume White, Western norms of child rearing and can therefore be seen to have the effect of marginalizing or even pathologizing families who do not fit this norm.

Consideration of attachment issues often takes place in a context of individualism (or "atomism," the tendency to focus on individuals and take no account of the wider social context in which individuals, groups, organizations, and whole societies operate) with little or no recognition of the impact of factors beyond the individual level. However, there is nothing inherent in the concept of attachment that prevents it from being developed into a more holistic approach.

Beyond Tradition

I have outlined three mainstream approaches to child development, each of which presents problems in terms of some degree of essentialism and/or atomism (that is, the tendency to neglect important wider sociological issues and remain narrowly focused on individuals in isolation). This is certainly not the whole purview of child development theory but should be enough to demonstrate that the traditional foundations of child development, while bringing certain valuable insights, also have significant flaws, particularly in terms of their tendency to rely on essentialism (neglecting agency) and atomism (neglecting wider sociological factors). In this regard they can be seen to fail to do justice to the complexities involved.

It could also be argued that traditional approaches failed to appreciate the diversity of development experiences. For example, disability issues rarely feature and yet disability is a major feature of the lives of a significant proportion of children. Excluding such factors contributes to a pathological view of disability (Higham, 2012). As Thompson and Thompson (2016) argue,

> Traditional approaches to life course development have also been criticized for failing to recognize the significance of disability. If too much emphasis is placed on so-called "able-bodied" norms, then there is a danger that disability is automatically defined as a problem. Although the term "differently abled" has never really caught on, it can be seen as significant in this context. If we are too rigid in determining what is normality without taking account of different forms of normality, depending on whether one has a physical impairment or not, then we run the risk of reinforcing negative images of people with disabilities. (p. 87)

A similar argument can be made in relation to same-sex relationships. When much of the classic literature relating to child development was written, homosexuality was seen as a mental illness, a moral abomination, or both. However, we now have a much clearer and less biased understanding of psychosexual development in relation to same-sex attraction and therefore have to give fuller consideration of the developmental experiences and needs of children and young people who do not fit a stereotypical heterosexual set of norms (DePalma & Atkinson, 2008).

Having reviewed some key aspects of traditional approaches to child development and identified a number of gaps and flaws, we can now consider how a perspective based on existentialism can encapsulate many of the strengths of traditional approaches while steering clear of their deficits.

The Existential Journey

What makes existentialism such a potent and useful explanatory framework is that it is rooted in a commitment to exploring fully what it means to be human. It is therefore not satisfied with biologically based explanations that speak of organisms rather than people (but does take account of biological factors) or with psychological approaches that rely on atomism and thereby fail to recognize the major impact of wider socio-political factors.

Existentialism is a holistic approach, insofar as it aims to understand not only the multiple dimensions of human experience, but also how they interact and form new sets of circumstances and spheres of influence on a constantly evolving basis. We can now begin to explore how this holistic and dynamic approach can cast considerable light on child development in general and on the significance of loss and grief in particular.

First of all, it is important to recognize that the very concept of childhood is socially constructed (Wyness, 2012). This means that it is not simply a "natural" stage of development in which the vulnerable young need to be protected while they grow and develop. Rather, what we now regard as childhood is something that has evolved historically from a set of social, political, and ideological developments (Cunningham, 2006). An illustration of this would be how different cultures and societies have not only differing perspectives on what is regarded as appropriate for a child (differences in the age of consent in relation to sexual intercourse, for example), but also different conceptions of what it means to be a child. For example, we no longer send children up chimneys, but extensive child labor is not uncommon in many cultures around the world.

One of the implications of recognizing that childhood is socially constructed is the need to acknowledge the powerful role of socio-political factors in shaping a child's experience. Poverty would be a sad but good example of this. Poverty can have adverse biological effects that can stunt growth and development (as a result of poor nutrition and damp housing, for example) as well as a psychological impact on self-esteem and aspirations (Lister, 2004). Sociologically, poverty can be seen as a key factor in relation to differential access to education, employment, health care, and various other social goods (Alcock, 2006). Arguably, poverty can also have an adverse effect in spiritual terms, a topic to which we will return below.

Linked to this is the significance of social capital. This is a concept which refers to the metaphorical wealth a person has as a result of their social connections (Castiglione, van Deth, & Wolleb, 2008; see also Jordan's [2007] discussion of the interpersonal economy). While some people will be rich in social capital (for example, as a result of having a wide range of friends and colleagues and membership of various groups and societies), others may have little or nothing to draw upon and can therefore be quite vulnerable due to a relative lack of social support when they encounter adversity.

Where a child is placed along this spectrum of social capital can have a major impact on their life chances and well-being. Trying to understand child development without consideration of this important social dimension means that a potentially very significant aspect of the human condition is being neglected; our efforts to understand are not fully connecting to human experience.

Existentialism also helps us to understand identity formation as a holistic and dynamic phenomenon, as opposed to the largely biopsychological emphasis on personality development that characterizes much of the earlier work on the subject and which can be criticized for its essentialism and underplaying of the significance of change in identity development (Thompson, 2010).

Existentialism portrays identity in the form of a journey. That is, our identity is a process of becoming, constantly evolving throughout our lives. This contrasts markedly with the dominant Western conception of the individual as a largely preformed personality on a journey. From an existentialist point of view, we are not relatively fixed individuals on a journey through life; we *are* that journey, an existential journey. This echoes the notion of "impermanence," characteristic of many Eastern philosophies which also emphasize human existence as a process of becoming (Billington, 1990).

In his early work, Sartre, the noted French existentialist, conceived of human existence as a process of self-creation (reflecting the influence on his philosophy of the nineteenth century thinkers, Kierkegaard and Nietzsche). Through the choices we make (closing some doors and opening others in the process), we shape who we are, we mold our identity: we are what we make ourselves. This early approach was criticized for lacking a sociological dimension, and so Sartre later developed his view to incorporate the influence of the social context. This latter, more developed view was captured in the idea that "we are what we make of what is made of us" (Sartre, 1973). What Sartre meant by this was that, while we do engage in a process of self-creation, we do so in a social context that is also a strong influence on us (in terms of such factors as socioeconomic class, culture and ethnicity, gender, religion, linguistic group, political regime, and so on). Sartre wrote of a dialectical relationship between our actions and reactions ("agency," to use the technical term) and the powerful formative influences of the circumstances that we are responding to; hence, we are "what we make of what is made of us." Our identity is forged by the ongoing interactions between the influences of the social world and our reactions to them in terms of choices made and decisions taken. That constant forging is what is meant by an existential journey, and it applies just as much to children as it does to adults.

This is sometimes referred to as the dialectic of subjectivity and objectivity—that is, the ongoing interactions of the subjective element (our choices, actions, and reactions: our agency—Archer, 2000) and the objective element (the social context described above). Each has a formative influence on the other.

While Sartre was writing about self-creation as a lifelong process, we can also see how his ideas apply specifically to child development. It takes us a long way from the simplistic idea of a child as an organism following a largely predetermined biological path of growth and development.

This approach avoids the problem of atomism identified earlier as it recognizes the key role of socio-political influences and constraints, but does not do so by losing sight of the individual as a unique person with agency. It therefore begins to do justice to the complex interactions of psychological and sociological factors.

Among the sociological factors are such key issues as language, communication, and culture. These play an important role because they connect people together in various ways—they are, in a sense, part of the glue that binds people together in meaningful ways. As Cross (2004) explains,

> Communication is a complex process, but we tend not to notice its intricacy, as for most of us "it just happens," rapidly and without conscious thought. Language is also easy to take for granted, because it is everywhere: we use language to talk about and organise our experiences; in order to build relationships; to learn about the world, and ourselves; and to think and imagine. (p. 17)

Patterns of communication form meanings and those meanings become institutionalized in the form of cultures. Those cultures then have a profound effect on structuring our life experiences and shaping our sense of who we are and how we fit into the wider world. We can therefore see that language, communication, and culture are important factors in relation to (i) child development and indeed human development more broadly across the life course; and (ii) the existentialist idea that a human being (child or adult) is not a fixed entity on a journey, but rather *is* that journey—each of us is our own journey, our own process of self-creation within a wider set of contextual factors that also influence and constrain us.

Among the important factors that will shape that journey will be the effects of loss and trauma. Although Bowlby's early work took account of loss issues in the child's life, much of the child development literature pays relatively little attention to them, even though, from an existentialist point of view, they can be seen as highly significant. This is because grief can be understood as an existential challenge, something that strikes at the heart of our very sense of self (Thompson, 2012). Indeed, grief—particularly traumatic grief—can contribute to what is known as "biographical disruption," a temporary loss of any clear sense of identity. In the immense confusion of such profound grief, we can lose any sense of being anchored or secure, we feel ill at ease with ourselves, perhaps not sure who we are any more. Such an existential challenge can therefore be understood as a spiritual crisis, a turning point in terms of the direction we take our life in, the beginning of a new chapter in our journey.

The idea of existential challenges—that is, challenges that are part of being human and not simply incidental to particular sets of circumstances—is a key part of existentialism. What an existentialist perspective on child development adds is a fuller understanding of human existence. For example, in addition to the biological, psychological, and sociological strands of development, we can see the significance of the less familiar notion of the ontological strand, which is about how we make sense of our reality, how we develop meaningful understandings of our life. Thompson and Thompson (2008) explain this in the following terms:

> Ontology is the study of reality or being. It is concerned with questions relating to existence: What is the nature of reality? and What does it mean to exist? This is an aspect of human development that is often neglected and sometimes does not feature even in major textbooks. Ontological development, in some respects, pulls together other strands of development, in so far as it gives us a basis on which to develop our identity. Ontology involves rising to the challenges of human existence. (p. 84)

This relates closely to the idea of spirituality. Many people automatically associate spirituality with religion, but it needs to be recognized that, while not everybody is religious, everyone—child or adult—has spiritual needs and faces spiritual/existential challenges. Existentialism gives us a sophisticated conceptual framework for addressing these issues (Thompson, 2007) and for developing our understanding of the child as a spiritual being.

We can see, then, that existentialism provides a platform for taking further our understanding of the child's reality. One particular "tool" or method for doing this is what is known as the "progressive-regressive method." This is a concept that has its roots in the work of Sartre (1973). It is a complex idea, but the core of the approach is the notion that if we want to understand the present, we need to look at not only the role of past influences (regressive) but also future aspirations and sense of direction (progressive) and how these interact and influence each other (progressive-regressive). This method can be used to understand broad social and political phenomena at a macro level and the experiences of an individual at a micro level.

For adults this can help cast light on their current situation by acknowledging the various ways in which past experiences interact with aspirations and plans for the future to shape key elements of the context for the present moment. For children, the same logic can apply, but with the added complication of growing awareness and understanding from infancy of the very notion of future and a sense of self-efficacy or recognition that he or she can play a part in shaping that future. The growing child searches for meaning and, as he or she begins to understand "temporal ekstases" (that is, meaningful notions of past, present, and future), a sense of identity and direction emerges and the journey of selfhood moves forward.

A related concept is that of the "existential project" (Sartre, 1958). As our journey moves forward through time, we "project" ourselves forward—that is, we throw ourselves forward into our lives. We engage with the situations we find ourselves in, make choices, take decisions, and construct meanings. Those meanings then shape how we engage with future situations and the people within them. The journey continues.

The Implications for Professional Practice

A wide range of professional groups work with children and young people and need to have at least a basic understanding of child development. Clearly a narrow and distorted understanding of child development that does not do justice to the complexities involved could prove highly problematic and misleading. Existentialism does not claim to offer all the answers, but it does provide a framework for extending and deepening our knowledge as a foundation for professional practice.

Space does not permit a detailed analysis of the consequences for the practice of adopting an existentialist approach, and so I will limit myself here to providing a few illustrative examples of some of the implications.

First of all, the holistic basis of existentialism makes it clear that we need to adopt a wider picture than has often been the case, one that incorporates not only biological elements but also psychological, sociopolitical, and spiritual dimensions of human experience. Central to this wider perspective is the recognition of diversity, and not just ethnic diversity. Differences in life experience in terms of gender, disability, religion, and sexuality are among the many dimensions of diversity that can also have a significant effect on the course of a child or young person's development.

The tendency to focus on the child as a biological organism leads to a predominant emphasis on what children have in common (as biological issues apply in the majority of cases to all children). Yet what makes each child a person in his or her own right is not just what children have in common but also how they differ in various ways, what is distinctive about certain groups, and of course, about each unique individual. All this then needs to be understood dialectically, as part of a set of dynamic interactions between and across the wider contextual factors (the set of strong cultural and social influences upon the individual) and his or her reactions to all this. From a professional practice point of view, this means that practitioners need to be attuned to a much wider range of issues affecting development than traditional approaches would have us believe.

Second, although we no longer regard children as "little adults" (Cunningham, 2006), there is a danger that we can go too far in the opposite direction, as if they are a different species; for example—by failing to see them as meaning-making creatures just as adults are. One example of this is the common tendency to refer to a child of unknown or unspecified gender as "it." To refer to an adult as "it" would normally be seen as derogatory or demeaning, and yet it seems to be acceptable to do so for a child. Practitioners therefore need to be aware of the dangers of overstating the differences between adults and children and thereby adopting a distorted picture of childhood.

Child development, as we have seen, can be understood as an existential journey, a perpetual process of self-creation in response to the circumstances we find ourselves in and the powerful influence of that wider context. Of course, children are different from adults in a number of ways, but we need to make sure that we do not impute differences where they do not exist. If we get this wrong, we could be engaging in age discrimination by, for example, denying children certain rights.

Third, we need to consider the question of age discrimination or "ageism" (S. Thompson, 2005). Ageism can be seen to apply to children and young people in relation to loss and grief through the medium of disenfranchised grief (Doka, 1989). The assumption that children "do not understand" loss and therefore do not need to be involved in discussions about such losses (Corr, 2000; Jackson, 2012) is not only discriminatory but also potentially abusive, insofar as there could be a major adverse emotional reaction to being denied the opportunity to grieve and mourn.

Going beyond reductionist approaches to child development which focus narrowly on biological or psychological processes by understanding children as persons in their own right (rather than as some sort of different entity in preparation for becoming persons at a later date) is key to the existentialist approach. As Silverman (2000) comments, "Children are not their stages of development" (p. 45, as cited in Rowling, 2003, p. 19). Existentialism understands human existence as a journey, and so childhood needs to be recognized as the early stages of that journey and not as some sort of precursor to it. Recognizing this puts professional practitioners in a stronger position to make sense of the complexities of a child's life, problems, challenges, opportunities, and potential.

CONCLUSION

Wyness (2012) makes the important point that:

> in recent years, childhood has become a far more contested phenomenon, with public commentary shifting between the reporting of its terminal decline through to the promotion of a new pluralized and culturally embedded version of the child (p. 45).

We should therefore be in a better position to move away from the traditional approaches to child development that present us with limited understanding of the realities of children's lives. Existentialist thought can play a part in helping us to do this.

The traditional debate about influences on children's behavior and development has tended to focus on the dichotomy between nature (biology) and nurture (upbringing). Some people have extended this by arguing that it is a matter of the interaction of nature and nurture, but in reality even this is too simplistic a view. Biological issues are important; biology is the vehicle through which we live our lives, but it is not the driver, as to put biology in the driving seat of our lives would be to deny the human agency that is at the heart of existentialist thought. So, it is perhaps best thought of as a matter of the complex interactions of nature; nurture; the influence of culture(s), social structures, divisions, processes and institutions; differential access to social capital; political processes; and the individual's reaction to all of the above plus an array of spiritual matters, whether religious or not.

In addition, there will be the effects of losses and how these have been managed by the individual and significant others around him or her, plus, of course, the influence of social chance (Sibeon, 2004). What happens to each of us is in part a matter of chance, of being in the right (or wrong) place at the right (or wrong) time.

It should be clear, then, that from an existentialist point of view, child development needs to be understood as far more diverse and complex than the long-standing idea that it is primarily a matter of the growth stages of an organism. We need to understand children more holistically if we are to do justice to the complexities involved. This is particularly the case where we are engaging with children and young people who are dying or grieving, as many of the issues discussed in this chapter will loom large in such circumstances. It is very much the case that loss issues can bring developmental matters into sharp relief.

Existentialism is not a philosophy that claims to have all the answers. Indeed, uncertainty and unknowability are key features of existentialist thought (Marino, 2004). However, it is to be hoped that this chapter has shown that there is much to be gained from shining an existentialist light on the complex subject of child development.

REFERENCES

Alcock, P. (2006). *Understanding poverty* (3rd ed.). Basingstoke, UK: Palgrave Macmillan.
Archer, M. S. (2000). *Being human: The problem of agency*. Cambridge, UK: Cambridge University Press.
Billington, R. (1990). *East of existentialism*. London, UK: Unwin Hyman.
Bowlby, J. (1953). *Child care and the growth of love*. Harmondsworth, UK: Penguin.
Bowlby, J. (1969). *Attachment and loss, Vol 1*. London, UK: Hogarth Press.
Bowlby, J. (1973). *Attachment and loss, Vol 2: Stagnation, anxiety and anger*. London, UK: Hogarth Press.
Castiglione, D., van Deth, J. W., & Wolleb, G. (Eds.). (2008). *The handbook of social capital*. Oxford, UK: Oxford University Press.
Corr, C. (2000). What do we know about grieving children and adolescents? In K. Doka (Ed.), *Living with grief*. Washington, DC: Hospice Foundation of America.

Cross, M. (2004). *Children with emotional and behavioural difficulties and communication problems: There is always a reason*. Philadelphia, PA: Kingsley.
Cunningham, H. (2006). *The invention of childhood*. London, UK: BBC Books.
DePalma, R., & Atkinson, E. (Eds.). (2008). *Invisible boundaries: Assessing sexualities equality in children's worlds*. Stoke on Trent, UK: Trentham Books.
Doka, K. (Ed.). (1989). *Disenfranchised grief: Recognizing hidden sorrow*. Lexington, MA: Lexington Books.
Erikson, E. H. (1977). *Childhood and society*. Harmondsworth, UK: Penguin.
Gambe, D., Gomes, J., Kapur, V., Rangel, M., & Stubbs, P. (1992). *Anti-racist social work education: Improving practice with children and families*. Leeds, UK: CCETSW.
Higham, P. (2012). Young children with physical impairments. In R. Adams (Ed.), *Working with children and families: Knowledge and contexts for practice*. Basingstoke, UK: Palgrave Macmillan.
Howe, D., Brandon, M., Hinings, D., & Schofield, G. (1999). *Attachment theory, child maltreatment and family support*. London, UK: Macmillan.
Hunt, S. (2005). *The life course: A sociological introduction*. Basingstoke, UK: Palgrave Macmillan.
Jackson, M. (2012). Children, grieving and loss. In R. Adams (Ed.), *Working with children and families: Knowledge and contexts for practice*. Basingstoke, UK: Palgrave Macmillan.
Jones, E. (1961). *The life and times of Sigmund Freud* (L. Trilling & S. Marcus, Eds. and Abr.), New York, NY: Basic Books.
Jordan, B. (2007). *Social work and well-being*. Lyme Regis, UK: Russell House.
Lister, R. (2004). *Poverty* (2nd ed.). Cambridge, UK: Polity Press.
Marino, G. (Ed.). (2004). *Basic writings of existentialism*. New York, NY: Modern Library.
Moore, C. (2005). The concept of development: Historical perspectives. In B. Hopkins (Ed.), *The Cambridge encyclopaedia of child development*. Cambridge, UK: Cambridge University Press.
Rowling, L. (2003). *Grief in school communities: Effective support strategies*. Philadelphia, PA: Open University Press.
Sartre, J-P. (1958). *Being and nothingness: An essay in phenomenological ontology*. London, UK: Methuen.
Sartre, J-P. (1973). *Search for a method*. New York, NY: Basic Books.
Sibeon, R. (2004). *Rethinking social theory*. London, UK: Sage.
Silverman, P. R. (2000). *Never too young to know: Death in children's lives*. New York, NY: Oxford University Press.
Thompson, N. (2007). Spirituality: An existentialist perspective. *Illness, Crisis & Loss, 15*(2).
Thompson, N. (2010). *Theorizing social work practice*. Basingstoke, UK: Palgrave Macmillan.
Thompson, N. (2012). *Grief and its challenges*. Basingstoke, UK: Palgrave Macmillan.
Thompson, N., & Thompson, S. (2016). *The Palgrave social work companion* (2nd ed.). London, UK: Palgrave Macmillan.
Thompson, N., & Walsh, M. (2010). The existential basis of trauma. *Journal of Social Work Practice, 12*(4).
Thompson, S. (2005). *Age discrimination*. Lyme Regis, UK: Russell House.
Wyness, M. (2012). The social construction of childhood: Sociological approaches to the study of children and childhood. In R. Adams (Ed.), *Working with children and families: Knowledge and contexts for practice*. Basingstoke, UK: Palgrave Macmillan.

CHAPTER 9
Children, Adolescents, and Catastrophic Loss: The Role of Spiritual Care

Peter Ford

Disaster is a mark of our time, whether natural disaster, as with a tornado or flood, or man-made disaster, such as a school or mall shooting or airline crash. Disaster that results in catastrophic loss can strike any community at any time, including the one in which you and I live, in one form or another. The way in which a community responds to that disaster can be critical to the survival of its citizens, including the way it responds to the special needs of its most vulnerable citizens.

When a disaster strikes, there will be sudden massive need for food, shelter, medical care, security, protection from further destruction, and communication. Disaster first responders will come from fire and rescue, emergency medical services, law enforcement, and the American Red Cross, cooperating with the regional VOAD (Voluntary Organizations Active in Disaster) to provide for the basic survival needs of the community.

Persons who are responsible for planning community and national-disaster response are realizing that another essential part of a community's—or the nation's—survival of disaster is emotional and spiritual survival. There also need to be spiritual and emotional first responders to provide spiritual and emotional first aid when disaster strikes.

A disaster can devastate the spiritual and emotional life and health of a community in an instant, changing it forever. The world, as the community has experienced it up to that moment, may never be the same again. This is why the focus of spiritual and emotional first aid must be focused on the community as a whole, not on individuals or groups of individuals. Everybody who lives in a community can be spiritually and emotionally affected by a disaster that strikes there. But there are two age groups within that community who are especially vulnerable. One vulnerable group is the aged—people for whom the life cycle is normally winding down. The other vulnerable group is children from birth through adolescence, for whom life is developing and expanding, full of new experiences, feelings, and perceptions. This chapter focuses on providing emotional and spiritual care of children while the disaster is underway and for a short time following the disaster. We will not be looking at spiritual or emotional care or therapy during the recovery period in the weeks and months and perhaps years after the disaster. We will focus instead on the period that the disaster itself is occurring and on the hours and perhaps a day or two after the disaster. And we will consider an action plan for providing spiritual and emotional first aid only. *But that first aid is critical to the future recovery from the disaster of the community, including its children.*

Before considering the spiritual and emotional care of children during a disaster, however, let's review the developing and expanding world of childhood. What inner resources, perceptions, and needs do children bring to a disaster experience and to the catastrophic losses a disaster brings with it?

Erik Erikson (1994) saw and described several stages of development as a child grows from babyhood to the teen years. At each stage, the child faces some specific conflicts and experiences some important events in his or her life that need to be resolved as a part of the task of growing up into normal adulthood. For the first 18 months of life, the basic conflict is trust versus mistrust. A basic event during this stage is feeding, and if the child is fed with reliability, care, and affection, the child will develop a sense of trust of the world and in his or her relationships. If feeding is associated with negative experience or can't be predicted or relied upon, the child will develop a pattern of mistrust.

From 2 to 3 years of age, the child faces conflict between autonomy on the one hand, and shame and doubt on the other. The focal point for this second stage of development is the experience of toilet training, when the child works to develop a sense of control over physical skills and begins to develop a sense of independence and autonomy. Failure at this stage of development will lead to feelings of guilt and shame.

For the preschool child from the third through the fifth year, the basic conflict is between initiative and guilt. The child discovers the world around him or her and explores that world. The child attempts to exert some control and power over his or her environment. If the child experiences approval in this attempt, he or she will begin to develop a sense of purpose. Disapproval of these attempts by persons most central in his or her life will result in a developing sense of guilt.

The school-age child from the sixth through the eleventh year struggles with the basic conflict between industry and inferiority. The child experiences all the academic and social demands and events of the school years. Success during the school years will lead to a developing sense of competence, while failure will lead to feelings of inferiority.

The basic conflict during adolescence, from 12 through 18 years, is identity versus role confusion. School is still a major stage for the important events of this stage of development, but the major experience is the development of social relationships. The task is to develop a sense of self in those social relationships. If the teen is successful in this task, the teen will develop the ability to stay true to himself or herself. Failure results in role confusion and a weak sense of self.

Abraham Maslow (1954) observed children and the way their lives unfold and develop. Maslow discerned several basic needs that must be met if the child is to develop into a healthy human being. The most basic need that Maslow saw is basic human survival needs such as food, shelter, warmth, safety, and security, to be filled in the human contact and care the child receives during the first 2 years of life. The second basic need Maslow observed was to be cared for and to be able to trust during a child's second through sixth years of life. This enables the development of cognitive functioning to successfully perform the activities of daily living. Maslow's third basic need is the need for love and belonging in interpersonal relationships during the child's 6th through 10th year. The next basic need is the need for intellectual and spiritual growth during the 10th through 14th year, when the focus is on developing self-esteem. The last basic need, self-actualization, builds on successfully meeting all the previous basic needs.

In addition to the theories of Erickson (1994) and Maslow (1954), there are some other realities about childhood that have a bearing on developing an action plan to care for the spiritual and emotional needs of children during a disaster. First, children's brains work differently from adult brains. Children simply do not think like adults:

- Children's thought processes focus on the self, with children's relationship with their environment developing as they develop psychospiritually from infancy through adolescence.
- Children's cognitive processes are egocentric. Children personalize what they hear, learn, and experience.
- To a child, hearing about an event more than once is the same as that event happening again. A replay of a news spot on TV means that whatever was reported two or three times or more, occurred two or three times or more.

Second, a child's grief is not the same as that of an adult, but it becomes more like adult grief as the child grows older:

- The younger the child, the more unable the child is to understand the finality of death.
- If a parent or loved one or pet is absent because of death, they expect that parent or loved one or pet to return alive.

Third, children have distinctive patterns of reacting to sudden change:

- There are gender differences. Girls and boys react differently. Boys externalize their reactions in behavior that can be disruptive and expose them to further trauma. Boys tend to have a longer recovery period than girls. Girls tend to internalize their reactions, which can result in depression and anxiety. Girls may be more willing than boys to talk about happened.
- Patterns of stress, conflict, abuse, or violence in a child's home can increase feelings of helplessness and insecurity when an unexpected event occurs.
- A child may regress to the behavior pattern of an earlier developmental stage if he or she experiences a difficult, frightening, or traumatic event.

Fourth, children are different from adults in their adaptive ability—their ability to cope or control how an event affects them:

- A child's adaptive capacity is being formed. It is in process, depending on the child's developmental stage.
- A child's adaptive capacity is influenced by his or her caregiver's response to an event. If a caregiver is overwhelmed by an event, the child's fears and insecurity will escalate, and long-term emotional, behavioral, and spiritual disorders are more likely. If the caregiver is calm and continues to nurture the child, the child's adaptive resources are more likely to activate.
- Children are more vulnerable than adults to the effects of a difficult event, but they also are highly resilient and can cope emotionally and spiritually through play, drawing, games, and singing.

These are some of the realities within the range of a normal childhood. It is a world of normal tasks and needs, a world of occasional difficult experiences, such as the death of a loved one, a pet, or a school friend. It is a world of nurture and support of the child to grow and develop into a healthy adult human being.

When disaster strikes, whether in the dark of the night or in the middle of a school day or hanging out at the mall or at home taking a bath, chaos suddenly explodes—a discordant hodge-podge of new and strange and scary sights, sounds, smells, people, and objects! To a young child, there are strange and frightening-looking people and big machines rushing around doing scary things that make an enormous and terrifying racket. But speaking through the mouth of a child, "I don't know what they're doing." "People are telling me things that make me sad, or scared, or angry." "Strange people are giving me strange food or taking me to strange places to get warm or get dry or to sleep." "My teddy bear is gone." "There are big people and other children with blood all over them being taken to the doctor." "There are people who are not moving. They are being put in big bags and being taken away." "There are people in scary uniforms making me do what I don't want to do. And not letting me do what I want to do." "There are people doing things and telling me things that help me feel just a little less scared." "But the noise and the smells and the scary-looking people just keep going, and I feel more and more like the whole world is just falling apart." "Everybody is yelling and screaming and there is all kinds of noise. It feels like everybody is full of scary feelings. Me too!" "I have feelings of emptiness. And I feel helpless, like I am about to fall apart inside. And nobody is acting normal." "Some people are saying bad things about God." "Some of them are shouting at God." "They are saying that if there really was a God, he wouldn't let anything like this happen if he really loved us." "But I love God. And I've been good." "Why is God doing this?" "People are crying and screaming about people they love." "Or that somebody has died." "Or that their house was destroyed." "Where is our house?" "Where is Mommy?" "And where are Grandpa or Grandma?"

If the disaster goes on and on, feelings of deep weariness set in for young and old alike, and for helpers as well as victims. A sense of despair deepens, and people are exhausted from helping or caring or hoping. Again from the mouth of a child: "I'm tired too." "So is Daddy." "I want Mommy!"

In this cacophony of sights, sounds, dirt, and pain, that child and others like him or her are experiencing the ways that a disaster assaults people's lives, overwhelms their senses, shatters their stability, shakes their hope, and terrorizes their very being. Children may experience any or all of these disaster realities directly. There are at least 12 disaster realities that affect everybody who is caught in the disaster area—and probably also in the community down the road. And these realities of a disaster can run on a collision course with the needs and the developmental tasks of children from infancy through adolescence. For this reason, because we cannot control the course of the disaster, we need to be ready to support children as the disaster plays itself out.

In looking more closely at some specific ways that each of the disaster realities affect children, and some interventions to help alleviate that effect, please think about what will work in your community for your children.

CHAOS

The first thing that may hit you when a disaster strikes is the Chaos—with a capital "C." Much or all of the familiar and the comforting of everyday life is suddenly gone, collapsing, or threatened. Predictability is destroyed. When that which is familiar and/or comforting has been destroyed and replaced by a frightening, terrifying chaos, children may be alive and uninjured but acting frighteningly different from normal.

Intervention with children in the midst of chaos includes providing something to trust—to help counteract the effect of the chaos on a young child. What is needed is a restored feeling of consistency. Keep children in touch with the "normal" or "routine" as much as possible to keep some sense of connectedness with normal life in order to bring the child down from a high level of anxiety, even though that anxiety can seldom be reduced to a normal level in the midst of the chaos of a disaster.

VISIBILITY

The next disaster reality is the loss or absence of visible sources of comfort and of the familiar. This may include the absence of people they know and love, possibly including parents or siblings or friends or neighbors. This loss of visible comfort and nurture may mean abandonment to a toddler by a parent who is normally present and active.

Intervention includes providing high visibility of people who bring reassurance. This includes people who are visibly filling specific helping functions to relieve the confusion, the fear, the pain, the hunger, the cold, the dirt, and the wet clothes. Intervention includes people who are visible as a calming, nurturing presence. Spiritual care providers can be especially helpful here by being visible to the child as someone the child already associates with spiritual and emotional comfort. And visibility also includes people who help restore visibility of loved ones for children.

COMMUNICATION

The third disaster reality is the necessity of truthful Communication. We must communicate with children truthfully and honestly at all times. There are no exceptions. Any misrepresentation, whether deliberate lying or careless omission of facts, can cause distorted thinking by the child. Children, especially older children and adolescents, will attempt to piece together truth out of the fragments of what they hear and experience. The result can be some frightening fantasies that may or may not have any relationship with truth. Teachers and parents know that children may be great observers, but they can be lousy interpreters.

Intervention by communication means to speak the truth—with reassurance. Tell them the facts they need to know about the disaster and at the same time tell them the facts they need to know about how people are being helped and protected. Give them reliable, honest information and present it simply and directly in a way that is appropriate for that child.

You may need to tell them truth that is not good news, but reassurance may mean that the child knows he or she can trust you to tell the truth, even when it may hurt. Your reassuring presence is then more convincing in a situation that appears to have no bright side or happy ending. This kind of truthfulness with reassurance is a way of giving hope, maintaining their trust in people, and allowing you to continue to serve as a source of strength. But answer only what the child asks and in the child's language. And don't tell more than the child asks or you may overwhelm the child. Finally, avoid offering reassurance if you don't know that it is true. Never say "Everything will be all right" or "I'm sure that you will go home soon" if you do not know that everything will be all right or you don't know for certain that they have a home to go back to.

SIMPLICITY

The disaster reality of Simplicity means focusing sharply on survival and survival only. Focusing on survival means to provide for the most basic needs for preservation of life such as food, shelter, warmth, clothing, safety, and security, and to do it as quickly as possible. And that may need to be done on a massive scale. Intervention through simplicity for spiritual caregivers means focusing on the emotional and spiritual survival of everybody, including children, taking into account children's distinctive developmental stages and needs. To demonstrate calm behavior and to model one's own inner peace is the core of simplicity for spiritual care providers. Your focused, direct, calm, and gentle activity among children is basic to assuring their spiritual and emotional survival of disaster.

Simplicity means being accepting and not judgmental or disapproving of age-appropriate behavior or of regressive behavior in response to the disaster. Simplicity means supporting children wherever they are, emotionally and developmentally. Simplicity means

- Do not demand that they be brave or tough. Let them cry, and be sure they have support and privacy so they can cry the way they need to.
- Do not try to make them talk about the disaster. Set them free and give them the tools they need to play or draw.
- Do not show your anger if they show strong emotions. Support them in their fear or anger or despair.
- Do not say things like "At least you survived," or how they should feel or act, or that they did something wrong to cause the disaster, but do listen to them and be accepting or at least neutral if they say any of these things.

Simplicity in a mass disaster with scores of distressed people may mean a compassionate glance and a healing presence instead of periods of reflective listening to a few, while scores of children and other people are in spiritual distress. Disaster spiritual care often needs to be focused on a group—on the community—not on individuals.

CONTROL

The purpose of Control is to provide safety for everybody and a stable situation for the care and treatment of victims. Even if children are out of immediate danger, they are at high risk during a disaster in ways that require strong control on the part of caregivers:

- Children may exhibit increased aggression, oppositional behavior, and decreased tolerance of frustration.
- If preschool and elementary school children repeatedly watch graphic images and repetitive reporting on TV, they may think that the disaster is happening over and over, and could be overwhelmed by fear and anxiety.
- Adolescents are subject to risk-taking behavior in a chaotic situation, including their need for privacy, which may cause them to try to go off to be alone. This coping behavior may land them in a more dangerous situation or area.

Spiritual care providers can play an important part in keeping control. But spiritual care providers are not at the disaster response site for the purpose of keeping things under control by telling people what to do. A key intervention by spiritual care providers for maintaining control is to encourage children to accept control by demonstrating the caring presence of a spiritual care provider that they may accept on the basis of experiences in their place of worship. Here is a trusted person available to interpret, listen to them, and respond to questions about why they are where they are. And the spiritual care provider can be accepted as a model to demonstrate calm, controlled behavior. A spiritual care provider can also be involved in helping children feel in control of something by encouraging them to choose the color they want for drawing, helping set up simple routines that help to reassure and normalize life a little bit, and distracting them from watching reruns of TV coverage of the disaster.

AUTHORITY

Authority, which is centralized in the Disaster Command Center, provides ongoing safety by making and implementing decisions as the disaster response progresses. These decisions may include temporarily controlling or curtailing individual freedom of movement for victims, family members, staff members, and disaster workers for the ongoing safety of the community. Freedom of movement is reduced or increased as circumstances change, and people are permitted to do things, such as going home, that they could not do an hour ago or a day ago. Authority also controls temporary loss of social norms that can occur during a disaster, and that can deepen the destructive effect of the disaster on children. Authority keeps a low profile. It is unobtrusive, but is alert, active, and quickly responsive. Spiritual care providers intervene to support authority by helping individuals to interpret decisions from the Command Center and perhaps to explain why such decisions are necessary for everybody's safety. To avoid raising anxiety in children and parents, do not express or support criticism of decisions or how the disaster response is being handled.

Spiritual care providers can strengthen authority by earning the direct trust of anxious disaster victims. We can do this by being strong, knowledgeable, compassionate, and safe to follow as a personification of authority. This trust can be earned by creating an atmosphere of safety, being a calming presence to anxious children and parents, and practicing an empathic attitude, understanding, and accepting of a child's experience as a normal reaction to an abnormal experience.

The spiritual care provider may also be authoritative by intervening with the central authority of the Command Center. For example, watch for, intervene as appropriate, and report any suspected child abuse—spiritual, emotional, verbal, physical, or sexual. Such abuse or neglect can occur as part of the breakdown of social norms during a disaster.

DISINTEGRATION

In a disaster, children experience the sudden and violent disintegration of their world—the world that has cradled and nurtured them all of their lives up to the moment the disaster struck. It is perhaps a smaller, more personal world that focuses on them and revolves around them because of their egocentric thinking patterns, but the resulting trauma of the collapse of the world around them is as devastating for children as it is for adults. Because egocentric thinking patterns are strongest in 3- to 5-year-olds, children of these ages may work harder than any other age at personalizing every scary or sad part of the disaster that they see, hear, or experience directly. And their developing relationship with their environment suddenly becomes very frightening, and the trauma of the disaster may make it very difficult for the child to overcome the sense that he or she is living in a frightening, scary world. For the youngest children (from birth to 18 months), the basic development issue is the conflict between trust and mistrust, and disaster can destroy trust in what is supposed to be predictable in their disintegrating world, including such basic patterns as eating. With all of this, a disaster can cause disintegration of basic developmental tasks of children from infancy through 5 years of age.

Disaster has a more general disintegrative effect on children from age 5 through adolescence. For example, watching repeated news reports of the disaster can make the disintegrative effects of the disaster seem to happen over and over again. Continuous TV watching can deepen the shock and numbness the child feels in response to the disaster. There can be cognitive disintegration in which the child plays the disaster and the trauma over and over in his or her head, deepening the apathy and feelings of unreality. There may be behavior that is regressive or aggressive, disrupted sleep patterns due to nightmares or even an obsession with violence. Intervention in the effects of disintegration begins with limiting exposure to the media. This includes television and handheld news devices.

Children need to be closely monitored for signs of behavior that may be harmful to themselves or others, with the purpose of intervention before the problem gets out of hand. Basic intervention includes giving the children something to trust in the midst of the chaos by providing a simple routine of care and affection that they can trust; that is reliable and that they can count on being there for them as their world falls apart. Such care can provide positive experience in the struggle between trust and mistrust for the infant to 18-month-old. It provides support for children struggling to build some control in their life as they learn to control bowel and bladder. It provides nurture for the child whose egocentric thinking patterns are forming the child's relationship to their environment.

Intervention can provide simple rituals that can offer quick comfort and reassurance when the child feels like the world is falling apart and may help to pull a little bit of that disintegrating world back together. Some specific ways that simple rituals can be helpful are

- For early adolescents, saying goodbye in the child's own way to a loved one who has died, through lighting a candle, praying, painting a picture, and such.
- For younger children, allow ritual to emerge and develop through play, drawing, singing, and such. Ritual or parts of ritual from the child's own faith tradition, if they have one, may help to slow disintegration by reinserting the comforting, reassuring, and healing. Timing is important; the ritual would need to be when the family needs it and not postponed. Ritual needs to be simple, short, and quiet to avoid disruption of care of other children.

EMOTIONS

The entire atmosphere of a disaster area will be filled with explosive emotional tension that comes from masses of distraught people reacting to a devastating event. The intensity, the volatility, and the real or potential expression of those emotions will likely be the strongest anyone in the community has ever experienced unless they experienced a previous disaster of similar magnitude. As a result of being caught up in this explosive emotional atmosphere, children may have distressing feelings with an intensity they probably have never experienced before. These are scary, frightening, overwhelming feelings. These feelings express their reaction to a world that has changed drastically or that may not even be there anymore. Emotional reactions are likely to be more severe if the child is a direct witness to, or victim of, the disaster. Fear is the dominant emotion of children reacting to disaster, including the fear that the disaster will happen again. The second most dominant emotion after fear is anger. Adolescents, with their normal patterns of emotional upheaval, can react especially strongly to the chaos, deaths, and losses of a disaster. So the presence of a significant number of adolescents may make the general emotional reaction to the disaster more complicated.

Intervention can begin very early in children's emotional response to the disaster, with a caring presence to help minimize the immediate trauma and to help reduce emotional damage later. At the same time, quick action to minimize fear, anxiety, and anger in children exposed to disaster is essential to communicate to them that some stability and routine are still present or are returning. Intervention can include providing for basic needs in a safe place away from at least some of the chaos to soften the emotional impact of the disaster. If possible, this safe place should also keep the children with as many of their parents and family members as are available to be with them. Take every opportunity to reassure the children that they are loved, that the disaster is not their fault, that they will be cared for, and that it is okay for them to feel upset or to emotionally "fall apart." Take children's feelings seriously. Provide space, time, necessary supplies, and permission to cry, be sad, talk about their feelings (if they want to talk), or to write or draw based on their feelings.

FRAGILITY

The atmosphere of a disaster response site is emotionally explosive. It is also emotionally and spiritually fragile. Fragility is the next disaster reality. The people you are assisting—victims, family members, disaster workers, and children—are emotionally and spirituality frail because they are in an unstable state. Their emotional and spiritual strength and resources have been shattered, leaving them vulnerable to new emotional and spiritual challenges. They can react unpredictably to the developing situation. An individual child may not react the way he or she would in "normal" circumstances. A normally stoic child may burst into tears. An emotionally expressive child may have no discernible reaction. A child may do things he or she would not do in "normal" circumstances. A common sign of this emotional frailty is shock and numbness.

A child may appear immune to what has happened or to ignore what he or she has seen or heard or experienced. But a calm or detached appearance may only be masking the pain and chaos within. The younger the child, the greater the likelihood that he or she will be severely upset by the sights and sounds of the disaster. However, it is also the case that any child with a history of loss, depression, or anxiety is at high risk for a severely maladaptive response to the disaster.

Children's fragile emotional state in disaster can create suggestibility. They may confuse fact with fantasy and create their own scary fantasy. They may lose their ability to keep things in perspective. They may be unable to block out troubling thoughts, and these thoughts may become obsessive. While a spiritually fragile child is vulnerable to proselytizing or persuasion to make religious commitments that promise quick and painless relief from spiritual or emotional distress, that proselytization or persuasion is likely to clash with the child's family's cultural or belief system. This clash can trigger further spiritual distress at exactly a time when they need all their spiritual resources to cope with the way the way the disaster has shaken or shattered their lives.

Interventions to control the effects of emotional fragility of child victims of disaster include

- Skepticism of seemingly calm or detached reactions to the chaos, with the readiness to sensitively but directly check out what may really be going on within
- Constant watchfulness to monitor and control unpredictable behavior that may be harmful to a particular child or to others
- Supporting the children's personal resources and the families' emotional and religious resources for coping with what they see, hear, and experience, and try to reconcile with their belief systems
- Controlling disruptive intrusions, including people with a religious agenda to convert or influence the children. Proselytizers must not be allowed in the disaster response site.

SPIRITUALITY

A disaster can slap a child hard in his or her developing spirituality. A common response of children to disaster is loss of trust. Loss of trust is especially strong for a child of 18 months or younger. If a child is not provided with something to trust during a disaster when so much else in the child's life is disintegrating, then mistrust may be an issue for the rest of that child's life. The child's take on life may be: You can't trust life. A child 3 to 5 years old is learning to exert some control on the environment around him or her. Disaster clobbers control. Everything around the child feels out of control. The child's egocentric thinking patterns may convince him or her that he or she has failed. And in the struggle between initiative and guilt, a sense of guilt may win out.

A child 6 to 12 years old is developing a sense of right and wrong as he or she copes with new social demands. The child is struggling with the conflict between industry and inferiority. A disaster is overwhelming. They can't cope with the trauma of disaster. The developing sense of right and wrong is slapped in the face. The seeds of inferiority are planted; then despair and guilt. Then there comes cynicism that life is not right—that wrong wins out in the end.

Adolescents are developing their value systems. Commitment and ideals are taken very seriously, even to becoming a sacred trust. Meaning and spirituality are becoming big realities for teenagers. The violence, destruction, and chaos of the disaster can deliver a body blow to all of these and prompt the cynical question,

"God is good?" And spiritual distress masked in sarcasm can overwhelm the adolescent.

Finally, there is the egocentric thinking pattern of childhood. From birth through adolescence, the focus is on the self as the child develops a relationship with the world around him or her. The child may personalize the disaster, deciding that he or she did something wrong to cause this to happen. The child may see the disaster as God's punishment of him or her for doing something terribly wrong. So the disaster is the child's fault, and the child is overwhelmed by guilt.

Intervention in this trauma to a child's developing spirituality requires a quick response by spiritual care providers to children's basic needs. This quick response to any need of the children encourages hope. The key is to spark some hope early in the disaster as children are first being affected and as they begin to cope with what is happening. This quick response is critically important because hope can disappear very quickly in the shock of disaster, at the precise time that hope is most needed for emotional and spiritual survival. If a child or family has religious beliefs or spiritual practices that they observe regularly, these beliefs or practices may provide some protection against the impact of the disaster. And they may also be a resource to draw from when coping with the effects of the disaster.

GRIEVING

Grief during a disaster can be massive, collective, and overwhelming. From the moment a spiritual caregiver arrives at the disaster response site, he or she is likely to encounter wave after wave of grieving that is stronger and more all-consuming than ever encountered before. People of the community are in the midst of experiencing multiple, sudden, cataclysmic loss of prized possessions, and the deaths of people they hold most dear in the world. Such loss after loss after loss can lead to raw, overwhelming mass grieving by victims, family members, friends, disaster workers, and children. But, as mentioned above, the children may not be grieving the way the adults are grieving. For example, a younger child is likely to be grieving the absence of parents, brothers, sisters, pets, and toys around him or her because the child can't see them. Younger children typically have had less direct experience with death. They may not understand the permanence of death. They may be waiting for Mommy or Daddy or a sibling or a pet that has died, to come back. They do not understand that, at death, all life functions cease completely and permanently. During the years of normal childhood development, children have the time to develop understanding by degrees that

- Death is irreversible and permanent.
- Death is final. All life functions cease completely.
- Death is inevitable. No living being escapes death.
- Death is physically caused by an impersonal process. Death is not punishment of the child for doing something wrong. (Gullo, 1985)

During a normal childhood, the child gradually becomes able to experience the death of a loved one as a personal loss. But in a disaster, a child experiences all at the same time many types of abnormal, overwhelming death that can result in traumatic grief. Deaths in a disaster might (a) be sudden and unexpected, (b) involve violence or mutilation, (c) be perceived as random or preventable, (d) multiple with many dying around the child, (e) witnessed by a child who is also at risk of death from the same cause, or (f) parental death, whether real or perceived.

A child's grieving during a disaster may not be a simple dynamic in direct response to immediate loss. Grieving by a child can be complicated because it may be connected to other disaster realities on a continuum. The continuum starts with the disintegration of the child's world, making the child emotionally and spiritually fragile. This fragility can predispose the child's spirituality during the disaster to experiencing survivor's guilt. The continuum can then extend to and overlay the child's emotional and spiritual pain with the belief that she caused the death of the loved one for whom she grieves. The continuum of intensifying pain can last as long as the disaster lasts. The disaster realities may gain strength, increasing the danger of long-term emotional and spiritual injury unless there is effective intervention.

Effective intervention with grieving children during a disaster needs to be done in broad strokes. There is not the time or the setting to provide grief therapy when we are in the midst of a disaster, but what can be provided is support that makes hope possible. This can include

- Providing a nurturing setting away from the chaos.
- Making the spiritual caregiver visible as a symbol of life beyond the chaos.
- Allowing direct contact with comforting people, pets, toys, or objects that have survived, or can serve as stand-ins
- Providing clear, direct communication without clichés: Say the words "dead" and "died," not "passed on," "passed away," "went to be with the Lord," or the problematic "sleep with the angels."
- Offering truthful communication that balances describing what happens to the body after death occurs with any religious beliefs the family may have about death, including violent death.
- Understanding and validating what the child feels and why.
- Giving the child permission to cry or grieve in the child's own way.
- Encouraging expression of grief through the child's own creative resources and talents.
- Encouraging rituals/memorials either individually or with family/ co-religionists.
- Seeing the body of the dead parent or loved one.

DURATION/RESPONDER DANGER

Duration—the length of the disaster and the dangers to everybody if the disaster extends from hours into days or even weeks—can have an effect that includes not only the child victims of the disaster, but also the children of disaster first responders and other disaster workers. The dangers of a prolonged disaster to children include

- Prolonged and intensified loss of security, of comforting routine, and possibly of hope. There may even be a second wave of disaster events and possibly more losses or deaths.
- Longer duration causes more psychological damage and more damage to children's extended social environment than a disaster of shorter duration.
- Exposure to a disaster for a month or longer puts children at higher risk of developing posttraumatic stress disorder (PTSD) and/or criminal behavior.
- Potential increase in antisocial behavior in the community as a whole, such as violence against children, including sexual violence. Prolonged disaster increases the risk of further trauma to children from people in the community—people they may trust and want to please, or at least to not upset.
- Potential fallout on the children of disaster first responders and other disaster workers who themselves are affected or injured emotionally or physically. These children may be vulnerable to neglect or even abuse from a hurting or distracted parent. If a disaster worker dies, and that disaster worker was also a parent, the child will experience traumatic grief with the same intensity as any other child whose parent died in the disaster.

For disaster spiritual care providers to intervene effectively in a prolonged or extended disaster, the first thing we need to do is to keep a constant supportive presence for victims, families, and workers throughout the entire disaster response. There is a need to work in partnership, including in shifts, with other care providers to maintain the safe place, the nurturing atmosphere, and the support children need during a disaster response, including the continuing strength of our healing presence. This quality of healing presence is the most important thing a spiritual caregiver can give during a prolonged disaster.

For child disaster victims during a prolonged disaster, spiritual care providers are in a continuing position of trust to observe and interpret emerging signs of regressive behavior or antisocial behavior in the children themselves and at the same time, we are in an extended authoritative position to monitor, report, and act as child advocates to the appropriate authorities for any signs we see of abuse or violence against the children even as we continue to provide direct emotional and spiritual support to child victims for the duration of the disaster. This means that spiritual caregivers must also care for ourselves even as we care for others, so that we can continue to stay alert, watchful, and ready to intervene as needed. Caregivers, too, will need to take breaks to eat, take showers, sleep, be with family, stroke the cat, pat the dog, or watch the fish in the aquarium. Self-care includes family care. Families need care and love during the disaster. Caregivers and their families all need some time together during the disaster to support and nurture each other during a chaotic and traumatic time.

It is also essential to the long-term health of families of all other disaster first responders and disaster workers to spend quality time together during a disaster. A vitally important part of our intervention as disaster spiritual care providers is to indirectly support the children of disaster workers by directly supporting their parents. We will be working alongside other disaster workers and will have opportunity to hear from them how their children are coping, how their spouses are handling the situation, to listen for signs of need or trouble at home with children or spouse, and to assist in setting up safety nets as needed for families of disaster workers.

CREATING AN ACTION PLAN

The emotional and spiritual first aid that we help provide to children at the time of the disaster can reduce the long-term emotional and spiritual injury to those children. Only in recent years, after several major disasters, have we become aware of the long-term emotional, mental and spiritual health consequences for persons of any age struck by a disaster. But now that we do know it, we can develop an effective action plan for providing spiritual and emotional care of the one dozen, or one hundred, or one thousand, or ten thousand, or however many children when disaster strikes the community in which we live.

The action plan needs to be oriented to the community of children; that is, to the entire group, while allowing as much as possible for limited individual attention as needed and as time or resources are available. Because of the probable scale of needs and the urgency of effective response to those needs, individual attention is likely to be limited. We need to answer two basic questions when creating an action plan for the spiritual and emotional care of children during a disaster:

- What principles must we follow?
- How can we most effectively intervene?

Principles

To alter the effects of a disaster on children, what must we include when developing the action plan? What features, qualities, and characteristics must the action plan have in order to be effective and to fit with the overall community or institutional disaster response plan? The list below is representative of the principles we need to follow when developing an action plan for the emotional and spiritual care of children during a community disaster:

- Have one single purpose; that is, stabilization, not therapy.
- Keep it simple for quick and easy implementation.
- Be supportive but not obtrusive.
- Make the plan one that is quickly effective to provide timely results.
- Spiritual helpers must be accountable to overall disaster authority.
- Use only available resources that are close at hand.
- Keep it lean so as not to use too many limited resources that may be needed elsewhere.
- Have a clearly defined purpose for each part of the disaster spiritual care action plan.

- Have each part focused to provide effective, specific interventions.
- Provide for special needs or situations of the child population of your community.
- Focus the action plan on interventions for children, but it may assist others as well, such as parents.
- Tailor it to serve the distinctive needs or situation of your community.
- Include awareness of the cultural patterns and belief systems of your community.

The list above is general. It is not complete. The reason that it is not complete is that it does not include any considerations that are distinctive to your community.

Intervention

How do we provide the basic interventions in the kind of emotional and spiritual distress that disaster causes in children? And how do we do this on a mass scale? What structured actions are needed to do the job?

Below is a list of basic interventions discussed earlier in this chapter. How can an action plan be set up to provide these interventions on a mass scale? Or to make it more personal and focused? What kind of action plan would you set up to provide these interventions on a mass scale in your community?

- Model calm, accepting, nonjudgmental behavior.
- Visible symbols of nurture: parents, family, chaplain/pastor, teachers, friends.
- Grandparent volunteers trained to listen, assess, support, facilitate, and participate in coping activities and simulate the nurturing grandparent-grandchild relationship.
- Support children in their vulnerability and nurture their resilience to facilitate successful coping.
- Provide a safe place where children can process their experiences and express their fears.
- Encourage comforting routines to help neutralize the effects of the chaos.
- Provide tangible, practical assistance as requested or perceived.
- Be generous with small comforts, such a drink of water or a blanket.
- Provide tangible comfort items, such as teddy bears.
- Offer empathic communication and reassurance.
- Allow the children to communicate about disaster-related events and their reactions.
- Reassure them that sadness, including crying, is normal and necessary.
- Do not minimize their losses. Acknowledge those losses as real and normal.
- Predict what will happen next as much as you truthfully can to help alleviate anxiety.
- Support the children's adult caregivers, including their parents.
- Obtain parental permission as appropriate and as parents are available. Besides being legally necessary, this affirms that parents are in charge and are the authority for the care of their children. It acknowledges and strengthens the parent-child bond.

- Delegate simple, closely supervised, responsibilities to older children and adolescents, as appropriate, to channel their need to take meaningful action, and to strengthen their developing value system, which includes responsibility toward others.
- Pay special attention to children at high risk for PTSD and other emotional outcomes.
- Music can be a mixed bag. Monitor and control it to avoid upsetting or irritating other disaster victims and families. What is comforting for one child or family may agitate others.
- Prayer, meditation, chants, and rituals may be used if they provide comfort and fit the belief systems and cultural background of the children and their families.

The action plan below (Ford, 2012) incorporates the principles listed above and provides structure for the interventions described above for large-scale emotional and spiritual care of children during a disaster. The action plan includes input and wisdom from three gifted people who have devoted their professional lives to different aspects of childcare and nurture, each one with healing compassion for children who are in pain. They are Tanya Armstrong, Child Life Coordinator at Winchester Medical Center (WMC) in Winchester, Virginia; Connie Ordower, retired school counselor and currently a chaplain at WMC; and Trena Fisher, Director, Child Care, at WMC. Tanya, Connie, and Trena, thank you for sharing so generously and insightfully in this sacred task of caring.

ACTION PLAN: EXAMPLE

Plan well ahead of time and plan cooperatively. Don't be a lone ranger. To be most effective, disaster emotional and spiritual care for children should be an integral part of the community or institution's overall plan for disaster spiritual childcare. In the same way, the childcare segment of the overall disaster plan must establish a working relationship with, and accountability to, the community or institutional authority responsible for planning and directing disaster response. This includes an understanding of which authority will activate disaster childcare if it is needed and to whomever the coordinator of the child spiritual and emotional care providers is to report to during a disaster.

Set up a staging area for uninjured children to be together with uninjured/available parents, siblings, and/or other relatives as the basis for the action plan. Disaster workers present may include volunteer grandparents and spiritual care providers together with childcare staff.

Observe or decide ahead of time whether uninjured children with no parents present are likely to be upset if they stay in the same staging area where other children are together with their parents. If so, provide a different area for children whose parents are not present, staffed with volunteer grandparents, if available.

Make resources, support, and quiet space separate from the staging area, quickly available for the normal emotional and spiritual/ritual needs of children and their families during the disaster.

Keep a confidential assessment checklist to provide a quick, simple, and accurate way for staff and volunteers to record and communicate symptoms, impressions, or danger signs of spiritual, behavioral, or emotional difficulties in coping with the disaster, either in the present situation or in the future.

Develop and follow a clear procedure for staff and volunteers to triage with basic (first aid) interventions for special needs or circumstances, such as

- Quiet/private place to pray, draw, cry, and such or to reunite children with parents to minimize the risk of PTSD.
- Monitor and intervene as necessary to quickly calm or defuse situations of conflict or tension within family groups.
- Monitor and intervene quickly as necessary to defuse behavioral problems or make them less disruptive to other distraught children or families.
- Support and facilitate family groups who are going back to their homes, as allowed. This may be a part of the beginning of the recovery phase. (See the last paragraph below.)
- Control or eliminate news media overload, such as news media replays of the disaster.

For injured or dead children, intervention is focused on parents:

- Provide a staging area different from the one described above. These parents may support each other as they share the uncertainty or tragedy.
- Monitor and support family groups as they wait for news or developments.
- Support the child or family's initial grief reaction.
- Keep a log of injured children being cared for in a different location, and provide spiritual and emotional care to children and parents (if present) as needed and appropriate.

If you support family groups as they are allowed to return home, your focus of providing spiritual and emotional care will shift from emotional and spiritual first aid to supporting the transition from the initial disaster response to the recovery period after the disaster. Be ready to terminate your current role, and if there is an announced need and you choose to respond, to transition to providing care during the recovery period in the days, weeks, months, and perhaps years after the disaster.

INVITATION

Please draw from the example action plan whatever you find useful as you develop an action plan for the emotional and spiritual care of the children of your own community if a disaster strikes. As stated at the beginning of this chapter, disaster, whether natural or man-made, is a mark of our times. As we respond to each disaster, we learn more about how to care for each other during a disaster. Now we have an opportunity to learn from each other.

REFERENCES

Erikson, E. (1994). *Identity and the life cycle*. New York, NY: Norton.
Ford, P. (2012). *A disaster spiritual care primer*. Independent Publisher.
Gullo, S. V. (1985). On understanding and coping with death during childhood. In S. V. Gullo, R. R. Patterson, J. E. Schowalter, M. Tallmer, A. H. Kutscher, & P. Buschman (Eds.), *Death and children: A guide for educators, parents and caregivers*. Dobbs Ferry, NY: Tappan Press.
Maslow, A. H. (1954). *Motivation and personality*. New York, NY: Harper.

CHAPTER 10
Helping Bereaved Children in the Schools

Linda Goldman

Educators and students can exist in a more healthy living and learning environment by acknowledging the special needs of the grieving child. Foremost is the complex relationship between loss issues and a child's ability to function in and out of the classroom. To create a safe haven for learning for all young people, the needs of the grieving child must be addressed in a new and fresh way within our school systems. Children's grief should be seen as an ongoing life process that is approachable through words, activities, nonverbal communication, and accountability. Educators can use this understanding to create a protected environment for parents, teachers, and children to acknowledge and process challenging feelings (Goldman, 2012, p. 26).

TODAY'S GRIEF ISSUES

Many times caring adults rely on the prevailing myth that children are too young to grieve. When a child is capable of loving, he or she is capable of grieving. Children and teens are often born into a world of loss and grief issues that exist inside their homes and wait for them outside in their neighborhoods. Girls and boys are becoming increasingly traumatized by these prevailing social and societal loss issues in their homes, in their schools, and in their communities.

A large percentage of our children globally face the loss of the protection of the adult world, as grief-related issues of suicide, homicide, war, terrorism, violence, and abuse infiltrate their outer and inner worlds. Issues involving shame and secretiveness when death is caused by such occurrences as suicide can create fear, isolation, and loneliness, which can be far more damaging than the original loss. Natural disasters ranging from earthquakes to tornados wreak havoc involving death and destruction of property. Current family issues including adoption, divorce, immigration, deployment, homelessness, deportation, and imprisonment reflect loss through separation for many youngsters.

Death and nondeath-related loss permeate childhood. There are basic categories of childhood loss impacting students that include death, loss of a relationship, loss of environment, loss of skills and abilities, loss of self and self-esteem, loss of external objects, loss of routines and habits, loss of the protection of the adult world, and loss of privacy (Goldman, 2014, p. 9). Often after a death, many of these categories arise as secondary losses.

COMMON SIGNS OF CHILDREN'S GRIEF

Parents, educators, and other caring adults need to become familiar with the common signs of grief in order to normalize them for students. We then can develop ways to work with the bereaved young people within the school system.

Sophie was a fourth-grade client whose dad had died of cancer on her 9th birthday. During our grief therapy session, she explained the rage she felt toward her teacher, Mrs. Pastor. The first week of school, Sophie told her that her Dad had died during the summer. Mrs. Pastor never responded and never addressed the subject again. Sophie was furious and vowed not to speak to anyone else in school about this death. She explained through tear-filled eyes, "I wish Mrs. Pastor would have given me a hug, said she was sorry, and promised to be there if I ever wanted to talk about my father." Educators must develop age-appropriate language to respond to grieving children and ways to acknowledge the death has occurred. This helps normalize feelings and create discussions on these sensitive topics.

Understanding that many bereaved students don't like to feel different is an important concept for school personnel. When youngsters experience the death of a loved one, they sometimes choose not to talk about it. This may give them a sense of control over their lives, help normalize what has happened, or allow time to understand thoughts and feelings.

Kate was 11 years old when her brother died of suicide. She expressed shame and stigma about the death and had difficulty sharing her thoughts and feelings. In her struggle to normalize her brother's death, Kate creatively developed the following definition of suicide and explained its meaning (see Figure 10.1) (Goldman, 2001, p. 37).

Brandon was playing on the school basketball team at the final play-off game. Most of the parents of team members came to the event to support their children. Brandon scored the final basket that won the victory for his team. Nick, Brandon's coach, ran over to Brandon to congratulate him, and all the other boys and their parents joined in the celebration.

"Where's your dad?" Coach Nick asked. "He's working today and couldn't come," Brandon replied. Coach Nick was unaware that Brandon's father had died of a sudden heart attack 3 months earlier. Brandon wanted to "appear normal" and decided to avoid mentioning his father's death. If his school had maintained a policy of requiring a mandatory "grief and loss inventory," Coach Nick could have accessed this tool and identified Brandon as a grieving child. The school guidance counselor can serve as liaison to identify grieving children to all school

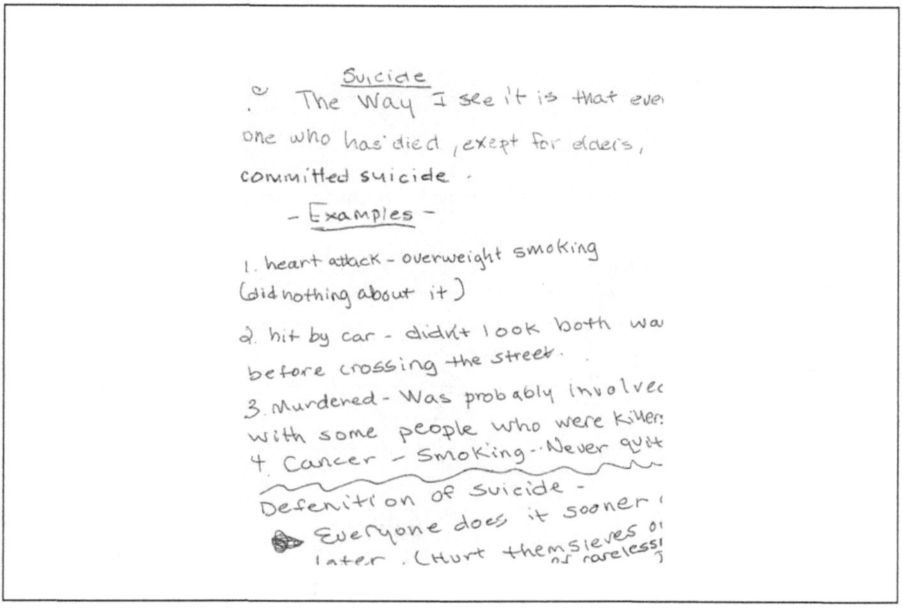

> Suicide
>
> The way I see it is that every one who has died, exept for elders, committed suicide.
>
> – Examples –
>
> 1. heart attack – overweight smoking (did nothing about it)
> 2. hit by car – didn't look both ways before crossing the street.
> 3. Murdered – was probably involved with some people who were killers
> 4. Cancer – smoking – never quit
>
> Defenition of suicide –
> Everyone does it sooner or later. (Hurt themsleves or careless)

Figure 10.1.

personnel who work with the grieving child. Figure 10.2 illustrates the loss and grief inventory (Goldman, 2014) that can serve as a valuable tool of communication and information for educators.

IDENTIFY THE WHOLE CHILD

Name _____ Age ____ Grade ____
Address _____ Date of birth _____
Phone number: _____ Today's date _____

REFERRAL INFORMATION

Reason for referral _____

Source for referral _____

IDENTIFY RECENT SIGNIFICANT LOSS

Relationship of deceased to the child _____
Facts about the loss (who, what, where, when?) _____
_____
_____

156 / CHILDREN, ADOLESCENTS, AND DEATH

Who told the child? _____

How was the child told? _____

Deceased's date of birth _____ Date of death _____

PREVIOUS LOSS AND GRIEF HISTORY [Include significant dates involved in prior losses.]

Divorce or separation_____ Date _____
Moving _____ Date _____
Friend moved away _____ Date _____
Past deaths _____ Who? _____ Date _____
         Who? _____ Date _____
Pet Deaths _____ Date _____
Parent(s) changing job _____ Date _____
Parent(s) losing jobs _____ Date _____
Fire _____ Date _____ / Robbery _____ Date _____
Natural Disaster _____ Date _____
Deployment _____ Deportation _____ Other _____ Date _____

INHERITED FAMILY LOSS (example grandparent killed in a war)
_____
_____

FAMILY UNIT

Single parent _____ Divorce _____
Unmarried _____ Adoption _____
Natural parents _____ Blended family _____
Same sex parents _____
Living with grandparents _____

FAMILY HISTORY OF CHRONIC CULTURAL LOSS

Drugs _____ Injury _____
Crime_____ Unemployment _____

MEDICAL HISTORY

Significant parent illness _____
Significant children's illness _____

PREVIOUS SCHOOL HISTORY

Grades _____
Progress _____
Participation _____

ASSESSMENT HISTORY

Standardized tests _____ Date _____

Speech and language evaluation _____ Date _____

Educational assessment _____ Date _____

Psychological evaluation _____ Date _____

IDENTIFY CHILD'S ATTITUDE TOWARD SIGNIFICANT OTHERS/SELF

Siblings _____

Parents _____

Friends _____

Pets _____
Self _____

LIKES AND DISLIKES

Interests Likes _____
         Dislikes _____
Abilities Likes _____
         Dislikes _____

PRESENT BEHAVIOR AT SCHOOL (Check those that apply)

Disruptive in school _____   Failing grades _____
Inability to concentrate _____   Increased absenteeism _____
Fighting with peers _____   Withdrawn _____
Using bad language _____   Very tired _____
Physical complaints (headache, stomach ache, etc.) _____
Nervousness _____   Other _____

IDENTIFY PRESENT BEHAVIORS AT HOME (Check those that apply)

Less interaction _____   Sleeplessness _____
Poor eating _____   Bed wetting _____
Clinging to parents _____   Nightmares _____
Increased perfectionism _____   Crying _____
Talks constantly about loss _____   Fighting with siblings or parents _____
Fears (of dark, noise, robbers, etc.) _____

IDENTIFY PRESENT BEHAVIORS WITH PEERS (Check those that apply)

More arguing _____ Less interest in play dates _____
Less communication with peers _____ Others _____

RECOMMENDATIONS

Team conference _____ In-school individual counseling _____
Referral to a counseling agency _____ In-school group counseling _____
Referral to a support group _____ Referral to a medical doctor _____
Testing _____

FOLLOW-UP

Monthly _____ Source _____ Date _____

Figure 10.2. Illustrates the loss inventory checklist.
Source: Goldman (2014, pp. 175–177).

Becoming familiar with the common signs of grieving children is essential for educators. Knowing how children and teens express grief through words and actions can help reduce their anxiety and the anxiety of those caring adults that surround them. It is common for a grieving child to

- Imitate behavior of the deceased,
- Want to "appear normal,"
- Need to tell the story over and over again,
- Enjoy wearing or holding something of loved one,
- Speak of loved one in the present,
- Tend to worry about health and health of surviving loved ones,
- Create their unique spiritual belief system. (Adapted from Goldman, 2009, p. 105)

AWARENESS OF BEREAVED CHILDREN IN SCHOOLS

Children are often told they "need to move on and get over their loss." Educators and other healthcare professionals must recognize and incorporate into our grief awareness the ongoing journey of children processing grief and trauma. Each person is unique, and the grief experience is unique to each individual.

Students may use homework and assignments to express life issues of which their teachers might not be aware. Ten-year-old Lila wrote a poetry assignment about the death of her Uncle Bryan. He died suddenly of a heart attack while jogging. The following poem expresses her love for her uncle and signaled to her teacher that she was a grieving child (Goldman, 2014, p. 41).

Uncle Bryan Is a Flower Blooming by Lila
When he comes light-jogging
Into my arms . . . he delights me.
Like a child getting his own pet,
And I still love him.
He always was playing sports
And he puts a smile on my face
   When he comes light-walking into my heart
   He opens his arms to me
   Like vines wrapping around a tree
   . . . and I love him.
Even though he is gone
Uncle Bryan is a flower blooming
   . . . that fills me with joy

Educators can engage students in schoolwork that allows expression and also completes an education task. Christopher, a 10th-grade student, shared profound feelings about the sudden death of his friend Doug in a poetry homework assignment. Christopher was then identified as a grieving student.

Doug by Cristopher
You played a bold game of basketball,
Even though you were dizzy and wanted to fall.
You jumped high and shot well,
Which led us to victory at the sound of the bell.
   We slapped five and bragged to the other team,
   For the game had ended much like a dream.
   We left the building and went to the parking lot.
   And found the Caravan in the same spot.
We pulled out of the school and rolled over a bump,
A few seconds down the road I heard a large thump.
I turned around to see what fell,
And in the dark it was hard to tell.
   I soon realized it was Doug draped over the seat.
   I held him up and checked for a beat.
   He looked through me as if I were a ghost,
   He sat in his seat as motionless as a post.
He was a happy kid that didn't deserve to die.
For he was a friend on whom you could always rely.
He lived for soccer and tried his best,
Which is all you can ask from a kid now at rest.

The following was a heartfelt response by his teacher: "These are well-written. I realize that comfort and well-meant words often sound trite, but I offer them anyway. I truly admire your strength. I hope writing these poems were as much a comfort to you as they were an enjoyment to me." 50/50 A+ (Goldman, 2014, p. 174).

Ashley was a third grader whose mom had died in a car crash when she was in first grade. The class was making Mother's Day gifts, and Ashley was suddenly inundated with memories as peers began talking about their moms. She burst into tears and ran out of the room. Mr. Jones, her teacher, rushed after her. Ashley shared that her mom had died 2 years ago, and it was still painful to remember her. Mr. Jones admonished Ashley. "It's been two years since your mom has died. You need to get over her and move on!" Ashley said she hated her teacher for saying that and explained she wanted to be able to remember her mom and share memories. "The last thing I want to do is to forget my mom!" she shouted.

Mr. Jones could have responded to Ashley in a more compassionate way and perhaps that would have enabled her to safely express challenging feelings in school. One useful procedure is creating an agreement with Ashley to choose a designated safe adult in school to speak with when she missed her mom.

After Ashley explained her story in grief therapy, she decided she would like to light a candle to remember Mom. I then invited Ashley to participate in another intervention. I asked if she would like make a symbolic mother's day card for her mom, write a poem to her mom, or plant a flower in her memory. Letter and poetry writing are grief therapy techniques that allow children to create concrete ways to communicate the death of a loved one. Figure 10.3 is a letter Ashley wrote to her mom on Mother's Day (Goldman, 2014, p. 60).

INTERVENTIONS FOR BEREAVED CHILDREN

Children gain a greater understanding of themselves when they can express previously hidden emotions. The awareness of unrecognized feelings also allows educators, parents, and other caring adults to be more in touch with what is going on in the grief process. Grief feelings and thoughts are continuous and ever-changing, inundating their lives like waves on the ocean. These thoughts and feelings may arrive without warning, and children feel unprepared for their enormity in a school

Figure 10.3.

setting. It is essential that school personnel be trained in recognizing the following needs of the bereaved child:

The bereaved child needs to acknowledge a parent or sibling who died by using his or her name or sharing a memory.

- The bereaved child needs to tell his or her story over and over again.
- The bereaved child needs to use tools such as drawing, writing, role-playing, and reenactment to safely project feelings and thoughts about the loss and present life outside of themselves.
- The bereaved child needs to be allowed to go to a safe place outside the classroom when these unexpected, overwhelming feelings arise without needing to explain why in front of fellow classmates.
- The bereaved child often is preoccupied with his or her own health and the health of loved ones. Providing a reality check, such as allowing the child to phone the surviving parent during the school day or to visit the school nurse, can reassure boys and girls that they and their families are okay.
- The bereaved child needs to use memory work to create a physical way to remember their feelings and share them. Memory books are a collection of drawn or written feelings and thoughts that allow the child to reexperience memories in a safe way. The books serve as useful tools to enable children to tell about the person who died and open discussion. Kids can tell about how the person died and share funny, happy, or sad memories. (Goldman, 2012, p. 29)

Educators can use a grief and loss inventory (Goldman, 2014) as a tool for creating and storing history on the grieving child throughout his or her academic life. This history includes all losses and important dates of birthdays and deaths of loved ones that may have a great impact on the child through the years. Figure 10.4 is a memory book example by 7-year-old Danny, who illustrates through artwork the way he perceived his dad's death (Goldman, 2001, p. 126).

Educators can use the concept of "teachable moments" to create a spontaneous lesson, calling upon a life experience that is happening in "The Now." The death of

Figure 10.4. Memory Book

Ms. Nolan's class's goldfish, Goldie, was a huge loss to the kindergartners. Goldie's death during school provided a teachable moment wherein the children could express their feelings about death and commemorate their loss with a burial ritual and memorial service.

Classroom teachers can provide a safe haven for the grieving child by

- Allowing the child to leave the room if needed,
- Allowing the child to call home if necessary,
- Creating a visit to the school nurse and guidance counselor periodically,
- Changing some work assignments,
- Assigning a class helper,
- Creating some private time in the day,
- Giving more academic progress reports.

Schools can help children commemorate a death in the school by

- Creating a ceremony, releasing a balloon with a special note, lighting a candle,
- Creating a memorial wall with stories and pictures of shared events,
- Having an assembly about the student,
- Planting a memory garden,
- Initiating a scholarship fund,
- Establishing an ongoing fundraiser with proceeds going toward a designated charity,
- Placing a memorial page and picture in the school yearbook or newspaper,
- Sending flowers to the grieving family. (Goldman, 2012, p. 29)

GRIEF IN IDENTIFIABLE POPULATIONS: ADD, LD STUDENTS, BULLYING AND VIOLENCE, LGBTQ YOUTH, AND HOMELESSNESS

Every student is unique, and every student needs to be protected and cared for in the school community. Grieving and traumatized children often become those most at-risk and most vulnerable to learning and bullying/victimization issues. These issues among our children have reached epidemic proportions. As concerned educators, we may ask ourselves how our children are expressing unresolved and unexpressed grief and trauma that can so often result in challenging behaviors. The seemingly apparent answer has been poor grades, detachment, learning problems, depression and low self-esteem, with the extreme responses including violence, crime, drugs, promiscuity, depression, suicide, and homicide.

GRIEF AND ADD, LD

Children can be misdiagnosed with attention deficit disorder and learning disabilities after their experience with traumatic grief and loss. Hyperactivity, distractibility, impulsivity, and inability to concentrate are common grief symptoms that too often become the behavioral criteria to diagnose learning problems.

Seven-year-old Sam was a second grader whose older sister Sally was murdered in a drive-by shooting the day before Christmas. He came back to school after the winter holiday with extreme restlessness and frequent swings of emotional outbursts and withdrawal. This continued for several months, along with a decrease in attention and school performance. The behaviors continued well into third grade, where Sam's teacher expressed concern that he might be exhibiting signs of attention deficit. She suggested to his mom that Sam receive an evaluation by his pediatrician. Sam was placed on medication for quite some time. He continued to have the nightmares and bed-wetting that began with his sister's death. Sam had become a part of the learning-disabled population, and his hidden grief and its symptoms remained buried.

Artwork can be used as a grief therapy tool to help children recognize unresolved grief feelings and buried or frozen blocks of emotion. Sam's drawing (Figure 10.5) illustrates the deep grief of an elementary school child, detached from his soul, and masking overwhelming feelings with a smile, common for the young child (Goldman, 2001, p. 40).

Sam eventually became a member of a school-based grief therapy group, attending for several months with four other children between the ages of 6 and 9, led by his guidance counselor. Children made memory books commemorating loved ones and shared photos and stories. Gradually Sam's concentration in school became more focused; eventually, he was taken off the medication. He continued to attend a children's bereavement group in a neighboring hospice program for the remainder of the school year.

We, as caring adults, need to be educated in learning the common signs associated with the complexities of grief and trauma. Gaining an understanding of many feelings, including angers, anxiety, and depression, which occur with bereavement, can be a crucial tool in differentiating between grief related issues and ADD or LD.

The bereaved child in the classroom may

- Become the class clown,
- Become withdrawn and unsociable,

Figure 10.5. A Student and his Grieving Soul.

- Bed-wet or have nightmares,
- Become restless in staying seated,
- Call out of turn,
- Not complete schoolwork,
- Have problems listening and staying on task,
- Become overly talkative,
- Become disorganized,
- Show reckless physical action,
- Show poor concentration around external stimuli,
- Show difficulty in following directions,
- Cry unexpectedly,
- Get stomachaches and headaches.

BULLYING AND VIOLENCE

Bullying is grossly misunderstood and largely invisible, but its results often mirror the reactions in youth who experience trauma and loss, such as anxiety, panic, rage, and self-hatred. Too many kids admit they have been bullied at some point during their school experience, often resulting in poor grades, detachment, learning problems, and depression.

The Bureau of Justice Statistics' Indicators of School Crime and Safety report from 2007 indicated that 28% of youth between 12 and 18 years of age were bullied at school in the past six months, with about one fifth of those stating that it happened at least once or twice a week (Dinkes, Cataldi, Lin-Kelly, & Snyder, 2007). Results from Hinduja and Patchins research (2010) indicated that "experience with traditional bullying and cyberbullying is associated with an increase in suicidal ideation in bullying and cyberbullying victims and offenders were almost twice as likely to have reported that they attempted suicide as youth who were not victims or bullies" (p. 216) and "with regard to clinical implications, the small but significant variation found in suicidal thoughts and actions based on bullying and cyberbullying suggests that all forms of adolescent peer aggression must be taken seriously both at school and at home" (p. 217). Bullying needs to become paramount for educators in order to change thinking and consciousness for children and adults to see bullying-victimization encounters as dangerous to students.

Bullying is no longer an innocuous schoolyard activity or sibling interchange. Young people who engage in tormenting, teasing, and abusing others are beginning to be seen as legitimate offenders exhibiting criminal actions. Many schools not only implement a zero-tolerance policy for violent behavior, but along with expulsion, are currently referring chargeable offenses to the criminal justice system. Clearly, our children cannot stop bullying or violence without guidance, modeling, and absolute support from the adult world. Caring adults must vigilantly create no-bullying policies and use no-bullying curricula.

A potentially powerful concept for children to integrate at a young age is that being a bully is anything but "cool." Another essential understanding for youngsters is the difference between telling and tattling. Even preschoolers can recognize that "Tattling is telling on someone to get them into trouble. Telling is reporting something to prevent trouble" (Goldman, 2005c, p. 13).

One 6-year-old, Alice, relayed her story of being picked on and called names for being overweight. She ran home to be comforted by her mom, tears streaming down her face. "Stop that crying," her mother demanded, as she ordered her to go back and handle it herself. Alice felt that was impossible and avoided her tormentors whenever she could.

Adults can become role models in actions and words, never allowing verbal abuse, physical threats, or sexual innuendos to be tolerated by immediately stopping harassment at any level. Ignoring insulting or offensive words, even in passing, continues the cycle of promoting ideas of inferiority and marginalization. It is mandatory that our educational systems stand up against any racial, cultural, or homophobic slur in order to promote the acceptance and mental health of all.

Bullying is seen to be an imbalance of power. All too often bullying-victimization circumstances such as glances, threats, verbal harassment, and malicious gossip are invisible to parents and professionals and fall under their radar screen of awareness. Yet we must recognize the unmistakable relationship between juvenile homicide, suicide, and repressed rage from years of bullying, taunting, intimidation, isolation, and abuse by students in our nation's schools.

It is apparent that one of the answers to social violence may be the prevention of bullying behavior. Many publicized suicide/homicide rampages were committed by perpetrators who themselves were victims of prolonged bullying that went unnoticed. Clichés such as "Boys will be boys" or "Handle it yourself" can leave young people in hopeless situations to handle alone, often manifesting in outward rage or inner self-hatred. Vossekull, Fein, Reddy, Borum, and Modzeleski (2002) present the U.S. Secret Service and U.S. Department of Education findings of the Safe School Initiative and the implications for the prevention of school attacks in the United States. One of the key findings was that "Many attackers felt bullied, persecuted or injured by others prior to the attack" (p. 12). They continue,

> In a number of the incidents of targeted school violence studied, attackers described being bullied in terms that suggested that these experiences approached torment . . . the prevalence of bullying found in this and other recent studies should strongly support ongoing efforts to reduce bullying in American schools. Educators can play an important role in ensuring that students are not bullied in schools and that schools not only do not permit bullying but also empower other students to let adults in the school know if students are being bullied. (pp. 35–36)

School shootings are a reflection of society, wherein no student, no matter the age, is exempt. From Columbine to Sandy Hook Elementary, kids' exposure to violence, either directly or through the media, is prevalent. Educators react in many ways. One student made the following poster (Figure 10.6) to send to Columbine after the rampage. "In memory of lives lost at Columbine High," signed by every student and every faculty member (Goldman, 2014, p. 173).

166 / CHILDREN, ADOLESCENTS, AND DEATH

Another school experienced a violent rampage, wherein several students and a teacher were shot and killed. During a class discussion of this traumatic event, one little first grader, Annie, was emotionally frozen. As other classmates were sharing their feelings and concerns, Annie couldn't speak. She just sat at her desk and drew this picture (Figure 10.7) (Goldman, 2005, p. 98).

> Then a community is educated about recognizing hurtful behaviors, its members are more likely to intervene. Another aspect is firm actions and boundaries to create a zero tolerance for bullying at home, in the schools and throughout the community. Still a third aspect is guidelines and procedures established in families and educational systems that allow a safe harbor for those victimized by bullying and expedite action against those that perpetuate abusive behaviors. Only then can we begin to eliminate the imbalance of power so inherent in the challenge of eliminating the dangers of bullying for our children.(Goldman, 2005c, p. 15)

Figure 10.6. A Columbine Poster.

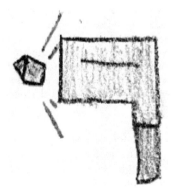

Figure 10.7. Drawing of Trauma.

LESBIAN, GAY, BISEXUAL, TRANSGENDER, AND QUESTIONING YOUTH (LGBTQ)

"Do not let a homophobic moment go by. Correct them. Change their minds. They speak from ignorance, as they probably have never really interacted with a gay person before" (an anonymous teen). School personnel have long understood that a fair and inclusive education is threatened when students' physical and emotional security is endangered. The hostile environment that exists for LGBTQ students in many of our schools is all too apparent. Sexual orientation and gender identity are topics that have become a subject of enormous interest and speculation by the media. LGBTQ young people today are far more visible and active in expressing themselves and facing homophobic barriers head-on to demand equality in relationships, economics, politics, and spirituality.

Schools are our student's homes away from home and the place they spend the majority of their time. LGBTQ adolescents need to be guaranteed their environment is safe. All students deserve to learn in an environment that is supportive and friendly. Kidspeace Institute defines a safe space as "one where there are student and adult allies who can help shape a program or school culture that is accepting of all people, regardless of sexual orientation, gender identity, expression, or any other difference" (Goldman, 2008, p. 159).

Hostile environments within schools are distressing for our LBGTQ youth. Young people are targeted for atypical behavior and coming out as LBGTQ, and become victims of bullying and harassment. This distress too often culminates in anxiety, depression, suicide ideation, or physical and emotional harm. GLSEN is the Gay, Lesbian, Straight Educational Network. GLSEN's 2009 School Climate Survey (Kosciw, Greytak, Diaz, & Bartkiewicz, 2010) reported 9 out of 10 LGBT students experienced harassment at school. The following statistics reflect the world our LBGTQ teens live with in their educational environment and underscore their need for love, friendship, acceptance, advocacy, and safety in our schools.

- According to the National School Climate Survey, 52.9% of LGBT students were harassed or threatened by their peers via electronic media, often known as cyberbullying (Kosciw et al., 2010).
- Lesbian, gay, or bisexual youth who reported high levels of family rejection in adolescence were 8.4 times more likely to have attempted suicide (Ryan, Huebner, Diaz, & Sanchez, 2009).
- Nearly two thirds (61.1%) of students reported that they felt unsafe in school because of their sexual orientation, and more than a third (39.9%) felt unsafe because of their gender expression (Kosciw et al., 2010, p. 3).
- Approximately 29.1% LGBT students missed a class at least once and 30.0% missed at least one day of school in the past month because of safety concerns, when compared to the general population of secondary school students (Kosciw et al., 2010, p. 5).

- LGBT students who were more frequently harassed because of their sexual orientation or gender expression had grade point averages almost half a grade lower than students who were less often harassed (Kosciw et al., 2010).
- Derogatory remarks such as "faggot" or "dyke" were often heard by 72.4% of students at school; 88.9% reportedly heard "gay" used in a negative way often or frequently at school; 40.1% reported being physically harassed at school because of their sexual orientation; and 18.8% were physically assaulted because of their sexual orientation (Kosciw et al., 2010, p. 3).

Peers constantly taunted Alex, a tenth grader. "You're gay, you're a faggot, go play with the girls" were words hurled at him throughout the day. Everyone heard but did nothing—not teachers, not classmates, not friends. Alex attempted suicide at the end of the year. He told his mom he just couldn't take it anymore. The pain caused by ridicule can produce vulnerability, low self-esteem, and hopelessness. The Massachusetts Youth Risk Survey (MDE, 2009) states that lesbian, gay, and bisexual youth are up to four times more likely to attempt suicide than their heterosexual peers. This suicide ideation can decrease with increased social support for LGBTQ teens and the awareness of the abusive quality of words that carry hateful and derogatory connotations.

The following ideas suggest what school systems can do. Schools can

- not assume heterosexuality in students, faculty, and friends;
- use the words "lesbian and gay" in a positive manner during everyday conversation;
- teach methods to stop homophobic harassment of students and faculty;
- educate athletic staff and students to reduce bias often found in locker rooms and gyms;
- be sure dances, proms, and social events are inclusive of the entire student population;
- collaborate with staff to create a united front to address diversity and combat all forms of prejudice and oppression;
- recognize the role of peer allies in helping to create a change in school climate;
- begin Gay/Straight Alliance (GSA) groups to dialogue about LGBTQ issues;
- establish a "safe zone," with a familiar sticker on the door of a guidance counselor, school nurse, coach, or administrator, signifying to all students that this is an empathetic, supportive, safe person to speak with;
- provide a place to display written information and brochures detailing support groups, the school policy, and implications on sexual harassment, legislation, and community activities for the LGBTQ community;
- participate in No Name Calling Week in schools, a campaign to stop verbal abuse sponsored by GLSEN (Gay, Lesbian, Straight Educational Network). Figure 10.8 was a prizewinner entitled "Junky Words." The artist clearly illustrates that hurtful words, including "gay," should be thrown away (Goldman, 2008, p. 181);

Figure 10.8. No Name Calling Contest Winner.

- provide resources for LGBTQ students, such as COLAGE (Children of Lesbians And Gays), GLSEN: Gay, Lesbian and Straight Education Network, and the Family Pride Coalition (Goldman, 2008, pp. 189–190).

School personnel can join with students and parents as a like-minded community determined to change the prejudice and bias that remains in school climates. This goal can be accomplished by transforming cultural indoctrination and societal stereotyping into a paradigm of equality for every student, regardless of sexual orientation or gender identity, with all the rights and privileges that accompany that freedom.

HOMELESS CHILDREN

Homelessness can produce a condition that is detrimental to the healthy development of children and create stressors and continuing losses for them in school as well as with family. The following statistics give an overview of negative outcomes due to poverty, poor nutrition, lack of shelter, and violence. One in 45 children experience homelessness in America each year—over 1.5 million children. Children experiencing homelessness

- Are sick four times more often than other children;
- Go hungry at twice the rate of other children;
- Have high rates of obesity due to nutritional deficiencies;
- Have three times the rate of emotional and behavioral problems as non-homeless children;
- By age 12, some 83% had been exposed to a least one serious violent event;
- Are four times more likely to show delayed development;
- Are twice as likely to have learning disabilities as non-homeless children (National Center on Family Homelessness, 2010).

170 / CHILDREN, ADOLESCENTS, AND DEATH

Carlos was age 16 when his father was deported, labeled "illegal" by the system. He was destitute. Instantly he had no parent, lost his home, was brought to live with a distant relative, and changed from his home school. Angry and rebellious, he left his aunt's home, sometimes living with friends and sometimes living on the streets. Figure 10.9 depicts the sentiments of many youth in this situation, stating, "No human being is illegal" (Goldman, 2014, p. 132).

McCoy-Roth, Mackintosh, and Murphey (2012) report the impact of homelessness on young children and practices and guidelines crucial to educational responsibility. These authors emphasize that homelessness has increased in this century, producing more homeless shelters, yet many families are not using these programs. They explain that the "Lack of regular, stable housing, and the resulting transitions, can negatively affect children's development, including their physical, social-emotional, and cognitive development (p. 2).

Particularly noteworthy for school systems is the idea that "homeless children may be at greater risk for social-emotional and behavior problems in schools, as well, especially when they lack certain abilities (e.g., focusing attention, self-control) associated with academic achievement" (McCoy-Roth et al., 2012, p. 3) Thus, early school experience for homeless children can be beneficial in providing stability and routines that are otherwise nonexistent.

The following guidelines, from *Child Trends*, can help enhance the environment for learning by creating a broader definition of homelessness and greater access to federal funds. Adequate mental health supports, reliable transportation, and play-based centers for homeless children can improve emotional and physical well-being.

1. Childcare and preschool programs should consider prioritizing homeless children during enrollment, similar to the way Head Start does.
2. Reduce barriers to enrolling young homeless children in early learning programs.
3. Improve coordination of programs serving young homeless children.

Figure 10.9. Teen Drawing about Deportation.

4. Transitional housing programs, including shelters, should provide services that support the physical and social-emotional needs of young homeless children.
5. Support homeless children's participation in early childhood programs by providing transportation to programs or by providing services in easily accessible locations (McCoy-Roth et al., 2012, pp. 5–7).

CONCLUSION

We are *powerless* to control the losses and catastrophic events our children may need to face. But by honoring their inner wisdom, providing mentorship, and creating safe havens for expression, we can *empower* them to become more capable and more caring human beings. (Goldman, 2005a, p. 74)

What we can mention, we can manage. This idea is a useful paradigm for educators to understand when formulating a safe environment for the grieving child. If professionals in the school system can acknowledge and express thoughts and feelings involving grief and loss, they can serve as role models for the ever-increasing population of students experiencing traumatic loss.

Today's children face a kaleidoscope of grief and loss issues ranging from school shootings, terrorism, and hurricanes to a parent's deportation, homelessness, or imprisonment. Girls and boys are bombarded daily with graphic images of violence and sexuality. They are threatened by bullying at school and by cyberbullying on their computers. Educators must create guidelines to support children through their grief journey, protect them in school during vulnerable times, and make their classroom an oasis of protection to explore life issues with support and guidance.

Educators can provide grief vocabulary, resources, crisis and educational interventions, preventions, and "postventions" in order to create an oasis of safety for bereaved children within the school system. By opening communication surrounding loss and grief issues, caring adults can build a bridge between the world of fear, isolation, and loneliness to the world of truth, compassion, and dignity for the grieving child.

Our hope is to create resilient girls and boys that meet the challenges of modern life. These difficulties assuredly will include stress and anxiety as they cope with arduous situations. Although events may be disturbing, we can encourage young people to ultimately "feel they are surmountable. Building our children's capacities to positively endure, adapt, and overcome life adversities with optimism is our ultimate goal" (Goldman, 2005b, p. 273).

REFERENCES

Dinkes, R., Cataldi, E. F., Lin-Kelly, W., & Snyder, T. D. (2007, December). Indicators of school crime and safety: 2007. *Bureau of Justice Statistics*. Retrieved from https://nces.ed.gov/pubs2008/2008021a.pdf

Goldman, L. (2001). *Breaking the silence: A guide to help children with complicated grief* (2nd ed.). Taylor & Francis.

Goldman, L. (2005a). *Children also grieve*. London, UK: Kingsley.
Goldman, L. (2005b). *Raising our children to be resilient: A guide to help children with traumatic grief*. New York, NY: Taylor & Francis.
Goldman, L. (2005c, Fall/Winter). The bullying epidemic. *Healing Magazine*, 12–15.
Goldman, L. (2008). *Coming out, coming in: Nurturing the well being and inclusion of gay youth in mainstream society*. New York, NY: Taylor & Francis.
Goldman, L. (2009). *Great answers to difficult questions about death: What children need to know*. London, UK: Kingsley.
Goldman, L. (2012). Helping the grieving child in the schools. *Healing Magazine*, 26–29.
Goldman, L. (2014). *Life and loss: A guide to help grieving children* (3rd ed.). New York, NY: Taylor & Francis.
Hinduja, S., & Patchin, J. (2010). Bullying, cyberbullying, and suicide. *Archives of Suicide Research, 14,* 206–221.
Kosciw, J. G., Greytak, E. A., Diaz, E. M., & Bartkiewicz, M. J. (2010). 2009 National School Climate Survey. *GLSEN*. Retrieved from http://www.google.com/url?url=http://www.glsen.org/download/file/NDIyMw%3D%3D&rct=j&frm=1&q=&esrc=s&sa=U&ved=0CBQQFjAAahUKEwiUqM6xss7GAhVC04AKHekbAis&usg=AFQjCNEctXZPXZq3nkochrRqWCF7cODVGA
Massachusetts Department of Education (MDE). (2009). Massachusetts Youth Risk Behavior Survey. *Mass.gov*. Retrieved from http://www.doe.mass.edu/cnp/hprograms/yrbs/
McCoy-Roth, M., Mackintosh, B., & Murphey, D. (2012, February). When the bough breaks: The effects of homelessness on young children. *Child Trends: Early Childhood Highlights, 3*(1), 1–11. Retrieved March 24, 2014, from http://www.childtrends.org/wp-content/uploads/2012/02/2012-08EffectHomelessnessChildren.pdf
National Center on Family Homelessness. (2010). *Children*. AIR: American Institutes for Research. Retrieved March 24, 2014, from http://www.familyhomelessness.org/children.php?p=ts
Ryan, C., Huebner, D., Diaz, R. M., & Sanchez, J. (2009). Family rejection as a predictor of negative health outcomes in White and Latino lesbian, gay and bisexual young adults. *Pediatrics, 123*(1), 346–352.
Vossekull, B., Fein, R., Reddy, M., Borum, R., & Modzeleski, W. (2002). *The final report and findings of the Safe School Initiative: Implications for the prevention of school attacks in the United States* (pp. 1–54). Washington, DC: United States Secret Service and United States Department of Education.

CHAPTER 11
A School Counselor's Role in Bereavement Counseling

Arthur McCann

PERSONAL REFLECTIONS

The death of a student is something you never forget—over my nearly 40 years of work as teacher, a school counselor, and Director of Guidance, one of the most challenging experiences to deal with personally and professionally is the death of a student. The closer the relationship, the more profound the loss. As surprising as it may seem, by the end of high school, as many as 40% of adolescents have experienced the loss of a peer and 90% the loss of a family member (Gurwitch & Schonfeld, 2011). There are so many constituencies in need of the school counselor's attention in the immediate aftermath of the death of a student that it can be difficult to know what to do first and where to turn for direction. Even if one has a religion or belief system to which one is committed, it is very hard not to become rattled by the loss of a child. The apparent unfairness and inscrutability of a supreme being who would allow such an occurrence can shake one's beliefs to the core. Consequently, the school counselor is in the unenviable position of needing to acknowledge his or her own reaction to the loss and process it in order to assist students and colleagues with the grief process, often with very little lead time. It should be acknowledged that there may be times when the school counselor is so personally grief stricken (because of the closeness of the relationship and/or the triggering of the memory of past losses) that he/she is unable to assist others with the grieving process. Under such circumstances it is arguably more prudent for such school counselors to not actively engage in grief counseling with others when they may first need to do so for themselves. There may be roles other than grief counselor that such a person can play in the healing process that would be generally helpful to the family and/or school community. I clearly remember a number of students who died while I was a counselor at their school. (Their names have been changed to protect their privacy and that of their families.)

- **Louis** died of leukemia in his junior year at Holy Cross High School. A colleague and I visited him in the hospital. While we engaged him in conversation about school, he went into a most humorous imitation of his English teacher, Bro. Karl, who had a distinctive manner of speaking.
- **Matthew** was a model student. In addition to being a strong student academically, he was very engaged in many extracurricular activities including peer counseling. He died in a car accident. A memorial scholarship was set up in his memory.
- **Lori** died from "huffing"(inhaling the contents of an aerosol can). North High School was her "home" school, even though she was placed out of district in a special school at the time of her death, because her needs could not be met in a traditional high school setting. The school community was so moved by her death that it did a variety of things to support her family, including taking up a collection to purchase a casket and cemetery plot. Although North was a public school, when a number of fellow Latino students approached the Chair of our Special Education Department expressing a need to offer prayers in Lori's memory, she immediately received permission from our principal for her and some classmates to go to the local church, where she arranged for a priest to lead the group in a prayer service. I accompanied the group as a school chaperone.
- **David** died from a chronic heart condition. His parents had come from Ghana. They gave us no warning in advance from parents and David's older brother just showed up at the school and began telling people. Our school psychologist and I went to the hospital to support the family and they led us into the hospital room where we saw his body with tubes still attached, left over from the medical staff's efforts to resuscitate him. Students spontaneously began to decorate his locker with memories of his life. When it was discovered that he had been keeping a journal of his reflections upon his life, these were put into a book format and bound and copies made and distributed to those who attended a ceremony and a dedication at the school library in his memory.
- **Vanessa** died of an ill-defined chronic condition, probably heart related. The solemnity of the grieving process and religious prayers at her family's home is something I will never forget. The men wore black arm bands and the older brother was unshaven and clad in a torn shirt. The "rent garment" is a Jewish tradition.
- **Joanne** was a talented and gifted junior/senior peer leader and field hockey player, whose mother was an M.D. and father in the finance industry. She had to wear a babushka to school when her hair fell out during chemotherapy and courageously followed her schedule of rigorous classes, whenever physically possible. I will never forget her sitting in my peer leadership class fully engaged despite all she was going through. In her memory her family donated a gazebo for students to gather in front of school.

THE DEATH OF A FACULTY MEMBER

The death of faculty members presents its own special challenge. This can leave a void that at times is seemingly impossible to fill. Often surviving faculty, depending on their age, health, and experience with loss, can experience an intense preoccupation with their own mortality and/or a resurfacing of unresolved issues surrounding the loss of a significant other. If receptive, such faculty should be offered the opportunity for some short-term grief counseling with an eye toward a possible referral, if and when further counseling may be needed. This is one of the many ways in that school counselors can be a valuable resource to their colleagues. An important caveat of which to be conscious is the critical need for confidentiality and for such counseling to be brief and transitional in nature, leading to a reliable referral when warranted.

Loss of a colleague impacts not only students. Different faculty members, as an artifact of their history in the school, personalities, teaching styles, and degree of involvement with colleagues and supervisors can leave behind them an array of different emotional responses from students and faculty. Some of these can be uncomfortable to express in a public forum such as a classroom or larger gathering. Some faculty have a history of active, positive engagement with so many members of the school community that their death is experienced as a profound loss by many. Whereas the death of others who maintained a much lower profile may not seem to have as significant or widespread an impact on the school community. There are yet others whose style of interacting with students and colleagues was more abrasive and confrontational, whose death may leave students and colleagues with very mixed emotions. When explaining to a music teacher's class what we knew of their teacher's death and offering an opportunity to ask questions or share their feelings or memories, one student pointed out how the deceased teacher could, at times, say some rather hurtful things to his students. The counselor's response was validating to the student, acknowledging that one's death does not make us eligible for sainthood and that it is OK. It is normal to remember both the negative and the positive things about people after they die.

On the other hand, when a very highly esteemed Social Studies teacher passed away years later, there was such a compelling need felt in the school community to acknowledge her contributions that students and faculty organized a committee that planned a touching tribute held on a weekend, and her husband and children attended. In the immediate aftermath of this faculty member's death, when asked to address the faculty at an emergency meeting before school on the morning after we had received the sad news, I was reminded of the importance of never making a public statement comparing the impact of the loss of one faculty member to the impact of the loss of another, even when confident about the accuracy of the statement. Doing so can unnecessarily detract from the effectiveness of other suggestions to faculty by inadvertently upsetting colleagues who either felt close to the colleague in question or felt a need to be a champion of his/her memory.

There have also been times when a teacher played such an integral role in a department, or was so well thought of by students who used her services, that the department felt a natural desire to have a portion of their suite devoted to a grieving space during the first day after her death. Our Pupil Personnel Team (PPT) made sure there was always a member available on-site every period to help in any way needed.

Sometimes a group will find symbols that immediately remind them of the recently deceased faculty member to be a source of consolation. When checking on how the girl's field hockey team was doing as they were gathered together in a library conference room, an "unofficial assistant coach," who also happened to be a school counselor, indicated that the girls wanted to get the letter "G" to add to their uniforms to remind them of their beloved "Coach G." In this case, my role was to contact a colleague who had a side business manufacturing team uniforms to see if he could get a sufficient supply of letters for the girls' uniforms. Under the rubric of recognizing that often people feel a need to do something tangible to help out in times of grief, it became apparent that all they wanted me to do was to make the contact and that others would take care of picking up the letters and helping the girls get them sewn onto their uniforms. It is important to also know when to back away and let others take charge. That is important because it is something that is not always easy for us as helpers to do.

Deaths of Multiple Colleagues

The deaths of multiple colleagues in a relatively short period of time can be a disconcerting experience. It can rattle even the most emotionally balanced and stable of educators. After losing several colleagues in a row in a relatively short period of time, it is difficult not develop a visceral, almost primitive, response of worrying "Who will be next?" or "Is this place cursed?"

Such a reaction can come even from a loss that does not involve death. I have witnessed such an experience in a school where the principal retired rather abruptly in the middle of the year. It became critical that the members of the school community, students and faculty alike, receive reassurance that they would be taken care of. Consequently, while an extensive search for a new principal was initiated as expeditiously as possible, the superintendent, a highly respected dean among secondary educators in the region, took over as principal during the school day and tended to his other responsibilities later in the day. His daily presence in the school, symbolized by the playing of music over the PA from his arrival at 7:00 a.m. until first period at 8:00 a.m., fostered a calming and reassuring atmosphere that was helpful to students and faculty alike. In the search for a new principal, it became apparent that the school community needed a dynamic and personable leader who could help heal the wounds and present warm reassurance in the aftermath of loss and feelings of abandonment.

Loss of a Leader

The loss of a leader has some special issues connected to it. One such leader was Mark, the principal of a high school in a suburban school district, who died of lung cancer. Such a loss can prove unsettling for a school community. At an assembly in which the superintendent addressed student concerns about the loss of their principal, he had to reassure them that his death from lung cancer was in no way connected to the recently identified asbestos that was part of the school's infrastructure, as was the case in many other school buildings of similar vintage. In fact, the principal had been a smoker for decades, a habit he had been working hard to overcome in the years immediately preceding his death. Expressing concerns that their school might be unsafe was perhaps also a way of expressing their fears of going forward without the support of their principal who had been a kind and compassionate leader and even a father figure for some. In offering a sign of continuity of leadership an assistant principal was appointed as the interim principal until a comprehensive search could be conducted. In the meantime to address the concerns of students and faculty, after a thorough assessment an extensive asbestos abatement period was planned for the following summer.

THE IMPORTANCE OF HAVING A CRISIS PLAN

What we found most helpful over the years was to have a crisis plan of action that the entire Pupil Personnel Team (PPT)/Crisis Team (consisting of administrators, school counselors, school psychologists, and social workers) was trained for and prepared to implement immediately. Often this plan would be fine-tuned at a meeting called as soon as feasible after the news of a death in the school community was received. Frequently this news was received after school hours by the principal who would call the other administrators and the head of the Crisis Team. My responsibility as head of the Crisis Team would be to call everyone, to share the information that was known at that time (which often was incomplete), and ask them to attend a meeting before school the next morning in the principal's office to receive further information and refine our plan of action to meet the unique needs of the situation.

Typically, in the case of the death of a student, all of the student's teachers would be invited to this meeting as well so that they could be briefed on the latest information and share their ideas with the Crisis Team regarding such areas as identifying which other students would be likely to be most profoundly impacted by the student's death. Typically this would include friends, teammates, fellow club members, and such. Unless there was a reason not to, such as in the case of the loss of a faculty member, a grieving area was usually established in an all-purpose room that was about the size of two classrooms and permitted flexible seating. Usually, chairs would be placed in small circles and it was insured that there was an ample supply of water and tissues available. I would set up a schedule for the day so that the room was always staffed by a Crisis Team member who was comfortable helping students and faculty express their grief and share their memories of the deceased. Often there would be a need for more than one Crisis Team member to be present, especially during the early periods when the news was fresh and during the lunch periods when more students were free to drop in.

After the loss of a student or teacher, throughout the course of the day, a Crisis Team member would visit each of the classes in that person's schedule to provide an opportunity for students to receive clear and accurate information within the scope of what the next of kin was comfortable with us sharing. Opportunity would also be provided for sharing of memories about the person. Information would be shared about the grieving process as well as the opportunity to drop by the grieving room or to meet with their school counselor or another Crisis Team member privately, if they were more comfortable with that.

In the case of the loss of a teacher, some colleagues needed some private time in their department area to grieve with colleagues, especially if the news was a shock to them. Other times, they actively invited faculty from other departments and students to drop by throughout the day. In either case, the PPT always offered to have a member available to be of support, and usually our presence was most welcome.

A general trend that we noticed is that as the school day progressed, it was very important that we had one or more PPT members circulate throughout the school building to ascertain whether some spontaneous grief sites sprang up that needed our attention. When they did, we always offered to be of assistance and through our presence would help in any way we could. Another trend that often occurred was that, as we entered the latter periods of the school day, fewer students and faculty came to grieving areas and fewer questions were asked or memories shared during classroom presentations. It appeared as though the school community had reached a saturation point and just needed to quietly absorb and process what had transpired throughout the day.

Debriefing at the end of the day and planning for the future can be a critical part of the crisis plan for many reasons:

- Often it is the first time for the Team and the students' teachers or teachers' colleagues to fully process how things went throughout the day.
- There is a need to identify members of the school community (students and teachers) who may need individual outreach and follow-up from members of the Crisis Team. The names of students who appeared so distressed that their parents needed to be called (some of whom may have gone home early) should also be shared at this time.
- Plan for the next day and the near future—setting up a large book in which students and faculty may share their memories of the deceased, which would in turn be presented to the next of kin at an appropriate time, creating a committee that could plan some memorial activity, sharing information about funeral services, arranging for class coverage, and dividing follow-up responsibilities, planning for a Crisis Team member or another faculty member who was especially close to the family to become the liaison between the family of the deceased and the school to coordinate important follow up activities.
- Taking a page from Critical Incident Stress Debriefing, this is also a time for the members of the Crisis Team to share how they personally are coping with the loss as well as the stress of assisting other members of the school community with the grieving process. Members can also be encouraged to share strategies that help them cope with the stress of such a day. The crisis team leader needs to be especially vigilant about and attentive to a team member who manifests signs of stress and follow up appropriately.

HOW TO LEAD A CRISIS TEAM EFFECTIVELY

Lead by example, be able to step back and take in the big picture. One of the challenges that a leader of the Crisis Team faces in helping the school community in its time of loss is to continually assess where his/her own skills and those of fellow team members can be most effectively utilized. At times, a survey of the school building will reveal that a substantial group of students and/or faculty are gathering and grieving in a completely unexpected location. In such circumstances, it is important to redeploy resources and send a grief counselor to where they are needed, which is not always the designated area. Ideally, the Crisis Team members who are providing grief counseling should be those already assigned to the school and those who are familiar to students. These are usually the personnel with whom students are most comfortable sharing in times of crisis and bereavement. However, it is recognized that, at times, because the usual PPT members are either immobilized or otherwise unavailable, or the crisis is of such a profound and/or traumatic nature, such as the loss of multiple lives simultaneously, that it is necessary to bring in grief counselors from outside the building.

PROVIDING SUPPORT

Support Groups for Students Dealing With the Loss of a Parent

When it becomes evident that the school community contains enough students of similar developmental level who have experienced the recent loss of a parent, offering an ongoing support group can go a long way toward helping students with the grieving process. Hearing that other students have had similar feelings and experiences in dealing with the loss of a parent can be a source of reassurance and support. Even quieter students, less likely to open up in a group, can vicariously benefit from hearing others share their feeling and experiences. Although publicizing the death of a student's parent on a broad-scale basis would usually be inappropriate, offering the student, with the permission of the surviving parent, the opportunity to participate in a support group could be construed as a positive attempt to acknowledge the importance of this event in the student's life while also facilitating the healing process.

Support Groups for Students Dealing With Their Parents' Divorce

Although seen by some as not as profound as the death of a parent, most students experience the divorce of their parents as a very real loss of what they once had as an intact family. Because approximately 50% of marriages end in divorce, the provision of support groups to students may have to be limited, either to those who have experienced this loss very recently, and/or those whose behavior or academic performance appear to have been negatively affected by the experience. The potential benefits are similar to those who participate in a bereavement support group. The experience of learning they are not alone in their observations and feelings about the dissolution of their parents' marriage can be very reassuring and comforting. The opportunity to express feelings that they might otherwise not and receive validation for same can be a source of both relief and empowerment.

Providing Death Education Classes

According to Stevenson and Powers (1987) in a paper entitled, "How to Handle Death in the School: Ways to Help Grieving Students," another viable way in which school counselors and properly trained teachers can prepare students to cope with loss in their lives is to include a course on death education in the Secondary School Curriculum. The benefits of same include, but are not limited to

> preparation for coping with future losses, improved communication, increased knowledge and academic skills, lessening of death related anxiety and fear, greater feeling of personal control of life, life is felt to be more precious, greater appreciation of cultural diversity, and possible therapeutic effects. (pp. 6–11)

COUNSELOR SELF-CARE

A tendency that many helpers have, especially in time of crisis, is to consume all our available energy in helping others to the point at which we forget to take care of ourselves. The more significant or comprehensive the trauma that we are addressing, the more likely we can become susceptible to this trap. The counselor has a responsibility to self and clients to prevent compassion fatigue by tending to our own physical and emotional needs.

A condition which must be addressed by counselors is *Compassion Fatigue*, also known as secondary traumatic stress, nearly identical to PTSD, vicarious traumatization. This is similar to emotional contagion, "defined as an affective process in which an individual observing another person experiences emotional responses parallel to that person's actual or anticipated emotions" (Figley, 2002, p. 2). Perhaps the best way to prevent Compassion Fatigue is to develop *Compassion Satisfaction*, which Stamm (2002) has identified as a protective factor, a positive side of compassion that counterbalances the negative. She developed a Compassion Satisfaction and Fatigue (CSF) Test to help estimate risk of burnout and compassion fatigue.

To help be aware of and to prevent Compassion Fatigue, a counselor can

- Develop a capacity for humor,
- Gain a sense of achievement and satisfaction from setting achievable work standards,
- Acquire adequate rest and relaxation,
- Develop and regularly use an array of stress reduction methods,
- "Let go" of work,
- Apply critical incident stress debriefings and stress management (CISD/M) plans and actions as needed when crises arise. (Figley, 2002)

RECOMMENDATIONS FROM THE LITERATURE

The following are some recommendations from the professional literature and other valued resources designed to assist the school counselor in helping the school community grieve.

After reflecting on the steps we developed for our Crisis Team to follow in the aftermath of the death of a student or faculty member, I took the opportunity to turn once again to the classic, *What Will We Do? Preparing a School Community to Cope With Crises*, edited by Robert G. Stevenson (2002) to see how our practices compared to those recommended. It was reassuring to note in the chapter entitled, "School Based Grief Crisis Management Programs" by David K. Meagher, that over time we had developed a plan that covered the critical elements, including

- "making the facts of the even known to all appropriate persons . . .
- controlling the spread of rumors about the cause of death . . .
- planning for the inclusion of students in scheduled mourning rituals . . .
- providing grief support services to all members of the community . . .
- referring to non-school services when necessary and appropriate . . .
- assessing the effectiveness of the process . . . and revising where necessary . . .
- scheduling a follow-up assessment of needs." (pp. 50–51)

Although we were fortunate to have an excellent Crisis Team of professionals that were able to go into action at very short notice and were effective at assisting students and colleagues, alike in times of trauma, we probably did not give sufficient attention to the possible role that peer helpers could have played in this process as well. In a chapter entitled, "Helping Peers to Help Themselves: The Role of Peer Support in Times of Crisis," Stevenson (2002) persuasively articulates a vital role that properly trained "natural helpers" and "student leaders" can play as part of the school's response in a time of crisis. The reason why I am concerned that we did not think of this role is because we had such a vibrant peer leadership program in our school that they, in fact, ran our advisory groups on the freshman and sophomore levels under the supervision of faculty advisors and the ongoing training from our school counselors, social workers, and health education teachers. In light of the fact that students often first share concerns with peers before becoming comfortable enough to do so with adults, these trained peer leaders truly could have played a vital role in our crisis plan as well. This is certainly a possible role to keep in mind for schools that already have a cadre of trained peer helpers.

The School Counselor's Book of Lists, edited by Blum and Davis (2010), contains some excellent suggestions for helping both teachers and students deal with the grieving process. The following is a list of suggested interventions for working with students:

- Be proactive in providing help.
- Encourage student to draw support from friends and family.
- Encourage self-care (exercise, rest, and healthy diet).
- Listen without judging.

- Encourage talking about loss, while being mindful of the stages of grief (denial or shock, fear, anger, guilt, depression or sadness, and acceptance).
- Invite sharing of memories.
- Encourage resumption of normal activities. (List 7.18)

Another valuable resource provided by Blum and Davis (2010) clarifies our role in helping teachers after the death of a student:

- When speaking with bereaved parents, be supportive; only give suggestions when requested, ask what they would like shared with other students.
- Offer to visit class to tell the students what happened.
- Prepare the teacher (or offer to collaborate) to tell classmates.
- Match information with the students' developmental ability to understand.
- Communicate that life is precious and precarious.
- If death is by suicide, do not glorify and do not try to explain why it happened.
- Be truthful, honest, and accepting.
- Coordinate follow-up steps with teacher and administrator.
- Inform the faculty in the way the parent(s) or guardian(s) desires (if possible).
- Pay special attention to siblings and special friends of the deceased child. (List 7.20)

An edition of *School Counselor* (2011) entitled "Crisis in the Schools: Natural Disasters, Terrorism, Violence and Death—Help Students Prepare, Adjust and Move On" contained five articles that identify practical and worthwhile steps that school counselors can take to help in times of crisis. The following suggestions from Gurwitch and Schonfeld (2011) in this edition help identify ways we, as school counselors, can support students in times of trauma:

- Initiate the conversation
- Validate feelings and experiences
- Answer questions and correct misinformation
- Educate students and caregivers about common reactions
- Help students identify positive coping strategies
- Identify triggers or reminders
- Encourage return to extracurricular activities
- Encourage activities that promote help and healing
- Maintain regular communication with teachers and caregivers
- Be available for the immediate, short-term, and long-term counseling.

The National Center for School Crisis & Bereavement has a website hosted by St. Christopher's Hospital for Children in Philadelphia, Pennsylvania (http://www.stchristophershospital.com/pediatric-specialties-programs/specialties/693), which has a substantial array of resources that will walk even the most inexperienced school counselor through a step-by-step process for developing a well-trained Crisis Team to implement a comprehensive and effective crisis plan. In addition to traditional print resources for faculty, there are booklets for parents as well a comprehensive teacher-training module that contains the presenters' notes. There is also a website, www.schoolcrisiscenter.org, created by Scholastic through funds from the New York Life Foundation on how schools can support grieving students. The resources available on this website include the following:

- Guidelines for Responding to the Death of a Student or School Staff
- Guidelines for Schools Responding to Death by Suicide
- A Teacher Training Module
- Helping Grieving Students—A Webcast
- Guidelines for Parents and Schools for the Anniversary of Sept. 11
- Helping Schools Respond to Crisis
- Parent Guides
- Programs and Services
- Psychological First Aid

LOSS OF A STUDENT THROUGH SUICIDE

If personally dealing with and helping the school community heal in the aftermath of a student death by natural causes, such as illness or accident, is difficult, then helping oneself and the school community cope with the loss of a student to suicide can become an extraordinary challenge. However, based on research and experience, there are some very specific suggestions of "do's and don'ts" and sample materials from the American Foundation for Suicide Prevention (AFSP) and the Suicide Prevention Resource Center (SPRC), considered to be two of the leading organizations in the country for suicide prevention. These suggestions can be helpful to school counselors in their efforts in both suicide prevention and in facilitating healing in the aftermath of a suicide. These are contained in a 48-page manual available online, entitled, *After Suicide: A Toolkit for Schools* (2011), available from AFSP and SPRC. This manual seems to more than adequately address the earlier concerns of Ryerson and Kalafat in their chapter entitled, "The Crisis of Youth Suicide" in *What Will We Do? Preparing the School Community to Cope with Crisis* (2002), that there were "no universally accepted guidelines for managing this public problem [suicide]." In this classic reference, the authors capture well the emotional response of the school community to the loss of a student or faculty member through suicide, identifying the emotions of "grief, remorse, guilt and shame" (Ryerson & Kalafat, 2002) in both students and faculty as ones that are frequently experienced in the aftermath of suicide.

Some of the critical recommendations from AFSP and SPRC to school counselors include the following: It is important to strive to treat all deaths, including suicide, in the same way. Because adolescents are vulnerable to the risk of "suicide contagion," we should not do anything that could potentially "simplify, glamorize or romanticize the student and his or her death" (AFSP/SPRC, 2011, p. 8). It is also appropriate to emphasize to students that those who commit suicide are struggling with depression and anxiety. Of course, it is also crucial to let students know that help is available to any who may be struggling with anxiety, depression, or suicidal thoughts. Students should be informed of the easiest and most direct way of accessing this help as well. As was mentioned above in preparing for any crisis or emergency, having a crisis response plan in place that can be activated quickly and efficiently is essential. Trying to create one on the fly in the immediate aftermath of a crisis just adds even more stress to an already challenging situation and runs the risk of missing some important elements that should be addressed. A comprehensive program related to suicide should include three critical components: prevention, intervention, and postvention (Ryerson & Kalafat, 2002). It truly seems that in their creation of this manual, AFSP and SPRC (2011) have left no stone unturned in their efforts to prepare school counselors and administrators for anticipating virtually every conceivable issue that might emerge in the aftermath of a student's death by suicide. The recommendations are well grounded in theory and research and are formulated in a clearly organized and pragmatic checklist format. For those relatively new at helping a school community in the aftermath of a crisis such as a student's suicide, this resource even contains sample agendas for meetings and sample statements for various constituencies.

With resources such as *After a Suicide: A Toolkit for Schools* (2011) at our disposal, school counselors can feel a bit more confident as we respond to the challenge of helping the school community heal in the aftermath of such a tragedy as the suicide of a student. For more on the topic of helping children and adolescents cope with loss due to suicide, please see the chapter in this book by Janet S. McCord and Rebecca S. Morse entitled, "Seasons of Love: Measuring a Child's Life after Suicide."

CONCLUDING REMARKS

After reflecting on what I have shared above about the procedures, practices, and policies we developed for helping the school community in times of crisis, there are some practices that, if incorporated, after being modified to suit the needs of a particular school community, could very likely enhance the effectiveness of a Crisis Team. First, although the introduction of a freestanding course on death education could prove to be very challenging as anything other than an elective that a small percentage of upperclassmen could fit into their schedule, extracting some of the more crucial units and integrating them into the already existing freshman and sophomore Advisory Programs as well as integrating a few of the more challenging units into the existing junior year health education curriculum could better prepare students for dealing with the inevitability of experiencing the death of someone they know before they graduate high school.

Second, time should be set aside during each academic year, even those years when the school is not impacted by a crisis, for the Crisis Team to engage in professional development that would improve their currency with the literature regarding best practices for helping the school community in times of crisis. Convening the Crisis Team to review recent crises that occurred in other schools and to learn from strategies that were effectively employed to assist the school community and to discuss their potential applicability would all be very worthwhile activities in which to engage. The literature clearly urges us to plan ahead and prepare during periods of calm for the crisis that will arrive sooner or later. Even schools with reasonably effective crisis plans need to invest time every year to critique and improve them and to upgrade the team members' skills.

Third, the Crisis Team, in turn, can and should update faculty through presentations at faculty meetings and through the media regarding new information about best practices and any consequent changes in the Crisis Plan. Finally, having a Crisis Team and Crisis Plan in place to be truly effective needs to be part of a much more comprehensive plan that all faculty members implement every day of the year; one that cultivates a positive school climate built on mutual respect and trust. When this is in place, the school community is much more likely to respond as well as humanly possible in times of crisis. When it is not, even the best designed plans fail.

Although the school counselor's role and responsibilities have expanded over the years beyond individual meetings with students to include engaging students, parents, and faculty in an array of settings ranging from small group discussions to classroom lessons and auditorium presentations, at the heart of our effectiveness is still our capacity to form relationships with students, parents, and colleagues based on mutual respect and trust. The groundwork that we lay on a daily basis to develop these relationships is what gives us credibility, confidence, and strength when we have to stand in front of a class and tell them that their classmate or teacher just died or to stand in front of an auditorium of one hundred colleagues at 7:00 a.m. and give them suggestions regarding how to help their students grieve when they receive news of a death in their school community. Although these responsibilities may weigh heavily on our shoulders at times, we embrace them because this is our mission in life.

REFERENCES

American Foundation for Suicide Prevention and Suicide Prevention Resource Center (AFSP/SPRC). (2011). *After a suicide: A toolkit for schools*. Newton, MA: Education Development Center.

Blum, D. J., & Davis, T. E. (2010). *The school counselor's book of lists* (2nd ed.). San Francisco, CA: Jossey-Bass.

Figley, C. R. (Ed.). (2002). *Treating compassion fatigue*. New York, NY: Brunner-Routledge.

Gurwitch, R. H., & Schonfeld, D. J. (2011, September/October). Support traumatized students: Help students learn to address and deal with traumatic incidents or loss with a few key actions. *School Counselor, 49*(1). 10–13.

Ryerson, D., & Kalafat, J. (2002). The crisis of youth suicide. In R. G. Stevenson (Ed.), *What will we do? Preparing the school community to cope with crises* (2nd ed.). Amityville, NY: Baywood.

School Counselor. (2011, September/October). *Crisis in the schools: Natural disasters, terrorism, violence and death—Help students prepare, adjust and move on.*

Stamm, B. H. (2002). Measuring compassion satisfaction as well as fatigue: Developmental history of the compassion satisfaction and fatigue test. In C. R. Figley (Ed.), *Treating compassion fatigue*. (pp. 107–122). New York, NY: Brunner-Routledge.

Stevenson, R. G. (Ed.). (2002). *What will we do? Preparing the school community to cope with crises* (2nd ed.). Amityville, NY: Baywood.

Stevenson, R. G., & Cox, G. (Eds.). (2007). *Perspectives on violence and violent death.* Amityville, NY: Baywood.

Stevenson, R. G., & Powers, H. (1987, May). How to handle death in the school: Ways to help grieving students. *Education Digest, 2*(9).

SECTION 3

Death and the Family

This section contains chapters that can help to answer the following questions:
- Why do people kill themselves?
- How can a child's life be "measured" after they have experienced a loved one's suicide?
- How can we explain a suicide death to a child/teen?
- What is grief like after suicide?
- What can help adolescents who may be at higher risk of suicide?
- What specific factors must be examined when helping grieving urban, minority children?
- What techniques have been helpful for those working with grieving Latino children?
- In what ways may the grief of African American children and adolescents differ from other groups?
- What can grandparents do to help grandchildren deal with grief and with the approaching death of the grandparents themselves?
- What are the legacies that a grandparent can leave to a grandchild that may help with the child's grief?
- What protective measures should parents and counselors take to ensure that children and adolescents can handle loss?
- How honest should parents and counselors be when talking to children and adolescents about death?
- What is the psychological impact of the death of a child on the bereaved parents?
- What is the role of benefit-finding and sense making in predicting adaptation to bereavement?
- What evidence-based guidelines and procedures inform grief therapy for bereaved parents?

CHAPTER 12
Seasons of Love: Measuring a Child's Life After Suicide

Janet S. McCord and Rebecca S. Morse

The Broadway musical *Rent* opens with the cast singing "Seasons of Love," asking how we measure a loved one's life (Larson, 1996). Collins, one of the characters, asks if a life is measured "in truths that she learned, or in times that he cried, in bridges he burned or the way that she died," (Larson, 2008). Loosely based on Giacomo Puccini's *La Bohème*, the Tony Award- and Pulitzer Prize-winning musical examines the lives of young artists struggling to survive and create in New York City's East Village. It peers closely at what is real about life and what is sometimes tragic about struggle, pain, suffering, and death. Finally, the song concludes with the thought that maybe one measures a life in terms of love. For many adults who are bereaved after suicide, a lifetime is measured in tears also in guilt, fear, shame, and stigma. For children bereaved after suicide, these same issues permeate every stage of life and can have far-reaching effects on psychosocial development.

In one of the most comprehensive literature reviews on the impact of suicide on children and adolescents, Cerel and Aldrich (2011) summarize research indicating that between 7,000 and 12,000 children are parentally bereaved due to suicide each year (Small & Small, 1984), and that approximately 60,000 youth under age 18 are bereaved every year because of the suicide of a relative (Pfeffer, Martins, Mann, & Sunkenberg, 1997). They go on to cite Pfeffer, Karus, Siegel & Jiang (2000) who suggest that the actual number of children bereaved annually because of the suicide of a parent is most likely between 10,000 and 20,000, much higher than Small and Small (1984) suggest. This number may seem relatively small compared to the estimated 2.5 million youth under age 18 who will experience the death of a parent each year (Howarth, 2011), yet the number is significant and will probably increase in tandem with the number of suicides among active duty military and veterans (Kemp & Bossarte, 2012).

Children and teens bereaved after death by suicide may have numerous and/or complex questions. Obviously, there may be more questions or concerns, depending on the significance of the deceased person to the child, such as a parent, sibling, other family member, friend, or some individual who was influential to that child. Whether or not the child knew him or her is less important than the perceived significance, such as the death of a public icon, that is, a famous actor, athlete, or musician. The questions this chapter seeks to address are those that children or teens might ask after a death by suicide as they strive to understand what happened and seek ways to respond.

Most of the research on children and teens bereaved by suicide tends to focus on the bereavement responses of young people after parental suicide death, but parental suicides are not, regretfully, the only suicides children and teens might experience. Therefore, the focus of this chapter is geared toward bereavement after parental suicide, but bereavement after the suicide death of a sibling, friend, acquaintance, or some other significant person (sports hero, musician, actor, other) will present similar challenges.

WHY DO PEOPLE KILL THEMSELVES?

There are a great many "why" questions following a death by suicide. Even for those who have studied suicide for years, suicide is difficult to understand. Although there are certain commonalities across suicides, every suicide, to some extent, consists of elements that are unique to the individual who has died. The enigmatic nature of suicide has fascinated sociologists, psychologists, practitioners, biologists, and artists alike. Suicide is always set in a social and cultural context, and themes of self-destruction pervade art and literature, sometimes with devastating results. For example, the "Werther Effect" is so named because of the rash of "copycat" suicides inspired by *The Sorrows of Young Werther* (Goethe, 1774) at the time of publication (Schmidtke & Häfner, 1988).

Copycat or "contagion" behaviors are a social media phenomenon that continues to be considered influential, and historically even led to media censorship of death-related material, specifically suicide, in an attempt to curtail its effects (Hegerl, Kohberger, Rummel-Kluge, Gavert, Walden, & Mergl, 2013; Schmidtke & Häfner, 1988). In more recent times, families occasionally bring lawsuits against artists by drawing connections between music and suicides, such as the case brought in 1990 against the heavy metal band Judas Priest and CBS Records by the families of Raymond Belknap and James Vance, who shot themselves in a churchyard after becoming intoxicated, high from marijuana, and listening to Judas Priest's song "Stained Class" (Rohter, 1990). It is important to note, however, that music, art, and literature do not have a causal relationship with suicide; rather, the ideas expressed via media may serve as validation for the feelings of hopelessness and despair that the suicidal individual is experiencing.

In considering the question of why people die by suicide, it is useful to consider historical and contemporary theories about suicide. Berman, Jobes, and Silverman (2006) have suggested that theories about suicide can be grouped under three conceptually based categories: sociological, psychological or social-psychological, and neurobiological. Emile Durkheim was the first suicide theorist in the late

19th century. A sociologist and social psychologist from France, Durkheim viewed suicide as a fact of society and was interested in examining the differences between different societies. Psychoanalytical theories of suicide range from Freud's (2007) perspective of suicide as externally focused hostility turned against the self, to Karl Menninger's (1956) notion that every suicide includes the wish to kill, to be killed, and to die. These theories may have a certain face-validity, but they often neglect environmental or contextual factors that are innate to answering the question of why a person might engage in suicidal behavior.

David Jobes (Berman et al., 2006) theorized that suicidality sometimes falls on a continuum between an intrapsychic orientation (with a focus on internal psychological pain, typically a male) and an interpsychic orientation (with a focus on interpersonally generated pain, typically a female). Thomas Joiner (2007) further theorized that every suicidal behavior requires three interpersonal elements: acquired capacity for lethal self-injury, a perception that one is a burden on others, and a perception of social isolation or lack of connection to a social group in what he calls "thwarted belongingness."

Developmental and family-system theories contribute a great deal to our understanding of child and adolescent responses to suicide, as well as potential for suicidal behaviors. Research suggests that the role of relationships, in particular the quality of attachment within those relationships (as opposed to the number of relationships), are important in understanding the risk for adolescent suicide as well as the protective factors that help mitigate these effects (Agerbo, Nordentoft, & Mortenson, 2002; Borowsky, Ireland, & Resnick, 2001; Evans, Hawton, & Rodham, 2004; Wright, Briggs & Behringer, 2005). A study by Bostik and Everall (2007) demonstrates that adolescents' perceived experiences of quality attachments and relationships were important to overcoming suicidality, suggesting that interpersonal elements are a key factor in suicide for this age group.

As early as 1988, Israel Orbach (1988), based on a careful examination of both clinical experience and research data, argued that "self-destructive tendencies in children, and to some degree in adolescents, are strongly linked to familial processes rather than to personality factors" (p. 7). Orbach further suggests that suicidal children are ambivalent about both life and death, and exhibit four types of attitudes of repulsion and attraction toward life and death that can profoundly influence relative suicidality (p. 209). Attraction to life is influenced by feelings of love and security in interpersonal relationships, whereas repulsion toward life is reflective of the level of painful experiences such as abuse, rejection, and alienation. Attraction to death is characterized by a belief that death is somehow superior to life and that death is a "place" or "mode" of safety and all-embracing love, and in adolescents, this can be related to existential issues (meaning of life) in which death is romanticized. In this theory, attraction to death is a powerfully motivating force for suicide. Conversely, repulsion can act as a protective factor against suicide by perceiving death as irreversible and frightening or as a "place" or "mode" of punishment or eternal solitude (Orbach, 1988).

The link between suicide and suicidality on the one hand and nonlethal self-injury on the other hand is not clear. Some researchers have suggested that adolescents who engage in self-injurious behaviors are at an increased risk for suicide ideation and attempt; however, a recent study found that those who engaged in nonsuicidal self-injury were more likely to experience early depressive symptoms, anxiety, and suicidal ideation than those who actually attempted suicide (Kim et al., 2015).

Behavioral and cognitive theorists have addressed suicide from a learned behavior perspective. Shneidman (1980, 1985) was one of the first to recognize the importance of cognition and suicide in his discussions of cognitive constriction and ambivalence, followed closely by the work of Beck and colleagues (Beck, Steer, Kovacs, & Garrison, 1985; Brown, Jeglic, Henriques, & Beck, 2006; Rush & Beck, 1978). Building on this, Rudd, Joiner and Rajab (2004) have suggested that suicidal individuals can be treated effectively using a cognitive-behavioral model that incorporates multiple variables (behavioral, cognitive, affective, motivational) that help the patient understand the time-limited aspect of suicidal crises and help the suicidal individual understand his or her own unique "triggers," emotional regulation, distress tolerance, interpersonal factors, social reinforcement, self-awareness, and skill acquisition. One of the reasons that cognitive-behavior therapies (CBT) are reported to be effective may be due to the fact that they target these cognitive distortions (Ellis & Ellis, 2006). In one of the few clinical control studies to have explored these distortions, Jager-Hyman, Cunningham, Wenzel, Mattei, Brown, & Beck,(2014) found greater cognitive distortion in those who had attempted suicide than in a psychiatric control group.

Decades of practical experience and research led Shneidman to formulate his theory of "psychache" as the cause of suicide (1995, 1996), which can be viewed conceptually as a multifaceted "cube." Along one axis of the cube is "press," with a second axis termed "perturbation" and a third axis named "psychache" Shneidman's term for psychological pain (Shneidman, 1995). "Press" refers to any pressures that affect an individual's feelings or behaviors. "Perturbation" is the individual's level of "upsetness" or agitation. "Psychache" is the subjective experience of mental suffering. Each axis ranges from level 1 (low) to 5 (high) and meet in a 5-5-5 cubelet, the point at which an individual is most at risk of suicide. According to this theory, suicide is the result of intolerable (for that person) psychological pain or suffering, caused by thwarted or unfulfilled psychological needs. Pain and suffering in the mind combined with sufficient agitation and stress, Shneidman argued, are sufficient to drive suicidal thinking and action in a needful individual. The point of clinical intervention is to get the individual out of the 5-5-5 cubelet.

Building on Shneidman's approach, Jobes (2006) created a phenomenological structural model drawing on multiple theories, starting with psychological suffering and moving toward understanding suicide as a coping mechanism. His Collaborative Assessment and Treatment of Suicidality (CAMS) treatment framework, begins with assessing psychological pain, stress, and agitation, and subsequently introduces additional key concepts: hopelessness (Beck, Steer, Kovacs, & Garrison, 1985), self-hate and the need for escape (Baumeister, 1990), and the behavioral perspective (will the person kill him/herself?). The CAMS approach is a treatment philosophy rather than a new therapy and can be used with any clinical therapeutic approach. Once suicidality has been identified, CAMS begins with the Suicide Status Form

(Jobes, 2006) a multipurpose tool used by the client and clinician at every session to jointly assess suicidality (including suicide risk), create or update a treatment plan, track the ongoing suicide risk, and document clinical outcomes. At the close of every session, the client and clinician together identify five alternative coping mechanisms that can be used by the client if crisis looms, and these are written on a card that fits in the wallet. If the client goes into crisis, his or her responsibility is to try the strategies (part of the safety plan) and if the crisis is not reduced, the client can turn over the card and call the clinician directly. The idea of CAMS is to address the suicidality first and in an overtly collaborative way by identifying and addressing the specific drivers of suicide, enhancing reasons for living, reducing reasons for dying, and motivating the individual to learn new coping skills. Once the suicidality is ameliorated, the clinical treatment plan can shift to address the underlying issues that may have led to the suicidal crisis in the first place.

Valach, Michel, Dey, and Young (2006) and Valach, Michel, Young, and Dey (2006) examine the notion of suicide as a coping mechanism from a slightly different perspective. Their research and clinical experience with those who attempted suicide demonstrates that social processes are prominent in suicidal thinking and that the suicidal act is a joint social process rather than an individual one, since it occurs in a social context. Furthermore, suicide is a goal-directed action. Viewed this way, suicidal processes are similar to other goal-directed processes throughout life and, as such, can be interrupted or circumvented.

Based on the notion of suicide as a goal-directed action, Michel and Gysin-Maillart (2013) developed the Attempted Suicide Short Intervention Program (ASSIP), a four-session clinical intervention used with suicide attempters. An initial videotaped interview offers insight into the suicidal "career" of an individual and fosters a collaborative working relationship between the clinician and client. After completing the videotaped interview, the client and clinician meet a second time and view the video together, stopping at points and allowing the client to fill in the backstory or augment the narrative. During this time, the client and clinician collaboratively identify potential vulnerabilities and stimuli, or "triggers," and discuss the elements that might go into a safety plan. Between the second and third session, the clinician creates a written version of the narrative and prepares a version of the folded personalized emergency card called a ("Leporello," referring to printed material folded into an accordion-pleat style sometimes known as a concertina fold) which fits in the wallet and contains helpful information, including phone numbers and individually targeted strategies for ameliorating a crisis. (The term "Leporello" refers to printed material folded into an accordion-pleat style, also sometimes known as a concertina fold.) During the third session, the written narrative is discussed and the Leporello is examined for accuracy, and any changes are made between the third and fourth meetings. The narrative is viewed by the client and the clinician a third time during the fourth meeting to facilitate safety protocol rehearsal, and the four session intervention is followed by regular outreach contacts (letters) over two years.

Indeed, protocol rehearsal is key in many CBT approaches, as well as in these two promising suicide-specific treatment approaches, as a form of cognitive script-writing and maintenance. A "script" is any rehearsed (in real-life through practice, repetition, or mentally via imagined scenarios) behavioral response in a given situation or context. It affords the individual an opportunity to create, rehearse, and utilize more adaptive behavioral "scripts" when in a vulnerable or stimulating situation. Tools like a crisis card in CAMS or the Leporello used in ASSIP can be helpful reminders of the newly learned adaptive life skills.

It is difficult, if not impossible, to concisely answer the question "Why do people kill themselves" is difficult, if not impossible. Shneidman (1996) said it best:

> Stripped down to its bones, my argument goes like this: In almost every case, suicide is caused by pain, a certain kind of pain—*psychological* pain, which I call *psychache* (*sīk-āk*). Furthermore, this psychache stems from thwarted or distorted psychological needs. In other words, suicide is chiefly a drama in the mind. (p. 4)

He goes on to say that suicide is multifaceted and includes "biological, biochemical, cultural, sociological, interpersonal, intrapsychic, logical, philosophical, conscious, and unconscious elements" (p. 5). In short, no matter the risk factors, social context, or mental health status, people kill themselves because they are in intractable pain and are unable to conceive of life without intolerable suffering.

THE NEXT STEP: WHAT HELPS?

The concept of children and young adults experiencing bereavement and grief due to suicide is hardly novel. What is new is the increased recognition of the needs and challenges these individuals incur after a suicide-related loss. Additionally, we can learn from the experiences of adults who were, as children, parentally bereaved because of suicide. Research indicates that the death of a parent is one of the most traumatic events a child can experience. Statistically, being related to someone who dies by suicide puts one at higher risk for suicidal behavior. The American Association of Suicidology's list of risk factors includes history of suicide in the family, parental history of hospitalization for major psychiatric disorder, and a tolerant/accepting attitude toward suicide. Based on the information thus far presented, the higher risk for suicide might include those "biological, biochemical, cultural, sociological, interpersonal, intrapsychic, logical, philosophical, conscious, and unconscious elements" identified by Shneidman (1996, p. 5), and it could be argued that for the suicide-bereaved child, survival means grappling with the acceptability of suicide as a problem-solving strategy and separating that from the act of the parent.

But is this true? Research on bereavement trajectories for parentally bereaved children due to suicide, compared to nonviolent death, offers mixed results. Brown, Sandler, Jenn-Yun, Xianchen, and Haine (2007) analyzed data from the Family Bereavement Program and found that cause of death is a weak predictor of the need for intervention services and that other variables such as level of functioning, beliefs about self, and family environment were more important. They also found that cause of parental death is not a predictor with respect to risk and protective factors associated with problem outcomes.

The studies by Cerel, Fristad, Weller, and Weller (1999, 2000) offer a very different view. Their analysis of the experiences of 26 suicide-bereaved (SB) children compared to several hundred nonsuicide-bereaved (NSB) children suggests that SB children were more likely to experience anxiety, anger, shame, were more likely to have preexisting behavioral problems, and displayed more behavioral and anxiety symptoms throughout the first two years after the death compared with NSB children (Cerel et al., 1999).

Other researchers suggest that a child's developmental stage at the time of experiencing a loved one's death is an important variable, not only because of the loss impact but because death conceptualization is so closely linked to cognitive development (Nagy, 1948; Koocher, 1973) seminal studies. Children between 6 and 8 years of age understand the finality of death, but full understanding, including the absence of personal culpability for the death, may be elusive (Childers & Wimmer, 1971). They may be anxious and emotional, especially after a parent's traumatic death, and may exhibit symptoms of traumatic stress over time (Christ, 2010).

Grief is a journey and a process of adjusting to life after a significant loss. But suicide as a traumatic loss brings additional circumstances that can make healing more difficult. Children tend to move in and out of grief response, periodically revisiting a loss. Often, grief "work" is done through play instead of words. When the death itself is traumatic, especially if preceded by other traumatic experiences, the trauma can impede the grief process. Thoughts of how the person died or, in the case of some suicides, remembering the earlier trauma of suicide attempts, can lead to frightening images, dreams, and memories. Children may experience trauma if they found the deceased or were present when police or first responders arrived to process the scene. Sometimes the memories are blocked from conscious memory, but the traumatic response is still evident in its aftereffects.

Traumatic reactions in children can be caused or exacerbated by multiple factors. Family or individual psychopathology, prior trauma, lack of support systems, avoidance, lack of opportunities to process the trauma, or isolation can make the situation worse (Schuurman & Decristofaro, 2010). Some individuals may report intermittent episodes of traumatic reactions. These may consist of nightmares to waking events similar to classic posttraumatic stress disorder-type "reliving" (Gilbertson, Orr, Rauch, & Pitman, 2008).

Additionally, older children and young adults may experience survivor's guilt for what they did or didn't do or what they did or didn't feel (authors' unpublished anecdotal experience). For example, a child who grows up with a parent who has repeatedly attempted suicide may feel anger or may distance him or herself as much as possible from the suicidal parent, and when bereaved after that parent's death may experience profound regret, self-recrimination, or magical thinking. Magical thinking includes fantasy, "all or nothing" thoughts that the person has more control over events than he/she actually does—the notion that he/she could have prevented the suicide "if only." One anecdotal example is a woman who thought her father would never have killed himself "if only" she had stayed home on the night he died.

After a suicide, families sometimes struggle with what to tell the children. Wanting to protect children from additional pain and suffering is a natural desire, but wisdom from the field of child bereavement at-large suggests that it is best to answer questions with simple, truthful answers that inform without overwhelming a child with details that were not sought. It is beneficial to avoid euphemisms that children sometimes find confusing, such as "passed on" or "went to Heaven." A simple "died" or even "died by suicide" may suffice, without hiding the fact that the death was self-inflicted.

For example, in the experience of the one of authors, it has been helpful to compare death education for children with that of sex education—keep it brief, honest, and titrated to the child's developmental level. When a 4-year-old asks where babies come from, she isn't asking for details on ovulation and insemination, but rather, how do they get here? A simple answer such as "from inside Mommy's tummy" or "the baby has to live inside. Mommy to keep it warm and safe until it is big enough to come out and play with you" may suffice, whereas that would be an inadequate answer for a 9-year-old on the precipice of adolescence.

A similar construct can apply here: "Daddy was very sad, and his heart was so broken we couldn't fix it, but the pieces of his heart that worked loved you, and he is very sorry that he hurt you when he died" may be perfectly acceptable for a younger child, but would be appallingly inappropriate for an older child who can understand notions of mental pain and suffering and is familiar with suicide. Parents can tell the children that their significant person died because he wanted to end the pain, explaining that he was wrong to end the pain that way but he could not think clearly, his judgment was clouded by the pain, and he made a poor decision (McCord, 2014).

Younger children may wish to be with the person who died and worry that these thoughts are the same as the ones that caused their loved one to die. Parents can explain that these two situations are different and can encourage the child to tell a trusted grown-up if she ever does think about suicide. In fact, parents can help their children to identify an adult at school to whom they can go if they feel anxious or afraid in the future (McCord, 2014). Because suicide is a traumatic death, bereaved children can be at risk of depression and substance-abuse issues. Brent, Melhem, Donohoe, and Walker (2009) demonstrated in their two-year study of 176 children (ages 7–25) that following traumatic and sudden death including suicide, there are many effects of parental bereavement from the time of death through the second year postdeath, in particular depression during the second year. Youth whose parents died by suicide showed the highest risk for subsequent depression and for alcohol and substance abuse, but only a longer-term study would show whether or not those parentally bereaved by suicide actually suffer long-term effects of bereavement compared to other bereaved youth.

Being cognizant that children and teens are at higher risk of suicide themselves after a significant person in their lives has died by suicide, it is important to recognize that some children are afraid that they too will die by suicide. Suicide is an extremely meaningful event in any child's life, and the impact may be seen many years later. It is not unusual for child survivors of parental suicide to fear they will kill themselves when they reach the age of their parent at the time of death (Avrami, 2005; Loy & Boelk, 2013), what Avrami called the Agonizing Question: "I thought that when I will reach her age at suicide—it will happen to me, too," (2005, p. 71). It is important to be supportive of these individuals' feelings and thoughts and not dismiss their concerns, as that may serve to alienate the them and exacerbate any unresolved grief or fear and anxiety they are experiencing.

WHAT FINALLY MAKES THE DIFFERENCE?

Losing a parent to suicide rocks the assumptive world of a child, and at some point, there must be appropriate resolution and reconstruction of that internal perspective in order to adapt to the loss and heal. A narrative approach to healing after suicide the Tripartite Model of Suicide Bereavement (Sands, Jordan, & Neimeyer, 2011), focuses on key themes that emerge in bereavement after suicide: the relationship of the survivor with the deceased, the self, and the community. This approach is a "process of adaptation in recursive meaning-making processes concerned with the intentional nature of suicide, reconstruction of the death story, and repositioning of the suicide and pain of the deceased's life" (Sands et al., 2011, p. 262).

Grief support groups can allow participants to control their healing, to make meaningful decisions regarding level of engagement, and to overcome barriers to processing traumatic memories. For traumatized individuals for whom control is often elusive, well-facilitated groups can help the bereaving to move toward levels of pre-loss functioning. It is important though, particularly in the case of bereavement due to suicide, that the group is selected carefully. It is human to compare weight, grades, income and even Christmas decorations, but unfortunately, this can be an issue in group-counseling settings as well. In a recent, albeit short-running situational comedy, *Go On* (Silveri, 2012), actor Matthew Perry's character attends a loss and bereavement support group and in accordance with the character's career (sports-radio talk show host), creates a chart wherein all the other individuals in the group rank their "trauma" or loss with everyone voting on the "winner" (the person with the "greatest" loss). This competitive approach may not be as overt in a real-world support group but may still be insidiously evident, particularly in the case of suicide. A person bereaved due to cancer may see the person who was bereaved due to suicide as partly responsible or having experienced a less significant loss, since the person who died by suicide "chose" to die, whereas their loved one(s) did not. Because of this, it may be most helpful, when possible, to find a support group that focuses specifically on loss due to suicide. It "levels the playing field" of grief, where experiences may be more similar and individuals more supporting of one another.

Children and teens who are bereaved because of suicide may find it helpful to identify ways to memorialize the dead. They might compile a recording of favorite music, create a candle, or draw a picture. Parents and other trusted adults can help children and teens identify concrete coping strategies that help, for example, talking about the deceased, writing in a journal, playing with clay, planting a flower, or even mindfully taking a walk in the sunshine (McCord, 2014).

CONCLUSION

In the end, how does one measure a life—especially after death by suicide? The brief overview of this chapter is merely one attempt to understand the child's perspective of suicide. The path of post-bereavement development is complex; it turns and twists down myriad roads, sometimes with substantial obstacles, as well as momentous triumphs. In the end, the life of the surviving child is measured in terms of love—the love received from the person who died by suicide, the love of caring adults during the bereavement journey process, and the love of self that is finally embraced.

REFERENCES

Agerbo, E., Nordentoft, M., & Mortensen, P. B. (2002). Familial, psychiatric, and socio-economic risk factors for suicide in young people: Nested case-control study. *British Medical Journal, 325*(13), 74

Avrami, S. (2005). "I wish he had died in the war": Suicide survivors—the Israeli case. *Omega: Journal of Death and Dying, 51*(1), 65–75.

Baumeister, R. F. (1990). Suicide as escape from self. *Psychological Review, 97*, 90–113.

Beck, A. T., Steer, R. A., Kovacs, M., & Garrison, B. (1985). Hopelessness and eventual suicide: A 10-year prospective study of patients hospitalized with suicidal ideation. *American Journal of Psychiatry, 142*, 559–563.

Berman, A., Jobes, D., & Silverman, M. (2006). *Adolescent suicide: Assessment and intervention* (2nd ed.). Washington, DC: American Psychological Association.

Borowsky, I. W., Ireland, M., & Resnick, M. D. (2001). Adolescent suicide attempts: Risks and protectors. *Pediatrics, 107*(3), 485–493.

Bostik, K. E., & Everall, R. D. (2007). Healing from suicide: Adolescent perceptions of attachment relationships. *British Journal of Guidance & Counselling, 35*(1), 79–96. doi: 10.1080/03069880601106815

Brent, D., Melhem, N., Donohoe, M., & Walker, M. (2009). The incidence and course of depression in bereaved youth 21 months after the loss of a parent to suicide, accident, or sudden natural death. *American Journal of Psychiatry, 166*(7), 786–794. doi: 10.1176/appi.ajp.2009.08081244

Brown, G. K., Jeglic, E., Henriques, G. R., & Beck, A. T. (2006). Cognitive therapy, cognition, and suicidal behavior. In T. E. Ellis (Ed.), *Cognition and suicide: Theory, research, and therapy* (pp. 53–74). Washington, DC: American Psychological Association. doi: 10.1037/11377-003

Brown, A. C., Sandler, I. N., Jenn-Yun, T., Xianchen, L., & Haine, R. A. (2007). Implications of parental suicide and violent death for promotion of resilience of parentally bereaved children. *Death Studies, 31*(4), 301–335.

Cerel, J., & Aldrich, R. S. (2011). The impact of suicide on children and adolescents. In J. R. Jordan & J. L. McIntosh (Eds.), *Grief after suicide: Understanding the consequences and caring for the survivors* (pp. 81–92). New York, NY: Routledge/Taylor & Francis.

Cerel, J., Fristad, M. A., Weller, E. B., & Weller, R. A. (1999). Suicide-bereaved children and adolescents: A controlled longitudinal examination. *Journal of the American Academy of Child and Adolescent Psychiatry, 38*(6), 672–679.

Cerel, J., Fristad, M. A., Weller, E. B., & Weller, R. A. (2000). Suicide-bereaved children and adolescents: II. Parental and family functioning. *Journal of the American Academy of Child and Adolescent Psychiatry, 39*(4), 437–444.

Childers, P., & Wimmer, M. (1971). The concept of death in early childhood. *Child Development, 42*, 1299–1301.

Christ, G. (2010). Children bereaved by the death of a parent. In C. Corr & D. Balk (Eds.), *Children's encounters with death, bereavement and coping* (pp. 169–194). New York, NY: Springer.

Ellis, A., & Ellis, T. E. (2006). Suicide from the perspective of rational emotive behavior therapy. In T. E. Ellis (Ed.), *Cognition and suicide: Theory, research, and therapy* (pp. 75–90). Washington, DC: American Psychological Association. doi: 10.1037/11377-004

Evans, E., Hawton, K., & Rodham K. (2004). Factors associated with suicidal phenomena in adolescents: A systematic review of population-based studies. *Clinical Psychology Review, 24*(8), 957–979.

Freud, S. (2007). *On murder, mourning, and melancholia*. London, UK: Penguin Books.

Gilbertson, M. W., Orr, S. P., Rauch, S. L., & Pitman, R. K. (2008). Trauma and posttraumatic stress disorder. In T. A. Stern, J. F. Rosenbaum, M. Fava, J. Biederman, & S. L. Rauch (Eds.), *Massachusetts General Hospital comprehensive clinical psychiatry* (chap. 34). Philadelphia, PA: Mosby Elsevier.

Goethe, J. (1774). *Die leiden des jungen Werthers (The sorrows of young Werther)*. Leipzig, Germany: Weygand'sche Buchhandlung.

Hegerl, U., Kohburger, N., Rummel-Kluge, C., Gravert, C., Walden, M., & Mergl, R. (2013, March 20). One followed by many?—Long-term effects of a celebrity suicide on the number of suicidal acts on the German railway net. *Journal of Affective Disorders, 146*(1), 39–44.

Howarth, R. A. (2011). Promoting the adjustment of parentally bereaved children. *Journal of Mental Health Counseling, 33*(1), 21–32.

Jager-Hyman, S., Cunningham, A., Wenzel, A., Mattei, S., Brown, G. K., & Beck, A. T. (2014 August). Cognitive distortions and suicide attempts. *Cognitive Therapy and Research, 38*(4), 369–374. doi: 10.1007/s10608-014-9613-0

Jobes, D. A. (2006). *Managing suicidal risk: A collaborative approach*. New York, NY: Guilford Press.

Joiner, T. (2007). *Why people die by suicide*. Cambridge, MA: Harvard University Press.

Kemp, J., & Bossarte, R. (2012). Suicide data report 2012. *Department of Veteran's Affairs*. Retrieved July 28, 2014, from http://wdata rww.va.gov/opa/docs/suicide-data-report-2012-final.pdf

Kim, K. L., Galvan, T., Puzia, M. E., Cushman, G. K., Seymour, K. E., Vanmali, R., et al. (2015, February). Psychiatric and self-injury profiles of adolescent suicide attempters versus adolescents engaged in nonsuicidal self-injury. *Suicide and Life-Threatening Behavior, 45*(1), 37–50. doi: 10.1111/sltb.12110

Koocher, G. P. (1973). Childhood, death and cognitive development. *Developmental Psychology, 9*, 369–374.

Larson, J. (1996, August 27). *Rent* [original Broadway cast videorecording]. New York, NY.
Larson, J. (2008, April 1). *Rent: The complete book and lyrics of the broadway musical.* New York, NY: Applause Theatre & Cinema Books.
Loy, M., & Boelk, A. (2013). *Losing a parent to suicide: Using lived experiences to inform bereavement counseling.* New York, NY: Routledge
McCord, J. (2014). *Why suicide? Support after a death by suicide.* Selected Independent Funeral Homes.
Menninger, K. (1956). *Man against himself.* New York, NY: Mariner Books. (Original work published 1938.)
Michel, K., & Gysin-Maillart, A. (2013, May 30–June 1). *ASSIP: Attempted suicide short intervention program.* Presented at the Aeschi West Conference, Vail, CO.
Nagy, M. (1948). The child's theories concerning death. *Journal of Genetic Psychology, 73,* 3–27.
Orbach, I. (1988). *Children who don't want to live: Understanding and treating the suicidal child.* San Francisco, CA: Jossey-Bass.
Pfeffer, C. R., Martins, P., Mann, J., & Sunkenberg, M. (1997). Child survivors of suicide: Psychological characteristics. *Journal of the American Academy of Child & Adolescent Psychiatry, 36*(1), 65–74. doi:10.1097/00004583-199701000-00019
Pfeffer, C. R., Karus, D., Siegel, K., & Jiang, H.. (2000). Child survivors of parental death from cancer or suicide: Depressive and behavioral outcomes. *Psycho-Oncology, 9*(1), 1–10.
Rohter, L. (1990, July 17). 2 families sue heavy-metal band as having driven sons to suicide. *The New York Times.* Retrieved from http://www.nytimes.com/1990/07/17/arts/2-families-sue-heavy-metal-band-as-having-driven-sons-to-suicide.html
Rudd, M. D., Joiner, T., & Rajab, M. H. (2004). *Treating suicidal behavior: An effective, time-limited approach* (Treatment Manuals for Practitioners). New York, NY: Guilford Press.
Rush, A. J., & Beck, A. T. (1978). Cognitive therapy of depression and suicide. *American Journal of Psychotherapy, 32,* 201–219.
Sands, D. C., Jordan, J. R., & Neimeyer, R. A. (2011). The meaning of suicide: A narrative approach to healing. In J. R. Jordan & J. L. McIntosh (Eds.), *Grief after suicide: Understanding the consequences and caring for the survivors* (pp. 249–282). New York, NY: Routledge/Taylor & Francis.
Schmidtke, A., & Häfner, H. (1988). The Werther Effect after television films: New evidence for an old hypothesis. *Psychological Medicine, 18,* 665–676. doi: 10.1017/S0033291700008345
Schuurman, D., & Decristofaro, J. (2010). Children and traumatic deaths. In C. Corr & D. Balk (Eds.), *Children's encounters with death, bereavement and coping* (pp. 257–274). New York, NY: Springer.
Shneidman, E. S. (1980). Suicide. In E. S. Shneidman (Ed.), *Death: Current perspectives* (pp. 416–434). Palo Alto, CA: Mayfield.
Shneidman, E. S. (1985). *Definition of suicide.* New York, NY: Wiley.
Shneidman, E. S. (1995). *Suicide as psychache: A clinical approach to self-destructive behavior.* New York, NY: Aronson.
Shneidman, E. S. (1996). *The suicidal mind.* New York, NY: Oxford University Press.
Silveri, S. (2012). *Go on.* Television show.
Small, A. M., & Small, A. D., (1984). Children's reactions to a suicide in the family. In N. Linzer (Ed.), *Suicide: the will to live vs. the will to die* (pp. 151–169). New York, NY: Human Sciences Press.

Valach, L., Michel, K., Dey, P., & Young, R. A. (2006). Linking life- and suicide-related goal directed processes: A qualitative study. *Journal of Mental Health Counseling, 28*(4), 353–372.

Valach, L., Michel, K., Young, R. A., & Dey, P. (2006). Suicide attempts as social goal-directed systems of joint careers, projects, and actions. *Suicide and Life-Threatening Behavior, 36*(6), 651–650.

Wright, J., Briggs, S., & Behringer, J. (2005). Attachment and the body in suicidal adolescents: A pilot study. *Clinical Child Psychology & Psychiatry, 10*(4), 477–491. doi: 10.1177/1359104505056310

CHAPTER 13
Dealing with Loss and Grief of Minority Children in an Urban Setting

Fernando Cabrera and Robert Stevenson

If the grief process that follows a death has universal components and is experienced cross-culturally, the way it is expressed varies substantially between cultures. It also differs in expression between children of different social and economic levels. This chapter begins with an important assumption: that is that the experiences of death, dying, and bereavement with minority children in the urban setting are significantly influenced by the culture in which they occur. Those who wish to help such children need to understand those differences.

In today's cities, there are things to which young minority people must adapt. In many ways, death is the most painful adaptation for all members in minority families. Whereas in White America death has become more privatized and invisible, it is more public and visible in urban areas (Murray, Toth, & Clinkinbeard, 2005). General areas in which differences exist, especially those that might apply to children and adolescents, include the following: (a) extent of ritual attached to death (e.g., importance of attending funerals, degree to which funerals should be costly, and types of acceptable emotional displays); (b) need to see a dying relative; (c) openness and type of display of emotion; (d) appropriate length of the mourning period; (e) importance of anniversary events; (f) roles of men and women; (g) roles of children and extended family; (h) beliefs about what happens after death, particularly related to ideas of suffering, fate, and destiny; and (i) whether certain deaths are stigmatized (Walsh & McGoldrick, 1991).

There are a number of factors to consider when dealing with loss and dying issues with minority urban children.

WORLDVIEW

The first factor is the child's worldview. Western cultures stress individualism and self-advancement. Decisions are made by the individual. Most urban minority cultures have a collectivist worldview and typically engage in group decision making. In an urban context, a child's grieving and decision making take place in the context of the family and significant others.

COMMUNICATION AND CUES

A second factor is communication. In other cultures, and with most adults, what is said receives the greater focus. That is "high content." In urban minority communities, and with children in those communities, "high context," that is, how things are said is more important. Minority children listen with their eyes. They tend to focus on nonverbal communication (Okun, Fried, & Okun, 1999).

TIME FACTOR

Children in many urban minority communities tend to be "present oriented." This can make them less likely to plan in advance and less likely to make appointments or to be on time. This is not always a sign of resistance. This differs from the dominant American culture, which tends to have a "monochronic orientation," meaning that Americans prefer to do one thing at a time and are focused on the efficient management of time (Chung & Lim, 2005).

LOCUS OF CONTROL

The locus of control refers to one's perceived ability to control external factors in the environment. It is seen as the point from which control spreads. In Western culture, the locus of control is seen as internal—people determine their own individual destiny and control their own environment. Urban cultures tend to experience an external locus of control—control coming from "outside forces." For example, disease may be attributed to an individual who is believed to hold a grudge or an angry ancestor. There is potential to blame God for any misfortune, creating a spiritual crisis for a child—"Why did God take my mother?" The other side of this is that a child may also find safety and reassurance from an outside force who is in "control" of everything (Rotter, 1975).

TRUST FACTOR

Trust is a most important issue for urban minority children, as it is for many urban minority communities. There is a generational suspiciousness. Trust is earned through unspoken, genuine action. Having an agenda can help these children to feel secure. To build such trust, sincerity is essential for any caregiver. Passion on the part of a caregiver may turn into suspicion if children judge it to be coming from ulterior motives. The agenda may well be to help, but allow the person himself/herself to elicit the help. Ask, "What is it that you hope to get from this meeting?" Don't prescribe what they need. Instead, allow them to share it with you. They may be concerned about control or a helper trying to take over. Do not act paternal or maternal. Allow the person to have a voice and to use it. When counselors come with their own agenda, rather than eliciting the agenda from the client, they may say, "You are not here the way we are and you don't know what we go through." One solution for this is to connect early with the client. It can establish, and be the foundation on which to build, long-term bonding.

CONTACT POINT (FIRST CONTACT)

Those who connect early after the incident have greater chance for credibility and bonding with the family and child. One program that has used this principle of first contact effectively is the S.N.U.G. Program. "SNUG" is guns spelled backwards. The letters stand for

S = Street intervention/Stopping violence

N = National, state, and local funding

U = Use of celebrities and centers

G = Gangs/Guns/Gainful employment

SNUG seeks to reverse the growing presence of weapons among young people in urban minority communities. The program places mentors with real-life street experience into neighborhoods affected by violence. They work to help gang members—mostly teens and young adults—find ways to avoid violence. SNUG team members take to the streets, often late at night or in the early morning hours. Most of the outreach workers have served prison time or experienced life as a gang member. This has helped build trust early on. SNUG also contributes to the community by paying for participants to get summer jobs and educational counseling. The SNUG workers are there early and immediately help young people begin to take action and to make positive changes (DeBoer, 2012).

In contrast to the successful SNUG model, now active in New York City for several years, latecomers may be seen as opportunistic, even those who are from the same cultural group. There can be a credibility factor established when you are the first to show up.

SPIRITUALITY AND RELIGION

Hope is essential. Remember, many in these communities feel there is an external locus of control. In communities of people of color, spirituality is very important because it provides connectedness. People word it in various ways: "Religion gives us a place to which we often go when we don't have answers." "It is the one place we can go where we can give ourselves permission to ask 'Why did it happen?'" and "We don't have to have the answer." Another believer said, "As long as the higher power, God, has the answer and control, all is well. It gets us to the place where it is OK to not fully not understand and allows us to talk about it."

One of the challenges in working with an adolescents who have not been practicing religion the way he/she feels he/she should may be the feeling of guilt that can arise if he/she goes back to that community of faith for support. Since so many in urban settings go back to religious and or spiritual institutions for burial ceremonies, acceptance can also be a big issue. A pastor, priest, or spiritual leader often is called on to help make the funeral plans after a death. This early presence allows them to be included in helping find an answer to the question "Why did this happen to (our loved one)?"

ECONOMIC FACTOR

A study conducted by the Organization for Economic Cooperation and Development (OECD, 2011) found that 25.8% of American children are raised by a single parent, a number high above the 14.9% average seen in the other 26 countries surveyed. Among African Americans, the rate nearly tripled, with 67% of African American children relying on a single parent (Kids Count Data Center, 2012). Finances can be a reason for limited support during the grieving process. For example, this can happen when the immediate family lives in one state, but most of the extended family, a potentially strong support system, lives some distance away and cannot come to the ceremonies, or remain there afterward, for financial reasons.

A CULTURE OF VIOLENCE

A study of elementary school children in New Orleans revealed that over 90% of the children had witnessed violence, over half had been victims of some form of violence, and over 40% had seen a dead person. Virtually all ethnic minority children in South Central Los Angeles had witnessed a homicide or a shooting of a person by age 5 (Dubrow & Garbarino, 1989). Another study found that 40% of the mothers in the New Orleans sample, and 20% in the Washington, DC, sample said their children were worried about being safe. Similar proportions of the children reported feeling "jumpy" and "scared" (Osofsky, 1999).

Shooting incidents in urban areas are typically concentrated in a small number of neighborhoods. In New York City, there are 76 police precincts; 44% of the total shooting incidents occur in only 15% of police precincts and 82% are in only 40% of police precincts. In addition, data shows that violence is concentrated in certain neighborhoods within each precinct. The 2013 report from the Gun Violence Prevention Task Force claimed that the experiences of Task Force member showed that within some neighborhoods, violence is concentrated among a particular segment of the population: predominantly young men between the ages of 14 and 24. They concluded that because violence is often concentrated in urban, high-poverty neighborhoods of color, one group of those at risk of gun violence consists predominantly of young men of color (Gun Violence Prevention Task Force, 2013, pp. 16–17).

As listed in the NYC.gov website, in New york City in 2012, Black New Yorkers, who make up 23% of the City's population, represent 60% of those murdered; nearly 40% of all victims were male blacks aged 16 to 37, while 4% were Asian. 60% were Black, 27% were Hispanic and 9% were White. Of the 419 Homicide Victims in NYC 86% of black males aged 16 to 21 were killed with a gun 46% of New Yorkers are non-Hispanic white or Asian, yet these groups represent only 13% of those murdered. (NYC.gov, 2013)

Who is it that is harmed by firearm violence? Men aged 45 years and older bear the greatest burden of suicide. However, it is young urban Black men aged 15 to 24 years who bear the greatest burden of violence-related firearm deaths and injury. Non-Hispanic Blacks had the highest firearm homicide rate (11.4 deaths/100,000); this rate was over four times higher than that for Hispanics, who had the next highest rate (2.6 deaths/100,000). (NYC DOH, 2010; NYC DOHMH, 2011) However, with gun-related suicides the picture is reversed and it is the most-rural areas that have a fourfold higher rate than the most urban ones: 2.75 versus 0.7 suicides per 100,000 kids (CBS KBTX, 2010) For youth in rural areas, the most pressing issue is hopelessness; in the urban areas it is fear. Hopelessness can lead to suicide, while fear is a factor that can increase the likelihood of violence against others.

THE FACTOR OF STIGMA

Stigma may be connected with a death.

Those working with grieving young people need to find out the details of a death. Certain types of death (e.g., suicide or stillbirth) can carry a stigma in a community. Also, certain types of death may be especially traumatic for that cultural group (e.g., homicide or death of a child).

Stigma of Counseling Services

This may exist in some who believe that "mental health care is for crazy people." This is often the case in minority communities. Institutions created this stigma, partly because people from minority communities don't see counselors who look like them, so they think, "They can't understand me." This presents a difficulty with any youth who were raised thinking that counseling is for "crazy people." Dr. Cabrera, one of the authors of this chapter, has shared that he was one of those raised this way! Caucasian families do take their children to counseling (family, divorce), so by the time they are confronted with a loss, they are not unfamiliar with the counseling process.

Stigma of the Inner City

The inner city is often stigmatized. For example, the Bronx evokes many negative thoughts (i.e., Fort Apache, "The Bronx is burning," etc.), and in neighboring New

Jersey, many of the cities such as Paterson, Newark, and Camden have a stigma associated with them because of their high levels of crime and violence. This situation can cause minority inner-city youth to feel misunderstood, underrated, and underserved. They do not believe that "outsiders" can understand their situation. They feel that their efforts do not matter because they sense a powerless to change things. And they often do not receive the same support available to young people in nearby suburbs.

LANGUAGE FACTOR

The language you use when working with these young people in urban settings can effect receptivity. Those seeking to help need to use empowering language. It is often counterproductive to say things such as "I am here to help you." It is better to say, "I am here. Now, what do *you* think I can do that may help?" Avoid language that appears patronizing. Words alone are not the only thing playing a role here. In urban minority communities, body language and tone of voice often speak louder than the actual meaning of words.

Hispanic Americans make up 13.5% of the total population, but they represent only 4.8% of deaths (CDC, 2014). Why is that? There has been some question about the accuracy of this information, but one explanation comes from the fact that some do go back to their country of origin for their final days of life (Dr. Cabrera's grandfather, for one). Healthier members may then be selected by the family to come to America. Also, young people make up the highest percentage of the Latino population. For example, in Texas the student subpopulation is 8%–10% higher than total of the rest of the state. Main causes of death among Latinos are heart disease and cancer. But among youth, the highest causes of death are homicide and HIV.

HELPING URBAN LATINO CHILDREN

The following points can be helpful to keep in mind when working with Latino children in urban settings.

Understand That Hispanic Children Often Seek to Maintain Their Bond With the Deceased

Latino children will often seek to maintain their bond with the deceased. It is uncommon for a Hispanic to mention obtaining "closure" or "moving on." These terms often associated with the older, "breaking ties" model of grief. This continuing attachment to the deceased can help children transition from the past to the future. There are a variety of ways in which Hispanic children and teens maintain bonds with a lost loved one:

- Dreams: In many Latino families, children are asked, "Did you dream about _____ (the deceased person)?" These dreams are felt to be a form of connecting, and young people may feel upset if they do not dream about the deceased loved one.

- Storytelling: Storytelling includes the Latino children's vivid recall of one's last interaction with the deceased and extended family remembrances. One student who told and retold the story of his last time with the deceased said, "Instead of talking about his death, we need to talk about how he lived." It can be helpful to provide a time for the family to tell and share their stories about the deceased. A variation of this point is seen in Cuban culture, where wakes not only offer an opportunity to honor the life of the recently deceased and to share stories of the person, but may also become a site of exiled reconnection.
- Keepsakes: Cherished objects that were used by the deceased, such as toys or a special blanket, are kept in a special place as form of connection.
- Sense of Presence: Latino children often speak of an enduring sense of presence of the deceased. "God took my Mami, but sometimes I can feel her around me." There is a benevolent aspect to this "presence," in which the deceased one takes the form of the child's "guardian angel." This feeling is interpreted in Latino families as a sign of good things to come and continuity.
- Spiritual Connection: Faith-based beliefs also helped children stay connected to the deceased. Latino adolescents say they will be reunited with their deceased loved one in the afterlife. Above the door of some of the Latino children's bedroom there may be a prominent picture of the Virgin of Guadalupe. The Virgin of Guadalupe is a powerful Mexican and Mexican American religious and cultural symbol exemplifying the protection offered to all by the Mother of God. Even after becoming adults and despite Latino children's crises of faith, the Latino adolescents do not abandon the comfort of cultural/religious symbolism that appears to connect him/her to deceased loved ones.
- The "Near" Connection: First-generation Latinos often described the dilemma of where to bury their parents—in the United States or country of origin? If they are buried in the country of origin, then they would feel obligated to go back to their country of origin to be close to the gravesite. Children are often considered in this decision, so they can have access to pay respect at their relative's gravesite.
- Picture Memorials: Latino youth often displayed pictures of the deceased in funerals, especially when it is of another youth. In some Latino groups, these pictures are part of home altars, a permanent and constant reminder of the deceased. Some of these small home altars are quite elaborate and intense. They may include religious figures and pictures, a lit glass candle, several plants, and vases with flowers. At times, when a sudden and unexpected violent death of a fellow youth occurs, a graffiti mural may be painted. A parallel to this in the African American community would be the creation of memorial t-shirts with a likeness (photo or artwork), and the name (or nickname) of the deceased. The date of the death may also be included or a statement to the deceased.

Those working with Latino youth need to find a way to show honor and respect. It is important to find out how best to show respect or what kind of behavior is expected in mourners in their culture. Remember, not all Latino/Hispanic cultures are the same in their traditions and observances. In some Latino cultures, such as Puerto Rican and Dominicans, human touch demonstrates respect for grieving Latino individuals and is an important gesture for professionals to include in their support of the family.

Familismo

It is essential to earn the trust of those with whom one will be working (both the young people themselves and their families. Vazquez (2009) states that this trust is called *Familismo*. In Latino culture, family is considered to be more important than the individual members who make up the family. There is both interdependence and a feeling of "oneness" (Falicov, 1998). Cooperation among the immediate family members is expected. This does not only involve the immediate family, it includes aunts, uncles, and close friends as well (Comas-Diaz, 1997). Members of this extended family may have to take on an obligation to share responsibility in rearing children, provide financial and emotional support, and make decisions about issues that affect the family (Santiago-Rivera, Arredondo, & Gallardo-Cooper, 2002).

The *compadres* (godparents), who can be blood relatives or friends, play a vital role in the family. The *comadre* (godmother) and *compadre* (godfather) are considered "co-parents" and, through a formal religious ceremony, are given the right of passage to help rear a child or children in the family. The *compadres* also participate in traditional family celebrations and funerals (Falicov, 1998; Marin & Marin, 1991).

Hispanic Cultural Values—Personalismo, Respeto, Simpatia

Personalismo

This is a value associated with the Hispanic culture, and it is based on building and maintaining significant interpersonal relationships (Gillette, 2013). According to the Chadwick Center, *personalismo* encourages warm and friendly relationships as opposed to impersonal or formal interactions in everyday life; it is an expectation among Hispanics that they will be treated in a caring and respectful manner. Because of this Hispanic cultural value, it is critical for healthcare professionals to find a way to reach Hispanics on this personal level, regardless of language or other barriers.

Respeto and Simpatia

Addressing an older person by their last name is often a sign of respect to older persons (*Senor* or *Senora*). The importance of *simpatia* in Latino culture has been corroborated by empirical findings. Triandis, Marin, Lisansky, and Betancourt (1984) examined dimensions of *simpatia* in a sample of Latino and non-Latino male Navy recruits and found that Latino males ascribed more importance to aspects such as respect, loyalty, dignity, and cooperation than their non-Latino male counterparts. Both *personalismo* and *simpatia* are characteristic of a collective worldview (Levine & Padilla, 1980; Marin & Marin, 1991).

Help the Child to Express Grief Through Rituals

In rituals immediately after a death, there are prayers for the soul of the deceased. The Rosary is repeated. This is a series of repetitions of two prayers (often holding prayer beads called rosaries). The two prayers are the *Prade Nuestro* (Our Father) and *Ave Maria* (Hail Mary). There is typically a Mass in a church and procession to the burial site. Blessing with holy water by the priest before the burial completes the final ceremony (Lobar, Youngblut, & Brooten, 2006).

The funeral is often preceded by a Mass or Memorial Service. There are also nine days of prayer (called "novena") as part of the ritual. The novena is repetitive prayer said by the family and friends every night for nine nights during the grieving period. Some families say the rosary every month for a year after the death and then repeat it on each anniversary. Wearing black or dark colors shows respect for the deceased. This may continue among adults for a year, and sometimes with widows or grieving mothers, for many years after the death. It is less common among children. Adolescents sometimes may not be sure what is expected of them at this time. Should they resume typical dress (as children do) or should they wear mourning colors (as adults)? This is an important topic to address with adolescents and their families.

Many Hispanic survivors commemorate the loss of their loved ones with promises or commitments. These promises are taken very seriously and failure to honor them can be considered a sin. Young people may make extreme commitments immediately after a death and can then feel guilty for not having fulfilled their commitment to the deceased. During the time of grief, with the length varying from one week to a year among different Latino groups, there is to be no entertainment (such as watching television or listening to the radio or to music) and no attending social events.

As was said earlier, there can be clear differences among Latino groups. Puerto Ricans show greater outward demonstrations of grief than other Hispanic groups (Grabowski & Frantz, 1991). However, Mexicans are found to have more understanding and acceptance of death than other Latino countries. Death is portrayed in Mexican statues, art, literature, and history. There is a cultural familiarity with death: on the *Dia de los Muertos* (Day of the Dead), relatives feel an obligation to remember and honor the dead (Brandes, 2007).

On the Day of the Dead, children are given a chance to think about death and talk about experiences or fears they might have had regarding death. Instead of being something that is hushed and terrifying, death takes its natural place as a necessary part of life. A ritual celebrating remembrance of dead loved ones by reminiscing, partaking of the deceased's favorite foods, lighting candles, and visiting the cemetery.

Hispanic families do not like to talk about a DNR (Do not resuscitate). It is regarded as a big responsibility, and they fear other family members may accuse them of "killing their loved one" if they sign such a document without consulting all of the family members. Hispanic families, believing that death comes when "it will come" are sometimes resistant to hospice care as well (Whitfield & Baker, 2014).

Be Conscious of Possible Language Issues

Be sure to have some materials available in Spanish—and be sure the translation is accurate. Grief, for example, may be referred to as *dolor* (pain). While the grief process can be painful, it is felt to also be a healing process. These two words convey different meanings. It is important to be able to express oneself in a native language when one is experiencing a trauma, and a counselor needs to be able, if possible, to allow the person to do that. Death can often be a trauma for those left behind. For that reason, if a counselor is not bilingual, a referral may at times be appropriate.

Other Considerations

Fatalism and Anticipatory Grief

Contraction of serious diseases are often seen as a death sentence; helping to prepare the person for eventual death may ease the intensity of grief for survivors.

Presence at Death

There is value in being with a dying relative so that any unresolved conflicts may be resolved before the death. Many used to die at home, but the trend toward institutions as the location of death has been rising in minority communities.

Grieving Practices

Open expressions of grief are acceptable. However, there is a pronounced lack of emotional expression by males—males do not grieve openly, needing to be strong.

Other Points

Among Latinos, there is a preference for burials versus cremation. Children are not discouraged from viewing the deceased in the casket (but they may choose not to do so). What is important is giving a young person the choice and allowing them to know what they will see and what they may experience if they choose to view the deceased.

HELPING AFRICAN AMERICAN CHILDREN AND ADOLESCENTS

As was the case with Latino children and adolescents, there are points that can be helpful in working with grieving African American children and adolescents.

Rituals

African American death rituals vary widely as a function of religious affiliation. In general, the funeral often involves a large gathering of family and friends to pay respect to the deceased. African Americans in urban areas traditionally have a viewing of the deceased in the house before the funeral (Lobar et al., 2006). "Flower girls" (actually adult women) may walk with the pallbearers during the funeral procession. In African American rituals, explicit outward demonstrations of emotion are common, particularly among women and children who identify as Southern Baptists or among those who are recent African immigrants (Schoulte, 2011).

Bond

African Americans children, much like Latino children, demonstrate a closer bond with the deceased compared to their White counterparts—they are similar. African American children often seek out certain activities to remind themselves of the deceased or conversations they had with the deceased.

Good Death

For African American families, the idea of a good death is often related to the amount of control a person believes he/she has in the process of dying and the degree of closure achieved. This is a significant factor when dealing with a sudden death caused by violence

Outside Network

African Americans are more likely to become socially involved with members outside of their immediate family, such as other members of their church. While family is important, they are more likely to receive social support for comfort and condolence from people outside of the family. This includes support from outside people for their children (Carr, 2004).

Economic Trap

After a violent death, there can often be a fear that the person (or group) who did the shooting will come "after me and my children." That fear exists among children and adolescents as it does among adults. Often African Americans can't afford to move out of their neighborhoods to save their other surviving children and this can be a source of fear and parental guilt. Other than in their churches, African American communities do not have enough centers dealing with grieving and there are not sufficient funds available to create new centers. Perhaps this economic trap is a contributing factor to the way in which African American youth are not able to see an end point to their grief. White children are more likely to believe their grief will have an end than are African American children/adolescents, who see grief going on with no fixed end in sight.

Celebration of Loss of Life

It can be typical in urban settings to have a time for anyone to speak up about something positive they would like to celebrate or remember about the deceased during the funeral services. The origin for this celebration of the life of the deceased is in the oral tradition of African storytelling. It provides a time to honor accomplishments and what the person contributed to the community. The storytelling helps families and friends to see death as a time of rest from trials and labor. The person is now more likely to be seen by family and friends as "Resting in Peace." The deceased, having accomplished so much—as told in the stories—can rest in peace without shame or guilt. The honor provided to the life that was lived provides a strength-based form of grieving for family and friends.

Rituals of Honor including Shrines, Pictures, and Reunions

Shrines are seen more frequently in the inner city than before. They are becoming such an issue that the city may seek to remove the flowers, lit candles, and objects (teddy bears or toys for children, pictures of the deceased for all ages) as quickly as possible. Family reunions allow for expression of the ties that remain after a death. For the younger generation, photographs, a t-shirt with picture of the deceased, buttons (again with a picture or name) appear and may be worn for a time as a visible symbol of grief. A young person may wear a "rest in peace necklace" instead of keeping the funeral program or adding to a shrine.

Funeral Director's Role

Funeral directors are highly involved in preparations for mourning and burial, and funeral service professionals are accorded a high status in the African American community. The funeral directors are a good source of information about cultural observations in a community. They may be able to provide counselors and others with materials that explain the rituals and symbolism that are part of funerals in this community.

"Singing Through It"

Children are often included in the singing of songs or hymns and in reciting poems. Some services are a "Going Home" celebration. While the service reflects cultural standards and expectations of the African American community, the personality of the service is also a reflection of the personality of the deceased.

Other Points

A shared meal among grieving loved ones is commonplace after the wake and funeral. A life has ended, but for those taking part in this meal, it is a reminder that life will go on. Children become part of this "family reunion" at and after the funeral.

In the African American community, cremation is seldom used as an option. In some faiths, embalming may also be frowned upon or banned outright. In many African traditions, embalming is forbidden. One young man was an exchange student, along with his brother, at an American college. His brother died and the family required that the body be shipped home to his village for burial. He faced this dilemma. The body needed to be sent home as soon as possible, but he was not able to find an airline that would transport the body unless it was embalmed. He took it upon himself to have the body embalmed and never informed his family. The guilt he felt over this decision plagued him for some time. Without understanding the cultural sanctions he had violated, a counselor might find that he/she was unable to be of help.

In some urban African American communities it is common to mourn by dressing in white as a symbolic gesture of resurrection and hope. The most common mourning colors worldwide are either black or white. In African American communities it is common to see adults wearing black, while the children wear white.

The isolation felt by some African Americans can be reinforced by the place of death. African Americans die outside their home, such as in a hospital, more often than all other urban ethnicities.

What happens to urban minority youth if these factors are ignored can have consequences that can last throughout life. Adult African American males are often reluctant and resistant when it comes to counseling. Lee and Bailey (2006) point out that "historically, achieving masculine privilege has not been a birthright for African American males (as it has been for their white counterparts). Social and political forces have combined to keep African American males from assuming a traditional masculine role." They point out that this process has been an integral part of "the dynamics of oppression and racism that have pervaded the Black experience in America." These two counselors, African American themselves, show how the African American male has been seen an object of fear; denied the ability to exercise masculine privilege and power through life-sustaining employment and the ability to support a family; subject to feelings of rage, frustration, powerlessness, and hopelessness in the dynamics of personal development; and developed coping mechanisms and survival strategies to overcome social resistance. They also point out ways that early counseling can mitigate such multigenerational history of loss and help young men to cope more effectively when they encounter deaths and other losses in their lives. It has been pointed out that the sooner loss-related issues are addressed, the easier it may be to find more effective ways of coping. That is also the case with African American youth. Knowledge of the special issues they face when coping with grief can be beneficial for counselors and others who work with them.

GUIDELINES

Lee and Bailey (2006, pp. 93–112) offer guidelines for counseling African American men, which include the following points:

- Develop rapport
- Pace the engagement of the actual counseling process
- Prepare to self-disclose
- Encourage introspection
- Explore spirituality
- Be sensitive to racism
- Conduct psychoeducational counseling with a primary focus of the counseling process to develop new skills or behaviors to deal more effectively with social or behavioral challenges.

Adult African American males have many issues. The time to start helping African American males to deal with their issues connected to loss is when they are young. As statistics can show, life in urban centers can be difficult for minorities. For both Hispanic and African American urban youth (children and adolescents), the present is a critical time, a time of crisis. It is critical in that it holds the potential for each individual to succeed or fail, based on the course they choose and the help they receive in dealing with their issues. Helping adults (parents, counselors, teachers, and others) can make a clear difference in the way such young people see and experience their world.

REFERENCES

Brandes, S. (2007). *Skulls to the living, bread to the dead: The Day of the Dead in Mexico and beyond.* Malden, MA: Blackwell.

Carr, W. (2004). Philosophy and education. *Journal of Philosophy of Education, 38*(1), 55–83.

CBS News & KBTX Staff. (2010, May 31). Child gun deaths as common in rural as urban areas. *KBTX.com.* Retrieved from http://www.kbtx.com/health/headlines/94916809.html

Centers for Disease Control and Prevention (CDC). (2014). *Minority health: Hispanic and Latino populations.* Retrieved from http://www.cdc.gov/minorityhealth/populations/REMP/hispanic.html

Chung, L. Y., & Lim, S. S. (2005). From monochronic to mobilechronic—Temporality in the era of mobile communication. In K. Nyiri (Ed.), *A sense of place: The global and the local in mobile communication* (pp. 267–282). Vienna, Austria: Passagen Verlag.

Comas-Diaz, L. (1997.) Mental health needs of Latinos with professional status. In J. G. Garcia & M. C. Zea (Eds.), *Psychological interventions and research with Latino populations* (pp. 142–165). Needham Heights, MA: Allyn & Bacon.

DeBoer, H. (2012, January 25). Gun violence reduction in small U.S. cities. *OLR Research Report 2010-R-0061.* Retrieved from http://www.cga.ct.gov/2012/rpt/2012-R-0061.htm

Dubrow, N. F., & Garbarino, J. (1989). Living in the war zone: Mothers and young children in a public housing development. *Child Welfare, 68,* 3–20.

Falicov, C. J. (1998). *Families in therapy: A guide to multicultural practice.* New York, NY: Guilford Press.

Gillette, H. (2013). *What is personalismo and why is it important in health care?* Retrieved from http://voxxi.com/2013/09/18/hispanic-personalismo-health-care/

Grabowski, J., & Frantz, T. (1991). Latinos and Anglos: Cultural experiences of grief intensity. *Journal of Death and Dying, 26*(4), 273–285.

Gun Violence Prevention Task Force. (2013). *Gun Violence Prevention Task Force recommedations.* Retrieved from https://www.scribd.com/doc/124384563/Gun-Violence-Prevention-Task-Force-Recommendations

Kids Count Data Center. (2012). *Children in single parent families by race.* Retrieved from http://datacenter.kidscount.org/data/tables/107-children-in-single-parent-families-by#detailed/1/any/false/868,867,133,38,35/10,168,9,12,1,13,185/432,431

Lee, C. C., & Bailey, D. F. (2006). Counseling African American male youth and men. In C. Lee (Ed.), *Multicultural issues in counseling: New approaches to diversity* (3rd ed., pp. 93–112). Alexandria, VA: American Counseling Association.

Levine, E. S., & Padilla, A. M. (1980). *Crossing cultures in therapy: Pluralistic counseling for the Hispanic.* Monterey, CA: Brooks/Cole.

Lobar, S. L., Youngblut, J. M., & Brooten, D. (2006). Cross-cultural beliefs, ceremonies, and rituals surrounding death of a loved one. *Medscape.com.* Retrieved from http://www.medscape.com/viewarticle/525639

Marin, G., & Marin, B. V. (1991). *Research with Hispanic populations.* Thousand Oaks, CA: Sage.

Murray, C. I., Toth, K., & Clinkinbeard, S. S. (2005). Death, dying and grief in families. In P. C. McKenry & S. J. Price (Eds.), *Families and change* (3rd ed.). Thousand Oaks, CA: Sage.

New York State Department of Health. (2012). *Statewide Planning and Research Cooperative System (SPARCS).* Retrieved from https://www.health.ny.gov/statistics/sparcs/

New York City Department of Health and Mental Hygiene. (2011). *Data & statistics.* Retrieved from http://www.nyc.gov/html/doh/html/data/data.shtml

New York City, (2012). *Murder in New York City,* retrieved from NYC.gov/February, 2016.

Okun, B. F., Fried, J., & Okun, M. L. (1999). *Understanding diversity: A learning-as-practice primer.* Pacific Grove, CA: Brooks/Cole.

Organization for Economic Cooperation and Development (OECD, 1012). Retrieved from http//www.oecd.org/statistics/

Osofsky, J. D. (1999, Winter). The impact of violence on children. *Domestic Violence and Children, 9*(3), 33–49.

Rotter, J. B. (1975, February). Some problems and misconceptions related to the construct of internal versus external control of reinforcement. *Journal of Consulting and Clinical Psychology, 43*(1), 56–67.

Santiago-Rivera, A. L., Arredondo, P., & Gallardo-Cooper, M. (2002). *Latinos and la familia: A practical guide.* Thousand Oaks, CA: Sage.

Schoulte, J. C. (2011). Bereavement among African Americans and Latino/a Americans. *Journal of Mental Health Counseling, 33*(1), 11–20.

Triandis, H. C., Marin, G., Lisansky, J., & Betancourt, H. (1984). Simpatia as a cultural script of Hispanics. *Journal of Personality and Social Psychology, 47*(6), 1364–1375.

Vazquez, C. I. (2009). *Parenting with pride Latino style: How to help your child cherish your cultural values and succeed in today's world.* New York, NY: HarperCollins.

Walsh, F., & McGoldrick, M. (1991). Loss and the family: A systems perspective. In F. Walsh & M. McGoldrick (Eds.), *Living beyond loss* (pp. 1–29). New York, NY: Norton.

Whitfield, K., & Baker, T. (2014). *Handbook of minority aging.* New York, NY: Springer.

CHAPTER 14
When a Grandparent Dies

Richard Gilbert

Hillary Clinton titled her book on children, *It Takes A Village* (2006), drawing on an old adage she quoted on a number of occasions, "It takes a village to raise a child." The message was clear. Children (and teens) are part of what makes for a village and are both our present and our future. Children (and teens, understood) are also among the most vulnerable members of this village. Chicago just delivered some horrific numbers. Often they were innocent victims of gang activity. Others were drive-by. The majority of them were intraracial. In the same period over 200 children were seriously wounded in similar situations. What can parents and grandparents do? How do we prepare the children?

Children are facing increased violence, even in rural areas. We have saddled our children with a debt that may never be paid. Declining populations accompanied by changing demographics have left many communities in a state of unrest, with particular challenges for school districts and emergency services. Current tax bases frequently are found short of the mark with local programs. In my own community of 35,000, several schools have 90% of their children living below the poverty level. We now send them home with special packets of food so that they have something to eat on the weekends along with breakfast and lunch at the school.

So much has happened. Some changes bring improvement while others bring more burdens. Still the village remains central to it all and, even with "traditional families" evolving into many traditions, revisions, and updates, we still find the three flowers in the "family garden." These growing flowers are structure and symbolic structure for living that can be the most effective for our children and our communities.

FAMILY AS CONTEXT

As we and others approach the end of life, two hazards rise to the surface: death and financial burdens. They present themselves as the total sum of a person's life. We ignore them as much as we can, but at the end we die, and for most people, the family faces the burden of remaining bills, a financial challenge that often threatens the dreams and ambitions of children.

We live our lives, relationships rise and fall, some goals are met while others turn to dust; judgment and mourning remain. The importance of family is measured by the definition and purpose the members place on it. It also is influenced, for good or otherwise, by the economy, meaningful jobs, safe neighborhoods, city services, good neighbors, and friends. They symbolically represent effectiveness as the gathering place that represents help, hope, and happiness. Family and home are definitive places—the gathering, the staging area that simultaneously identifies itself as a center of conflict and a temple of healing. We seek to face and shape our future as these same conflicts work tirelessly to defeat our best intentions and roles. Family is what and who we count on. Keep that point in mind as death enters a family and everything seems to crumble.

Family is so important for all of us and for the community, the listening and affirming must apply to all family units (including single parents) and not the mythological "traditional family"—Mom, Dad, two children, a dog, and two cars in the garage. "Home, sweet home," likely embroidered and placed near the entrance to your house, has been reshaped, shattered, even shunned, as some attempt to put on the brakes for these new families and relationships. If we are to be a healthy society, with meaning contained in that wall hanging handed down from your grandmother, we must continue to explore, express, and expand who we are and what we do. Strong families mean strong communities.

When a family faces a death, it also draws the children to "viewing" death, even when shielded or interrupted by innocence of children or child's age and development. They can shield the children from the trauma of death and loss. Some of these efforts can provide welcomed respite. Others can delay or disrupt what ought to be their grief journey. It is often the grandparent who reaches out, knows what the children want for lunch, their favorite toys, and their playmates. They also have that special tie that binds grandparent and child for occasions when the child may feel stuck or stumped. Children recognize when something is wrong, often assuming it is something they have done. All adults known by the child may be sought by the child. Grandparents have an instinct that picks up on the concerns of the child even when nothing is said or done. Grandparents may know more than the parents know about some things—when you pick up the children after school, making sure the cookies are already. Many feel safe and refreshed when a grandparent is there to greet them. The grandparents have instincts that help them assess what the child may be thinking about. You earn that privilege when the child loses a mitten or a button of his coat, because you can fix it. You know when there is an appointment that child must attend. The grandparents are there and they are prepared to address any questions when they are asked. "Grandpa always misses whiskers when he shaves (I think he does that on purpose) and has a hug and kiss for the child. Grandpa often smells, but his smile is so special and he always has a piece of candy in his pocket for the child. Those are things that kids remember!"

Children can handle some of the disruption of death and grief, but they are sustained by routine, love, and some answers when they ask a question. Grandparents know the routine and are trusted by the children when a change is called for. Routine is important. Two children in elementary school were sitting together in the cafeteria.

One was passionately eating his lunch while the other lad sat very still, looking off into space. The hungry eater asked, "I thought you were hungry. Why aren't you eating your lunch?" The boy replied, "Every Monday is jelly sandwich day. Just jelly. No peanut butter. That's Thursday. I get a piece of fruit (today it is pears) and grapefruit juice. I hate grapefruit juice! My Mom knows that, but if it is Monday you *must* have grapefruit juice."

This was not the routine, but an interruption. When death enters the picture, routine often takes flight and children need to establish new routines.

As children go through their phases of independence, privacy, space, and ownership, they often communicate through tantrums. Protest may not get the desired results, but the children get "a moment of their time" from the adults in their lives. "This is *my* room," shouted the granddaughter in fourth grade. Her grandmother knows this! Now the family, because of my grandmother, have taken over *my* room and stripped me of identity, sanctuary, familiarity, and structure. School often provides the structure and rituals that build on the lifestyle at home. In times when the home life is disrupted, the school can observe this and when observations point to a particular person, feeling, or issue.

None of us dare overreact when the child is pushing toward tantrum except for reasons of safety. Intervention may be both justified and expected, but how the adults (i.e., school personnel) react can both redirect and/or push away the child who desperately seeks understanding and nearness.

Children want the familiarity of schedule, yet fight the rigidness. Structure is essential for all of us, but especially for children and teens. Structure is an annoyance for some and a threat for others, but, as the recent discussion on luncheon menus, we have both safety and clarity. Of course it might be nice if, at least once, we can have grapefruit juice on Friday. Sameness means predictability and, when we know what is happening, there is reassurance and safety. And it is trust and dependability when everything else seems to be in chaos. It is also a good prelude to grief work with children. Grief knocks down and rips apart, much like having the wrong lunch on Monday. We should understand that. As adults we know grief in chaos. When grandchildren are in that chaos, how will a grandparent help?

Grief and sorrow tend to disrupt things, thriving on the chaos that follows. This is what made the Monday grapefruit juice issue so important. The child is now on a schedule determined by the school bus and family members to piece together something we might recognize and get ready for. It is a new day, even while everything takes on a different sense of urgency. We may be oblivious to the needs of a child who is less concerned with picking the right casket and more about the luncheon schedule. It may just be that the grandparent will stop and really listen.

Janice Nadeau (1998) has an international reputation for her work on the impact of loss within families. She is a strong guide on family meaning, how it does or does not function, and both the tensions that families face and the abiding strength and bond that can bring them into and beyond these times of loss. She moves us from the primary focus on individuals and loss to an investigation of family grief. She emphasizes, How family members interactively make sense of their experience may well determine both outcomes and coping. This interactive process, referred to as *family meaning-making*, is said to occur in a variety of family events, traditions and rituals, and not just those that follow a death. (Hess & Handel, 1959) Nadeau notes (1998),

> Hess and Handel coined the term *family worlds* to capture the notion of family as a finite province of meaning, having its own consistent logic of knowing that applies within the family world of knowing that applies within the family world but not outside it. (p. 1)

Years have elapsed since Nadeau's pivotal work. It would seem that progress on understanding "family" has moved forward at a snail's pace. Any concept or body evolves at its own pace—to a point. For many families, that evolution is spinning out of control. Emergence surrenders to the rat race of emergency, challenging what we believe family living was meant to be.

Sharon and I became grandparents at 64. After Andrew, we were 67 when Adam bounced into our lives. We are thrilled by these two gifts. They surprise us, rarely annoy us, and easily make us laugh. Make no mistake about it. The hugs are great. It has required many adjustments. We are back on the clock. Taxi service to preschool, playtimes, library time, circle time, and music. Medical matters, including keeping track of what is due when, are time-consuming, especially when I have enough trouble monitoring my own appointments. We help financially, step in when there are emergencies, sometimes begrudge the "interruptions," then, when PopPop and Mama get a hug from two handsome young lads wearing big smiles, we manage to feel renewal. It is not only developing new traditions with regard to the care of the children, it also is the reward of knowing that you also were good parents.

We haven't entirely forgotten the hectic paces we endured when we both were working at very demanding jobs. Beepers can be painful intrusions. We keep asking Allison (our daughter) about Andrew's bus schedule, when the school day ends, required school supplies, and what we need to get from the physicians. We aren't that old and cranky, and try not to behave that way with our daughter. We started pushing our daughter because the information was not forthcoming. We are learning that we must go by the school timetable even as it seems unreasonable. Things are moving now, but how do we know if everything is in place?

The seminal work of Price, Price, and McKenry (2010) introduces us to the Parent-Child Subsystem (p. 239). It focuses on a shared history that is disrupted by divorce. These are some of the results from changes in routine; all of these are like "deaths" to a child.

- Possible relocation or moving in temporarily
- Multiple changes that affect both parents and children
- Typical routines of daily life also are disrupted, renegotiated, or face short-term suspension. Children ask tough questions and their timing often is off the mark. "Will you walk me to the bus stop?" or "Do you know how to fix a peanut butter and jelly sandwich?" "What is proper dress for school?"

"Scouts meet after school. Is the uniform ready?" "I need to return books to the library."
- Some subsystems emerge because of the destruction of the original-couple disruption or dissolution by death. Like divorce, everything is gone and yet the "responsible parent" is still around.
- Grandparents, parents, and children will need to negotiate and renegotiate a daily schedule. Don't worry if you don't like it. It can be very static.
- Stress is in all families, and this includes these redefined families. Stress can be soothing or heightened by involving the children in the planning.
- Loyalties can be stressed and produce conflicts.

Hooyman and Kramer (2006) have produced a standard-setting book that speaks to many interrupted life experiences. *Living Through Loss: Interventions Across the Life Span* gives meaning to context and context to meaning. In their discussion of grandparents providing primary care, they point out that, "Although some grandparents gain tremendous pride, love, and feelings of being needed from caregiving, they nevertheless face numerous losses " (p. 317). Some examples of loss emerging from this new arrangement are listed here:

- Retirement time or income that they had anticipated in a child-free old age.
- Dreams of their multigenerational family
- Friends who pursue their leisure instead of being constrained by childcare responsibilities.
- Shame for their adult children's inability to care for their own children. (p. 317)

Every issue or symptom is different and also as varied, as are the stories that represent current life history. Some of the reference points cited above are important when understanding the features discussed in this story.

The rules have a way of changing, as do the "players." No one has a clear picture of how the life game is meant to be played. There are as many stories as there are parents: single parents, both parents working, divorce, blended families, death, war (and returning veteran parents), fiscal crises, same-sex parenting. Do we have working models that define today's family? Has there ever been one specific description that we are expected to model? Of course not. The specifics come over the long haul, prophetically reported and commented upon as we find ourselves again setting the standards for family! Did this cycle work? Is it working now? Who will assess, shape, and implement the new tomorrows while sustaining us today. These changes often become that deep hole. The darkness frightens us and the helplessness from being beyond rescue washes over grandparents, parents, and children.

Family as concept has been defined, disrupted, reconfigured, and oftentimes moved beyond anything we could identify. Some families are bound together by gender, with mothers, daughters, sisters, and grandmothers (and others) becoming the definitive standard for their families. Mothers or mothers and fathers are often juggling multiple jobs, parenting, becoming parents to their families, facing challenges that put enormous pressure on children, and heighten the worries weighing down the parents and their children. The treadmill effect is evident. All of these extra jobs (at least financially) infringe upon our complicated lives—shortages of energy and more than mite fair aches and pains. For all of these resources there remain those families in which love, the sharing of sorrow, and the pathway of hope are blocked or broken or otherwise tarnished by the secrets and resultant shame from secrets revealed.

UNDERSTANDING THE POWER OF INTERDEPENDENT

There are many diagrammatic approaches to identifying the key components we are looking at in this chapter. Remember from the start that we are encouraging interdependence. That inhibits people, especially children. We all bounce around among three lifestyles: dependent, interdependent, and independent. They can take radical departures from the base definitions we give to them.

There are many ways to use concentric circles. Set within one another, they provide a way of identifying those closest to us (of course we are in the center circle) while allowing those who are further out the place they occupy in this fabric as they move in and out. Some who had no meaning to the other often become central. There are many whom we consider "the nearest and dearest," who may slide into the back rows for a time. Not necessarily anything personal, but we are wandering on unfamiliar soil.

The model preferred for this is a large planter, round, with low side walls and filled with soil. Three plants are transferred to the pot. One is a tall, mighty plant. In matters of tenure and experience, we might link that plant to the grandparents. While there are many possible exceptions, the parents are the primary decision makers, guides, interpreters, and providers for the family, including the children. In this situation, the need for active grandparent involvement is quite strong in many families. Children quickly pick up on mixed messages. The parents must be the parents, but veteran helpers are always needed.

The plant for the grandparent(s) is transplanted into the same planter, with a gap in the center for the child or children. Each one gets his or her plant, young, ready to grow, and thriving on the rich soil also providing nurture for the parents and grandparents. We stretch our roots, seek our nourishment, and stand as tall as we can against the winds of the world. As a grandparent helping my wife take care of two grandchildren every day, I think we are doing a good job with two good kids. It rewrites our lives for a time, fills our calendars, and pinches our wallets. Who would seek retirement and miss all of this?

The focus of this book is children and teens. That is where we will look. There are more than children in this garden. As growth takes place there are changes for each "plant." These changes can push us apart. Seldom do these changes link us to common paths and tasks.

GRANDPARENTS: SKETCHING TODAY'S PICTURE

I was adopted. My paternal grandparents died when I was a toddler. My maternal grandmother died two weeks before my seminary graduation. She was my grandmother, mother, best friend, *Scrabble* partner, pinochle partner, and spiritual director, who reached my heart despite that nagging pain that someone didn't want me, love me, or find me suitable. She knew what it meant to be a grandmother, and I learned to become a man, pursue a career, fall in love (Gram was at our wedding), and how to be a grandson. Now I add the credential of grandparent as we share these tales, memories, and hopes with Andrew and Adam.

Like any group with a shared name or job description, there are both the markers we would expect to see in today's grandparents, some generalities and stereotypes that are both hurtful and harmful, and a multigenerational revolution set to define what we want in today's grandparents. All characteristics are framed by those making the observations and drawing the conclusions. Those who are observers in grief can find their observations changing as capriciously as everything else in life. Grandparents cannot always be the steadying shoulder and the guiding hand. And grandparents will someday die too!

WHAT DO GRANDPARENTS LOOK LIKE?

Like anything else, it really depends on what the observer sees and who the reviewer is. These are some comments about grandparents from many years of pastoral care and counseling:

1. She is so classy and bears an uncanny resemblance to Elizabeth the Queen Mother.
2. He always tried to "manage us." His mind wandered more frequently, but we wouldn't dare say anything. He was our corporate head.
3. Grandpa had been sick for years. In many ways he died long ago. He seems to know nothing of his surroundings or his family. My bedroom became his hospital room. He lived his last two years in the family home. He had very little connection with reality.
4. They look old, often seem lost in space, don't always match clothes properly, and, at best, smell like Right Guard deodorant.

GRANDPARENTS HAVE DEFINED GOALS, SPECIFIC VALUES, AND EXPECTATIONS

Grandparents are human, have feelings, have likes and dislikes, love me (but that doesn't always guarantee approval), seem to find specific ways to nurture us as we proceed to and through this new challenge or expectation, and are very good at spotting our "ouchies" and doing the "right kind of medicine." They can be our best friends. They understand my parents and their decisions and choices, but they do not always agree with them. They believe in "tomorrow." They also like ice cream, which is so cool!

GRANDPARENTS HAVE THEIR SHARE OF HURTS, PAIN, LOSSES, AND CHALLENGES

When a grandparent dies, or "is gone" due to creeping senility or Alzheimer's, a child may believe that "Nothing will ever be quite the same again." That can be as traumatic for a 14-year-old as with any elder. It also can be seen as a new adventure, another marker—"I am growing up." Many teens and young adults don't have the benefit of experience to trace what is happening in more relevant ways and what this may mean to us and do to us. Most older adults are veterans of pain, broken bones, diseases, hurt feelings, disappointments, and such, and their own history both interprets the significance of these experiences and provides some scale or yardstick to help the older adult assess possible pathways to resolution. The price of quality medical care, more and more knowledge, antibiotics can run very high. Even with good medical care, there is always that price to pay. As many physicians have said, doctors don't fool God and you don't save patients. They just postpone death for a time. Grandparents know this all too well, and grandparents hurt. They have trouble sleeping. Pain is real. They spend too much time waiting in doctor's offices. Medicare and its supplements provide much calm, but it doesn't smooth all of the other turbulence.

GRANDPARENTS ARE TO GRANDCHILDREN AS A MASK AND SHIN GUARDS ARE TO A BASEBALL CATCHER

Our intent is not only to stress the importance of grandparents to young children (and even teens), but also to point out that, as much as we come to life when we are with our grandchildren and always carry a lot pictures, it comes with a price. Retirement plans are put on hold. There are more expenses than anticipated, and sleep patterns will change. Resources on grief and children remind us of many requirements for caring for children. The number one need is to keep the structure predictable.

Parents need the grandparents to keep in touch. They will know everything is going well because the grandparents oversee things at home. Grandparents need to communicate, to take time for simple meetings, gather in the rest of the family, or at least the siblings. Share stories that you remember. Stability is crucial and it is the place where we should start with each grandchild. Grandchildren (and at times their parents—the grandparent's children) can be very bright, focused, and hardworking, but they are still children.

GRANDPARENTING IN TODAY'S WORLD

Yesteryear's grandparents would be hard-pressed to find any landing field in what we define as today's "modern family." A book that helps us shape that picture of the modern family is *Help! I'm Raising My Grandkids: Grandparents Adapting to Life's Surprises*, by Harriet Hodgson (2012). It manages to transcend recent generations and expectations. Much of that which they write for today would have been equally true generations back. Don't be fooled. When a grandparent is thrust into a parenting role (full time or part time), nothing has changed and everything has changed. Mark this carefully and clearly.

We always stress that we let the children be themselves and speak for themselves. This "ground rule" has not changed, and today's "modern child" can do quite well at it when important guides and resting points are in place. Following the model in Hodgson's book offers a structure that also would work in small groups. This would allow grandparents to share and receive clarification, information, and hugs!

WHY THIS? WHY NOW? NOW WHAT?

These questions are crucial. We will never answer them completely because that would mean that the subject is closed and the issues have all been addressed. This is not going to happen. They will soften for a time and will also serve as good markers to measure where we are, how far we have come, and if we are on the right track.

When our daughter called and announced that, at 38, she would bear us a grandchild, we considered ourselves to be ready. Who were we kidding? We had planned to retire and move to Galesburg to be with the family. We both had lost our jobs. A good time to move? There was an air of caution, occasionally fear, because our foundations had a very disjointed fit. That is not an unusual situation for today's grandparents. It all sounded supremely grand, and it was and is. But make no mistake here, however, every step of the way seemed to be a battle. We fell into a new learning curve and it was a pretty hefty curriculum. It also was wonderful.

Lifting the Fog

In our case, freedom, as we had known it, was severely compromised. We couldn't sleep in, lounge around in our bed clothes, or decide to go out for breakfast. What we had forgotten was that families are built on understanding, communication, trust, lots of patience, and forgiveness, learning, walking away from moments, words or actions best left for another time and, above all, keeping your sense of humor. Make lists, then make more lists. It is a turning point when a grandparent has lists, but has stopped writing them in ink.

GRANDPARENTS HAVE VALUES, DREAMS, NEEDS, AND PROBLEMS

In researching these significant concerns, statistics can be a difficult matter to address. The "senior" segment of our society is growing rapidly, outpacing the other age and social groups. Linda Goldman, contributor to this book, therapist, counselor, author, and educator, is among the best when children/teens need help and also for the parents, grandparents, and professionals who, however reluctantly, are called in to care for grieving children and teens. In the third edition of her book, *Life & Loss: A Guide to Help Grieving Children* (2014), Linda gives us the facts, the numbers, and the ramifications for many dimensions of children and loss. A few of them are listed here because it is so important that we both consider the complexities of each story and each griever, and also clarify what each caring person should understand are the needs "out there" and what can be reasonably expected from them. She introduces this section with this tough reality: "Today's children live in a world of experiences and memories inundated with children's loss and death issues. The following statistics illustrate the picture of the grieving child as the norm in the present millennium" (p. 4).

A. Death: "The death of a parent, which is experienced by 4% of children in Western countries, is consistently rated as one of the most stressful life events that a child can experience" (p. 4).
B. Divorce: "Half of all divorces involve minor children, with 1 million children a year joining the ranks" (p. 5).
C. Grandparents raising children: "Almost 7.8 million children under age 18 live in homes where the householders are grandparents or other relatives (10.5% of all children under 18)" (p. 5).
D. Children with a parent in prison: "53% of the 1.5 million people held in U.S. prisons in 2007 were the parents of one or more minor children. This percentage translates into more than 1.7 million minor children with an incarcerated parent... African American children are 7 and Latino children 2.5 times more likely to have a parent in prison than White children." (p. 6)

These are but a few of the many of life's twists and turns that call for the help of an adult in supporting the children and the families as independent units. Some grandparents back into this childcare role. Everything is worked out—pension, medical care, housing, social networks—and the call comes for help. Some younger grandparents are both doing the babysitting and looking for babysitters who can suit their scheduling needs. There are many things a grandparent/caregiver has to learn:

- When the children are wound up, not listening, not cleaning up their toys, and such, a grandparent can laugh about it. After all, grandparents are not the parents, but grandparents providing childcare. We get the fun and they get the work. We can go home when it seems necessary.
- Grandparents now are juggling multiple schedules and may still be working. There are clubs, sports teams, theater groups they have joined.

These demand time, often hard work, and you can't just sleep in the next day to catch up
- Life patterns and routines are firm. When conflicts arise, what do you do? This reminds us how little control we have. New boundaries and protocols seem to unfold daily. One of the toughest ones to both honor and enforce is, "We are now off duty."
- All grandparents know that their grandchildren are "gifted." We are grandparents and we know this. We also acknowledge that caring for these gifted children costs money, from school lunches to field trips to play trips to college and their care involves time. This takes a toll on any grandparent.
- These new responsibilities do not necessarily represent losses in life. Grandparents may be thrilled and happy to help. There are times when grandparents feel resentful, usually because they feel taken advantage of. It requires carefully crafted conversation, mutual respect, trust, and a lot of patience.

Harriet Hodgson, in the aforementioned book, *Help! I'm Raising My Grandkids: Grandparents Adapting to Life's Surprises* (2012), provides some encouragement, reassurance, plus lots of helpful hints. It paints good landscapes for working grandparents that is both lovely and realistic. These are not easy arrangements we must face. They are emotionally demanding, physically exhausting, money draining, and so much more.

The demands of childcare quickly diminish nagging problems or tough challenges that come to those who are adults and grandparents. We have our feelings and we still are very much in control. That control, however, is a rude awakening for those who want to meet our buddies for coffee every morning, for the neighbors who talk over the hedges about our yards and our families, the job that seems to scratch your needs and anticipated pleasures of your "to-do" lists, is plagued with so many side challenges, opportunities, and disappointments that our own frame of reference, health, and our marriage remain in a frequent state of chaos.

Grandparents can become easy prey for "specials" on everything from reverse mortgages to bargain funerals. We have witnessed so much in life and want to share it with grandchildren. What happens if health fails or death comes? Are we prepared enough so that the surviving partner can continue taking care of the grandchildren and yet maintain reasonable financial security? Will there be enough of the "right" medical care for spouse, children and grandchildren? A grandparent needs to address this and must see to that while he/she still can? Again the key question, "Who will take care of my spouse if I can't?"

How do we express our spiritual values, unanswered questions, or circumstances that tend to cut us off from the spiritual and religious resources that have been vital fixtures in our lives? At least in the Christian tradition, older adults are the largest segment of adults and usually the most fiscally generous. They want only to serve their God in a meaningful way, yet often feel overlooked. "Are my portions now so small that they are outweighed by the cost of the gasoline to drive over here? Is this what God thinks of me?" Who will address her spiritual needs? She has several grandchildren who attend there. What must they be thinking?

WHAT IS TO BECOME OF US, OUR CHILDREN, AND OUR GRANDCHILDREN?

Many questions have been presented in this chapter. There are many more questions. All of them seem pertinent to us personally as well as suitable markers when talking with other "working grandparents." These questions struggle with issues of life and death, of justice and fairness, and also doing what we can for our children and grandchildren. If we have at least put the questions before you we have accomplished a lot.

Put all of this together in your thinking, planning, and doing and you may just be the one who will make a difference for children and grandchildren.

- How did we get into this mess? Is there a nearby exit?
- What of family conflicts and coping? Who can see the big picture? Are there any shortcuts?
- Are you on the alert for "guilt?" It can be a monster lurking about.
- Do your grandchildren tell you how much they love you? Do you remember to tell them that they are included in the family gatherings and funeral time?

THE CONTRACT

For most of us, this understanding is not a written document cosigned by two witnesses and an attorney. Some do need this in order to facilitate communication and trust and also to provide a written schedule that helps the family, but it also can provide details for medical appointments, babysitters, play time, and the few less-familiar affairs that can catch us by surprise and leave us unprepared for whatever the day has planned.

Communicate. A challenge with a contract is that it can't guarantee that all of the tasks will be known, understood, and completed. Nothing replaces communication except more communication. It means having more details to juggle with schedules and more intrusion into days that are otherwise "normal."

THE WEDGE

Wedges are walls, things that divide or prompt us to travel a different road. Sometimes we devise our own wedges, much like "time-outs" for rest, to catch up on chores, to vacation, or just to get away from the children. It is important to remember that this new "childcare" is not just watching the children while their parents get some chores done. It can become a radical departure from what we would consider "normal."

We approach our older years with anticipation of free time, more control over schedules, and, as one friend reminded, to go fishing at 0430 when he wants to sleep in 'til noon. When we think of the responsibilities of childcare and our awareness of its intrusion, we might speak of it as "a wedge intruding on the present wedge."

In *How to Cope With Mental Illness in Your Family: A Self-Care Guide for Siblings, Offspring, and Parents* (1998), authors Marsh and Dickens provide a very clear picture of life "in the later years." We are not suggesting that this is a mental illness issue or that we should anticipate its presence. Nevertheless we should keep its possibility in mind. We are making use of their discussion of "late adulthood." This does warrant some clarification. More contemporary discussions of these years would speak of them as "later years." They are not necessarily the "end of the line," though that can be looming in the darkness. For our purposes it is like east/west. In one direction and in the other one road with the choice of turning right or left. We find our aging, or that of our spouse/partner, the engines of failing health, more aches and pains, diminishing funds, more deaths among family and friends, a need for a more structure in a residential setting that offers convenience, assistance, and safety. Generally it means one spouse now has two "jobs" and there is the risk that both might suffer. The "working partner" has doubled his or her workload when they too might be facing the same perils now experienced by their partners.

Marsh and Dickens (1998) speak of "late adulthood" as "a new set of challenges and opportunities for most of us. During this phase we often adapt to more restricted vocational, financial, and social circumstances" (p. 70). It can require us "to attain a sense of meaning and coherence in our lives" (p. 71). It can also be a time to enhance our present lives by providing opportunities for a "period of successful aging that is marked by growth, vitality, and creativity" (p. 70).

It has not been mentioned before, but Marsh and Dickens speak about these new developing phases, which include "a personal legacy, an occupational legacy, an interpersonal legacy, and a family legacy" (1998, p. 71).

FINALLY . . . THE END

There is much more to be said on this subject. More and more children and teens need that honest caring from the adults in their lives and even from classmates or teammates. While here I had more to say about children than teens, they deserve the same any of us would ask in a similar situation—to have us listen; to be surrounded, but with lots of room; to understand how the mid-teen boy, after the death of his father, may need to juggle being the man of the house when he just wants to be a little boy who knew how much his parents loved him. He wants to sneak off with his friends. It was happier throwing the football around. He needs to know that Dad would understand.

The planter I spoke of earlier is real and it is life. A pediatric social worker used a similar approach many years ago, working with middle school students, families, and friends after a popular teacher died a horrible, violent death. How will plants fill her planter? Aging has created its own planter for me. Then the arrival of Andrew and Adam put that one planter on hold. Of course it is still there and I don't want it to sneak up on me. I don't need everyone telling me how to tend my garden. I remember shocking some friends when I tried to rescue my mother's garden. She was proud of her flowers, and the friends failed to accept any issues I might have had with my mother or the risky allergies waiting for me in the garden. That didn't matter. "Get those weeds out of the garden. Your mother would be very disappointed." Even allowing for that woman's sorrow because my mother and she were close friends for years, I put on my clergy hat long enough to stay reasonably calm and polite (which sounds more like my father!), turned to the woman, and said, "My mother took many years to die. I know that mother was so proud of the garden. I live five states away and can't be there, so right now I am helping my mother by reminding anyone who stops by to 'remember the weeds.'"

Children bear the gift of honesty, hope, and trust. In their innocence, they often remind us of our own pain and helplessness, not grasping that isn't in how you say it, but in how you share. Andrew was at his great grandmother's funeral. Like everyone else, he threw a rose on the casket in the grave. He had many questions and still has many questions that he hasn't yet put into words, but his first agenda was family, and meeting his cousins for the first time. Adam joined the family when Grandma died. They both shared their rose, though I think Adam may have wanted it back!

Never think a child isn't grieving for someone or something special. They may not know or understand what they are feeling. A favorite toy becomes a good friend. Teens may grieve with selected friends rather than their parents. They may be rougher on defense in the football game. They will make it as we listen, hang around, and not pout when it seems like the teens have forgotten us.

I have a friend who taught death education in high school for 25 years. Each year he would ask his students, "What can you do now to make it easier for those left behind when you die?" It has helped his students to not put things off and to try to deal with business now. They tried to not leave any "I Love You" left unsaid. The same question could be useful for grandparents. This chapter has highlighted some of the many roles that grandparents play in their families. What can be done to help those left behind when death does arrive? When is the time to do that? Well, since none of us know for sure, I would guess the best time is right now.

REFERENCES

Clinton, H. R. (1996). *It takes a village: And other lessons children teach us.* New York, NY: Simon & Schuster.

Goldman, L. (2014). *Life & loss: A guide to help grieving children* (3rd ed.). New York, NY: Routledge.

Hess, R. D., & Handel, G. (1959). *Family worlds: A psychological approach to family life.* Chicago: University of Chicago Publishing.

Hodgson, H. (2012). *Help! I'm raising my grandkids: Grandparents adapting to life's surprises.* Createspace.

Hooyman, N., & Kramer, B. (2006). *Living through loss: Interventions across the life span.* New York, NY: Columbia University Press.

Marsh, D., & Dickens, R. (1998). *How to cope with mental illness in your family: A self-care guide for siblings, offspring, and parents.* New York, NY: Penguin Putnam.

Nadeau, J. (1998). *Families making sense of death.* Thousand Oaks, CA: Sage.
Price, S., Price, C., & McKenry, P. (2010). *Families & change: Coping with stressful events and transitions.* Thousand Oaks, CA: Sage.

CHAPTER 15
Difficult Conversations: Children, Adolescents, and Death

Carolyn Cullen

In the past 60 years, mental health professionals have made great strides in understanding how children perceive the world, in how they learn, think, and feel. This knowledge base is critical in helping parents, caregivers, and counselors answer children's questions about death. Many organizations have developed educational pamphlets and books to help caregivers of grieving children. There is less information about how to talk to all children about death. The U.S. Government published an informational booklet, "Talking to Children about Death" (NIMH, 1979). The National Institutes of Health (NIH) updated the NIMH booklet in 2006 with roughly the same information. The information in both government publications is largely based on the work of experts who have worked with children and families. This chapter looks at some of the expert advice and empirical studies that specifically look at our current understanding of talking to children about death. It attempts to answer questions about how honest adults should be with children and adolescents about death and how to protect them from anxiety associated with the topic.

It is noteworthy that most of the popular work on talking to children about death is drawn from practical wisdom. In regard to helping bereaved children, Schuurman (2003–2004) points out, "there is an unfortunate gap that exists in tying together clinical experience and solid research findings" (p. 418). Much of what we know about talking to normal children comes from direct experience of adults who have spent a lot of time working with children and families affected by death. In addition, many experts on death and dying come from religious backgrounds since they are often brought in to help families when medical personnel can no longer prolong life. This chapter provides arguments for opening up conversations about death with all children, not just sick children or children affected by death and loss. Furthermore, some of the barriers to talking openly will be presented as well a presentation of the developmental model used to provide a framework for talking to young people about death. A case vignette for each developmental phase will be used to illustrate some of the issues. Lastly, some good children's storybooks will be listed to provide the reader with a way to open up a conversation and normalize the topic of death when speaking with children.

THE CASE FOR TALKING TO CHILDREN AND ADOLESCENTS ABOUT DEATH

There are undeniable truths about death that can be difficult for adults to confront, let alone explain to children. As Benjamin Franklin famously noted, there are two things in life that are certain: death and taxes. Taxes might be avoided, but death is inevitable, universal, and permanent. Unlike separations that might be temporary, death is the final ending to life on earth. Noppe and Noppe (2004) summarize five important principal concepts about death: universality (everyone dies), irreversibility (death is permanent), nonfunctionality (the body stops working), causality (there are reasons for death), and noncorporal continuation (idea of spirituality or afterlife). As children move toward adult maturity, they develop a greater capacity to understand these key concepts. Adults can play an important role in helping children to understand these concepts gradually over time through active listening, simple explanations, and reassurance.

Some adults believe that children should be shielded from knowing, thinking, or talking about death because it is too painful and potentially traumatic. According to this perspective, childhood should be occupied by play and happiness, and there is no room for such macabre topics like death. In general, thanatologists (those who study death and dying) believe that essential notions about the end of life ought to be shared with a child as a normal part of living in the world around them. Accordingly, the subject of death should not be avoided or covered up. As soon as the child shows readiness to learn and understand, adults can listen to their questions and begin a conversation. Death educators point to the fact that children are very aware of the world around them and observant of nature's life cycle. For example, children routinely witness death in everyday experiences: plants in winter, animals in nature or household pets, characters in cartoons, video games, fairytales, and movies. Children also hear stories about death in the media and from adult conversations.

Talking about death in everyday life before a child is directly affected by death might be easier to do because there is less emotional involvement (NIH, 2006). Hilliker (2013) encourages adults to use teachable moments to promote truth-telling with children, helping them to understand death and loss. The exact approach in which to bring up the topic of death with children is not clear-cut. For example, Schuurman (2003–2004) advocates using nonfiction children's books to explain death in a factual, direct way, which some in the field believe to be too intrusive. Clearly the level of openness about talking about death will depend largely on the child's cognitive and emotional readiness to have such a discussion as well as other factors described later in the chapter. The idea of striking a balance when talking about death with children is captured well by Bugge, Darbyshire, Rokholt, and

Haugstvedt (2014). They describe balancing between shielding and including, and also balancing informing and frightening.

Perhaps the best argument for talking openly to children about death is that children have the emotional capacity to experience loss at a very early age. Children are able to experience the negative emotions surrounding temporary loss, commonly known as separation anxiety. This understanding is earned through a child's normal separation with a caregiver in infancy and early childhood. Bowlby (1960), the forebear of attachment theory, was the first to draw a parallel between an infant's separation with his/her adult caregiver and the adult experience of loss and grief. In his observation of infants who were removed from their mother and familiar surroundings, Bowlby found a pattern of protest, despair, and detachment, which he correlated with adult grief and mourning. If babies and young children are capable of cognitive and emotional awareness about separation, children might benefit from ongoing short conversations about death as they become aware of it. As grief counselor Rabbi Earl Grollman (1990) clarifies,

> A child growing up today is more aware of death than you may realize. Grief is a deeply felt human emotion, as normal as playing, laughing, crying, or sleeping. Grief is a way of saying, "I miss you," or, "I'm sorry for all the things I've said and done." When you avoid children's reactions, you may magnify fears and replace reality with fantasy and psychological defenses. (p. ix)

An adult's ability to invite a child's questions and reactions to death is quite another story.

CHALLENGES IN TALKING TO CHILDREN AND ADOLESCENTS ABOUT DEATH

Even for motivated and well-meaning adults, talking to children about death has many challenges. First and foremost, our society has been called death denying and death-defying. We put off thinking about death and try to prolong youthfulness well into adulthood. The market is filled with age-defying products that capitalize on adults' fears about growing old. In fact, the subject of death and dying is often thought of as taboo, shrouded in darkness, and not to be brought up in normal conversation. Grief counselor and community educator Primo (2013) often finds that adults with whom he works—school administrators, teachers, and parents—"like to sweep death under the rug and act as if things are normal" (p. 12). Developing openness in this context takes courage.

Another challenge to talking openly about death is that it requires an adult to confront anxiety about mortality and the complex negative emotions associated with death. The idea that life can end abruptly or naturally brings up negative feelings of discomfort: hurt, anxiety, sadness, fear, despair, and even anger. Adults might want to deflect acknowledging these negative emotions with children. For example, a child observes to her mother that old people die, and the mother responds by focusing on how great heaven is. It is quite common to use avoidance to ward off the negative feelings associated with endings (Gitterman & Germain, 2008). Findings in brain imaging suggest that putting negative feelings into words can actually help normalize difficult experience and may ultimately play a role in promoting positive mental and physical health (Lieberman et al., 2007).

Adults who have unresolved issues around loss can be stymied by conversations about death, creating even more of an incentive to keep an especially painful topic secret so as not to trigger upset. Family therapist Imber-Black (2014) describes the "paradoxes of protection" whereby such secrets are kept to protect others but end up creating harm. The harm is done when family members can sense the anxiety and discomfort but cannot put their finger on the source. This can happen when children sense that talking about death is not okay with an adult. In the best-case scenario, the child in this situation finds another adult with whom it is safe to wonder and talk about death. In the worst case scenario, the child internalizes the anxiety and develops a belief that talking about death is anxiety-provoking and taboo.

Interestingly, a review of the literature suggests that fear of death generally decreases with age (Neimeyer, Wittkoski, & Moser, 2003). This might be because adults become more accustomed to personal mortality through their experience with death and dying. As adults move through the life cycle, they might gradually gain competency in witnessing death and dying, which might help develop a mature perspective of life coming to an end. This idea is supported by Bluck, Dirk, Mackay, and Hux's (2008) finding that adult hospice volunteers with more death experience had lower levels of anxiety toward death than volunteers with less experience. These same adults were able to use death-related memories to add meaning to their lives and help form social connections with others. Another study found that parental warmth of the surviving parent actually served as a buffer against the negative effects of losing a parent (Haine, Wolchik, Sandler, Millsap, & Ayers, 2006). The authors identified communication skills, namely, active listening, as an important component of parental warmth. These findings suggest that overcoming the stress associated with facing death is a life skill that adults can learn and master so they can talk openly about it with the next generation.

A third challenge to inviting children to talk about death is lack of knowledge about how to go about doing it in a sensitive and caring way. The rest of this chapter attempts to address "the how" of talking to children about death. Likewise, this chapter will also address when it is appropriate to omit certain information in order to protect children from overstimulating facts that might cause excessive worry or fears of abandonment. Honesty is the best policy, with the caveat that adults must be well-attuned to what information a given child can handle at any given point. The prevailing developmental model will be used, which has one think about a child's cognitive maturity. Also, other important factors will be discussed that should be considered in opening up conversations.

THE DEVELOPMENTAL MODEL

The developmental model is described well by Koocher (1974), who looked at age and how children respond to four questions about death. The questions were open-ended and asked children to (1) Describe what causes death, (2) Can death be reversed, how? (3) When does death occur? and (4) How do people die? According to Koocher, children's understanding of death follows developmental lines of childhood in three stages: preoperational, concrete operational, and formal operational. He found that children's ideas about death were different at each stage of development, supporting the idea that cognitive maturity was an important factor in a child's understanding of death. In the following three sections, each developmental stage is described and its bearing on a child's understanding of death during that stage.

Preschool Age (Preoperational)

Case Vignette

A father of a 3-year-old son is driving home late one night. His son is in the backseat quiet with exhaustion from staying up well past his bedtime. Suddenly out of the silence and darkness, his son asks him pointedly, "Daddy are you going to die?" The child's father pauses a moment before responding, "No Buddy, Daddy's not going to die."

Children between the ages of 3 and 5 are naturally curious and explore the world through observation and play. They are egocentric, meaning they process the world around them as if they are the center of the universe. The child may mistakenly believe that he is the reason for both good and bad events. It is important to be aware that children might blame themselves for bad events and reassure them that this is not the case. The child's responses to death may seem cold or unemotional as he figures out how death directly impacts him. For instance, a 5-year-old girl may suddenly start to cry because she will no longer be receiving gifts from her recently deceased grandmother. Or she may experience "magical thinking" whereby reality and imagination are intertwined. On the one hand, children might believe they can possess supernatural powers or have special benevolent guardians who protect them. On the other hand, young children can also become frightened of monsters or other evil figures of their imagination.

Death might be difficult to explain because the child tends to think in concrete terms. He is not developmentally equipped to understand concepts outside of the here and now. Consequently, death may be seen as reversible and not permanent. For example, a child might believe that someone can come back to life even after seeing the dead person in an open casket. Experts urge adults to talk about death in a simple and concrete way, avoiding euphemisms that might stimulate a child's fantasies and create misunderstandings (NIH, 2006).

How then can a parent respond to a preschooler asking if the parent will die? In the case vignette above, the father lies, perhaps to both avoid his own anxiety and prevent upsetting the child. Looking at the question using a developmental lens, one begins to wonder what is stimulating the child's question. Is the child afraid to fall asleep for fear of losing his father? How does he perceive dying? What happened during the day that might have triggered this question? Within this context, the parent has more options than "yes" or "no." He might clarify the question and ask his son what is making him wonder about it. He might reassure him that it is OK to fall asleep and he will talk to him in the morning. He might also silently reflect on how his son has become more aware of the life cycle and how this question shows his son's greater cognitive capacity and awareness.

Elementary School–Aged Children (Concrete Operational)

Case Vignette

A mother recounts the following story about her 7-year-old daughter. Her daughter overhears a news report that a famous actor has been found dead with a needle in his arm. Alarmed at this, the girl turns to her mother and asks, "Was he sewing?" The mother senses her daughter's fear (the mother likes to sew) and succinctly and assuredly answers, "No, I don't think so."

The school-age child begins to move beyond egocentricity and gains the understanding that there are forces in play that may have nothing to do with him or her. The child gains greater awareness that death is universal and irreversible and begins to understand causality. While children at this age begin to understand the causes of death, they might still hold onto contingency notions or view death as avoidable (Varga & Paletti, 2013). "They harbor the idea that somehow they can escape through their own ingenuity" (NIH, 2006, p. 4). In addition, while they might understand that there are different reasons that cause death, they might have difficulty understanding the full processes of how death occurs. For example, they might understand that people die of old age, but they may not understand the exact cause of what makes the body stop working.

In the case vignette, the young girl is alarmed by the news of someone's death and is wondering about the cause of the death. The child seems to be alarmed that the actor might have died of sewing since the activity seems harmless and her mother likes to sew. The mother intuits the daughter's fear and assures her that the death was not from sewing. The conversation is succinct and possibly fraught with unsaid emotion such as fear and worry. The mother might want to invite the child to talk more openly about her ideas and feelings. The mother could also help the child develop her understanding of what can cause one's body to stop functioning: a wound from a sharp object or overdose on drugs. Again, looking from a developmental perspective, the parent can celebrate the child's curiosity and greater capacity to understand that death is irreversible and consider what makes someone die.

Adolescents (Formal Operational)

Case Vignette

A mother is frustrated that her teenage daughter does not want to spend time with her ailing grandmother. Her daughter never visits or calls her grandmother on the phone. Instead, her daughter prefers to spend time with her friends.

Beginning around age 11, adolescence is a time of rapid growth accompanied by physical, cognitive, and emotional changes. Susillo (2005) aptly describes how death is counter to late adolescent experience,

> In adolescence, the focus is on life, limitless potential, and passionate vitality. The adolescent's subjective experience is a cauldron of conflicting forces of change and growth. The body's development and sexual urgency are exhilarating and alarming; the rapidly expanding cognitive competencies are exciting; the anticipated landscape of adult power and privilege is tantalizing and so near. (p. 500)

By the time children reach adolescence, the majority have had some personal experience with death. As many as 90% of adolescents have known a family member or friend who has died (Ens & Bond, 2007). While most teens have experience with death, studies show that they feel the most emotional upset by the loss of a friend who is close to them (Servaty-Seib & Pistole, 2006–2007). This may be because of the importance of peer relationships during this developmental phase.

In addition to the importance of peer relationships, adolescents tend to engage in thrill-seeking or risky behaviors that can lead to death. Some researchers believe that this can be explained by the adolescent's budding cognitive recognition of death and concomitant fear of aging. During adolescence, teenagers gain the ability to think in more abstract terms wherin they are better able to understand the finite quality of life, understand the processes that bring life to an end, and potentially develop a spiritual understanding of death. These cognitive milestones can be scary and may lead adolescents to engage in risky behaviors in an attempt to cheat death. Popham, Kennison, and Bradley (2011) found that college students who held ageist attitudes and behaviors also had high levels of risk-taking behaviors (sex, drug, and alcohol use). Popham et al. suggests that risk-taking behavior in adolescents may be related to fear of aging. On the other hand, high-risk adolescent behaviors might also be a product of incomplete brain development, which thrives on stimulation during this developmental phase (Noppe & Noppe, 2004).

According to a recent news article, young people are very interested in learning to talk openly about death. Hayakaki (2014) reports that a Death in Perspective college course at Kean University in New Jersey has a 3-year waiting list. In addition, Hayakaki notes increased interest in talking about death through social events such as death dinners, salons, and cafés in cities all over the country. This optimistic perspective might be overstated, as suggested by Eckerd's (2009) study, which found that only one fifth of respondents from Midwestern psychology undergraduate programs offer courses on death, dying, and bereavement.

In the case vignette above, the adolescent girl is engaging in normal teen behavior and her lack of involvement with her grandmother might have many factors. The mother can be reassured that her daughter is engaging in developmentally appropriate behavior prizing peers over adult relationships. It is also possible that her daughter is avoiding her grandmother because she has greater cognitive capacity to understand her impending death. The mother can also take solace in the fact that her daughter is gaining independence and developing her own identity through her greater reliance on friends. This understanding can help the mother frame the issue of spending time with the grandmother as a choice for her daughter to make recognizing the complex emotions that the daughter might be facing.

Critique of the Developmental Model

Bluebond-Langner, DeCicco, and Schwallie (2012) critique the developmental model for its limits in terms of usefulness in talking to children about death. They point out that the linear, sequential nature of the developmental model does not accurately reflect the reality of children's reactions to death. For example, understanding about death is influenced by cultural background, religious beliefs, community context, and emotional reactions such as anxiety. These influences might contradict what we would expect from a child in a certain age range. What's more, children are able to hold two contradictory beliefs at the same time and might express different beliefs to different adults.

While it is true that the developmental model is based on thoughts and cognitive ability and does not take into account emotions and attachment level or style, it is an important starting point for understanding how children's reactions to death might differ dramatically from adults' perspectives. In addition, it is critical to think about environmental factors that might also be important to the child's understanding of death. In a recent study, Bonotti, Leondari, and Mastra (2012) found that children's previous experience with death was correlated with a better understanding of death through more mature death concepts. In support of the developmental model, they did find that older children have a better understanding of causality than younger children. However, they also found that 11-year-olds appear to regress on the concepts of irreversibility and nonfunctionality. They attribute this to the ability to think on a more abstract level and incorporate spiritual and religious notions that are not strictly biologically bound. Similarly, Hunter and Sullivan (2008) found that a child's age and previous death experience were correlated with a more mature understanding of death. These two studies show the continued relevance of looking at age and using the developmental model. Certainly, examining children's understanding of death is a complex undertaking and requires further empirical research.

THE USE OF CHILDREN'S BOOKS

Children's storybooks are a good tool to open up a conversation about the human life cycle. Books can guide adults who are anxious about conversations about death. In fact, reading children's books may be soothing to adults. Children's books can be an effective and nonthreatening way for both parent and child to begin to tackle the complex emotions associated with death. Hare (1993) put together a comprehensive list of children's fiction books that deal with varying types of death and loss. The following list of books is adapted from Hare's list and includes more recent award-winning and/or highly rated books on the subject. Books that were no longer in print were not included in the list. The book list is arranged by age group and is by no means an exhaustive list on the subject. This list does not include nonfiction because a story about someone else is a gentler way to introduce the topic of death and loss. The child can draw inferences from a fictional story, and she can then relate directly (or not) to the theme.

Counselors can use fiction as an adjunct in their therapeutic work with both children and adults (Detrixhe, 2010). Detrixhe (2010) discusses the value of fiction over nonfiction in providing bibliotherapy through the work of Pardeck and Pardeck. First, through identification, the reader can recognize himself in the life and problems of a character in a book. Second, the reader can experience catharsis or emotional release that might not otherwise have taken place. Lastly, the reader can develop insight by becoming aware of an issue in his life, recognizing that others face the same difficulty, and discovering new ideas and values that can be helpful. The use of fictional books is an excellent way for adults to help children cope with grief, and it is important for adults to familiarize themselves with good books before introducing them to children (Stevenson, 2008; Stevenson & Stevenson, 1996).

As discussed throughout this chapter, understanding a child's developmental phase is an important piece of understanding concerns about death and dying. That said, adults should also consider the cognitive and emotional readiness of the child to talk about death as well as take into account sociocultural factors. Therefore, the age brackets are meant to merely serve as a guide in selecting titles that might be appropriate, but caregivers should use their own judgment. Adolescent books were not included since many books read by this age group include death and loss. Lastly, adults and older children may enjoy books aimed at younger children. As Hare (1993) explains, "Children and parents may find emotional release and comfort through the simple poetic language and illustrations of younger children's books" (p. 8).

Ages 3 to 6

Aliki. (1979). *The Two of Them*. West Caldwell, NJ: Greenwillow Books.
   Describes the loving bond between a grandfather and his granddaughter and how hurt feelings follow his death; for older children in this age group. Ages 4 to 8.
Demas, C. (2004). *Saying Goodbye to Lulu*. Published by author.
   When her dog Lulu dies, a girl grieves but continues with her life.
dePaola, T. (1973). *Nana Upstairs and Nana Downstairs*. New York, NY: G.P. Putnam's Sons.
   Four-year-old Tommy enjoys his relationship with both his grandmother and great-grandmother and eventually learns to face their inevitable deaths.
Donahue, M. (1988). *The Grandpa Tree*. Niwot, CO: Roberts Rinehart.
   The story covers the lifecycle of trees, from the time a seed is dropped by a bird, grows, and finally turns to sawdust, makes a home for new trees, and becomes a seed again.
Karst, P. (2000). *The Invisible String*. Camarillo, CA: DeVorss & Company.
   A mother explains to her young children that she is connected to them through an invisible string. The story helps children deal with separation anxiety by

introducing the idea that loved ones are emotionally connected to them even if they are not physically there.

Klassen, J. (2012). *This is Not My Hat*. New York, NY: Candlewick Press.
A little fish steals a big fish's hat and tries to run and hide. The ambiguous ending allows children to consider the little fish's demise when the big fish is shown entering the hiding place and reappears wearing the hat again.

Seeger, L. V. (2007) *First the Egg*. New York, NY: Roaring Brook Press.
Shows the life cycle of plants and animals in nature.

Varley, S. (1984). *Badger's Parting Gifts*. New York, NY: Lothrop, Lee & Shepard.
A wise old Badger is worried about his friends' suffering after his death. The story shows how his friends are comforted by Badger's memory when they recall how he has helped each of them.

Wilhelm, H. (1985). *I'll Always Love You*. New York, NY: Crown.
A child's sadness at the death of a beloved dog is tempered by the remembrance of saying every night, "I'll always love you."

Ages 6 to 9

Buscaglia, L. (1982). *The Fall of Freddie the Leaf*. Thorofare, NJ: Charles B. Slack.
This allegorical tale relates the phenomena of life and death through the experiences of Freddie the leaf and his wise friend Daniel. Designed to help adults explain permanent loss to children.

Miles, M. (1971). *Annie and the Old One*. Boston, MA: Little Brown.
Annie is a young Navajo girl who refuses to believe that her grandmother, the Old One, will die. Sadly, Annie learns that she cannot change the course of life from her grandmother who explains the cycle of life and death.

Smith, L. (2011). *Grandpa Green*. New York, NY: Roaring Brook Press.
A child explores the life of his late great-grandfather with his grandfather in a topiary garden of memories.

Thomas, J. (1988). *Saying Good-bye to Grandma*. New York, NY: Clarion Books.
When her Grandmother dies, 7-year-old Suzie goes back with her parents to visit the small town where her mother grew up to attend the funeral with extended family. She experiences the sadness and comfort of family rituals related to death.

Viorst, J. (1971). *The Tenth Good Thing About Barney*. New York, NY: Atheneum Books.
A classic book about a boy heartbroken by the death of his cat, Barney. His parents help him plan a funeral and encourage him to remember 10 good things about Barney.

Ages 9 to 11

Adler, C. (1990). *Ghost Brother*. New York NY: Clarion Books.
Twelve-year-old Wally's older brother has been killed in an accident, but his spirit reappears when Wally least expects it to help him reach a goal.

Applegate, K. (2012). *The One and Only Ivan*. New York, NY: HarperCollins Children's Books.
The story of a gorilla in captivity who loses his best friend but goes on to honor her legacy.

Coerr, E. (1977). *Sadako and the Thousand Paper Cranes*. New York, NY: Putnam.
Eleven-year-old Sadako is dying of leukemia. This real-life Japanese story portrays Sadako's hope for eventual health and her final acceptance of death.

Holm, J. L. (2007). *Penny from Heaven*. New York, NY: Random House.
Set in the 1950s, 11-year-old Penny spends a summer getting to the bottom of how her father died before she was born. Shows how opening up families secrets surrounding death is difficult but ultimately worthwhile.

Jukes, M. (1985). *Blackberries in the Dark*. New York, NY: Knopf.
This story revolves around 9-year-old Austin, who spends the summer after his grandfather's death with his grandmother. Grandmother and grandchild cope with their grief by sharing activities that grandfather loved.

Kadohata, C. (2008). *Kira-Kira*. New York, NY: Atheneum Books.
A Japanese American family faces discrimination in the 1960s South and suffers the loss of one daughter who dies from an illness. Her surviving sister overcomes her grief and rallies her family to be more hopeful.

Smith, D. (1973). *A Taste of Blackberries*. New York, NY: Crowell.
This story depicts the emotions and memories of an 11-year-old boy who learns to cope with the loss of his best friend who loved playing in the sun and eating blackberries.

White, E. (1952). *Charlotte's Web*. New York, NY: Harper & Row. Pictures by Garth Williams.
A classic story about a special friendship between Charlotte the spider and Wilbur the pig. Charlotte helps Wilbur see that despite her death, she will live on in Wilbur's memories.

REFERENCES

Bluck, S., Dirk, J., MacKay, M. M., & Hux, A. (2008). Life experience with death: Relation to death attitudes and to the use of death-related memories. *Death Studies, 32*, 524–549.

Bluebond-Langner, M., DeCicco, A., & Schwallie, M. N. (2012). Children's views of death. In A. Goldman, R. Hain, & S. Liben (Ed.), *Oxford textbook of palliative care for children* (2nd ed., pp. 68–77). New York, NY: Oxford University Press.

Bonotti, F., Leondari, A., & Mastra, A. (2012). Exploring children's understanding of death: Through drawings and the death concept questionnaire. *Death Studies, 37*, 1, 47–60.

Bowlby, J. (1960). Grief and mourning in infancy and early childhood. *Psychoanalytic Study of the Child, 15*, 9–52.

Bugge, K. E., Darbyshire, P., Rokholt, E. G., Haugstvedt, K. T. S., & Helseth, S. (2014). Young children's grief: Parents' understanding and coping. *Death Studies, 38*(1), 36–43.

Detrixhe, J. J. (2010). Souls in jeopardy: Questions and innovations for bibliotherapy with fiction. *Journal of Humanistic Counseling, Education, and Development, 49*(1), 58–72.

Eckerd, L. M. (2009). Death and dying course offerings in psychology: A survey of nine Midwestern states. *Death Studies, 33*, 762–770.

Ens, C., & Bond, J. B. (2007). Death anxiety in adolescents: The contributions of bereavement and religiosity. *Omega: Journal of Death and Dying, 55*(3), 169–184.

Gitterman, A., & Germain, C. B. (2008). *The life model of social work practice* (3rd ed.). New York, NY: Columbia University Press.

Grollman, E. A. (1990). *Talking about death a dialogue between parent and child*. Boston, MA: Beacon Press.

Haine, R. A., Wolchik, S. A., Sandler, I. N., Millsap, R. E., & Ayers, T. S. (2006). Positive parenting as a protective resource for parentally bereaved children. *Death Studies, 30,* 1–28.

Hare, J. (1993). *Understanding the grief of children* [Brochure]. Corvallis, OR: Pacific Northwest Extension.

Hayakaki, E. (2014, March 6). Why college students are dying to get into 'death classes.' *The Wall Street Journal.* Retrieved from http://www.wsj.com/articles/SB10001424052702304104504579377160102817476

Hilliker, L. (2013). An enlightened (and relieved) death educator: The value of truth telling with children. *Illness, Crisis, & Loss, 21*(4), 361–364.

Hunter, S. B., & Smith, D. E. (2008). Predictors of children's understanding of death: Age, cognitive ability, death experience and maternal communicative competence. *Omega: Journal of Death and Dying, 57*(2), 143–162.

Imber-Black, E. (2014, April 4). Will talking about it make it worse? Facilitating family conversations in the context of chronic and life-shortening illness. *PubMed.gov.*

Koocher, G. (1974). Talking to children about death. *American Journal of Orthopsychiatry, 44*(3), 404–411.

Lieberman, M. D., Eisenberger, N. I., Crockett, M. J., Tom, S. M., Pfeifer, J. H., & Way, B. M. (2007). Putting feelings into words: Affect labeling disrupts amygdala activity in response to affective stimuli. *Psychological Science, 18*(5), 421–428.

National Institute of Mental Health (NIMH). (1979). *Caring about kids: Talking to children about death* (DHEW Publication No. 79-939). Rockville, MD: Author.

National Institutes of Health (NIH). (2006). *Talking to children about death.* Bethesda, MD: Author.

Neimeyer, R. A., Wittkowski, J., & Moser, R. P. (2003). Psychological research on death attitudes: An overview and evaluation. *Death Studies, 28,* 309–340.

Noppe, I. C., & Noppe, L. D. (2004). Adolescent experiences with death: Letting go of immortality. *Journal of Mental Health Counseling, 26*(2), 146–166.

Popham, L. E., Kennison, S. M., & Bradley, K. I. (2011). Ageism and risk-taking in young adults: Evidence for a link between death anxiety and ageism. *Death Studies, 35,* 751–763.

Primo, J. M. (2013). *What do we tell the children?* Nashville, TN: Abingdon Press.

Schuurman, D. L. (2003–2004). Literature for adults to assist them in helping bereaved children. *Omega: Journal of Death and Dying, 48*(4), 415–424.

Servaty-Seib, H. L., & Pistole, M. C. (2006–2007). Adolescent grief: Relationships category and emotional closeness. *Omega: Journal of Death and Dying, 54*(2), 147–167.

Stevenson, R. (2008). Helping students cope with grief. In K. J. Doka & A. S. Tucci (Eds.), *Living with grief: Children and adolescents.* Washington, DC: Hospice Foundation of America.

Stevenson, R., & Stevenson, E. (Eds.). (1996). *Teaching students about death: A comprehensive resource for educators and parents.* Philadelphia, PA: Charles Press.

Susillo, M. V. (2005). Beyond the grave—Adolescent parental loss letting go and holding on. *Psychoanalytic Dialogues, 15*(4), 499–527.

Varga, M. A., & Paletti, R. (2013). Life span issues and dying. In D. K. Meager & D. E. Balk (Eds.), *Handbook of thanatology* (2nd ed.). New York, NY: Routledge.

CHAPTER 16
The Presence of Absence: The Struggle for Meaning in the Death of a Child

Robert A. Neimeyer and Wendy G. Lichtenthal

One Father's Grief

The expression of grief of this sort knows no gender; it is as gender-neutral as stone. What has struck me so profoundly lately, some 18 months after Graham was torn from our family, has less to do with the symptoms of this pain—the loneliness, the constant tears, the loss of sleep, the gripping shame—and more to do with its dimensions.

As an aside, let me state that Graham was a person of great measure—by which I mean, he measured everything! From the youngest age, he was fascinated with the tallest building, the oldest living person (he wrote her a letter at age 8, in French, with help of a dictionary and his French-speaking grandfather), the richest man (Bill Gates became his idol for many reasons), the highest IQ, etc. Of course, this quantitative orientation had a lot to do with his becoming a passionate lover of math, music, and the pulse of life in all its forms.

It strikes me as darkly ironic, then, that this thing that so occupies my being, unquestionably the largest, heaviest, and most omnipresent thing I have ever encountered, is . . . an absence. It is an absence that is more present than the present. I am continually amazed at how ubiquitous it is; how it insinuates so thoroughly and fluidly every crevice of my consciousness. It's as if a large crystal globe had been dropped and, as it hit the floor, exploded into a million directions, the splinters embedding themselves invisibly into every aspect of my life. As I finish my shower and stretch the towel across my back, I recall wrapping up a freshly scrubbed cherub, barely two years old, as he wriggled in delight; our silly mutt has eyes that are the same shade as Graham's; Graham and a cadre of his techie pals could have fixed the Obamacare website in a week, and would have asked nothing for it, etc.

Our lives are divided into many spheres, but by convention, we keep these separate. Yet Graham's absence infiltrates these disparate spheres with a laughing randomness, making a mockery of convention and throwing into great relief how absurd our petty attempts to compartmentalize life are under the

glare of such overwhelming loss. Nothing is as present as his absence. How is it that something I have been living with so intimately, remains so ineffable?
—Brian deWit, bereaved father of Graham, who died tragically at age 23[1]

* * * *

Of the countless losses that human beings confront over the course of a lifetime, the death of a child may be the most devastating. By definition such losses are tragic, in that they violate the implicit law that children should outlive their parents. Likewise, the cause of death—whether occurring *in utero*, in the perinatal period, in childhood, or beyond—typically compounds parents' suffering, occurring suddenly in the wake of an accident or act of violence, or as a function of fetal abnormality, disease, or unknown causes. Whatever the timing and whatever the cause, such losses can challenge the felt biological imperative of the caregiving bond (Bowlby, 1980), underscoring parents' ultimate helplessness to ensure the safety of their children.

Research on bereaved parents underscores the heavy toll most suffer in the aftermath of their children's death. Mothers and fathers contending with such tragic loss are at greater risk of numerous psychosocial challenges, including depression, psychiatric hospitalization, marital disruption, and even mortality(Li, Laursen, Precht, Olsen, & Mortensen, 2005; Li, Precht, Mortensen, & Olsen, 2003; Oliver, 1999; Rogers, Floyd, Seltzer, Greenberg, & Hong, 2008). They are also believed to be at heightened risk of complicated grief (CG, also referred to as prolonged grief disorder), which is characterized by persistent preoccupation with the loss and its aftermath (Prigerson et al., 2009). While it is common for bereaved parents to grieve for the remainder of their lives, many parents find a way to coexist with their grief. Parents suffering from CG, however, experience more debilitating symptoms and related impairment in functioning and find it more difficult to adapt to their ever-present pain.

Our goal in this chapter is threefold. First, we will summarize our research on the experience of the death of a child, underscoring its impact across multiple studies. Second, we will review our findings concerning the quest for significance in parental bereavement, situating this work in the context of our broader program on meaning making as a central dimension of grieving. Finally, we will conclude by sketching some promising practices in grief therapy that are coherent with this perspective, and anchor these briefly in some selective case studies. In sum, we seek to orient readers to the relevance of meaning-based concepts and methods in understanding and addressing the unique struggles of parents facing life's most tragic loss.

---

[1] Brian requests that we include his actual name, as well as that of his son, as a means of honoring his son's life while also acknowledging his death. We open this chapter on parental grief with his words in the hope of conveying more vividly than any research summary or clinical commentary could the lived reality of an ineffable loss. In doing so, we intend to speak to the hearts as well as the minds of readers who work alongside bereaved parents to find some way forward in the wake of a shattering death.

THE IMPACT OF PARENTAL BEREAVEMENT

As noted above, several studies converge on the conclusion that the death of a child puts mothers and fathers at risk for quite serious psychological and medical outcomes. Our own research reinforces this conclusion and suggests the multifaceted nature of this impact. For example, in one study of 54 African Americans within five years of the homicide of a family member, the majority of whom were parents of the deceased, nearly 20% met diagnostic criteria for posttraumatic stress disorder (PTSD), and over 50% met criteria for clinically significant depression as well as CG. Results also suggested high comorbidity for the three conditions, with virtually all of those suffering from PTSD also reporting mood disorder and prolonged, preoccupying grief following the murder of their loved one (McDevitt-Murphy, Neimeyer, Burke, & Williams, 2012). Worryingly, although anxiety and PTSD symptomatology declined significantly across the years, no such trend was evident with respect to bereavement-related depression and CG. Neither depression nor CG appeared to remit significantly as a function of time, suggesting the clear utility of clinical intervention (Neimeyer & Currier, 2009).

A second study of bereaved parents suffering the death of a child from a broader set of causes (though mainly accidents and illness) underscores these concerns. Investigating 157 predominantly Caucasian parents, we discovered that potentially 30% of those bereaved 6 months or more met criteria for this form of prolonged and intense grieving regardless of cause of death (Keesee, Currier, & Neimeyer, 2008), which is triple the rate reported in studies of bereaved spouses (Prigerson et al., 2009). Thus, across samples that vary in ethnicity and mode of death, our research supports the general conclusion that being the parent (and especially the mother) of the deceased is a confirmed risk factor for CG (Burke & Neimeyer, 2013). More comparative research is needed, however, on relative risk for poor outcome as a function of cause of death, as it is possible that the sudden accidents that are a leading cause of death in childhood compound the complications of such loss, relative to causes of death that permit greater anticipation, closeness, and caregiving of the child, as in progressive illness.

LOSS AND THE QUEST FOR MEANING

Like other psychologists with a broadly humanistic-existential orientation, we consider the "effort after meaning" to be a defining feature of human activity (Kelly, 1955), and one that has particular relevance in the context of highly stressful life events (Frankl 1992). Specifically with reference to bereavement, we take as a starting point the proposition that grieving crucially entails the attempt to reaffirm or reconstruct a world of meaning that has been challenged by loss (Neimeyer, 2001). That is, the absence of a significant person can perturb the basic self-narrative that confers on our lives a sense of continuity, identity, and purpose, woven together with the lives of others (Neimeyer, 2004): as one young couple recently noted in their first session of grief therapy following the death of their only child, "It's as if all future chapters in our life story have been erased." Accordingly, bereavement prompts two key forms of narrative activity, as we both strive to process the "event story" of the death itself (what happened, why, and its implications who we are and how we live now), and attempt to access the "back story" of our love relationship with the deceased, in a way that restores a sense of connection and secure attachment (Neimeyer & Thompson, 2014). As mourners gradually integrate the loss into those global meaning systems that structure their sense of autobiographical identity over time, we and others have proposed that they will experience fewer symptoms of preoccupying and complicated grief (Boelen, van den Hout, & van den Bout, 2006; Park, 2010), and perhaps even report significant personal growth in the process (Neimeyer, 2006).

Over the past decade we have conducted numerous studies that support this argument. For example, adults who are better able to "make sense" of their loss report fewer symptoms of complicated grief across the first 2 years of bereavement (Holland, Currier, & Neimeyer, 2006), and the failure of such sense making appears to be a powerful mediator that explains much of the impact of violent death on survivors (Currier, Holland, & Neimeyer, 2006). Moreover, whereas a struggle to find meaning in the loss predicts future levels of grief-related distress, reports of sense making in the early months of bereavement predict higher levels of well-being a full 18 to 48 months in the future (Coleman & Neimeyer, 2010). In another longitudinal study, mourners who were able gradually to integrate the experience into their meaning systems also reported fewer symptoms of complicated grief over time (Holland, Currier, Coleman, & Neimeyer, 2010). Finally, evidence supports the incremental validity of our measure of meaning integration following loss, as it makes a unique contribution to the prediction of mental and physical health outcomes even when demographic background of the mourner, his or her level of complicated grief, and the circumstances of the death are taken into account (Holland, Currier, & Neimeyer, 2014).

One dimension of mourners' response to a death has drawn our particular attention, namely, their efforts to make meaning of the loss in terms of their spiritual belief system. Although one's religious meaning system can be a great resource in times of adversity (Park, 2013), evidence indicates that many people struggle greatly with their faith and faith community in the wake of loss, especially when that loss is tragic. For example, our research on African American homicide survivors, nearly all of whom endorse a Christian view of God as omniscient, omnipotent, and compassionate, has documented that a substantial minority report a prolonged spiritual crisis in the aftermath of their loved one's murder, one marked by a sense of alienation from and anger with both God and their spiritual communities (Burke, Neimeyer, McDevitt-Murphy, Ippolito, & Roberts, 2011). Moreover, such "negative religious coping" is associated with higher levels of CG, both with this population and in samples that are more broadly based in ethnicity and cause of death (Burke & Neimeyer, 2014). In keeping with our conception of the centrality of sense making in bereavement, inability to integrate the loss into the mourner's meaning system appears to mediate between the experience of spiritual struggle and CG (Lichtenthal, Burke, & Neimeyer, 2011). Accordingly, we have recently constructed and validated a measure of what we are terming "complicated spiritual grief," whose component factors of "Insecurity with God" and "Disruptions in Religious Practice" predict CG even after more general measures of "negative religious coping" are taken into account (Burke et al., 2014). This highlights how not all "meanings made" are adaptive, particularly when global meanings (meanings about oneself and the way the universe works) are challenged (Bonanno, 2014; Park, 2010).

Finally, we should emphasize that as unspeakably onerous as the death of a loved one can be, it can yield growth as well as grief, contributing to the survivor's spiritual or philosophic gravitas, sense of compassion for the suffering of others, personal strength in the face of adversity, revised and clarified life priorities, and appreciation for life's beauty as well as its sadness. Empirically, we find that this form of posttraumatic growth is most likely when the pain of grieving is sufficient to prompt reconsideration of the mourner's previous assumptions and ways of being, but not so overwhelming as to be paralyzing (Currier, Malott, Martinez, Sandy, & Neimeyer, 2012).

THE QUEST FOR MEANING IN THE LOSS OF A CHILD

As in our broader research program on meaning reconstruction in loss, we have been particularly concerned with bereaved parents' ability to find sense and significance in the very present absence of their child from the family. In our study of a large group of mothers and fathers losing their children an average of 6 years previously to both natural and violent causes, we found that sense making accounted for 5 times as much of the intensity of their normal grief symptoms (e.g., crying, missing their children), and fully 15 times as much of the symptoms of CG (e.g., intense and disruptive yearning for the child's presence; feeling that the future is without purpose) than did other factors such as the number of months or years that had elapsed since the loss or whether the death was natural or violent (Keesee et al., 2008).

But what forms of meaning making are associated with more favorable grief outcomes? To answer this question, we carefully coded the content of parents' narrative accounts of their sense making and benefit finding regarding the loss and analyzed which themes in their meaning making were associated with fewer complications (Lichtenthal, Currier, Neimeyer, & Keesee, 2010). In terms of sense making, nearly half of the parents reported making "no sense" of their children's deaths, though others drew on a broad range of natural, spiritual, biological, and behavioral attributions to account for their child's dying. By comparison, only 20% of the parents were unable to identify some unsought benefit or life lesson in the tragedy, whereas the great majority reported some form of personal growth or learning in the wake of the experience. Of these themes, those involving making sense of the loss in terms of its being "God's will" and the potentially more secular belief that the child was no longer suffering were associated with less distressing grief symptomatology, as were benefit-finding themes suggesting enhanced spirituality and changed priorities in life. A further analysis of these patterns focused on meaning-making themes that characterized different causes of death (Lichtenthal, Neimeyer, Currier, Roberts, & Jordan, 2013). Results indicated that more than half of violent loss survivors could not make sense of their loss, as compared to one third of nonviolent loss survivors. Overall, there was overlap in sense-making strategies across different causes of death, with many parents invoking spiritual and religious meanings and the cultivation of empathy for the suffering of others. Nonetheless, violent-loss survivors described the imperfection of the world and brevity of life more frequently in their narrative responses than parents who lost a child to natural causes, who in turn were more likely to find benefit in the loss in terms of personal growth. Violent-loss survivors—and especially those losing a child to homicide—also reported enhanced appreciation of life more frequently than survivors of nonviolent losses, and surviving a child's suicide was specifically associated with a change in priorities in the sample (Lichtenthal et al., 2013). Thus, parents contending with the pervasive absence of a deceased child vary greatly in their meaning making, and the outcome of this process is predictive of their ultimate adjustment to this tragic loss.

IMPLICATIONS FOR TREATMENT

In light of the apparent centrality of meaning making in adapting to the loss of a child, it is encouraging that contemporary grief therapists are generating a great range of practices that facilitate both processing the event story of the death and accessing the back story of the relationship. Here we mention a few of these, briefly anchoring them in case studies and gesturing toward the growing scientific literature that illustrates their role in grief therapy and the support for their usefulness.

Talking About Talking

For many bereaved parents, and especially those whose children are taken from them suddenly or through unexplained causes, finding some way to understand the circumstances of the death and its implications for their life as a family is an early emotional imperative. But by the same token, approaching this anguishing knowledge in the silence of one's own thoughts and feelings or more audibly with one's spouse or therapist can trigger a cascade of overwhelming grief, horror, or anger, provoking understandable experiential avoidance. Thus, the ambivalence of many parents toward engaging the story of the loss in the presence of another calls for respect and negotiation rather than insistence on confrontation with the death story in all its painful reality. This stance contrasts with the common therapeutic assumption that grief work involves only direct and unvarnished acknowledgement of the loss, with anything less representing a form of denial that blocks successful adaptation (Stroebe, 1992).

The importance of negotiating the relative value of talking and not talking about the death is nowhere clearer than in couples therapy, as partners engage in a dynamic process of coordinating their mutual entry into and out of painful consideration of their child's death or absence (Hooghe, Rober, & Neimeyer, 2011). In keeping with the privileging of "sharing emotions," "open communication," and "intimate conversation" in much of the literature on grief, *not* communicating about a shared loss typically has been viewed skeptically as "withholding," "cutting off," or even a "conspiracy of silence" regarding a death in the family. In recent years, however, empirical research has raised doubt concerning the generally assumed beneficial effect of emotional disclosure and social sharing of a troubling event. In the context of bereavement, for example, selective and flexible avoidance of one's grief can play a helpful role in promoting restoration and resilience (Boelen et al., 2006; Bonanno, 2014; Stroebe & Schut, 2010). This shifting balance between speaking about the loss and remaining silent is dialectical, in the sense of reflecting an inherent tension, common in northern European and American cultures, between sharing one's experience and holding it privately, especially when the experience is as ineffable and irreversible as the death of a child. It is also dialogical, unfolding not only within but also between spouses who contend with an ongoing interplay between seeking intimacy in their attempts at meaning making with their partner and safeguarding themselves and their partner from conversations that trigger mutual pain (Hooghe et al., 2011). Intensive qualitative research has illuminated this process of "cycling around the emotional core of sadness" in the context of one couple's loss of an infant daughter to cancer, highlighting the intrapersonal and interpersonal processes by which parents regulate their proximity to the painful story of the death to balance their need to feel close to their child with their equally significant need not to be swallowed by despair (Hooghe, Neimeyer, & Rober, 2012). In view of this dynamic interplay of opposing needs, explicitly discussing with parents the advantages and disadvantages of talking directly about the event story of the loss, and how they might move toward and away from it, could represent a compassionate preliminary to more exposure-based methods to follow.

Just three weeks after the death of their apparently robust 2-year-old son, Braden, to unknown medical causes, Brenda and Cory were nearly paralyzed by shock. On the one hand, they felt an irresistible urge to engage the story of his dying, which remained shrouded in mystery from the horrible morning that Cory found him lifeless in his small bed, unresponsive to his or the paramedic's urgent efforts at resuscitation. With the press to make sense of what had transpired, the 6 to 9 weeks that they would have to wait for an autopsy loomed like an eternity. At the same time, the darkness of the death threatened to engulf them whenever their eyes met, or when one or the other sought to engage the unspeakable story of what they had seen, felt, or feared. In the first session of conjoint grief therapy, the therapist therefore invited a conversation of how it was for them to come in together for discussion of the loss, which of them felt the greater urgency to do so, how each signaled readiness or unreadiness for such a conversation, and the pros and cons of touching upon the death story in its intimate particulars. The resulting exchange prompted empathy for the sometimes converging, sometimes diverging need of each spouse, as Cory, for example, described his sense of "aloneness" with the images of his son's unresponsive body in his bed or on the hospital gurney, and Brenda acknowledged her need to "titrate the dose" of her grief by only gradually opening to such conversation, or by returning for brief periods to their home from their temporary refuge in the home of a friend. In this way, the couple, with the help of the therapist, explicitly began to define the "ground rules" for regulating their proximity to the loss and to one another, as they reckoned with the enormity of their child's absence and their need to find a foothold in the unknown terrain that stretched out before them.

Restorative Retelling

The death of a child often leaves parents with a profound rupture in the narrative of their lives, as they struggle to integrate the impossibility of the loss into the story of who they were and who they might now be. Violent death can complicate this dimension of narration of the loss, as the wordless imagery of the death scene, whether witnessed or imagined, spills ruminatively into consciousness, alternating with attempts at avoidant coping. Compounding the resulting suffering, the trauma of the story of dying commonly casts the parent as irrelevant and impotent to protect her child, denied any meaningful role in the inevitable replays of the circumstances of the death.

To counter the powerlessness of this repetitive psychic reenactment of the dying, Rynearson and his colleagues have devised systematic procedures for restorative retelling of the death narrative in a way that allows the story to be spoken, held, and witnessed in the responsive medium of psychotherapy (Rynearson, 2006; Rynearson & Salloum, 2011). By first encouraging the client or couple to "introduce the deceased" by sharing something of who he or she was in the context of the family, the therapist honors the humanity of the loved one and builds resources by anchoring the story of the loss in a longer story of love and ongoing connection, a motive and method also advocated by other narrative therapists (Hedtke, 2012). The therapist then supports the client in retelling the story of the loss in unhurried detail, assisting with processing the images and feelings that arise and helping the client share with a responsive other what previously was borne in private torment. Specific procedures that augment this retelling and promote greater mastery of the narrative of the traumatic dying have been detailed elsewhere, such as prompting the client to "braid" together external, internal and reflexive or meaning-oriented narration to form a more durable "through-line" in the midst of a difficult experience (Neimeyer, 2012). Recent evidence from an open trial of restorative retelling in the aftermath of violent death demonstrates that the procedure is well tolerated, with a significant decrease in symptom burden following the procedure (Saindon et al., 2014). Analogous "situational revisiting" of the story of the loss likewise plays a central role in evidence-based treatment for CG, which is especially efficacious following violent death (Shear, Frank, Houch, & Reynolds, 2005).

As a brilliant but troubled college student, Daniel had alternated between excelling in classes and succumbing to binges of drinking that challenged both his academic and social success. The decade that had followed college was similarly stormy, marked by lost jobs, a lost marriage, and several rounds of treatment for substance abuse. Finally, in his early 30s, he moved back into his parents' home, stabilizing for a time before sliding back into the recurrent cycle of substance abuse.

It was in this context that Daniel arrived at his parents' home late one night, obviously inebriated, when he was met by his mother, Carol. Exasperated, Carol broke off the ensuing confrontation between Daniel and his father about the son's behavior, suggesting "they all get to bed and return to the discussion in the morning." For Daniel, however, morning never came. As Carol began to worry about him as noon approached, she opened the door of his silent bedroom to a scene of horror instantly stamped in her mind: her son, tangled in the sheets, torso off the bed, the bedding awash in a swath of blood. Rushing to him as she screamed for her husband, she attempted resuscitation as he called emergency services. Arriving to the scene within 20 minutes, the first responders rushed Daniel's unresponsive body to the hospital, where his death—apparently of drug overdose, was confirmed. Tormented by the horrific imagery of the death scene as well as her guilt for not having recognized his condition that fateful night, Carol sought therapy a few months later.

After inviting Carol to share photos of her son on her iPhone and hearing stories of her pride and concern about his turbulent life, the therapist was struck by the power of the death narrative to eclipse any sense of secure connection to her son "in spirit," though Carol was a religious person. The therapist therefore introduced the possibility of doing a "slow motion replay" together of what she had seen, sensed, and suffered the morning she discovered her son's body, with the goal of helping her give voice to the silent story of the trauma, while being supported in managing the powerful emotions it triggered and in addressing the painful questions it posed. Bravely, Carol announced her readiness for this retelling, and the therapist began with the events of the night before, the disturbed night of sleep for Carol that followed, and the careful unpacking in sensory detail of what unfolded as she, with increasing apprehension, opened her son's bedroom door. Braiding together the horrific images—the tangled body, the purple face, the splash of congealed red blood spilling from his mouth across the white sheets—with the associated feelings that welled up in her, therapist and client gradually walked through the experience, tracing its objective and subjective contours and the struggle to make sense of his death that ensued. Finally, as the therapist asked what Carol would have done if she had been present to his dying, but unable to prevent it, she sobbed, "Just hold him, hold him . . . and tell him I loved him." Gently handing Carol a cushion, the therapist watched as she spontaneously hugged it tightly to her chest and tearfully affirmed her love for her precious if imperfect child. After a few minutes, she set the pillow aside, dried her eyes, and noted how she felt "flooded with comfort" following the retelling, and less alone in a tragic story. Together she and the therapist then reflected on further healing steps that could be taken, including responsive engagement with the partly parallel, partly unique grief of her husband following a shared loss.

Directed Journaling

As noted above, not all meanings constructed by grieving parents may be helpful to them. In fact, without direction, parents may develop narratives permeated with statements reflecting self-blame, anger at a higher power, or the unfairness of the universe. This may be in part why studies inviting the bereaved to write about their loss repeatedly (e.g., three to four times over the course of a week), but without specific instructions about how to shape their narratives, have generally not demonstrated that expressive writing is beneficial (Stroebe, Schut, & Stroebe, 2006). To facilitate engagement in potentially helpful meaning-making tasks, we conducted a randomized controlled trial of different types of expressive writing exercises (Lichtenthal & Cruess, 2010). We found that bereaved individuals who were directed to consider ways in which they either made sense of their loss (sense making) or to reflect on positive and meaningful consequences of their loss experience (benefit finding) reported lower levels of CG, depression, and posttraumatic stress symptoms, with greater improvements over time. Those directed to write about the positive byproducts of their loss showed the greatest improvements.

It should be noted, however, that participants in this study were not bereaved parents, and that on average, approximately 4 years had passed since their loss. Use of this approach with grieving parents should involve a careful respect of the parent's readiness to reflect on these ideas, remaining mindful of the findings we described above demonstrating that nearly half of parents report that they cannot make sense of their child's death. When parents make mention of this struggle and indicate a willingness to write, gentle prompt questions that may facilitate sense making include (a) Has there been any change between how you initially interpreted how [Child's name] died and how you interpret the loss now? (b) Are there any philosophical or spiritual beliefs that are helpful to you in understanding this loss? Or are there any beliefs that have been affected by the loss? (c) How has this loss influenced the direction of your life story? How, across time, have your dealt with this? (d) What qualities in [Child's name] that you admire do you believe shaped the way in which he/she lived and died? (see Lichtenthal & Neimeyer, 2012).

When parents begin to mention ways in which they may have experienced personal or relationship growth or valued changes in their priorities, writing prompts that may facilitate such benefit finding include (a) In your view, have you found any unsought gifts in grief? If so, what? (b) How has this experience affected your sense of priorities? Your sense of yourself? (c) What qualities in yourself have you drawn on that have contributed to your ability to coexist with your grief? What qualities of a supportive kind have you discovered in others? (d) What lessons about loving or living has your child or this loss taught you? (e) Has this profoundly difficult transition deepened your gratitude for anything you have been given? Is there anyone to whom you would like to express heartfelt appreciation now? (Lichtenthal & Neimeyer, 2012).

Jim came to therapy to process the recent loss of his 36-year-old son, Jeremy, to leukemia, frustrated and saddened that Jeremy would not allow him to be more actively involved in his care throughout his illness and especially as his condition deteriorated. Jim struggled to make sense of Jeremy's choices in medical care and relatively sudden death only 4 months after his diagnosis, wondering if he had pushed harder to be involved, whether Jeremy would have received treatment that could have prevented his death. As Jim continued to ask, "Why?" the therapist invited Jim to spontaneously write about Jeremy as a person and which of his traits may have influenced the choices he made during his illness. The therapist provided Jim with a pen and pad, and asked him to write down his reflections for 5 to 10 minutes. Jim then tearfully shared what he wrote, describing how Jeremy had grown up to be a caretaker, always looking out for friends and family. He noted how Jeremy had become increasingly concerned about the health and general well-being of his father and mother—Jim and his wife, Maggie—in recent years because of Jim's high blood pressure and his wife's recent diagnosis with Type 2 diabetes. He imagined that Jeremy was probably trying to protect them from the stress of being involved in making medical decisions and ultimately from the potential guilt that so many caregivers experience when a loved one dies. He reasoned that Jeremy likely sensed his prognosis was poor and wanted to prevent Jim and Maggie from investing in futile efforts. He concluded his writing by expressing his deep pride in his son and the man he became.

Meaning-Centered Grief Therapy

The processes of meaning reconstruction not only involve finding meaning in the loss, but also finding meaning in one's life and existence. Existential challenges are common following the loss of a child, as some parents perceive that the legacy they hoped they would leave through their child's life is threatened and their sense of identity as parent and protector is shaken. Meaning-Centered Grief Therapy (MCGT) is designed to address these existential issues in addition to facilitating meaning-making processes we described above. MCGT is based largely on Meaning-Centered Psychotherapy, a manualized intervention developed by Breitbart and colleagues (2010, 2012), which has demonstrated efficacy in enhancing meaning and purpose in advanced cancer patients. Meaning-Centered Psychotherapy applies the principles of Viktor Frankl's (1959/1984) logotherapy, helping cancer patients connect with valued sources of meaning in their lives while validating any suffering they may be experiencing through a series of didactics and experiential exercises. The adaptation of MCP into MCGT has been supported by the National Cancer Institute (R03 CA139944; K07 CA172216), and research is currently underway to pilot and refine the intervention for parents who lost a child to cancer at least 6 months ago who have elevated levels of CG.

MCGT for bereaved parents focuses on those sources of meaning and aspects of their identity most significantly affected by the loss while additionally applying other grief-related theoretical concepts, including attachment theory (Bowlby, 1978; Ronen et al., 2009), meaning reconstruction (Neimeyer, 2001), and cognitive-behavioral and schema work (Boelen, 2006; Lichtenthal, 2012). Bereaved parents are encouraged to connect to sources of meaning through creative acts (e.g., work, causes, deeds) and valued experiences of life (e.g., appreciation of love, beauty, and humor). Particularly relevant for parents is one of Frankl's (1959/1984) core principles: when faced with tragic circumstances beyond our control, we still have control over how we face these challenges; in this way, the attitude one takes toward life's challenges can be a source of meaning in and of itself (Lichtenthal & Breitbart, 2012). MCGT thus highlights the choices parents have in their day-to-day lives and who they want to be, the choices they have in how they create their personal story and their child's story, and the choices they have in how to honor and remember their child. Parents are given the opportunity to develop a Legacy Project to honor their child and reflect their personal values. In doing so, MCGT helps parents transform their caregiving and parenting roles so they may continue their bond to their deceased child in new, adaptive, and meaningful ways (Bowlby, 1978; Ronen et al., 2009) as they learn to coexist with their grief. Engaging in life in these ways despite the tremendous pain they experience may even cultivate a sense of pride, as only they know what a monumental feat it truly is to step out of bed each day and face the world.

Andy was a willful teenager—a lover of music, technology, and his close-knit group of friends. His mother, Susan, was "madly in love with him" despite the fact that the two had been butting heads more frequently in recent years. When Andy was diagnosed with Ewing's sarcoma at age 15, Susan and her husband, Mike, rallied, staying by the bedside of their only child virtually every day from diagnosis until Andy's death when he was 17 years old. Susan had quit her job as an executive at a succesful manufacturing company and her world became defined by caring for Andy. Following his death, she experienced a sense of emptiness and disconnection that she found difficult to put into words. She sought therapy around 14 months later, still feeling stuck and quite "raw," and was offered MCGT. As Susan responded to MCGT prompt questions to explore the most meaningful moments of her life, her therapist helped identify those sources of meaning and parts of Susan's identity that she had valued most; not surprisingly, being Andrew's mother topped the list. The therapist explored with Susan ways in which she could preserve that sense of identity, which for Susan was through staying connected to Andew's two best friends through text messages and regular dinners. Susan's value of being an industrious worker also became apparent, and so over time, the therapist worked with Susan to explore job opportunities that were congruent with a new set of priorities to help those who faced challenges in a nonprofit organization. Susan decided to use the Legacy Project assignment as the impetus to start a small but meaningful charity that she had wanted to create, but previously could not muster the energy to develop. The charity raises funds for pediatric cancer by hosting music concerts with local bands—something Andrew would have appreciated immensely.

CONCLUSION

Faced with what may be life's most tragic transition, the bereaved parents we have seen in our consulting rooms and in our research often struggle with a profound search for meaning in their loss and in their life in its aftermath. Impressively, most find ways to move forward even in the pervasive presence of absence, reconstructing rather than relinquishing their attachment to their children and extending the legacy of their children's lives in their own. We hope that the summary of our ongoing research and practice in this area provides encouragement for the many other therapists called to walk alongside such parents as they negotiate this traumatic transition and rewrite life stories transformed by loss.

REFERENCES

Boelen, P. A. (2006, January/February). Cognitive-behavioral therapy for complicated grief: Theoretical underpinnings and case descriptions. *Journal of Loss & Trauma, 11*(1), 1–30.

Boelen, P. A., van den Hout, M., & van den Bout, J. (2006). A cognitive-behavioral conceptualization of complicated grief. *Clinical Psychology: Science and Practice, 1*(13), 109–128.

Bonanno, G. A. (2014). Meaning making, adversity, and regulatory flexibility. *Memory, 21*(1), 150–156.

Bowlby, J. (1978). Attachment theory and its therapeutic implications. *Adolescent Psychiatry, 6*, 5–33.

Bowlby, J. (1980). *Attachment and loss: Loss, sadness and depression* (Vol. 3). New York, NY: Basic Books.

Breitbart, W., Poppito, S., Rosenfeld, B., Vickers, A., Li, Y., Abbey, J., et al. (2012). A pilot randomized controlled trial of Individual Meaning-Centered Psychotherapy for patients with advanced cancer. *Journal of Clinical Oncology, 30*(12), 1304–1309.

Breitbart, W., Rosenfeld, B., Gibson, C., Pessin, H., Poppito, S., Nelson, C., et al. (2010, January 19). Meaning-centered group psychotherapy for patients with advanced cancer: A pilot randomized controlled trial. *Psychooncology, 19*(1), 21–28.

Burke, L. A., & Neimeyer, R. A. (2013). Prospective risk factors for complicated grief: A review of the empirical literature. In M. Stroebe, H. Schut, P. Boelen, & J. van den Bout (Eds.), *Complicated grief: Scientific foundations for health care professionals* (pp. 145–161). Washington, DC: American Psychological Association.

Burke, L. A., & Neimeyer, R. A. (2014). Complicated spiritual grief I: Relation to complicated grief symptomatology following violent death bereavement. *Death Studies, 38*, 259–267.

Burke, L. A., Neimeyer, R. A., Holland, J. M., Dennard, S., Oliver, L., & Shear, M. K. (2014). Inventory of complicated spiritual grief: Development and validation of a new measure. *Death Studies, 38*, 239–250.

Burke, L. A., Neimeyer, R. A., McDevitt-Murphy, M. E., Ippolito, M. R., & Roberts, J. M. (2011). In the wake of homicide: Spiritual crisis and bereavement distress in an African American sample. *International Journal of Psychology of Religion, 21*, 289–307.

Coleman, R. A., & Neimeyer, R. A. (2010). Measuring meaning: Searching for and making sense of spousal loss in later life. *Death Studies, 34*, 804–834.

Currier, J. M., Holland, J. M., & Neimeyer, R. A. (2006). Sense making, grief and the experience of violent loss: Toward a mediational model. *Death Studies, 30*, 403–428.

Currier, J. M., Malott, J., Martinez, T. E., Sandy, C., & Neimeyer, R. A. (2012). Bereavement, religion and posttraumatic growth: A matched control group investigation. *Psychology of Religion and Spirituality, 18*, 65–71.

Frankl, V. E. (1959/1984). *Man's search for meaning* (Rev. ed.). New York, NY: Washington Square Press.

Frankl, V. E. (1992). *Man's search for meaning: An introduction to logotherapy* (4th ed.). Boston, MA: Beacon Press.

Hedtke, L. (2012). *Bereavement support groups: Breathing life into stories of the dead.* Chagrin Falls, OH: Taos Institute.

Holland, J. M., Currier, J. M., Coleman, R. A., & Neimeyer, R. A. (2010). The Integration of Stressful Life Experiences Scale (ISLES): Development and initial validation of a new measure. *International Journal of Stress Management, 17*, 325–352.

Holland, J. M., Currier, J. M., & Neimeyer, R. A. (2006). Meaning reconstruction in the first two years of bereavement: The role of sense making and benefit finding. *Omega: Journal of Death and Dying, 53*, 173–191.

Holland, J. M., Currier, J. M., & Neimeyer, R. A. (2014). Validation of the Integration of Stressful Life Experiences Scale—Short form in a bereaved sample. *Death Studies, 38*, 234–238.

Hooghe, A., Neimeyer, R. A., & Rober, P. (2012). "Cycling around an emotional core of sadness": Emotion regulation in a couple after the loss of a child. *Qualitative Health Research, 22*, 1220–1231.

Hooghe, A., Rober, P., & Neimeyer, R. A. (2011). The complexity of couple communication in bereavement: An illustrative case study. *Death Studies, 35*, 905–924.

Keesee, N. J., Currier, J. M., & Neimeyer, R. A. (2008). Predictors of grief following the death of one's child: The contribution of finding meaning. *Journal of Clinical Psychology, 64*, 1145–1163.

Kelly, G. A. (1955). *The psychology of personal constructs.* New York, NY: Norton.

Li, J., Laursen, T. M., Precht, D. H., Olsen, J., & Mortensen, P. B. (2005). Hospitalization for mental illness among parents after the death of a child. *New England Journal of Medicine, 352*(12), 1190–1196.

Li, J., Precht, D. H., Mortensen, P. B., & Olsen, J. (2003). Mortality in parents after death of a child in Denmark: A nationwide follow-up study. *Lancet, 361*(9355), 363–367.

Lichtenthal, W. G. (2012). Schema therapy for the lost relationship. In R. A. Neimeyer (Ed.), *Techniques in grief therapy: Creative strategies for counseling the bereaved* (pp. 139–141). New York, NY: Routledge.

Lichtenthal, W. G., & Breitbart, W. (2012). Finding meaning through the attitude one takes. In R. A. Neimeyer (Ed.), *Techniques in grief therapy: Creative strategies for counseling the bereaved* (pp. 161–164). New York, NY: Routledge.

Lichtenthal, W. G., Burke, L. A., & Neimeyer, R. A. (2011). Religious coping and meaning-making following the loss of a loved one. *Counseling and Spirituality, 30*, 113–136.

Lichtenthal, W. G., & Cruess, D. G. (2010). Effects of directed written disclosure on grief and distress symptoms among bereaved individuals. *Death Studies, 34*(6), 475–499.

Lichtenthal, W. G., Currier, J. M., Neimeyer, R. A., & Keesee, N. J. (2010). Sense and significance: A mixed methods examination of meaning-making following the loss of one's child. *Journal of Clinical Psychology, 66*, 791–812.

Lichtenthal, W. G., & Neimeyer, R. A. (2012). Directed journaling. In R. A. Neimeyer (Ed.), *Techniques of grief therapy: Creative strategies for counseling the bereaved.* New York, NY: Routledge.

Lichtenthal, W. G., Neimeyer, R. A., Currier, J. M., Roberts, K., & Jordan, N. (2013). Cause of death and the quest for meaning after the loss of a child. *Death Studies, 37*, 327–342.

McDevitt-Murphy, M. E., Neimeyer, R. A., Burke, L. A., & Williams, J. L. (2012). Assessing the toll of traumatic loss: Psychological symptoms in African Americans bereaved by homicide. *Psychological Trauma, 4*(3), 303–311.

Neimeyer, R. A. (Ed.). (2001). *Meaning reconstruction and the experience of loss.* Washington, DC: American Psychological Association.

Neimeyer, R. A. (2004). Fostering posttraumatic growth: A narrative contribution. *Psychological Inquiry, 15*, 53–59.

Neimeyer, R. A. (2006). Re-storying loss: Fostering growth in the posttraumatic narrative. In L. Calhoun & R. G. Tedeschi (Eds.), *Handbook of posttraumatic growth: Research and practice.* Mahwah, NJ: Erlbaum.

Neimeyer, R. A. (2012). Retelling the narrative of the death. In R. A. Neimeyer (Ed.), *Techniques of grief therapy: Creative strategies for counseling the bereaved* (pp. 86–90). New York, NY: Routledge.

Neimeyer, R. A., & Currier, J. M. (2009). Grief therapy: Evidence of efficacy and emerging directions. *Current Directions in Psychological Science, 18*, 252–256.

Neimeyer, R. A., & Thompson, B. E. (2014). Meaning making and the art of grief therapy. In B. E. Thompson & R. A. Neimeyer (Eds.), *Grief and the healing arts*. New York, NY: Routledge.

Oliver, L. E. (1999). Effects of a child's death on the marital relationship: A review. *Omega: Journal of Death and Dying, 39*(3), 197–227.

Park, C. L. (2010). Making sense of the meaning literature: An integrative review of meaning making and its effects on adjustment to stressful life events. *Psychological Bulletin, 136*(2), 257–301.

Park, C. L. (2013). Religion and meaning. In R. F. Paloutzian & C. L. Park (Eds.), *Handbook of the psychology of religion and spirituality* (2nd ed., pp. 357–379). New York, NY: Springer.

Prigerson, H. G., Horowitz, M. J., Jacobs, S. C., Parkes, C. M., Aslan, M., Goodkin, K., et al. (2009, August 4). Prolonged grief disorder: Psychometric validation of criteria proposed for DSM-V and ICD-11. *PLoS Medicine, 6*(8), 1–12.

Rogers, C. H., Floyd, F. J., Seltzer, M. M., Greenberg, J., & Hong, J. (2008). Long-term effects of the death of a child on parents' adjustment in midlife. *Journal of Family Psychology, 22*(2), 203–211.

Ronen, R., Packman, W., Field, N. P., Davies, B., Kramer, R., & Long, J. K. (2009). The relationship between grief adjustment and continuing bonds for parents who have lost a child. *Omega (Westport), 60*(1), 1–31.

Rynearson, E. K. (Ed.). (2006). *Violent death*. New York, NY: Routledge.

Rynearson, E. K., & Salloum, A. (2011). Restorative retelling: Revisiting the narrative of violent death. In R. A. Neimeyer, D. Harris, H. Winokuer, & G. Thornton (Eds.), *Grief and bereavement in contemporary society: Bridging research and practice* (pp. 177–188). New York, NY: Routledge.

Saindon, C., Rheingold, A., Baddeley, J., Wallace, M., Brown, C., & Rynearson, E. K. (2014). Restorative retelling for violent loss: An open clinical trial. *Death Studies, 38*, 251–258.

Shear, C. K., Frank, E., Houch, P. R., & Reynolds, C. F. (2005). Treatment of complicated grief: A randomized controlled trial. *Journal of the American Medical Association, 293*, 2601–2608.

Stroebe, M. (1992). Coping with bereavement: A review of the grief work hypothesis. *Omega: Journal of Death and Dying, 26*, 19–42.

Stroebe, M., & Schut, H. (2010). The Dual Process Model of coping with bereavement: A decade on. *Omega: Journal of Death and Dying, 61*, 273–289.

Stroebe, M., Schut, H., & Stroebe, W. (2006). Who benefits from disclosure? Exploration of attachment style differences in the effects of expressing emotions. *Clinical Psychology Review, 26*(1), 66–85.

APPENDIX
Questions and Answers

Since we are looking at questions and possible answers, it may be useful to look at some questions that are often asked by children and adolescents. The following questions and answers were collected from students in two suburban New Jersey high schools and in the urban center of Paterson. There are also some questions from their parents and teachers that connect to those questions. The answers are those that were actually used to respond to each question.

Q: Why do people die? (The "classic" question/variation of "Will you die?")
A: People die because they are too hurt, or too old, or too sick (very sick, not like a cold) that their bodies do not work. That is when they die. Everything that lives will one day die, but the people who care for you will do all they can to stay with you and to care for you.

Q: If you die, what will happen to me?
A: An adult who has planned for this can explain that there will be someone there to love the child and to care for him/her.

Q: What does a child "understand" about death and what role does age play?
A: Before age 2, children have little or no understanding of death. If they are aware of anything, it is that someone they love and need is "missing." In the early school years, kindergarten to about third grade, they see death as "reversible." From about third grade to fifth or sixth grade, they "personify" death (partly as a way of "avoiding" it). An adult understanding often develops at about age 10. Of course, in some areas where children view real death on a regular basis, such an understanding can come at a younger age.

Q: What information about death is "essential" for a child to understand?
A: A so-called adult understanding of death includes three points that an adult can assist a child to understand. The dead person no longer experiences anything (the body is nonfunctional), that the physical aspects of death last forever (death is irreversible), and that all living things will one day die (death is universal).

Q: Why is it that I feel so "alone" since my loved one died?
A: When we are unable to discuss our thoughts, feelings, and behaviors with someone who will listen, we may pull back or isolate ourselves from other people. This physical and emotional isolation can make us feel we are alone. In reality, this may not be true, even if we feel it is.

Q: Why do I have to die? Why does anyone?
A: Well, life is not always fair or easy, but it is worth being alive! We can spend a lot of time trying to answer the "why" questions and get nothing but greater frustration. Shift focus to a different question: "What can I do to handle these situations in my life that are so painful?" With this shift in focus, pain of loss can become more manageable and we may feel less helpless. This is the first step toward the healing part of the grief process.

Q: How can I avoid feeling like this again?
A: You probably can't. The only way that you may not experience these reactions again is if you never love anyone. Is that how you want to live? Any time that we decide to form attachments to a person, place, or thing, we run the risk of having these grief reactions if those attachments are broken. Life is a risk and so are the relationships we choose to make in our lives.

Q: What can I do if I think or feel so overwhelmed by grief that I start to think about suicide?
A: First, it is essential that you realize that suicidal thoughts are common enough to be considered "normal," but suicidal actions are not. It is not all right to continue with these thoughts and to allow a pattern to develop. In order to help yourself through this difficult time, you must risk reaching out to someone that you trust and who will listen and validate your reactions. You may first only be able to talk to a friend. A friend can help by listening and then by getting the person to get professional help. Reaching out for help is a sign of personal courage, not weakness. Please remember the oft-quoted observation that suicide is a permanent solution to what is often a temporary problem!

Q: What can I do or say to help a friend who is talking or acting as if he/she is contemplating suicide?
A: First, it is important to remember that you are not responsible for another person's life. But you can still be a special friend by getting them some professional help. Even if they may have asked you not to tell anyone, do not keep that confidence. This is too much for you to handle on your own. If they get angry at you for doing this, it is better to have them angry at you than to have them dead. If they are angry they may in time forgive you. If they die they never will. Remember to validate their feelings; don't tell them to "stop being silly" and don't ever ignore this behavior or treat it as if they are just seeking attention. Ask "Is this the worst things have ever been for you?" If they say no, you can remind them they have had the ability to cope with worse situations in the past. If they say yes, you know that this person is at risk.

Q: What should I avoid saying if I think that someone I am with may be considering suicide?
A: Do not "challenge" the person by saying that s/he is not serious. Do not weigh the pros and cons of suicide. This could be a signal that there are times when suicide is acceptable and could actually give a person "permission" to act on their thoughts/feelings.

Q: Can talking about suicide in school cause someone to make an attempt?
A: Addressing the tragic reality of adolescent suicide does not, by itself, cause suicide attempts. Talking about the issue can encourage them to understand and to better handle suicidal crises.

Q: My father (mother) is in the military. Will he/she die when they are away? (Related: Is it okay to tell him that his parent will be back?)
A: Tell him that you hope his parent will return. If you have a religious background, you can encourage the child to pray with you each day for his parent. Explain to him also that you are there to help take care of him/her, and other people in the family (grandparents, aunts, uncles) also care about him and would take care of him. He needs to be assured of his care and safety during this time. A child should not be told that the parent will not die because that is something we cannot guarantee. In the event that his father was killed, a child might feel that adults had lied to him and that he could no longer trust them.

Q: My counselor said I might want to attend a grief support group. How can a peer support group help me deal with my loss?
A: A peer support group provides an opportunity for you to meet other young people to share their thoughts and feelings, to understand that the grief process is "normal" but not comfortable, and to learn (or relearn) coping skills and new behaviors that will facilitate the grief process.

Q: Why do I need to attend a grief support group regularly or even every session?
A: If this is not a "drop-in" group, you need to be there every session because it is not fair to ask others to share their thoughts and feelings in the group and then to have to repeat these thoughts and feelings in another session if someone in the group was away for the last meeting.

Q: Why do my parents want so much for me to talk about this loss or the other losses in my life?
A: Parents want to help you. But they cannot really be of help unless you choose to share what sort of loss you may be dealing with or what may be going on in your life. After all, no decision can be better than the information on which it is based.

Q: Why are we told to not discuss any information that is shared in the group with anyone outside of the group?
A: Group members are told to not discuss any information that is shared by others in the group because confidentiality and having a safe place to risk sharing this information is essential to the group process and group dynamics. They can share their own information with anyone they choose. It is, after all, theirs.

Q: Why is it so hard to be different from other kids when you are an adolescent?
A: Sometimes we call this peer pressure. This is a time in life when you are trying to figure out who you are and what you want to do with your life. It can be a very

confusing time, and being different is often looked down upon by some young people. It may take courage to be different and to stand up for what you believe.

Q: Why is that I often think or feel or act as if I am never ever going to be happy again—that these grief reactions are never ever going to change?
A: The emotions that accompany loss hurt, and the healing of the grief process takes time.

Here are some tools that can help you to change and to be happy again:

- Hope
- Believe in Yourself
- Have Patience
- Learn about the Grief Process
- Share Your Thoughts, Feelings, and Actions with Others
- Risk Caring/Loving/Attaching Again

During the initial phases of the grief process, your reactions may be expressed through protest, despair, and detaching. Once you try to understand your losses, you begin to move toward the next phase, which is referred to as meaning. During this phase, we are trying to make some sense out of the losses that we have experienced and to begin shifting from the "Asking Why" to the "What Now" phase, which will enable us to explore, hope, and invest in ourselves and in new relationships. These phases can help us. It is at this time that you may begin to be happy again and to start to move on from your loss.

Contributors

Robert G. Stevenson, Ed.D., is senior professor in the Graduate Counseling Program, School of Social and Behavioral Sciences of Mercy College, NY. He has edited/authored a dozen boks and published over70 journal articles and book chapters. His most recent publications include: *Last Acts: The End of Life, Hospice and Palliative Care; Perspectives on Violence and Violent Death*; and *What Will We Do: Preparing a School Community to Cope with Crises.* He is a graduate of the College of the Holy Cross (BA), Montclair State University (MA) and Fairleigh Dickinson University (MAT and EdD). He developed the first independent high school death education course and taught it for 25 years. He is the recipient of the Wendel Williams Outstanding Educator Award, the ADEC National Death Educator Award, and the Founder's Award from the Center for Death Eduation and Bioethics for outstanding university teaching, research, publication and professional service in the field of death, dying and bereavement. In addition to his 30 hears as teacher, counselor and coach in secondary schools, he also was a founder of the Center for Help in Time of Loss, worked with parolees in a reentry program in Paterson, NJ, and was awarded the Defense of Freedom Medal by New York State for his work after September 11.

Gerry R. Cox, Ph.D., is a Professor Emeritus of Sociology at University of Wisconsin- La Crosse. He served as the Director of the Center for Death Education & Bioethics. His teaching focused upon Theory/Theory Construction, Deviance and Criminology, Death and Dying, Social Psychology, and Minority Peoples. He has over one hundred publications including twenty five books. He has served as editor of *Illness, Crisis, and Loss and for The Midwest Sociologist.* He is a member of the International Work Group on Dying, Death, and Bereavement, the Midwest Sociological Society, the American Sociological Association, The International Sociological Association, Phi Kappa Phi, and Great Plains Sociological Society. He served on the board of Directors of the National Prison Hospice Association.

Dr. Fernando Cabrera, Ph.D., has served as the NYC Council Member representing the 14th district in the Bronx since January 2010. His leadership positions in the NYC Council include Co-Chair of the NYC Council Black, Latino and Asian Caucus, Co-Chair of the Gun Violence Task Force, Chair of the Juvenile Justice Committee and Chair of the Technology Committee. Dr. Cabrera also serves as the senior pastor of New Life Outreach International in the Bronx, New York. He worked as the executive director of New Life for Youth rehabilitation program and as a middle school and high school guidance counselor in the New York City and Westchester school system. He is the former program director for the Mental Health and Counseling program at Mercy College, where also taught for 12 years. Dr. Fernando Cabrera earned his B.A. in Religion from Southern California College, M.A. in Counseling from Liberty University and Doctorate in Counseling from Argosy University.

Charles A. Corr, Ph.D., is a volunteer member of the Board of Directors of the Suncoast Hospice Institute (2000-present), an affiliate of Suncoast Hospice in Clearwater, Florida; Professor emeritus, Southern Illinois University Edwardsville; a member of the International Work Group on Death, Dying, and Bereavement (1979-present; Chairperson, 1989-1993); a member of the Association for Death Education and Counseling (1977-present); and Senior Editor of the ChiPPS (Children's Project on Palliative/Hospice Services) quarterly E-Journal on pediatric palliative/hospice care. Dr. Corr's professional work has been honored by the Association for Death Education and Counseling in awards for Outstanding Personal Contributions to the Advancement of Knowledge in the Field of Death, Dying, and Bereavement (1988) and for Death Education (1996), by Children's Hospice International in an award for Outstanding Contribution to the World of Hospice Support for Children (1989) and through the establishment of the Charles A. Corr Award for Lifetime Achievement [Literature] (1995), by The Dr. Robert Fulton CDEB Founder's Award from the Center for Death Education and Bioethics at the University of Wisconsin–La Crosse for Outstanding University Teaching, Research, Publication, and Professional Service in the Field of Death, Dying and Bereavement (2007), and by the 2008 MTF DonorCARE Award from the Musculoskeletal Transplant Foundation. Also, Dr. Corr received Research Scholar (1990), Outstanding Scholar (1991), and the Kimmel Community Service (1994) awards from Southern Illinois University Edwardsville. Dr. Corr's publications include over 100 chapters and articles in professional journals, along with more than three dozen books and booklets.

Carolyn Cullen, LCSW, Ph.D., is a faculty member at Mercy College's School of Social and Behavioral Sciences where she is involved in the training and supervision of graduate-level student clinicians. She earned her PhD in clinical social work at New York University. She has worked in the helping profession for over twenty years after earning her Master's degree from Boston College Graduate School of Social Work. She began her professional career in community agencies in New York City working with adults, children, adolescents, and families. She completed supervised clinical training at two mental health clinics specializing in trauma, loss, and addictions. In addition to working in academia, she maintains a psychotherapy practice in Pelham Manor, NY working with adults and couples.

CONTRIBUTORS / 269

Illene Noppe Cupit, a graduate of Temple University, is Professor of Human Development at the University of Wisconsin-Green Bay. She developed the Dying, Death & Loss course on her campus over twenty years ago. Dr. Cupit's research focuses on college student bereavement, adolescent grief, death education and developmental issues. Dr. Cupit recently coedited a book with Carla Sofka and Kathy Gilbert entitled, *Dying, Death and Grief in an Online Universe* (Springer Publishers, 2012). She also founded Camp Lloyd, a day camp for grieving children. She was the President of the Association for Death Education and Counseling for 2012-2013. In her minuscule spare time Dr. Cupit enjoys traveling, running, swimming, cycling, playing the piano, reading, cooking, and then eating the fruits of her labor!

Kenneth J. Doka, Ph.D., is a Professor at the Graduate School of The College of New Rochelle and Senior Consultant for the Hospice Foundation of America. Dr. Doka has written or edited over 30 books including three on children and adolescents' reaction to death, dying, grief, and loss, as well as over a 100 articles and book chapters. He is editor of *Omega: The Journal of Death and Dying* and *Journeys: A Newsletter to Help in Bereavement.*

Peter Ford has been Director of Pastoral Care and Lead Chaplain since 1977 at Winchester Medical Center, a level II Trauma Center in northwestern Virginia. He is a member of the Religious Society of Friends (Quakers) and is a recorded (ordained) Friends minister. After 9/11/2001 he collaborated with Reverend William D. Barton, an I.C.P.C. certified police chaplain at Ground Zero to train local clergy and chaplains in disaster response. From that collaboration came a written resource for clergy entitled "A Disaster Spiritual Care Primer." He holds a Master's degree in Pastoral Counseling, is a Board Certified Chaplain in the Association of Professional Chaplains (APC), an is certified in Thanatology by the Association of Death Education and Counseling (ADEC), and is a member of the American Academy of Experts in Traumatic Stress/National Center for Crisis Management AAETS/NCCM. Chaplain Ford is a member of the Religious Society of Friends (Quakers) and is an ordained Friends minister. Since retiring in 2014, he continues to work in disaster preparation focusing on spiritual care with the regional Volunteer Organizations Active in Disaster (VOAD).

Richard Gilbert, with his wife Sharon, moved to Galesburg, IL five years ago. He completed 35 years as an Anglican priest, working extensively in death education, training and counseling, health care, trauma, spirituality and spirituality/burnout. He has presented extensively throughout the U.S. and also in Canada and the United Kingdom. He does special work with resources. He currently has 34 bibliographies researched and upgraded for professionals. These compilations are free upon request. He has published several books and contributed to, or edited, others. He had a regular column in Bereavement and is the reviews editor for *Illness, Crisis, and Loss.* He currently is an adjunct faculty member on two campuses. At Mercy College (New York) he teaches are rotating list of graduate courses in the Graduate School of Social and Behavior Science and, at Benedictine University, Lisle, IL, a DL program on politics and ethics for the Masters in Public Health curriculum.

Linda Goldman is the author of several books, including and *Life and Loss: A Guide to Help Grieving Children, 3rd Edition, Children Also Grieve* and *Coming Out, Coming In: Nurturing the Well Being and Inclusion of Gay Youth in Mainstream Society.* She has been an educator in the public school system as a teacher and counselor for almost 20 years and has a private therapy practice in Chevy Chase, Maryland. She also teaches as an adjunct professor in schools and universities including Johns Hopkins Graduate School and Kings College.

Darcy L. Harris, Ph.D., FT, is an Associate Professor and the Thanatology Coordinator at King's University College at Western University in London, Canada, where she developed the undergraduate degree program in Thanatology. She maintains a clinical practice focused on issues related to change, loss, and transition. She has served on the board of directors for ADEC and is a member of the IWG. Her writings include *Counting our Losses: Reflecting on Change, Loss, and Transition in Everyday Life, Principles and Practice of Grief Counseling*, and *Handbook of Social Justice in Loss and Grief: Exploring Diversity, Equity, and Inclusion*.

Olyvia Kuchta is a recent psychology graduate of the University of Wisconsin-Green Bay. She is now pursuing her masters degree in Cognitive and Social Processes at Ball State University with future aspirations of becoming a social psychologist. Olyvia is an active researcher studying the topics of women in the workplace, female leadership, sexual assault, workplace diversity, and social media and death. Olyvia became interested in studying death because of her father's sudden death when she was in high school. When she entered college she began to research death in order to better understand the bereavement process, and thus help others. During her time at the University of Wisconsin-Green Bay she was a buddy at Camp Lloyd, a summer grief camp for children, where she put her research into action. Olyvia uses research to benefit the lives of others and the community as a whole.

Wendy G. Lichtenthal, Ph.D., is an Assistant Attending Psychologist and Director of the Bereavement Clinic in the Department of Psychiatry and Behavioral Sciences at Memorial Sloan Kettering Cancer Center (MSK) and Assistant Professor of Psychology in Psychiatry at Weill Cornell Medical College. She obtained her undergraduate degree at The University of Chicago and her doctoral degree at the University of Pennsylvania. She completed her clinical psychology internship at the Payne Whitney Clinic at Weill Cornell Medical Center and received specialized training in psycho-oncology research through a National Cancer Institute (NCI) T32-funded postdoctoral research fellowship at MSK, where she was Chief Research Fellow. Dr. Lichtenthal has led multiple National Institutes of Health-funded research studies on grief and bereavement, with a focus on meaning-making, prolonged grief, Meaning-Centered Grief Therapy, and intervention development. As a licensed clinical psychologist, she specializes in bereavement-related clinical work and teaching.

Arthur G. McCann, Ph.D., is the Chair of the Counseling Department and Director of the School Counseling program in the School of Social and Behavioral Sciences at Mercy College in Dobbs Ferry, New York. He earned his PhD in Counselor Education at Fordham University. He has over forty years of experience as a counselor and educator and maintains a private counseling practice. It is from his thirty years of experience as the coordinator of a high school crisis team in a suburban New York school district that he has drawn for his contribution to this book. Dr. McCann regularly makes presentations to school counselors in particular and to counselors in general at conferences sponsored by professional associations such as, American Counseling Association, American School Counselors' Association, Association for Specialists in Group Work, New York State School Counselors' Association, and at Long Island Counselors' Associations' Conference and Guidance Expo. He currently serves on the editorial boards for the *Journal of Hispanics in Higher Education* and the *Journal for Specialists in Group Work*. He is also the President of the Westchester Putnam and Rockland Counselors' Association.

Janet S. McCord, PhD, FT, Associate Professor and Chair of the Edwin S. Shneidman Program in Thanatology, teaches a broad range of topics in Marian University's online Master of Science in Thanatology. Under the direct supervision of Holocaust survivor and Nobel Peace Prize winner Elie Wiesel and UCLA Professor Emeritus Dr. Edwin S. Shneidman, she focused her doctoral dissertation (Boston University) on Holocaust survivor writers who killed themselves after the war, utilizing psychological pain theories of Dr. Shneidman to conduct literary psychological autopsies. She is a Certified Psychological Autopsy Investigator, and in April 2016 was installed as President of the Association for Death Education and Counseling. Her passions revolve around justice issues in death, loss and bereavement. Her research interests include suicidology, psycho-social readjustment of formerly abducted children in Uganda, and social stigma around mental health issues.

Dianne McKissock, OAM Dianne McKissock is the co-founder and former clinical director of The Bereavement C.A.R.E. Centre and The National Centre for Childhood Grief ('A Friend's Place') in Sydney, NSW Australia. A sociologist and Master Clinician with the Australian Association of Relationship Counsellors, Dianne began her counselling career in 1967 and has specialised in working with bereaved and dying children and their families since 1985. She has taught bereavement counselling skills throughout Australia and New Zealand, and in Canada, Greece, Malaysia and Hong Kong. Dianne is currently Clinical Supervisor for counsellors at 'A Friend's Place' and for palliative care social workers and psychologists working in other centres. She has published a CD of children's stories and numerous grief related books and articles. Dianne is a member of the International Work Group on Death Dying and Bereavement and in 1986 was awarded the Medal of The Order of Australia for her services to the bereaved community. She is currently semi-retired and lives with her husband Mal on the Central Coast of NSW.

Rebecca S. Morse, Ph.D., is a behavioral and developmental psychologist, and thanatologist who specializes in working with individuals she terms are "at the developmental bookends of life:" children, and the elderly. Much of her work has focused on those with developmental disabilities who are severely behaviorally disordered. She currently teaches at several Universities and Colleges on a broad range of topics in psychology, criminology, and thanatology from bereavement, children and grief, and traumatic loss to Victimology, and the psychological bases of criminal behavior. She currently serves on the Board of Directors for the Association for Death Education and Counseling. Previously Rebecca worked at the National Institutes of Health for over eight years on protocols for children and adults with rare genetic conditions and developmental disabilities, and continues to work with these individuals (and their families) in groups and 1-1, at home, school, workplace, and clinical in/out patient settings. Her research interests include aspects of grief such as social and personal risk factors, and their transactional relationship with resiliency, stress, coping, and attachment; and grief across the lifespan.

Robert A. Neimeyer, Ph.D., is a professor in the Department of Psychology of the University of Memphis and he maintains an active clinical practice. He has published over 25 books, including *Techniques of Grief Therapy: Creative Practices in Counseling* and *Bereavement in Contemporary Society: Bridging Research and Practice* (Routledge) and is editor of *Death Studies*. He has written over 400 articles and book chapters and his current focus is the use of grieving as a "meaning-making" process. He is a member of the American Psychological Association's Task Force on End of Life Issues. He received the Eminent Faculty Award from the University of Memphis and the Research Recognition and Clinical Practice Awards from the Association of Death Education and Counseling. He is a fellow of the Clinical Research Division of the American Psychological Association.

Stephanie Rabenstein, M.Sc. is a Registered Marriage and Family Therapist, clinical fellow and approved supervisor with the Ontario and American Associations for Marriage & Family Therapy in children's mental health at Children's Hospital, London Health Sciences Centre. She is an assistant professor in the Department of Psychiatry, Schulich School of Medicine & Dentistry, Western University in London, Ontario coordinating Resident family therapy training. She is also a play therapist teaching in the Canadian Association for Child and Play Therapy certification program. Stephanie writes about cross-cultural issues, trauma, and traumatic loss presenting on these topics across North America.

Harold Ivan Smith is a grief educator on the teaching faculties of Saint Luke's Hospital in Kansas City, MO and Carondolet Medical Institute in Eau Claire, Wisconsin. He earned a doctorate from Asbury Theological Seminary and the EdS from Vanderbilt University. His primary research focuses on grief of American presidents and their families. His books include, *Borrowed Narratives: Using Historical and Biographical Narratives with the Bereaving; When a Child You Know is Grieving;* and with Joy Johnson *What Does that Mean? A Dictionary of Death,*

Dying and Grief Terms for Grieving Children and Those Who Love Them. Smith is a member of the Association for Death Education and Counseling.

Neil Thompson is an independent writer and developer of online learning resources, based in Wales. He has held full or honorary professorships at four UK universities. He has qualifications in social work; training and development; mediation; and management (MBA), as well as a first-class honours degree, a doctorate (PhD) and a higher doctorate (DLitt). His latest book is The Authentic Leader (Palgrave Macmillan, 2016). Neil is a member of the International Work Group on Death, Dying and Bereavement. He tutors the Avenue Professional Development Programme, an online learning community for the people professions (www.apdp.org.uk). His website and blog are at www.neilthompson.info.

Index

(Page references followed by f indicates a figure.)

A to Z of Women in World History, The, 114
Abandoned children, 109
Abandonment, feeling of, 48, 137
Abductions, 70
Abortion, 14, 38, 40
Acceptance, 101, 206
Acceptor, child's coping style, 9
Accidental death, 109
Active listening, 236–238
Adaptive responses of children, 135, 142
ADD (attention deficit disorder), 162–164
Adolescents. *See also* Children; Grief
   coping with grief using cyberspace, 30–31, 93
   counseling at *A Friend's Place*, 63
   death of friends, 31, 38, 72, 76, 159, 177
   death of peers, 30
   development, death and technology, 29–30
   development stage and Internet use, 27–29
   developmental stage grief reactions, 48, 134–135
   discussing death with, 235–246
   Facebook, 31–32
   fear of aging, 241
   gang members, 205
   grief responses, 49–51, 232
   helping Latino, 208–212
   importance of friends, 28, 100–101, 167
   life-threatening illness, 28
   meaning-making, 26–27
   motherless daughters day, 64
   narrative psychology, 26–27
   needs of grieving/traumatized, 58, 139

[Adolescents]
   nondeath losses, 29
   other thanatechnological venues, 33–34
   physical complaints, 11, 15, 51–52, 161, 162
   reassurance. *See* Reassurance
   redefining mourning, 30
   religion, 141, 144, 206
   risk-taking behaviors, 10, 29, 139, 241
   schools helping externalize thoughts and feelings, 21
   self-narrative via technology, 34–35
   substance abuse by, 196
   suicides of, 183–184
   technology, 26–27
   Twitter, 32–33
Adoption, 38, 153
Afghanistan, 6
Africa, 17
African American youth. *See also* Adolescents; Children; Grief
   attending wakes and funerals, 7
   bond with deceased, 213
   economic trap for, 213
   funeral director's role, 214
   "good death" concept, 213
   guidelines for counseling, 215–216
   helping, 212–215
   honoring with shrines, pictures and reunions, 214
   incarceration rate of parents, 228
   outside network for, 213
   rituals, 212–213
   singing at funeral, 214
   thoughts and fears about death, 6

African Americans, responses after homicide, 249–250
After Suicide: A Toolkit for Schools, 183, 184
Age discrimination applied to disenfranchised grief, 129
Agerbo, E., 191
Aggressive behavior, 10, 14, 77, 139
Alcock, P., 125
Alcohol, self-medicating with, 11
Alcoholism, 11
Aldrich, R. S., 189
Allen, N. B., 94
Altruist, child's coping style, 10
Amazon.com, 107
American Academy of Child and Adolescent Psychiatry (AACAP), 72
American Association of Suicidology, 194
American Foundation for Suicide Prevention and Suicide Prevention Resource Center (AFSP/SPRC), 183
American National Biography, The, 112
American Psychiatric Association (APA), 76, 84
American Red Cross, 133
Amulets, 19, 75
Anger
  concealing fear, 10
  disaster response, 139, 142
  divorce response, 41
  grief response, 14, 163, 237
  at people not held accountable, 10
  secondary traumatization, 77
  suicide response, 195
  trauma response, 78
Anniversaries of death, 203
Antecedent loss, 117
Anthony, Sylvia
  The Child's Discovery of Death, 4
  The Discovery of Death in Childhood and After, 4
Anxiety
  female and male, 94, 135
  grief responses, 51, 77, 78, 163, 196
  leading to non-lethal injuries, 192
  relief, with art, 99
  schoolwork, 15
  separation, 94, 237
  sexual identity, 167

[Anxiety]
  suicide response, 183, 195
  using routines for reducing, 137
Apache traditions, children and death, 7
Apathy, 11, 14
Archer, M. S., 126
Armstrong, Tanya, 149
Arnett, J. J., 26, 28
Arnold, M., 34
Arredondo, P., 210
Artemieva, T. V., 7
Arts
  anxiety relief, 99
  benefits of, 91–95
  drawing, 21, 136, 139, 142, 161f, 163f, 198
  expressing grief thoughts and feelings, 21, 197–198
  music. *See* Music
  sociology of, 98–99
  storytelling. *See* Storytelling
  therapy, 64, 163
  types for children, 96, 100
Asia, 17
Aspirations and dreams, 103
Assessments, 60, 81–82
Association for Death Education and Counseling (ADEC), 17
Atkinson, E., 124
Atomism, 123–124, 126
Attachment relationships, as sources of support, 75, 191
Attachment theory, 123, 257
Attacks, verbal or physical, 10, 14
Attempted Suicide Short Intervention Program (ASSIP), 193
Attention deficit disorder (ADD), 162–164
Attig, Thomas, *Catching Your Breath in Grief... and Grace Will Lead You Home*, 99
Auchterlonie, J. L., 77
Australia, 16, 45
Avoidance symptoms, 77, 78, 237
Avrami, S., 197
Ayers, T. S., 238

Bailey, D. F., 215
Baker, T., 211
Balance in life, 101

Balk, D., 30
Banner, Lois W., 107
Barnes, M. F., 74
Barnes & Noble, 107
Bartkiewicz, M. J., 167
Battersby, J. D., 110
Bauman, R., 94, 95
Baumeister, R. F., 192
BBC (British Broadcasting Corp.), 16
Beck, A. T., 192
Behringer, J., 191
Belgium, 16
Belknap, Raymond, 190
Bendiksen, Robert, 17
Bengstson, V. L., 93
Ben-Porat, A., 84
Bereavement C.A.R.E. Centre (Sydney, Australia), 45, 59
Bereavement models
  Chaos Theory, 46–47
  Dual Process Model, 47
  Infinity Model, 47–48
  Bereavement support services, 45–67. *See also A Friend's Place* (Sydney Australia); Counseling and Counselors; Family therapy; School counselors
  adolescent service, 63
  appropriate locations for services, 54–55
  assessments, 60
  borrowed biographies, 107–117
  client needs and rights, 58
  clinical practice principles, 56–57
  differences from psychotherapy, 61
  directed journaling, 255–257
  family picnic event, 64
  family-focused interventions, 74
  home visits, 54–55
  hospital visits, 54–55
  individual counseling, 60–61
  length of support, 54
  meaning-centered grief therapy, 257–258
  motherless daughters day, 64
  reading to children, 91
  restorative retelling about child's death, 254–255
  school counselor's role, 173–186
  school recognizing grief, 158–160
  session structure, 62–63
  support groups, 61–62, 163

[Bereavement models]
  support strategies, 57–58
  target groups for, 52–53
  timing for providing support, 53–54
  training professionals and volunteers, 66–67
  25 things that can help children, 100–104
  weekend residential adventures, 63
Berman, A., 190, 191
Bernardon, S., 78
Best, S. R., 74
Betancourt, H., 210
Bettelheim, Bruno, *The Uses of Enchantment: The Meaning and Importance of Fairy Tales*, 94
Bible, 8
Bibliotherapy, 21
Billington, R., 125
Biological disruption of identity, 127
Birmingham Alabama church bombing (1963), 114–116
Black Women in America: An Historical Encyclopedia (Hine (Ed.)), 114
Blame, felt by children, 4
Blogs, 28, 93
Blos, P., 27, 28
Bluck, S., 238
Blue Banner Biography series, 113
Bluebond-Langner, M., 242
Blum, D. J., *The School Counselor's Book of Lists*, 181–182
"The Body" (King), 39
Body mutilation, 71
Boelen, P. A., 250, 253, 257
Boelk, A., 197
Boerner, K., 75
Bonanno, G. A., 251, 253
Bond, J. B., 241
Bonotti, F., 242
Book therapy, 21
Books, for children by age group, 242–245
Books, using borrowed biographies, 107–117
Bordewich, F. M., 18
Borowsky, I. W., 191
Borrowed biographies. *See* Historical and biographical loss narratives
Borum, R., 165
Bosnia, 6
Boss, P., 71

Bossarte, R., 189
Bostik, K. E., 191
Boundaries, 56–57
Bowlby, J., 123, 237, 248, 257, 258
Brabant, Sarah, 94
Bradbury, Ray, 115
Bradbury Chronicles, The (Weller), 115
Bradley, K. I., 241
Brandes, S., 211
Brandon, M., 123
Bravery, 11
Breaking the Silence: A Guide to Help Children with Complicated Grief: Suicide, Homicide, AIDS, Violence, and Abuse (Goldman), 96
Breitbart, W., 257
Brent, D., 196
Briere, J., 74, 76, 83
Briggs, S., 191
British Broadcasting Corp. (BBC), 16
British Columbia, 17
Brock, H., 93
Broken heart syndrome, 91
Brooten, D., 211
Brown, A. C., 194
Brown, E. J., 78
Brown, G. K., 192
Brown, J. E., 33
Brown, T. L., 95
Bugge, K. E., 236–237
Bullying, 164–169
Bunyan, Paul, 108
Burials vs. cremation, 212, 214
Burke, L. A., 249, 250, 251
Burlingame, M., 112, 115
Burns, Ken, 111–112
Bush, Barbara, *Reflections*, 111–112

Calhoun, L. G., 81
CAMS (Collaborative Assessment and Treatment of Suicidality), 192
Canada, 3, 15–17
Cancer, death due to, 74, 174
Cannon, Alice, 108
Car accidents, 30, 31
Caregivers. *See also* Families; Fathers; Grandparents; Mothers; Parents; Schools; Teachers
    children impacted by grief of, 82, 136

[Caregivers]
    empowering language, 208
    sincerity, 204
    traumatic loss for, 21
    traumatized, 83–84
Caring and sharing to help with loss, 102
Carlson, E., 70, 74
Carr, W., 213
Carter, M., 34
Carter, W. B., 6
Castiglione, D. (Ed.), 125
Cataldi, E. F., 164
Catching Your Breath in Grief . . . and Grace Will Lead You Home (Attig), 99
Catherall, D. R., 74
CBS News KBTX Staff, 207
CBS Records, 190
CBT (Cognitive-behavior therapies), 74, 192, 193, 257
CDC (Centers for Disease Control Prevention), 30, 208
Celebrity death, 40, 190
Centers for Disease Control Prevention (CDC). *See* CDC (Centers for Disease Control Prevention)
Cerel, J., 189, 195
Ceremonies, 64. *See also* Funerals; Rituals
CG (Complicated Grief). *See* Complicated Grief (CG)
Chants, 149
Chaos Theory, 46–47
Chapple, A., 71
Charities, 19, 258
Cheong, P. H., 33
Child, deceased
    bereavement impact on parents, 249
    Brian deWitt's story, 247–248
    directed journaling, 255–257
    implications for parents' treatment, 252–258
    loss and quest for meaning, 249–252
    meaning-centered grief therapy, 257–258
    measuring deceased's life after suicide, 189–198
    parents talking and not talking in therapy, 252–254
    Ray Bradbury, 114
    restorative retelling, 254–255
    struggle for meaning, 247–261

INDEX / 279

Child development
  asking why about death, 3–4, 8
  death knowledge by age, 4–5
  discussing death, 238–242
  grief response by developmental stage, 48, 91, 92, 195
  readiness for discussing death, 236, 243
Child development theories, 121–131
  Attachment theory, 123
  avoiding distorted views of childhood, 129
  beyond traditional approaches, 123–124
  biological focus, 121–122
  concrete operational, 239, 240
  death understanding by age, 4–5
  development by age and disaster reaction, 140–141, 143–144
  disabilities excluded from, 124
  Erikson's work, 122–123, 134
  essentialism, 122–125
  existentialism, 124–129
  formal operational, 239, 240–242
  Freud's influence, 122–123
  gender considerations excluded from, 123
  loss and trauma, 127
  Maslow's work, 135
  preoperational, 239–240
  professional practice implications, 128–129
  progressive-regressive method, 127–128
  racism inherent in, 123
  same sex relationships excluded from, 124
  in schools, 20
  social capital, 125
  sociological factors, 126–127
  socio-political factors, 125
  temporal ekstases, 128
Child Trends, 170–171
Childers, P., 195
Childhood Traumatic Grief, defined, 72
Children. *See also* Adolescents; Caregivers; *Child entries*; Families; Grief; Parents
  abandoned, 109
  age discrimination against, 129
  aiding dying, 91–93
  books by age group, 242–245
  cognition, 135

[Children]
  communicating through tantrums, 221
  competitive behavior in US, 96
  coping styles, 9–13
  death knowledge by age, 4–5
  death of friends, 39, 72, 76
  deceased. *See* Child, deceased
  development theories. *See* Child development theories
  developmentally or mentally impaired, 41
  discussing death with. *See* Death, discussing with children and adolescents
  disenfranchised grief. *See* Disenfranchised grief
  dying, 91–95
  experience of death and cultural expectations, 5–7
  fearing losing love, 10–11
  fearing losing respect, 11
  grief responses. *See* Disenfranchised grief; Grief
  helping Latino, 208–212
  with HIV, 8
  homeless, 153, 169–171
  importance of friends, 39, 100–101, 167
  language issues, 212
  life-threatening illness, 14
  minorities in urban setting, 203–217
  multiple or serial loss, 109
  needing to feel in control, 10–11, 20, 154
  needs of grieving/traumatized, 58
  neglected, 49, 140, 146
  nonverbal communication by, 18, 204
  orphans, 108
  Parent-Child Subsystem, 222
  physical complaints, 11, 15, 51–52, 161, 162
  protecting parents, 93
  reactions by developmental stage, 48, 134–137
  referring to, as "it," 129
  resilience, 108, 117
  routines and schedules for, 220–223
  serious physical injury, 14
  substance abuse by, 196
  sudden change reactions, 135–136
  suicides of. *See* Suicide, child or adolescent

[Children]
  traumatized, 83, 109. *See also* Spiritual care after disaster
  25 things that can help with loss, 100–104
Children of Lesbians And Gays (COLAGE), 169
Children's Television Workshop, 8
Child's Discovery of Death, The (Anthony), 4
Christ, G., 195
Christian beliefs, 8, 18, 250
Chung, L. Y., 204
Cities, minority children in, 203–217
Clay as therapy tool, 96
Clinical supervision, 56
Clinician perspective, 84–85
Clinkinbeard, S. S., 203
Clinton, Hilary Rodham, *It Takes A Village*, 219
Clinton, K., 29
Coe, R. M., 93
Cognitive-behavior therapies (CBT), 74, 192, 193, 257
Cohen, D. E., 110
Cohen, J. A., 72, 74, 78, 79, 80, 82
COLAGE (Children of Lesbians And Gays), 169
Cole, Nat King, 110
Cole, Natalie, 110–111
Coleman, R. A., 250
Collaborative Assessment and Treatment of Suicidality (CAMS), 192
Columbia-Presbyterian Medical Center (New York City), 8
Columbine high school murders (Colorado), 165–166f
Comas-Diaz, L., 210
Come to the Edge: A Love Story (Haag), 114
Comic strips, 94
Commire, A. (Ed.), *Women in World History*, 114
Communication, 18, 204, 221
Communities, 13–14, 29. *See also* Spiritual care after disaster
Compassion, 251
Compassion fatigue, 180
Compassion satisfaction, 180

Complicated Grief (CG)
  bereaved parents, 248
  Breaking the Silence: A Guide to Help Children with Complicated Grief (Goldman), 96
  child's symptoms, 91–94
  family meaning-making, 76, 250
  identifying families at risk for, 74
  posthumous disillusionment, 72
  prolonged grief, 72
  traumatic grief, 71–72
  using art, humor and music for, 93–95
Complicated spiritual grief, 250–251
Concentration difficulties, 78
Concrete operational development, 239, 240
Condoleezza Rice (Wade), 113
Connection to others, feeling
  bereavement therapy to regain, 250
Continuing Bond theory, 75
  group counseling for, 64, 197
  mother regaining, 258
  need for, 58
  religion and spirituality, 205, 209
  routines, 137
  social media for, 31, 34
  traumatic loss, 77
Continuing Bond theory, 75
Cooper, I., *Jack: The Early Years of Jack Kennedy*, 107
Coping
  adolescents, 139
  children's adaptive responses, 135, 142
  games for, 136
  help for disenfranchised grief, 42
  humor, art and music for, 91–104, 180, 197–198, 257
  school curriculum teaching, 17–18
Corr, C., 129
Corr, Charles A., 30
Corr, D. M., 30
Coulter, S., 73, 74, 78
Counseling and Counselors. *See also* Bereavement support services; Family therapy; Historical and biographical loss narratives; School counselors
  after death of child, 252–258
  art tools, 96
  borrowed biographies, 116

[Counseling and Counselors]
  client needs and rights, 58
  clinical considerations, 78–81
  clinical practice principles, 56–57
  clinician perspective, 84–85
  creating safety within family context, 79–81
  cultural and religious sensitivity, 57, 141, 144, 145, 174
  directed journaling, 255–257
  disenfranchised grief processing. See Disenfranchised grief
  drawing pictures to process grief, 95–96, 136, 139, 142, 161f, 163f, 198
  email counseling, 57, 63
  empowering language, 208
  existentialism framework for, 128–129
  first contact with minority children, 205
  funeral director explaining rituals and symbolism, 214
  group counseling, 61–62, 163
  guidelines for African American men, 215–216
  historical perspectives on family-focused interventions, 73–74
  home visits, 54–55
  hospital visits, 54–55
  individual counseling, 53, 60–61
  language issues, 208, 212
  meaning-centered grief therapy, 257–258
  mindfulness, 84–85
  online counseling, 93
  parents talking and not talking in therapy, 252–254
  Personalismo (interpersonal relationships) in Latin culture, 210
  reenactment, 161
  requests for counseling outside office, 55
  Respeto (respect), 210
  restorative retelling about child's death, 254–255
  rituals. See Rituals
  role-playing, 161
  Rule of 100, 57
  secondary traumatization in counselors, 84–85
  secondary traumatization in families, 76–77, 180
  self-care, 146, 180
  Simpatia (warmth, friendliness), 210

[Counseling and Counselors]
  staffing at *A Friend's Place* (Australia), 45
  stigma of counseling, 207
  stigma of inner city, 207–208
  storytelling. See Storytelling
  student not wanting to feel different, 154
  support strategies, 57–58
  talking with children after disaster, 139, 141–145
  texting with adolescent clients, 57, 63
  touch as sign of respect, 210
  training at *A Friend's Place*, 66–67
  treating both grief and trauma, 79–81
  using borrowed biographies, 107–117
  using fiction, 243–245
  value of family approach, 73
  work in sessions, 62–63
  writing to process grief, 142, 161
Couples therapy, 252–254
Cox, Gerry R., 7, 17, 96
Cremation vs. burials, 212, 214
Crenshaw, D., 41
Criminal behavior, 146
Crisis plan. See School crisis plan; Spiritual care after disaster
Cross, M., 126
Crosses, 19
Crossley, M. L., 27
Cruess, D. G., 256
Cultural sensitivity, 57
Culture of violence, 91, 164–166, 206–207
Cunningham, A., 192
Cunningham, H., 125, 129
Cupit, Illene Noppe, 27, 30, 31
Currier, J. M., 249, 250, 251, 252
Cyberbullying, 164–169
Cyberspace, learning and grieving in, 25–36
  adolescence development, death, and technology, 29–30
  coping by using Internet, 30–31, 93–94
  development stages of adolescence and using, 27–29
  embracing self-narrative via technology, 34–35
  Facebook, 31–32
  narrative psychology, meaning-making, teens, and technology, 26–27
  online memorials, 93

[Cyberspace, learning and grieving in]
  other thanatechnological venues, 33–34
  Twitter, 32–33
Cynicism, 143

Dalenberg, C., 70, 74
Darbyshire, P., 236–237
Davis, C. G., 76
Davis, T. E., *The School Counselor's Book of Lists*, 181–182
Day of the Dead (*Dia de los Muertos*), 211
De Keijser, J., 95
Death
  as abandonment, 48
  accidental, 109, 174
  adolescents death statistics, 30
  adult understanding of, 5
  African American children thoughts and fears, 6
  after long illness, 71, 74, 109, 174, 256–258
  aiding dying children, 91–93
  AIDS/HIV, 38, 41–42
  anniversaries of, 203
  beliefs about afterlife, 203
  Caucasian children thoughts and fears, 6
  celebrity, 40, 190
  of child, 112–113, 150, 207
  child being with dying relative, 203, 212
  Christian attitudes toward, 8
  committing crime leads to, 41
  concealing, 12
  as concrete person, place, or thing, 5
  conferences, 17
  cultural differences among American children, 6–7
  decision-making, 203–204
  denial, by children, 19
  differences between white and racial America, 203
  disillusionment after, 79
  DNR (Do not resuscitate) orders and Latino families, 211
  education classes, 4, 12–13, 14–16, 20, 180, 184, 241
  of father, 108, 110–111. *See also* Parents, death of
  by firearm violence, 207
  five concepts about, 236

[Death]
  of friend, 39, 136
  frightening children with, 12
  good death concept, 213
  grandparent, 136, 219–233
  grotesque aspect to, 71
  homicides, 30, 62, 109, 114–115, 153, 165–166f, 207, 249
  mass disaster, 71
  of mother, 41, 93, 111–113. *See also* Parents, death of
  natural disasters, 109, 133–151, 153
  of parent. *See* Parents, death of
  school shootings, 165–166f
  as separation, 5
  sibling, 14, 41, 51, 92, 112, 158–160, 163
  sleeping as a euphemism for, 12, 145
  socially discussing, 241
  stigma about cause of, 203, 207
  stories from different cultures, 18
  struggle for meaning in child's death, 247–261
  substance abuse, 109, 174, 254–255
  sudden, 51, 70, 71, 133–151
  Suicide. *See* Suicide
  terrorism, 91, 99, 153, 171, 182
  untimely, 70
  viewing body, 145
  violent, 70, 71, 114–115
  war, 153
Death, child learning and knowledge, 3–24
  acceptor coping style, 9
  altruist coping style, 10
  child development theories. *See* Child development theories
  child personifying death, 48
  children asking if parents will die, 9
  children asking why, 3–4, 8
  children feeling blame and guilt, 4, 10–11, 14, 143, 206
  as concrete person, place, or thing, 5
  cultural differences among American children exposure to death, 6–7
  cultural expectations and experience of, 5–7
  defier coping style, 10
  denial of, 19
  facilitator coping style, 10
  magical thinking, 4, 48, 195–196, 239

[Death, child learning and knowledge]
  optimist coping style, 10
  role of parents, 8–13
  role of schools, 13–16
  school support guidelines, 16–22
  as separation, 5
  submitter coping style, 10–13
Death, discussing with children and
    adolescents, 8–13, 235–245
  adolescents, 240–242
  after disasters, 138
  asking if parents will die, 9
  asking why about death, 3–4, 8
  avoidance, 237
  challenges, 237–238
  children's books by age group,
    242–245
  cognitive and emotional readiness, 236,
    243
  developmental model, 238–242
  developmental model critique, 242
  elementary school-aged youth, 240
  listening. *See* Listening
  paradoxes of protection, 238
  parent's role, 8
  preschoolers, 239–240
  reasons for, 236–237
  telling truth, 9, 138, 196, 239
  using borrowed biographies, 107–117
Death and Bereavement Around the World,
    3
Deblinger, E., 72, 78
DeBoer, H., 205
DeBourgh, Gregory A., 113, 115
Deceased child. *See* Child, deceased
DeCicco, A., 242
Decristofaro, J., 195
Defier, child's coping style, 10
DeGroot, J. M., 31, 32
Dekel, R., 73, 77
DePalma, R. (Ed.), 124
Deportation, 153, 170–171
Depression
  after homicide of family member, 249
  directed journaling for relieving,
    255–257
  grief responses, 15, 163
  leading to non-lethal injuries, 192
  passionate sadness vs., 49
  relief, with art, 99

[Depression]
  sexual identity, 167
  student response to suicide, 182
  symptoms, 49, 73
  traumatic loss, 78, 196
Despair, feeling of, 136, 143, 190, 237
Detrixhe, J. J., 243
Development stages. *See* Child
    development; Child development
    theories
DeWitt, Brian and Graham, 247–248
Dey, P., 193
Dia de los Muertos (Day of the Dead), 211
*Diagnostic and Statistical Manual of
    Mental Disorders, Fifth Edition
    (DSM-5)*, 76, 84
Diaz, E. M., 167
Diaz, R. M., 167
Dickens, R., *How to Cope With Mental
    Illness in Your Family: A Self-Care
    Guide for Siblings, Offspring, and
    Parents*, 231
*Dictionary of American Biography Online,
    The*, 112
*Dictionary of Canadian Biography Online,
    The*, 112
Dinkes, R., 164
Dinshtein, Y., 73
Dirk, J., 238
Disabilities excluded from child
    development theories, 124
Disabling accidents, 70
Disaster spiritual care. *See* Spiritual care
    after disaster
Disasters, natural, 6, 99, 153, 171
Disconnection to others, feeling of, 77
*Discovery of Death in Childhood and After,
    The* (Anthony), 4
*Discussing Death: A Guide to Death
    Education* (Mills), 20
Disenfranchised death, 41–42
Disenfranchised grief, 37–43. *See also*
    Grief
  age discrimination as part of, 129
  children experiencing, 39–43, 110–111
  contexts of, 37–39
  guilt leading to, 38
  helping children cope with, 42
Dissociation, 78
Distress, feeling of, 70

Divorce
  children books about, 107
  leading to disenfranchised grief, 38
  major loss for children, 41, 228
  Parent-Child Subsystem, 222–223
  support groups, 62, 179–180
Do not resuscitate (DNR) orders and Latino families, 211
Doka, Kenneth (Ed.), 95, 129
Doka, Kenneth J., 37, 38, 39
Dolls and dollhouses as therapy tools, 96
Donohoe, M., 196
Doron, G., 73–74
Dougy Center (Portland, Oregon), 59
Drama, 64
Drawing, 21, 136, 139, 142, 161f, 163f, 198
Dreams and aspirations, 103, 208
Drug abuse, 11
Dual Process Model, 47
Dubrow, N. F., 206
Dun, S. A., 96
Durkheim, Emile, 190–191
Dying children, 91–95. *See also* Child, deceased
Dyregrov, A., 96

Eckerd, L. M., 241
Economic factors, 206, 213
Education. *See* Schools
Edwards, Deanna, 97
Ein-Dor, T., 73–74, 75, 77
Eisenberg, N., 96, 99
Elder, Sandra, 15–16, 17
Eleanor Everywhere: The Life of Eleanor Roosevelt (Kulling), 113
Elkind, David, 28
Ellis, A., 192
Ellis, T. E., 192
Ellison, N., 25, 30, 31
Embalming, 214–215
Emotional numbing, 14, 77, 78
Emotional rubberneckers, 32
Emotions. *See also specific emotion*
  after disasters, 141–142
  expected norms, 38–39
  feeling something has died inside, 71
  in grief, 10–13
  numbness, 14, 77, 78

[Emotions]
  role model for expressing, 18
  suppressing, 94
Empathy, 140, 148, 252, 253
Encouragement for helping with loss, 103
Encyclopedia of Asian History, The, 114
Encyclopedia of Lesbian, Gay, Bisexual and Transgender History in America (Stein (Ed.)), 114
England, 4, 16
Ens, C., 241
Erikson, E. H., 122–123
Erikson, Erik, 134, 135
Escape, need for, 16, 192
Essentialism, 122–125
Europe, 3, 5
European Union, 16
Evans, E., 191
Everall, R. D., 191
Exaggerated startle responses, 78
Existentialism, 124–129

Facebook, 26, 28, 31–32
Facilitator, child's coping style, 10
Facing reality, helping with loss, 101
Facts of Death, The (BBC TV program), 16
Faculty death, 175–177. *See also* Grief; School counselors; Schools; Teachers
Falicov, C. J., 210
Families. *See also* Caregivers; Children; Grandparents; Parents
  abductions, 70
  adoption, 38, 153
  agreement about loss, 76
  AIDS/HIV, 38, 41–42
  being with dying relative, 203
  bereavement support services, 60–65
  bereavement support strategies, 57–58, 150, 160–162
  burial location decisions for immigrants, 209
  candidates for bereavement support services, 52–53, 154–158
  children asking if parents will die, 9
  children protecting parents, 93
  children worrying what will happen if parents die, 9
  children's coping styles for death, 9–13

[Families]
- children's support group for dealing with loss of parent, 179
- children's support group for divorce, 62, 179–180
- communication within, 230
- configurations of traumatic loss, 83–84
- as context, 219–224
- coping using humor, art and music, 91–104, 180, 197–198, 257
- death by substance abuse, 109
- death of child, 112–113, 150
- death of grandparent, 219–233
- death of parent. *See* Parents, death of
- death while committing crime, 41
- deployments, 153
- deportation, 153, 170–171
- disorganization in, 78
- divorce. *See* Divorce
- extended, 203
- father's grief, 247–248
- financial burdens of granparents, 219
- godparents (*compadres*) in Latino culture, 210
- home alters, 209
- immigration, 70, 153
- incarceration, 38, 41, 153, 171, 228
- life-threatening illness, 14, 28
- marriage problems, 248
- meaning-centered grief therapy, 257–258
- meaning-making, 76, 154, 158–162, 221–222, 249–252
- measuring a child's life after suicide, 189–198
- minority children in urban setting, 203–217
- motherless daughters day, 64
- pet loss, 38, 40, 114, 135, 162
- placement in foster care, 38
- providing social support, 76–77
- PTSD in. *See* Post-traumatic stress disorder (PTSD)
- rejecting child, 167, 191
- remarriage, 14
- resilience and reality, 81
- reunions, 214
- scholarship fund commemorating child, 162, 174
- school counselor's role, 154, 173–186
- seeking help from schools, 20

[Families]
- sensing presence of deceased, 209
- separation, 14, 62, 70
- sexual, emotional, or physical abuse, 70, 82, 135, 140, 146, 153, 191
- sibling stillbirth or miscarriage, 14, 38, 207
- sibling death, 14, 41, 51, 92, 112, 158–160, 163, 182
- sibling leaving home, 93
- single parents, 206, 220, 223
- stigma about cause of death, 203, 207–208
- stress in, 78, 135, 223
- sudden absence, 70
- suicide. *See* Suicide; Suicide, adult; Suicide, child or adolescent
- trauma-focused cognitive behavioral therapy, 74
- unemployment, 70
- violence in, 70, 135
- violent loss survivors, 252
- widowed dads support group, 64
- *Familismo* (trust), 210

Family therapy, 69–88. *See also* Bereavement support services
- assessments, 81–82
- clinical considerations, 78–81
- clinician perspective, 84–85
- complicated grief. *See* Complicated Grief (CG)
- configurations of traumatic loss, 83–84
- including children, 77–78
- interventions, 73–74, 81–82
- traumatic loss, 69–71
- value of, 73

Fatalism and anticipatory grief, 212

Fathers
- death of, 108, 110–111, 113
- grief of, 247–248
- widowed dads support group, 64

Fear, 10–11, 142, 153, 196, 237
Fear of aging, 241
Fear of losing love, 11
Fear of violence, 14, 207
"Feeling" rules, 38
Feifel, Herman (Ed.), 4
Fein, R., 165
Feldman, Zoe, "Lisa Frank Mixtape," 30
Female grief, 94, 135

Figley, C., 74
Figley, C. R., 84
Figley, C. R. (Ed.), 180
Firearms, 30, 206–207
Fisher, Trena, 149
Floyd, F. J., 248
Ford, Peter, 149
Forgiveness, helping with loss, 102
Formal operational development, 239–242
Foster care placement, 38
Frank, Anne, 97, 102
Frank, E., 254
Frankl, Victor. E., 249, 257
Franklin, Benjamin, 236
Frantz, T., 211
Fredman, S., 74
Free Willy, 40
Freedom for helping with loss, 103
Freud, S., 122–123, 191
Fried, J., 204
Friends of deceased child, 182
A Friend's Place (Sydney Australia), 45–67
 adolescent service, 63
 appropriate locations for services, 54–55
 assessments, 60
 client needs and rights, 58
 clinical practice principles, 56–57
 family picnic event, 64
 home visits, 54–55
 hospital visits, 54–55
 individual counseling, 60–61
 length of support, 54
 motherless daughters day, 64
 other services provided by, 63–66
 selecting staff and volunteers, 55–56
 service delivery model, 58–59
 session structure, 62–63
 support groups, 61–62
 support strategies, 57–58
 target groups for, 52–53
 timing for providing support, 53–54
 training professionals and volunteers, 66–67
 weekend residential adventures, 63
Friendship, 100–101
Fristad, M. A., 195
Frustration, 61, 139, 215, 240, 256
Fundis, R. J., 96
Funeral directors, 214
Funeral parlors and homes, 6

Funerals. *See also* Memorials; Rituals
 African American, 212–214
 burial location decisions for immigrants, 209
 burials vs. cremation, 212
 children attending, 42, 58, 93
 cultural differences, 6–7
 importance to minorities, 203
 informing school about, 178
 leaving gift in casket, 97
 Native American, 7
 pictures of deceased at, 209
 planning, 206
 in public spaces, 31
 religious services, 211–213
 selfies taken at, 33–34
 shared meal after, 214
 social media changing, 31
 storytelling, 213–214
 viewing body, 145, 212
 wakes, 209

Gallardo-Cooper, M., 210
Gambe, D., 123
Games, to cope with grief, 136
Garbarino, J., 206
Garrison, B., 192
Gaudry, E., 15
Gay, Lesbian, Straight Educational Network (GLSEN), 167–169
Gay/Straight Alliance (GSA) groups in schools, 168
Geller, S. M., 84
Gender considerations missing from child development theories, 123
Gender differences in grieving, 94, 135, 203
George, D., 114, 116–117
Gerhart, D. R., 84
Germain, C. B., 237
Gibbs, M., 34
Gilbert, K. R., 27
Gilbertson, M. W., 195
Gillette, H., 210
Gitterman, A., 237
GlobalWebIndex, 32
GLSEN (Gay, Lesbian, Straight Educational Network), 167–169
Go On, 197

INDEX / 287

Godparents (*compadres*) in Latino culture, 210
Goenjian, A., 78
Goethe, J., 190
Goldman, Linda, 153–155, 158–163, 165–171
  Breaking the Silence: A Guide to Help Children with Complicated Grief: Suicide, Homicide, AIDS, Violence, and Abuse, 96
  Life & Loss: A Guide to Help Grieving Children, 228
Goldsmith, D. J., 96
Gomes, J., 123
Gonzalez, D. J., *The Oxford Encyclopedia of Latinos and Latinas in the United States*, 114
Goodwin, Doris Kearns, 113
Gotlib, I. H., 94
Grabowski, J., 211
Grandparent, death of
  adolescents, 29
  children, 136
  facing end of life issues, 229
  family as context, 219–224
  understanding power of interdependent, 224
Grandparents, 219–233. *See also* Caregivers; Families
  as adults, 225–226
  becoming, 227
  children's perception of, 225
  emotional and physical support from, 220
  financial costs of child-raising, 229
  loss felt by raising grandchildren, 223
  personal financial burdens of, 219
  providing childcare, 228, 230–231
  raising grandchildren, 227, 228
  setting boundaries with family, 229
  spiritual values, 229
Gravert, C., 190
Greece, 3, 7, 16, 17, 59
Greenberg, J., 248
Greenberg, L. S., 84
Greytak, E. A., 167
Grief. *See also* Interventions
  ADD and LD children, 162–164
  adolescents redefining mourning, 30
  anniversaries of death, 203

[Grief]
  antecedent loss, 117
  art and music expressing, 95–98, 149, 197–198
  blaming God, 204
  borrowed biographies, 107–117
  celebrity death, 40, 190
  childhood innocence loss, 40, 51
  Childhood Traumatic Grief, 72
  clinical assessment of, 60
  closure, 208, 213
  comic strips helping with, 94
  common signs of, 11, 49, 154–158
  complicated. *See* Complicated Grief (CG)
  complicated spiritual, 250–251
  coping by singing, 135–136, 214
  coping with games, 136
  cultural practices, 203, 209, 212
  delayed expressions, 15
  Dia de los Muertos (Day of the Dead), 211
  disenfranchised. *See* Disenfranchised grief
  Dominican Republic culture, 210
  drawing pictures to process, 95–96, 136, 139, 142, 161f, 163f, 198
  emotional responses in schools, 183
  fairy tales, 94
  fatalism and anticipatory, 212
  father's, 247–248
  female and male, 94, 135, 203
  grief-work hypothesis, 92
  grieving space at school, 176
  inventory form for schools, 155–158, 161
  issues, 153–154
  keepsakes, 209
  learning to grieve, 16, 42, 51
  length of mourning period, 203
  love and, 153
  maintaining bond with deceased, 208, 213
  making promises or commitments, 211
  masked, 91
  meaning making from, 249–252
  Mexican culture, 211
  "moving on," 208
  narrative activity for processing, 250
  negative attachments, 39–40

[Grief]
  opportunity loss, 40
  parents, for child death, 150, 249
  play for helping with loss, 101, 136, 139
  posthumous disillusionment, 72
  postponed, 92
  prolonged grief disorder, 72, 248
  Puerto Rican culture, 210, 211
  reading to children, 91
  reenactment, 161
  rituals to express. *See* Rituals
  role-playing, 161
  romantic relationship ends, 40
  sadness. *See* Sadness
  safe place needed, 46, 54, 77, 142, 146, 148, 161, 168
  school curriculum teaching about, 17–18
  school recognizing, 158–160, 173–186, 196
  sensing presence of deceased, 209
  sibling death, 182
  societal norms, 38
  for someone not personally known, 91
  spiritual care after disaster. *See* Spiritual care after disaster
  spontaneous grief sites at schools, 178, 179
  storytelling. *See* Storytelling
  support groups, 53–54, 61–62, 93, 163, 179–180, 197
  tasks of, 117
  touch as sign of respect, 210
  trauma impeding, 195
  traumatic, 71–72, 78–79, 109
  treating with prescribed drugs, 49
  viewing body in home before funeral, 212–213
  wearing black or dark clothes, 211, 215
  wearing white clothes, 215
  writing, 142, 161
Grief responses
  anger. *See* Anger
  anxiety. *See* Anxiety
  appreciating life's beauty, 251, 252, 257
  broken heart syndrome, 91
  children's reactions to disaster and, 135–136
  in classroom, 163–164
  depression. *See* Depression
  diagnosed as learning disorder, 162–164

[Grief responses]
  drop in school grades, 15
  emotions, 10–13
  expressing love, 6
  fear, 153
  fear of losing love, 11
  fight, flight, freeze responses, 50, 51
  guilt. *See* Guilt
  hyperactivity, 162
  idealism loss, 40
  impulsiveness, 162
  increased daydreaming, 15
  increased somatic complaints, 11, 15, 51–52, 161, 162
  isolation, 153
  life priorities, 251, 252
  loss of self-esteem, 50–51, 99
  marriage problems, 248
  not wanting to feel different, 154
  pain, 212
  personal growth, 251
  reactions by child's developmental stage, 48
  reduced concentration and attention span, 15, 162
  reduced life span, 248
  regression, 48, 49, 50, 92, 135, 146
  sadness. *See* Sadness
  secretiveness, 153
  shame, 38, 153, 154, 182, 195, 247
  sleep difficulties, 11, 48, 247
  social withdrawal, 15, 77
  spiritual crisis, 127, 204, 250
  tendency to catastrophize, 51
Grief support services. *See* Bereavement support services
Grollman, Earl A., 237
Gross, J. J., 94
Group counseling. *See also* Support groups, program at *A Friend's Place*, 61–63
GSA (Gay/Straight Alliance) groups in schools, 168
Guardian angels, 209
Guilt
  emotional response in schools after suicide, 182
  felt by children, 4, 10–11, 14, 41, 143, 206
  leading to disenfranchised grief, 38
Gullo, S. V., 144

Gullo, Steven V., 5, 9
Gun Violence Prevention Task Force, 206
Guns, 30, 206–207
Gurwitch, R. H., 173, 182
Gysin-Maillart, A., 193

Haag, Christina, *Come to the Edge: A Love Story*, 114
Haddock, S. A., 77
Häfner, H., 190
Haine, R. A., 194, 238
Hamilton, Nigel, 115
Handel, G., 222
Handel, George, 113–114
Harasymchuk, C., 76
Hare, J., 242, 243
Harmony for helping with loss, 101
Harris, Darcy, 71, 83
Hart, K. E., 94
Haugstvedt, K. T. S., 236–237
Hawton, K., 191
Hayakaki, E., 241
Hedtke, L., 254
Hegerl, U., 190
Heirman, W., 30
Help! I'm Raising My Grandkids: Grandparents Adapting to Life's Surprises (Hodgson), 227, 229
Helping Bereaved Children: A Handbook for Practitioners (Webb), 96
Helplessness, 10–11, 18, 70, 135
Hemmings, P., 99
Hennighausen, K., 82
Henriques, G. R., 192
Hess, R. D., 222
Hicks, A., 113
High content and context communication, 204
Higham, P., 124
Hill, R., 73
Hilliker, L., 236
Hinduja, S., 164
Hine, D. C. (Ed.), *Black Women in America: An Historical Encyclopedia*, 114
Hinings, D., 123
Historical and biographical loss narratives, 107–117
  Abraham Lincoln, 112–113

[Historical and biological loss narratives]
  biographies, 110
  Birmingham Alabama church bombing (1963), 114–116
  Eleanor Roosevelt, 108–110, 113, 117
  George Handel, 113–114
  guidance for productive exploration, 115
  identify elements for borrowing, 108–112
  John F. Kennedy, Jr., 114–115
  Ken Burns, 111–112
  maximizing borrowed narratives, 116–117
  memoirs, 110–111
  Natalie Cole, 110–111
  Nelson Mandela, 109, 110
  search tips for researching, 112–114
  tasks of grief, 117
Historical perspectives on interventions, 73–74
Ho Chi Minh, 112
Hochschild, A. R., 38
Hodgson, Harriet, *Help! I'm Raising My Grandkids: Grandparents Adapting to Life's Surprises*, 227, 229
Hoge, C. W., 77
Holland, J., 72, 78
Holland, J. M., 250
Home alters, 209
Home visits, for grief counseling, 54–55
Homeless children, 153, 169–171
Homicides, 30, 62, 109, 114–115, 153, 165–166f, 207, 249
Hong, J., 248
Hong Kong, Jessie & Thomas Tam Centre, 59
Hooghe, A., 252, 253
Hooyman, N., *Living Through Loss: Interventions Across the Life Span*, 223
Hope, 97–98, 102, 143, 205–206
Hopelessness, 10–11, 18, 190, 192, 207
Hospital visits, for grief counseling, 54–55
Houch, P. R., 254
How to Cope With Mental Illness in Your Family: A Self-Care Guide for Siblings, Offspring, and Parents (Marsh & Dickens), 231

Howarth, R. A., 189
Howe, D., 123
Huebner, D., 167
Hughes, J. A., 95
Humor, 64, 91–95, 100, 180
Hunt, S., 122
Hunter, S. B., 242
Hupka, R. B., 96
Hutcheon, L., 98
Hutcheon, M., 98
Hux, A., 238
Hypersensitivity, 77
Hypervigilance, 78
Hypochondriasis, 51–52

Identity, biographical disruption, 127
Imber-Black, E., 238
Incarceration, 38, 41, 153, 171, 228
India, 7
Individual counseling, 53, 60–63
Indonesia, 18
Inferiority, feelings of, 143
Infinity Model, 45–48
Insecurity, feeling of, 135
Insomnia, 11
Instagram, 26
Internet, learning and grieving using, 27–31
Interventions
  after disasters, 137, 141–145
  for bereaved children, 160–162
  family-focused, 74
  for grieving students, 181–183
  Living Through Loss: Interventions Across the Life Span (Hooyman & Kramer), 223
  strategies for, 81–82
Introduction to the Interpretation of Fairy Tales, An (von Franz), 94
Iossifides, A. M., 7
Ippolito, M. R., 250
Iraq, 6
Ireland, M., 191
Irritability, 77
Isolation, 153
Israel, 6
"It," referring to child, 129
It Takes A Village (Clinton), 219
Itzhaky, H., 84

Jack: The Early Years of Jack Kennedy (Cooper), 107
Jackson, M., 129
Jager-Hyman, S., 192
Janoff-Bulman, R., 70, 71, 75
Japan, 7, 18
Jealousy, 77
Jeglic, E., 192
Jenkins, H., 29
Jenn-Yun, T., 194
Jessie & Thomas Tam Centre (Hong Kong), 59
Jewish traditions, children and death, 6
Jiang, H., 189
Jobes, D., 190
Jobes, D. A., 192–193
Jobes, David, 191
Jobes, G., 18
Joiner, Thomas, 191, 192
Jones, E., 122
Jordan, B., 125
Jordan, J. R., 197
Jordan, N., 252
Journaling
  directed, 255–257
  as form of storytelling, 100
  grief processing, 198
  used in memorial, 174
Joy, S., 41
Judas Priest, "Stained Class," 190
Jung, J., 96

Kalafat, J., "The Crisis of Youth Suicide," 183, 184
Kamp, J. (Ed.), *Notable Hispanic American Women*, 114
Kapur, V., 123
Karus, D., 189
Kasket, E., 28, 31
Kastenbaum, R. J., 31
Kauffman, J. K., 70, 71
Kean University (New Jersey), 241
Keesee, N. J., 249, 251
Kelly, G. A., 249
Kemp, J., 189
Kennedy, Caroline, *Poems to Learn by Heart*, 107
Kennedy, Jackie, 110, 114–115
Kennedy, John F. Jr., 114–115

Kennedy, Patrick, 114–115
Kennison, S. M., 241
Kids Count Data Center, 206
Kierkegaard, S., 125
"Kilroy was here" cartoon from World War II, 33f
Kim, K. L., 192
King, Stephen, "The Body," 39
"The Kingdom Where Nobody Dies" (St. Vincent Millay), 5
King's College Center for Education About Death and Bereavement (Ontario), 17
Kissane, D. W., 72, 74
Klass, D., 31, 75
Kohburger, N., 190
Koocher, G., 238
Koocher, G. P., 195
Korea, 7
Kosciw, J. G., 167, 168
Kovacs, M., 192
Kramer, B., *Living Through Loss: Interventions Across the Life Span*, 223
Kubotera, T., 7
Kulling, Monica, *Eleanor Everywhere: The Life of Eleanor Roosevelt*, 113

LaGrand, L., 40
Lakota traditions, children and death, 7
Language issues with children, 212
Larson, J., 189
Lassie, 40
Latino youth, 208–212, 228
Lau, K. J., 94
Laughter in Hell: The Use of Humor During the Holocaust (Lipman), 95
Laursen, T. M., 248
LBGTQ (Lesbian, gay, bisexual, and transgender), 124, 165, 167–169
Learning disorders (LD), 162–164
Lee, C. C., 215
Lee, C. S., 34
Legacy Project, 258
Lehmann, P., 81, 82
Lens, 19
Leondari, A., 242
Lesbian, gay, bisexual, and transgender (LBGTQ), 165, 167–169

Letter writing, 160–160f
Levenson, R. W., 94
Levine, E. S., 210
Levy, W. T., 108
Lewinsohn, M., 94
Lewinsohn, P. M., 94
Li, J., 248
Libraries, 114
Lichtenthal, Wendy G., 74, 76, 250, 251, 252, 256, 257
Liddell, Christine, 95, 96
Lieberman, M. D., 238
Life & Loss: A Guide to Help Grieving Children (Goldman), 228
Life and Death at School (LeDoS) Project (Belgium), 16
Life Balance, 101
Lim, S. S., 204
Lincoln, Abraham, 112–113
Lincoln, Nancy Hanks, 112
Lincoln, Sally, 112
Lincoln, William Wallace, 112–113
Lin-Kelly, W., 164
Liotti, G., 75
Lipman, Myra, 12
Lipman, Steve, *Laughter in Hell: The Use of Humor During the Holocaust*, 95
Lipsey, T. L., 74
"Lisa Frank Mixtape" (Feldman), 30
Lisansky, J., 210
Listening
  active listening, 236–238
  advice to parents, 51
  communication clues, 204
  disaster response, 139, 147–148
  disenfranchised grief, 42
  within family, 220
  grandparents, 221, 231–232
  grieving child not, 164
  to grieving children, 20, 79, 95, 102, 181
  to music, 97
  traumatic loss, 71
Lister, R., 125
Litz, B. T., 70
Living Through Loss: Interventions Across the Life Span (Hooyman & Kramer), 223
Living Thru Loss organization (Canada), 17
Lobar, S. L., 211, 212

Locus of control, 204
Logotherapy, 257
London, Ontario, 17
Loneliness, 10–11, 18, 93, 153, 247
Los Angeles, 206
Loss
　child development theories, 127
　of friend, 241
　multiple or serial, 109, 115
　25 things that can help children, 100–104
　types of traumatic, 70, 109
Loss of control, feeling of, 70
Love
　attraction to life, 191
　expressed through prayer, 104
　expressing, 6
　expressing on social media, 32, 34
　fear of losing, 11
　grandparents, 223, 230
　helping with loss, 101
　losing ability to give and receive, 11
　managing loss with, 101, 257
　Maslow basic need, 135
　poems expressing, 159
　retelling of death story to reconnect to, 254–255
Lowis, M. J., 95
Loy, M., 197
Lund, L. T., 77
Lyons-Ruth, K., 82

MacKay, M. M., 238
Mackintosh, B., 170
Madden, M., 25, 26, 33, 34
Magical thinking, 4, 48, 195–196, 239
Mahon, M. M., 93, 94
Male grief, 94, 135
Malinowski, S. (Ed.), *Notable Native Americans*, 114
Malott, J., 251
Mandela, Nelson, 34, 109, 110
Mann, J., 189
Mannarino, A. P., 72, 78
Marin, B. V., 210
Marin, G., 210
Marino, G. (Ed.), 130
Marriage problems, 248
Marrone, R., 91, 93, 95

Marsh, D., *How to Cope With Mental Illness in Your Family: A Self-Care Guide for Siblings, Offspring, and Parents*, 231
Marta, Suzy Yehl, 17
Martinez, T. E., 251
Martins, P., 189
Martinson, I., 12
Marwick, A., 25, 30, 31
Masked grief reactions, 91
Maslow, Abraham H., 135
Mass shootings, 91
Massachusetts Department of Education, Massachusetts Youth Risk Survey, 168
Mastra, A., 242
Matsakis, A., 74
Mattei, S., 192
McCann, L., 84
McCollum, E. E., 84
McCord, J., 196, 198
McCord, Janet S., 184
McCoyd, J. L. M., 92
McCoy-Roth, M., 170, 171
McCubbin, H., 74
McDevitt-Murphy, M. E., 249, 250
McGinnis, P. J., 96
McGoldrick, M., 203
McKenry, P., 222
McKinstry, Carolyn Maull, 114, 116–117
McKissock, Dianne, 46, 49, 55, 56, 57, 61, 62
McKissock, M., 46, 57
McNair, Denise, 116–117
McPherson, J. M., 112
Mead, G. H., 28
Meagher, David K., "School Based Grief Crisis Management Programs," 182
Meaning of Death, The (Nagy), 4–5
Meaning reconstruction, 257
Meaning-centered grief therapy, 257–258
Meaninglessness, feeling of, 70
Meaning-making by families, 76, 249–252
Media, news coverage, 135, 139, 141
Meditation, 149
Meese, J., 34
Melanesian mythology, 18
Melhem, N., 196

Memorials. *See also* Funerals
 buttons, 214
 Facebook, 31
 graffiti murals, 209
 helping with loss, 48
 Legacy Project, 258
 online, 93
 "rest in peace" necklace, 214
 in school yearbook or newspaper, 162
 in schools, 19, 21, 174, 178
 t-shirts, 209, 214
 for youth suicide, 197–198
Memories, 75, 104. *See also* Storytelling
Memory books, 19, 97, 161f, 163, 178
Memory garden, 162
Menninger, Karl, 191
Mergl, R., 190
Merimna (Greek agency), 3, 16, 17, 59
Merten, M. J., 32
Meyer, K. J., 30
Meyers, S. A., 94
Michel, K., 193
Mikulincer, M., 73–74
Military service, 73, 77
Miller, R. L., 112
Milliken, C. S., 77
Mills, Gretchen, *Discussing Death: A Guide to Death Education*, 20
Millsap, R. E., 238
Mindfulness, 84–85, 198
Minority children in urban setting, 203–217
 being with dying relative, 203, 212
 communication and clues, 204
 counselor's first contact with, 205
 culture of violence, 206–207
 economic factors, 206
 expressing grief through rituals, 211
 fatalism and anticipatory grief, 212
 grieving practices, 212
 helping Latino children, 208–212
 language issues, 208, 212
 locus of control, 204
 spirituality and religion, 205–206, 209
 stigma factors, 207–208
 time factor, 204
 trust factor, 204–205
 worldview of, 203–204
Miracles, 104
Miscarriage, 14, 38
Modzeleski, W., 165

Monochronic orientation, 204
Monson, C., 74, 77
Moore, C., 121
Moore, Thomas, 94
Morgan, John, 17
Morse, Rebecca S., 184
Mortensen, P. B., 191, 248
Moser, R. P., 238
Mother Teresa, 97, 102
Mothers, 41, 69–70, 79, 93, 107–108, 111–112, 249. *See also* Families; Parents
Mother's Day, 159–160
Mourning. *See* Grief; Grief responses
Mphakanyiswa, Gadla Henry, 109
Murders, 30, 62, 109, 114–115
Murphey, D., 170
Murray, C. I., 203
Music
 dying and bereaved children using, 64, 91–95, 97, 100, 197–198
 spiritual care after disaster, 149
Mussen, P. H., 96, 99

Nadeau, Janice, 221, 222
Nader, K. D., 71, 72, 78, 79, 80
Nagy, M., 195
Nagy, Maria, 48
The Meaning of Death, 4–5
Nansen, B., 34
National Association of Secondary School Principals, 17
National Cancer Institute, 257
National Center for School Crisis & Bereavement, 182
National Center on Family Homelessness, 169
National Centre for Childhood Grief (Sydney, Australia), 45, 58–59
National Child Traumatic Stress Network (NCTSN), 82
National Institute of Mental Health (NIMH), 235
National Institutes of Health (NIH), "Talking to Children about Death," 235, 236, 239, 240
National Library of Vietnam (Hanoi), 112
National Velvet, 40
Native American traditions, 6–7

Natural disasters, 6, 99, 109, 153, 171
Neimeyer, R., 72, 78
Neimeyer, R. A., 27, 109, 197, 238, 249, 250, 251, 252, 253, 254, 256, 257
Nelson, K., *Nelson Mandela*, 107
Nelson Mandela (Nelson), 107
Neria, Y., 70
Ness, M., 29
New Grove Dictionary of Music and Musicians, The, 113
New Jersey, 11, 207–208
New Orleans, 206
New York City, 205, 206–207
New York City Department of Health Mental Hygiene, 207
New York State Department of Health, 207
New York Times, 30
News coverage by media, 135, 139, 141
Nguyen, D. N., 112
Nickman, P. R., 75
Nietzsche, F.W., 125
NIH (National Institutes of Health), "Talking to Children about Death," 235, 236, 239, 240
NIMH (National Institute of Mental Health), 235
No Name Calling Week, 168
Nolan, Tom, 115
Nonverbal communication by children, 18, 204
Noppe, I. C., 29, 236, 241
Noppe, L. D., 29, 236, 241
Nordentoft, M., 191
Northern Ireland, 6
Notable Black American Women (Smith (Ed.)), Smith, J. C. (Ed.), 114
Notable Hispanic American Women (Telgen & Kamp (Eds.)), 114
Notable Native Americans (Malinowski (Ed.)), 114
Numbing, emotional, 14, 77, 78

Obama, Barack, 34
Oboler, S., *The Oxford Encyclopedia of Latinos and Latinas in the United States*, 114
Obsessive thinking, 143
OECD (Organization for Economic Cooperation Development), 206

Okun, B. F., 204
Okun, M. L., 204
Oliver, L. E., 248
Olsen, J., 248
Ontology, defined, 127
Optimist, child's coping style, 10
Orbach, Israel, 191
Ordower, Connie, 149
Oregon, 59
Organization for Economic Cooperation Development (OECD), 206
Orphans, 108
Orr, S. P., 195
Osofsky, J. D., 206
Otto, J., 96
Oxford Encyclopedia of Latinos and Latinas in the United States, The (Oboler & Gonzalez), 114
Ozer, E. J., 74

Padilla, A. M., 210
Palestine, 6
Paletti, R., 240
Palfai, T. P., 94
Panic, 78
Papadatos, Costas, 97
Papadatou, Danai, 7, 16, 97
Paradoxes of protection, 238
Parents. *See also* Caregivers; Families; Schools
  bereavement grief responses, 248
  children impacted by grief of, 82, 136
  children protecting, 93
  children's support group for divorce, 62, 179–180
  children's support group for loss of, 179
  concealing death, 12
  conflicts between, 78, 135
  death of. *See* Parents, death of
  death of child, 112–113, 150, 247–258
  death of non-custodial, 39
  deployments, 153
  deportation, 153, 170–171
  discussing death with children, 8–13, 136, 138, 196
  divorce. *See* Divorce
  dying from illness, 51
  empowering language, 208
  father's grief, 247–248

INDEX / 295

[Parents]
   frightening children with death, 12
   helping children cope with
      disenfranchised grief, 42
   helping children process grief, 51
   marriage problems, 248
   meaning-centered grief therapy, 257–258
   memorials. *See* Memorials
   motherless daughters day, 64
   mourning rituals. *See* Rituals
   Parent-Child subsystem, 222
   remarriage, 14
   role models against bullying, 165
   seeking help from schools, 20
   separation, 14, 62, 70
   sincerity, 204
   single, 206, 220, 223
   sudden absence, 70
   trauma-focused cognitive behavioral
      therapy, 74
   traumatized, 83–84
   unemployment, 70
   violent loss survivors, 252
   widowed dads support group, 64
Parents, death of
   Abraham Lincoln, 112–113
   appropriate responses from teachers, 154, 159–162
   children postponing grief, 92
   Eleanor Roosevelt, 108
   George Handel, 113
   helping children process grief, 160
   highest stress on child, 194, 228
   Ken Burns, 111–112
   mourning rituals for children, 159–160f
   Natalie Cole, 110–111
   Nelson Mandela, 110
   non-custodial, 39
   by substance abuse, 109
   sudden unexpected, 51, 136
   by suicide, 194
   using borrow biographies, 112–117
   warmth of surviving parent, 238
Park, C. L., 250, 251
Parkes, Colin Murray, 93
Patchin, J., 164
Pearlman, L. A., 84
Pennells, M., 97
Pernicano, P., 78
Pernice-Duca, F., 78

Personalismo (interpersonal relationships), 210
Pet loss, 38, 40, 114, 135, 162
Peterson, B., 32
Pew Center for Internet Research, 33
Pew Research Center, 25–26, 34
Pfeffer, C. R., 189
Photography as therapy tool, 96
Physical complaints, 11, 15, 51–52, 161, 162
Physical harm incidents, 70
Pictures, as ritual of honor, 214
Pilgrim, H., 78
Pistole, M. C., 241
Pitman, R. K., 195
Play for helping with loss, 96–97, 101, 136, 139
Plimpton, E. H., 5
Plopper, B. L., 29
Poems to Learn by Heart (Kennedy), 107
Poetry, 159–160
Poland, 7
Polliak, M., 73
Popham, L. E., 241
Portland, Oregon, 59
Posthumous disillusionment, 72
Postponed grief, 92
Post-traumatic stress disorder (PTSD), 70, 74, 76, 146, 149, 249, 256
Powerlessness, feeling of, 70
Powers, H., 180
Powers, H. L., 17
POZ, 8
Prayers, 7, 9, 101–102, 104, 149, 174, 211
Precht, D. H., 248
Preoperational development, 239–240
Preschoolers, discussing death with, 239–240
Present oriented in time awareness, 204
Price, C., 222
Price, S., 222
Prigerson, H. G., 72, 93, 248, 249
Primo, J. M., 237
Privacy, 34, 55, 83, 139, 221
Progressive-regressive method, 127–128
Prolonged grief disorder, 72, 248. *See also* Complicated Grief (CG)
Prominent Women of the 20th Century (Saari, P. (Ed.)), 114
Psychiatric hospitalization, 248

PTSD (Post-traumatic stress disorder), 70, 74, 76, 146, 149, 249, 256
Punching bags as therapy tool, 96
Purushotma, R., 29
Pynoos, R. S., 78

Rabenstein, Stephanie, 81, 82, 83
Racism inherent in child development theories, 123
Rage, 78
Rainbows program, 17
Rajab, M. H., 192
Rangel, M., 123
Rauch, S. L., 195
Reading stories related to grief and loss, 21
Reagan, Ronald, 110
Reassurance
    for adolescents, 33, 34
    after disasters, 137, 138, 148
    caregivers providing, 51
    discussing death with children, 236
    for parents, 60
    reducing trauma, 75
    rituals providing, 141
Reddy, M., 165
Reflections (Bush), 111–112
Regression, as grief response, 48, 49, 50, 92, 135, 146
Regret, feeling of, 195
Reidl, L., 96
Religious beliefs, 203, 250, 252
Religious sensitivity, 57, 141, 144, 145, 174
Religious services, 7, 210, 212–213
Religious symbols, 19, 209
Remorse, 183
Rent, "Seasons of Love," 189
Resnick, M. D., 191
Respeto (respect), 210
Reynolds, C. F., 254
Rice, Condoleezza, 113, 114, 116–117
Risk-taking behaviors, 10, 29, 139, 241
Rituals. *See also* Ceremonies; Funerals
    African American, 212–213
    burning secrets, 21
    Continuing Bond theory, 75
    end of year party, 64
    expressing grief through, 42, 95, 101, 141, 145, 149, 211–213

[Rituals]
    importance to minorities, 203
    Native American funeral, 7
    schools creating, 19, 162
Ritz, D., 110–111
Rober, P., 252, 253
Roberts, J. M., 250
Roberts, K., 252
Robinson, A. J., 29
Robinson, L., 93, 94
Rodham K., 191
Rogers, C. H., 248
Rogiewicz, 7, 12
Rohter, L., 190
Rokach, A., 93
Rokholt, E. G., 236–237
Romantic relationship ends, 40
Ronen, R., 257, 258
Roos, S., 71
Roosevelt, Eleanor, 108–110, 113, 117
Rotter, J. B., 204
Routines
    after disasters, 137, 139, 141, 142, 148
    creating sense of security and control, 58, 170
    forcing, 20, 77
    ignoring loss with, 116–117
    and schedules for children, 220–223
Rowling, L., 129
Rudd, M. D., 192
Rule of 100 in counseling, 57
Rummel-Kluge, C., 190
Rush, A. J., 192
Russell, C. E., 108
Russia, 7
Rwanda, 6
Ryan, C., 167
Ryerson, D., "The Crisis of Youth Suicide," 183, 184
Ryff, C. D., 95
Rynearson, E. K., 78, 79, 254

Saari, P. (Ed.), *Prominent Women of the 20th Century*, 114
Sacred place, creating, 100
Sadness
    children's short span of, 41
    grief response, 11, 50, 148, 182, 237, 251, 253

[Sadness]
  loss of self-esteem, 50
  modeling to children, 18, 110–111
  passionate, 47, 49
  suppressing emotions, 94
Safe place needed for grieving, 46, 54, 77, 142, 146, 148, 161, 168
Safe School Initiative, 165
Safety, creating during counseling, 80
Saindon, C., 254
Saleski, Z., 96
Salloum, A., 79, 254
Sanchez, J., 167
Sandbox as therapy tool, 96
Sanderson, J., 33
Sandler, I. N., 194, 238
Sands, D. C., 197
Sandy, C., 251
Sandy Hook Elementary murders (Conn.), 165
Santiago-Rivera, A. L., 210
Sarafino, 96
Sartre, J-P., 125–126, 127–128
Schlafly, Phyllis, 18
Schmidtke, A., 190
Schofield, G., 123
Scholastic Corp., 183
Schonfeld, D. J., 173, 182
School Counselor, "Crisis in the Schools: Natural Disasters, Terrorism, Violence and Death—Help Students Prepare, Adjust and Move On," 182
School counselors, 173–186. *See also* Counseling and Counselors
  acknowledge own reaction to loss, 173
  children experiencing divorce. *See* Divorce
  cultural and religious sensitivity, 57, 141, 144, 145
  death education classes, 4, 12–13, 14–16, 20, 180, 184
  death of faculty member(s), 175–177
  friends of deceased student, 182
  leading crisis team, 179. *See also* School crisis plan
  self-care, 180
  siblings of deceased student, 182
  student suicide, 183–184
  students' grief, 16–22, 162, 181–183

[School counselors]
  support group for divorce, 62, 179–180
  support group for loss of parent, 179
  talking with bereaved parents, 182
School Counselor's Book of Lists, The (Blum & Davis), 181–182
School crisis plan. *See also* Spiritual care after disaster
  bringing in outside grief counselors, 179
  care for team members, 178–179
  daily debriefing, 178
  faculty updates, 185
  importance of, 177–178
  leading team, 179
  planning, 20, 178–179, 182–185
  professional development for team, 184
  student peers, 181
Schools. *See also* Grief responses; Parents
  age-appropriate language, 154
  answering questions about death, 13–16
  avoiding silence, 18
  awareness of bereaved children, 158–160
  bringing in outside grief counselors, 179
  bullying, 164–166
  charity fundraiser commemorating student death, 162
  common signs of grief, 154–158, 163–164
  curriculum for loss, grief, and coping, 17–18, 162
  cyberbullying, 164–169
  emotional response after suicide, 183
  explaining abstract concepts with real objects, 19
  faculty member(s) death, 14, 166, 175–177
  Gay/Straight Alliance (GSA) groups, 168
  grief and ADD, LD, 162–164
  grief responses in assignments, 158–160
  grieving space, 176
  guidelines for support, 16–22, 162, 182
  helping bereaved children in, 153–172, 196
  helping child at his/her own development level, 20
  helping children with disenfranchised grief, 42
  helping externalize thoughts and feelings, 21

[Schools]
  homeless children, 169–171
  impacts of death and grief, 15, 153–154
  informing student body about funeral, 178
  interventions for bereaved children, 160–162, 181–183
  LBGTQ youth, 167–169
  loss and grief inventory form, 155–158, 161
  loss of leader, 176–177
  memorials in school yearbook or newspaper, 162
  monitoring bereaved child's health, 161, 162
  National Association of Secondary School Principals, 17
  No Name Calling Week, 168
  nonverbal communications, 18, 204
  offering help to parents, 20
  offering support for all ages, 20, 183
  partnerships with other schools, 21–22
  physical assaults, 167–169
  as positive role models, 18
  procedures for informing students, 17
  promote helping others as way to overcome negative feelings, 19
  rituals or memorials, 19, 21, 174, 178
  role models against bullying, 165
  safe place needed for grieving, 46, 54, 77, 142, 146, 148, 161, 168
  Safe School Initiative, 165
  scholarship fund commemorating student death, 162, 174
  security and structure from, 20
  sending flowers to grieving family, 162
  shootings with multiple victims, 165–166f, 171
  spontaneous grief sites, 178, 179
  sports uniforms with symbol for coach death, 176
  student not wanting to feel different, 154
  student peers, 181
  support organizations for, 17
  violence in, 91, 164–169
Schoulte, J. C., 213
Schultz, C., 71
Schut, H., 47, 75, 253, 256
Schut, H. A. W., 95
Schuurman, D., 195

Schuurman, D. L., 235, 236
Schwallie, M. N., 242
Scott, C., 74, 76, 83
ScuttlePad, 26
Secondary traumatization, 76–77, 84–85, 180
Secretiveness, 153
Secrets burning ritual, 21
Security, helping with loss, 14, 101
Seeley, J. R., 94
Self-care, 146, 180, 181, 231
Self-esteem, 50–51, 93, 99
Self-hate, 192
Selfies, 33–34
Self-injury, lethal. *See* Suicide
Self-injury, non-lethal, 191–192
Self-recrimination, 195
Seligson, H., 27, 30
Seltzer, M. M., 248
Senselessness, feeling of, 70
Sensitivity, religious and cultural, 57, 141, 144, 145, 174
Separating parents, 14, 62, 70
Separation anxiety, 94, 237
Servaty-Seib, H. L., 241
Sesame Street character with HIV, 8
Shame, 38, 153, 154, 182, 195, 223, 247
Sharing and caring for helping with loss, 102
Shatil, Jonathan, 96
Shaver, P., 73–74
Shear, C. K., 254
Shear, K., 72
Shneidman, E. S., 192, 194
Shock, 142
Shootings, 91
Shrines, 214
Sibeon, R., 130
Sibling
  death, 51, 92, 112, 158–160, 182
  leaving home, 93
  murder of, 163
  stillbirth, 14, 38
  suicide, 41, 154–155f
Siegel, K., 189
Sigel, R. S., 6
Silveri, 197
Silverman, M., 190
Silverman, P. R., 60, 129
Silverman, Phyllis, 92

Silverman, S. L., 75
Silverstein, M., 93
Simpatia (warmth, friendliness), 210
Simpson, M., 78
Singer, B., 95
Singing, 135–136, 214
Single parents, 206, 220, 223
Sleep difficulties
  from aging, 226
  depression symptom, 49
  disaster response, 141
  grief response, 11, 48, 247
  stress symptom, 73, 239–240
  trauma response, 78
Sleeping, as death euphemism, 12, 145
Small, A. D., 189
Small, A. M., 189
Smith, Harold Ivan, 109, 110
Smith, J. C. (Ed.), *Notable Black American Women*, 114
Smith, S. C., 97
Snapchat, 26, 28, 32
S.N.U.G. Program (New York City), 205
Snyder, T. D., 164
Social capital, 125
Social impairments, 78
Social media, 25, 28–30
Social support, 76
Sociological factors in child development theories, 126–127
Sociology of arts, 98–99
Socio-political factors in child development theories, 125
Sofka, C., 26
Sofka, C. J., 27, 29, 35
Solomon, Z., 73–74
Somatic complaints, 11, 15, 51–52, 161, 162
Somers, P., 16
Sommerfield, C., 78
South Africa, 8, 34
South America, 17
Souvestre, Marie, 109–110
Spielberger, C., 15
Spiritual belief systems, 250, 252
Spiritual care
  complicated spiritual grief, 250–251
  crisis, 127, 204, 250
  hope, 205–206
  minority children in urban setting, 205–206

Spiritual care after disaster, 133–151
  action plan, 147–149. *See also* School crisis plan
  action plan example, 149–150
  child development theories, 134–137
  children's grief, 135. *See also* Grief
  children's sudden change reactions, 135–136
  children's thought processes, 135
  disintegration, 140–141
  duration, 145–147
  earning trust, 140
  emotions, 141–142
  empathy, 140, 148
  first responders and disaster workers, 146–147
  fragility, 142–143
  grieving, 144–145
  helping children facing chaos, 137
  modeling calm, 139
  monitoring behavior, 141–145
  music, 149
  numbness, 142
  providing stability for victims, 139, 142
  rituals for grief, 141, 145
  safety, 139
  self-care, 146
  shock, 142
  spirituality, 143–144
  suggestibility, 142–143
  supporting authority, 140
  talking with children, 138–139, 141–145
  visible comforting, 137
  volunteers, 143, 148, 149
Spirituality for helping with loss, 102–103, 127, 205–206
St. Christopher's Hospital for Children (Penn.), 182
St. Vincent Millay, Edna, "The Kingdom Where Nobody Dies," 5
Stalfa, F. J., 72
Stamm, B. H., 180
Stand by Me, 39
Steer, R. A., 192
Stein, M. (Ed.), *Encyclopedia of Lesbian, Gay, Bisexual and Transgender History in America*, 114
Steinberg, A. M., 78
Stevenson, E., 243
Stevenson, E. P., 13

Stevenson, Robert G., 6, 13, 14, 17, 18, 91–92, 180, 243
Stevenson, Robert G. (ed.), *What Will We Do? Preparing a School Community to Cope With Crises*, 181, 183
Stigma factors, 154, 203, 207–208
Stoicism, 38
Storytelling
  Continuing Bond theory, 75
  death and dying stories from different cultures, 18, 94
  fairy tales, 94
  at funeral, 213–214
  Infinity Model use of, 47
  journaling, 100
  posting on social media, 28–29
  repeating, for grief process, 161, 209
  restorative retelling about child's death, 254–255
  in support groups, 63
  transmit emotional navigational skills, 108
Stress. *See also* Post-traumatic stress disorder (PTSD)
  after disasters, 135
  after parent's suicide, 195
  children's, 77–78, 171
  compassion fatigue, 180
  coping with. *See* Coping
  family, 77, 223
  life skill to overcome, 238
  music relieving, 98
  parent's, 257
  school crisis team debriefing, 178
  suicide factor, 192
Stroebe, M., 75, 253, 256
Stroebe, M. S., 47, 95, 252
Stroebe, W., 256
Stubbs, P., 123
Students. *See* Adolescents; Children; Schools
Submitter, child's coping style, 10–13
Substance abuse, 109, 174, 196, 254–255
Suggestibility, after disaster, 142–143
Suicidal thoughts, 164, 167, 168, 183, 190, 192
Suicide
  contagion, 182–183, 190
  contagion prevention treatments, 192–194
  fearing death by, 196

[Suicide]
  gun-related, 207
  risk factors, 194
  statistics on youth impact, 189, 194
  stigma of, 207
  theories, 190–194
Suicide, adult
  emotional response in schools, 183
  feeling worthless leading to, 11, 18
  Lakota traditions, 7
  Werther Effect, 190
Suicide, child or adolescent, 189–198
  adolescence death statistics, 30
  advice for school counselors, 182, 183–184
  attempts, 167–169
  due to bullying and cyberbullying, 164–169
  emotional response in schools, 183
  feeling worthless leading to, 11, 18
  grief support groups, 197
  helping bereaved youth, 194–197
  measuring a child's life, 189–201
  memorializing the dead, 197–198
  reasons for, 190–194
  sexual identity, 167
  sibling, 41, 154–155f
  Tripartite Model of Suicide Bereavement, 197
  Werther Effect, 190
Suicide Prevention Resource Center (SPRC), 183
Suicide Status Form, 192–193
Sumerian mythology, 18
Sunkenberg, M., 189
Support, attachment relationships, 75
Support groups
  after youth suicide, 197
  for grieving, 53–54, 93, 163
  students dealing with loss of parent, 179
  students dealing with parent's divorce, 62, 179–180
  widowed dads, 64
  work in sessions, 61–63
Support organizations for schools, 17
Support services, target groups for, 52–53
Survivor's guilt, 143, 195
Susillo, M. V., 241
Sweeney, C., 74, 76
Swift, C., 71

Taft, C., 74
Talismans, 19, 75
"Talking to Children about Death" (NIH), 235, 236, 239, 240
Tape recordings as therapy tool, 96
Tarabrina, N. V., 96
Tarrier, N., 78
Teachers. *See also* School counselors; Schools
　death of single or multiple, 14, 166, 175–177, 231
　emotional strain on, 21
　grief issues for, 175–178
　responding with compassion to student's grief, 158–160
　role models against bullying, 165
　school counselor helping, 182
　student not wanting to feel different, 154
　talking with bereaved parents, 182
　using age-appropriate language, 154
Tedeschi, R. G., 81
Teenagers. *See* Adolescents
Television, news coverage, 135, 139, 141
Telgen, D. (Ed.), *Notable Hispanic American Women*, 114
Temporal ekstases, 128
Terrorism, 91, 99, 153, 171, 182
Texting, 28
Therapy and Therapists. *See* Counseling and Counselors
Thomas, Abigail, 110
Thompson, B. E., 250
Thompson, Neil, 91, 121, 124, 125, 127
Thompson, S., 124, 127, 129
Time awareness, 204
Toth, K., 203
Touch, as sign of respect, 210
Toy figures as therapy tool, 96
Training, at *A Friend's Place*, 66–67
Trauma
　child development theories, 127
　family-focused trauma interventions, 73–74
　grief intersecting with, 78–79
　impeding grief process, 195
　NCTSN, 82
　secondary traumatization, 76–77, 84–85, 180
　sleep difficulties, 78
Traumatic grief, 71–72, 127

Traumatic loss, 69–71
Triandis, H. C., 210
Trojcak, Ronald, 6
Trust, 143–144, 204–205, 210
T-shirt memorials, 209
Tumblr, 26
Twitter, 26, 28, 32–33

United Kingdom, Winston's Wish, 59
United States
　Association for Death Education and Counseling (ADEC), 17
　children developmental discussions, 3
　children's competitive behavior, 96
　cultural differences about child's exposure to death, 6–7
　death statistics, 14
　Dougy Center, 59
　nonverbal communication, 18
　Sesame Street character with HIV, 8
　shielding children from death, 6
　terrorist attacks of September 11, 2001, 11
　TV program about death education, 16
University of Wisconsin-LaCrosse, 17
U.S Bureau of Justice, Statistics' Indicators of School Crime and Safety report (2007), 164
U.S. Department of Education, 165
U.S. Secret Service, 165
Uses of Enchantment: The Meaning and Importance of Fairy Tales, The (Bettelheim), 94

Valach, L., 193
Van den Bout, J., 95, 250
Van den Hout, M., 250
Van Deth, J. W. (Ed.), 125
Vance, James, 190
Vanden Berk, B. J., 96
Vanwesenbeeck, I., 30
Varga, M. A., 240
Vazquez, C. I., 210
Verbal abuse, 77, 159–160, 164–169
Vietnam, 112
Vine, 32
Violence, fear of, 14
Violence culture, 91, 164–166, 206–207

Violent loss survivors, 249–252
Virgin of Guadalupe, 209
Voluntary Organizations Active in Disaster (VOAD), 133
Volunteers, 54–56, 66–67
Von Franz, Marie-Louise, *An Introduction to the Interpretation of Fairy Tales*, 94
Vossekull, B., 165

Wade, Linda, *Condoleezza Rice*, 113
Wakes, 209
Walden, M., 190
Walker, M., 196
Wall Street Journal, 115
Walrave, M., 30, 34
Walsh, F., 203
Walsh, F. R., 70, 71, 73, 75, 76, 81
Walter, C. A., 92
War, 91, 153
Warhol, Andy, 99
Washington, DC, 206
Weariness, feeling of, 136
Webb, N. B., 71, 75, 77, 80
Webb, Nancy Boyd, *Helping Bereaved Children: A Handbook for Practitioners*, 96
Webb, Willyn, 116
Weigel, M., 29
Weisel, Elie, 95
Weiss, D. S., 74
Weller, E. B., 195
Weller, R. A., 195
Weller, S., *The Bradbury Chronicles*, 115
Wenzel, A., 192
Werther Effect, 190
What Will We Do? Preparing a School Community to Cope With Crises (Stevenson ed.), 181, 183

Whitfield, K., 211
Willcock, D., 16
Williams, A. L., 32
Williams, J. L., 249
Wilson, T. L., 95
Wimmer, M., 195
Winchester Medical Center (Virginia), 149
Winston's Wish (UK), 59
Withdrawal, 15, 77
Wittkowski, J., 238
Wohl, M. J. A., 76
Wolchik, S. A., 238
Wolleb, G. (Ed.), 125
Women in World History (Commire (Ed.)), 114
Worden, J. W., 37, 60, 92, 97, 117
World War II, "Kilroy was here" cartoon, 33f
Worthlessness, 12, 18
Wright, J., 191
Writing, expressing grief with, 21, 142, 161. *See also* Journaling; Storytelling
Wyness, M., 124, 129

Xianchen, L., 194

Young, R. A., 193
Youngblut, J. M., 211
Youth. *See* Adolescents; Children
YouTube, 25, 27, 34

Ziebland, S., 71
Zimmerman, T. S., 77
Zisooki, S., 72
Zupanick, C., 40
Zweig, A. R., 6, 7